The Greatest Jewish Stories Ever Told

The Greatest Jewish Stories Ever Told

Selected, retold, and introduced by

David Patterson

JD | JONATHAN DAVID PUBLISHERS, INC.
Middle Village, New York 11379

THE GREATEST JEWISH STORIES
EVER TOLD

Jonathan David Publishers, Inc.
68-22 Eliot Avenue
Middle Village, New York 11379

2   4   6   8   10   9   7   5   3   1

Library of Congress Cataloging-in-Publication Data

The greatest jewish stories ever told / [compiled] by David Patterson
    p. cm.
  ISBN 0-8246-0399-0
  1. Legends, Jewish. 2. Bible stories, English—O.T. 3. Talmud—Legends.
  4. Midrash—Legends. 5. Aggada—Translations into English.
  I. Patterson, David, 1948–
BM530.G74   1997
296.1'9—dc21   97-11943
                                                                      CIP
                                                                      r97

Design and composition by John Reinhardt Book Design

Printed in the United States of America

for my students

Acknowledgments

I would like to thank Patricia A. Rigsbee, Senior Copyright Research Specialist at the Library of Congress, for the work she did in certifying the copyright clearance on the stories that appear in the section "Modern Tales." I would also like to thank Judy Sandman for her diligent, meticulous, and excellent work in editing the manuscript for this book.

Contents

Biblical Tales

Talmudic Tales

Midrashic Tales

Kabbalistic Tales

Legends and Folktales

Tales of the Hasidim

Modern Tales

Preface

THE STORIES THAT APPEAR IN THIS VOLUME have generally been selected for their prominence within the many traditions of Jewish life. Since a tale requires a certain amount of time to enter the tradition and become of "one of the greatest," I have not included anything written in the last half century.

Most of the sources for these tales are familiar: the Bible, Talmud, Midrash, and Zohar. Many legends, folktales, Hasidic tales, however, derive from oral traditions that have found their way into many different sources, in a variety of forms, texts, and languages. While some of them may be attributed to this rabbi or to that sage, they are not the creations of specific authors but rather arise from the various religious and cultural communities where Jews have lived and died. In many cases, then, I do not name specific sources for these tales; rather, I have chosen to retell them based on my having received them from several sources, both written and oral. It should also be noted that I am the translator of the stories by Heinrich Heine, Shalom Aleichem, Isaac Babel, and S. Y. Agnon.

Introduction

IT IS SAID THAT WHEN Rabbi Yisrael Baal Shem Tov, founder of Hasidism, encountered some calamity threatening the Jewish community, he knew just what to do. Quietly he would slip off into the forest. There he sought out a special place, in which he would light a fire in a particular manner and say a prayer that he saved for just such emergencies. Having completed this ritual, the miracle of deliverance was accomplished, and the community was saved.

Misfortune has a way of returning to the Jews. And so, a generation later, the task of petitioning the Holy One for the miracle of deliverance fell to the Baal Shem's celebrated disciple, Rabbi Dov Ber, the Maggid of Mezeritch. Like the Baal Shem before him, the Maggid would go off to a certain place in the forest whenever disaster threatened the community. There he would cry out, "Oh, Lord, King of the Universe, hear me! Though I know the place in the forest, I do not know how to light the fire. Nevertheless my teacher has taught me the prayer. And this must be sufficient!" And so it was: the miracle of deliverance was accomplished, and the community of Israel was saved.

But still misfortune would return to the Jews, so that after the great Maggid had gone to join his fathers, Rabbi Moshe Leib of Sasov was entrusted with the task of intercession. Whenever catastrophe threatened the Jews, he would seek out the very same place in the forest where his masters before him had uttered their prayers. "Oh, Lord, King of the Universe, hear me!" he would cry out. "I cannot kindle the fire of the Baal Shem, and I never learned the prayer that he and the Maggid offered up to You. But, as You can see, I do know the secret place in the forest. And this must be sufficient." And so it was: for with these words the miracle of deliverance was accomplished, and the Jews were saved once more.

Finally the responsibility for seeking deliverance by the hand of God fell to Rabbi Yisrael of Rizhin. And yet, even as the breath of destruction was upon the community, Rabbi Yisrael stood in his study as though paralyzed, his head buried in his hands. In his despair he did not cry out but spoke hardly above a whisper, saying, "Oh, Lord, King of the Universe, have mercy! The secret of the Baal Shem's ritual of fire and his prayer for salvation are long forgotten. Here I stand before You, unable even to find the place in the forest. All I can do is tell the story. And this must be sufficient." And so it was: having told the tale of the fire and the prayer and the place in the forest, Rabbi Yisrael found the salvation he sought for the sake of the community.

More than a tale about four Hasidic masters, this is a story about storytelling and our stake in telling tales. It tells us what makes a Jewish story Jewish and what makes a Jewish story great. A Jewish story is much more than a story told by a Jew or a story told about Jews. A Jewish story is about God's relation to the Jewish people, their relation to God, and what those two relationships have to do with the way people relate to one another. It is about handing down a teaching and assuming responsibility. Therefore it is about a tradition that conveys what Jews hold dear, what Jews live for, and what Jews have to answer for.

In this tale, for example, we see the importance of being in the right place at the right time, the importance of establishing a presence before the one God who is known as *Hamakom*, "the Place." We see what is at stake in kindling a fire, in bringing light into the darkness of the world. Indeed, the first utterance of Creation is "Let there be light," and in that utterance lies the meaning of all creation: we are born into the world not only to bring light to darkness but to turn darkness into light. It is not for nothing that the Torah is said to be made of fire or that the religion of those whom God chose to be a light unto the nations is symbolized by a lamp, by a menorah. And the prayer? In this tale it is spoken not for the sake of self but for the sake of others. That is what makes it a Jewish prayer. That is what makes this story about presence and light and prayer a Jewish story. And that is what makes the story itself enough, even when the rites and rituals are forgotten.

According to one Jewish tradition, God created human beings because He likes stories. The mystics tell us that the basis for all creation is *chesed*, or lovingkindness. Looking at this tale about the telling of a tale, we realize that these two commentaries on creation

harbor a single idea: God likes stories because God loves human beings. The light born upon the first utterance of the Creator—the light
that precedes the luminaries of the heavens—instills human life with
its sanctity. Jewish stories not only are about that light and the sanctity it confers, but are a primary means of transmitting both: so often
hidden, that sanctifying light shines through Jewish stories. And Jewish stories show themselves through Jewish lives: to tell a tale is to
choose life.

In the first verse of one of the most ancient of mystical texts, the
Sefer Yetzirah (*Book of Creation*), it is written that God "created His universe with three books (Sepharim): with text (Sepher), with number
(Sephar), and with communication (Sippur)." The word here translated as "communication," *sippur*, also means "story." According to the
twelfth-century sage Yehudah ha-Levy, it signifies "the voice of the
words of the living God," by which all things come into being. Here,
then, is the intimate connection between the act of Creation and the
tale of Creation, which belongs both to the one who tells the tale and
to the one who listens to it.

The mystics further maintain that the book of books God consulted in the Creation is none other than the Torah, and that when
God gave the Torah, He gave not only the words but the silence
between the words. This teaching suggests that the world itself is
structured upon the tales told in the Torah. And what abides in the
silence between the words of the Torah? The silent Word by which
the being and the holiness of all is sustained; the Word that echoes
throughout the greatest Jewish stories ever told.

If the story, the *sippur*, is among the keys to Creation, it is also
among the pathways to God, as Rabbi Yisrael of Rizhin discovered.
Thus the most famous of all the mystical texts, the thirteenth-century
Zohar, makes a distinction between speaking, saying, and relating,
that is, story telling or *aggadah*. "Speaking and saying," explains the
Lubavitcher Rebbe, Rabbi Menachem Schneerson, in his book *Torah
Studies*, "come from the surface, not from the depth of the soul. The
mouth can sometimes speak what the heart does not feel. Even what
the *heart* says can be at odds with what the man truly wills in his soul.
. . . But 'relating' comes from the depths of a man's being." In the
depths of the soul dwells the Creator of all souls, the One who, in
His love for the human soul, loves stories.

That is why in the same work Rabbi Schneerson notes what we are taught in an ancient commentary on the Torah, the *Sifre* on Deuteronomy 11:22, urging us to study Jewish tales: "You wish to recognize the One who spoke and brought the world into being? Learn *Aggadah* for in *Aggadah* you will find God." And in the *Sifre* on Deuteronomy 32:14, we are told that "the blood of grape drunk for wine" refers to the tales that God pours, like wine, into the souls of all humanity.

Into this volume, then, are gathered not only the tales of a particular people but tales that affirm the sanctity of all people, tales of the sacred itself. Arranged in categories that reflect the history of their telling, these eternal tales declare the holiness and chosenness of all human beings, a chosenness that has its origin in the beginning of all things. We live in a world that has lost most of its ties to this origin, that has forgotten what is sacred and grown confused about what there is to hold dear. The secret place in the forest, the ritual of fire, and the special prayer have all receded into obscurity. But perhaps the memory of these tales will be enough to bring the deliverance that we so desperately need.

Biblical Tales

THE TALES IN THIS SECTION come from the oldest and holiest of Jewish texts: the Torah, the Prophets, the Writings. Also included are two tales from the Apocrypha. Many people believe that the Torah was given at Sinai and that the other portions of the Bible come from the mouth of God Himself. Whether or not this is true, it can surely be said that these tales arise from the earliest days of storytelling and have endured throughout the generations. Indeed, they have sustained the lives of thousands in times and places where, by all that is rational, life should have been extinguished. In these tales it is not merely the voice of a particular storyteller that speaks but the voice of the Spirit that is part of every soul. To attend to these tales is to hear something or someone who abides both within us and beyond us. These tales are the first utterances of why we live and why we die. These stories are the origin of all tales and form the basis of all human life.

The First Man and Woman

GENESIS 2:5–24

In order that no person may say to another, "My family, my people, my race is better than yours," God began His creation of humanity with a single human being. The first woman was created in response not just to Adam's loneliness but to a solitude that even the presence of God could not mitigate, a solitude that only the presence of another human being could overcome. God brings Eve to Adam not just to keep him company but to uphold him in a universe that is otherwise alienating and overwhelming. Adam, whose name means "human being," is placed in the garden not merely to enjoy its fruits but to work it and watch over it: he must see to it that the fruit he eats from the garden is transformed into an embrace of God and his fellow human being. Thus he sanctifies the earth of which he is made and the woman who is made from him.

No wild shrubs of the field yet existed on earth, and none of the wild plants had yet come up, for the Lord God had not yet brought rain to the earth, and there was no human being to till the ground. A mist rose up from the earth and watered the whole surface of the ground. And the Lord God took the dust from the ground and formed a human being. He breathed into his nostrils the breath of life, and Adam became a living soul. And the Lord God planted a garden in Eden, to the east, and there He placed the human being He had formed. He made to grow from the ground every tree pleasant to behold and good to eat from, with the Tree of Life in the middle of the garden, as well as the Tree of Knowledge of Good and Evil.

The Lord God took Adam and placed him in the garden of Eden to work it and watch over it. He commanded him, saying, "From every tree of the garden you may eat. But do not eat from the Tree of Knowledge of Good and Evil, for on the day you eat from it, you will surely die."

From the ground the Lord God formed every wild beast and every bird of the sky. He brought them to the human being to see what he would call them, and Adam named every animal and every bird of the sky and every wild beast. But he had no helper who might uphold him.

Said the Lord God, "It is not good for man to be alone."

God made Adam fall into a deep state of unconsciousness. Then He took one of his ribs and closed up the flesh where it had been. From the rib He had taken God built a woman, and He brought her unto Adam.

Said Adam, "Behold, this is bone of my bones and flesh of my flesh. She will be called woman, for she has been drawn from man."

Thus a man will leave his father and his mother and be joined with his wife; they will become one flesh.

Exile from the Garden

GENESIS 3:1–24

The emergence of the self-consciousness and self-centeredness removes us from our relationship to God and to our fellow human beings. Did God lie when He said that death would befall man and woman upon eating the forbidden fruit, which, significantly, is pleasing to the eyes? Assuming that God does not lie, in what sense may this be understood? Perhaps it is rooted in the loss of capacity to affirm our presence before God. When God asks Adam, as He asks us all, "Where are you?" he replies, "I was afraid. . . . I hid." Perhaps that is the death of which God speaks: on the day that we isolate ourselves from Him and from our fellow human beings, we remove ourselves from life.

The serpent was the most cunning of all the beasts that the Lord God had made. The serpent asked the woman, "Did God really say that you may not eat from any of the trees of the garden?"

The woman replied to the serpent, "We may indeed eat from the fruits of the trees in the garden. But as for the fruit of the tree in the middle of the garden, God said, 'Do not eat from it and do not touch it, lest you die.'"

Said the serpent to the woman, "You will not die. For God knows that on the day you eat from it your eyes will be opened, and you will be like God, knowing good and evil."

The woman saw that the fruit was good to eat, that it was pleasing to the eyes, and that the tree was a delightful way to gain intelligence. She took some of its fruit and ate. She gave some to her husband, and he too ate. Their eyes were opened, and they realized they were naked. So they sewed together fig leaves and made themselves loincloths.

They heard the voice of the Lord God walking in the garden in the afternoon wind, and the man and woman hid themselves from the face of God among the trees in the garden. God called to Adam and said to him, "Where are you?"

The man answered, "I heard Your voice in the garden. I was afraid because I was naked, so I hid."

"Who told you that you are naked?" asked God. "Have you eaten of the tree from which I commanded you not to eat?"

Adam answered, "The woman You gave to be with me offered me food from the tree, and I ate."

The Lord God said to the woman, "What have you done?"

The woman answered, "The serpent led me astray, and I ate."

The Lord God said to the serpent, "Because you have done this, you are more cursed than all the animals and all the wild beasts. You will crawl on your belly and eat dust all the days of your life. I shall create hostility between you and the woman, between your offspring and her offspring. They will strike you on the head, and you will strike them in the heel."

To the woman He said, "I shall greatly increase your agony in pregnancy. In anguish you will give birth to children. Your longing will be for your husband, and he will rule over you."

To Adam God said, "Because you listened to the voice of your wife and ate of the tree from which I commanded you not to eat, the ground will be cursed. In adversity will you reap your food from it all the days of your life. It will bear thorns and thistles for you, and you will eat from the grass of the field. By the sweat of your brow will you eat your bread, until you return to the ground. From it you were taken: you are dust and to dust you will return."

And Adam called his wife Eve, because she was the mother of all.

God clothed Adam and Eve and, "Behold, the human being has become like one of us, knowing good and evil. He must be kept from extending his hand to take also from the Tree of Life, for if he eats, he will live forever."

The Lord God cast Adam out of the garden to work the ground from which he had been taken. He drove out the human being, and to the east of Eden He stationed cherubim with a revolving sword of flame to guard the path to the Tree of Life.

First Blood

GENESIS 4:1–16

A case of brother killing brother, this story of the first murder suggests that every murder is a fratricide. It also implies that the violent death imposed upon creation is a rebellion against the Creator Himself. When God rejected Cain's offering, Cain killed Abel. Killing Abel, Cain set out to make himself as God. God asks Cain two questions: Where is your brother? and, What have you done? These two questions are variations of the question that God put to Adam: Where are you? Taken together, the three questions teach us at least two lessons: that we determine our presence in the world through our responsibility for our fellow human being, and that our relationship to our fellow human being is shaped by what we do. The punishment of Cain suits his crime. Sent into the land of Nod, which means "wandering," Cain is cut off from his dwelling in the human community, just as his crime cut him off from humanity.

Adam knew his wife Eve, and she conceived and gave birth to Cain, saying, "I have acquired a man through the Lord." She gave birth a second time, to his brother Abel. Abel became a keeper of sheep, while Cain worked the ground.

Time passed, and Cain brought some of the fruits of the ground as an offering to the Lord. Abel also brought an offering from the fattest of the firstborn of his flock. The Lord received Abel and his offering, but to Cain and his offering He paid no heed. Cain was enraged and fell into despair. The Lord said to him, "Why are you so angry? Why are you despondent? If you do good, will you not be accepted? If you do not do good, sin will crouch at your door. It lusts after you, but you can overcome it."

Cain and Abel were together in a field, and Cain rose up against his brother and killed him. And the Lord asked Cain, "Where is your brother Abel?"

"I do not know," he answered. "Am I my brother's keeper?"

The Lord said to him, "What have you done? The voice of your brother's blood cries out to Me from the ground. Now you are cursed from the ground that has opened its mouth to receive from your hand the blood of your brother. When you work the ground it will no longer offer up its strength to you. You will be a fugitive and a wanderer on the earth."

Cain replied, "My punishment is too great to bear! For You have banished me this day from the face of the earth, and I am to be hidden from Your face. I shall be a fugitive and a wanderer on the earth, and whoever finds me will kill me!"

And the Lord said to him, "Indeed. But whoever kills Cain will be punished seven times over."

And God placed a mark upon Cain, so that whoever might find him would not kill him. Cain went out from the presence of the Lord and settled in the land of Nod, which is east of Eden.

The Great Flood

GENESIS 6:5–8:22

While the biblical tale has some parallels with other flood tales that appeared in the Fertile Crescent as early as the third millennium B.C.E., the most famous being the Babylonian "Epic of Gilgamesh," the differences far outweigh any similarities. In the biblical story God alone—not a council of gods—decides to bring the world to an end. He does so not because people are disturbing His sleep, as in the Babylonian myth, but because people are committing violent acts against one another. The hero of the biblical tale is saved not because of the whim of some god or goddess but because of his own righteousness; the waters subside not due to the course of natural events but because "God remembered Noah." Unlike the Babylonian myth, the biblical account ends with a covenant between God and humanity.

The Lord saw that the evil of humanity was growing. Man's every thought and inclination was evil. The Lord regretted having made humanity on earth, and He was afflicted to His very core. He said, "I shall annihilate from the face of the earth the humanity I have created, from human beings to beasts and creeping things and birds of the sky. For I regret having made them."

But Noah found favor in the eyes of the Lord. He was a righteous man, a man without blemish. Noah walked with God, and Noah had three sons: Shem, Ham, and Yafet.

God said to Noah, "The end of all flesh has come before Me, for the land is filled with violence. Therefore I shall destroy the earth. Make yourself an ark of gopher wood. Seal it inside and out with pitch. Its length is to be three hundred cubits, its width fifty cubits, and its height thirty cubits. Put a skylight in its roof a cubit high, and place a door on its side. Make an upper, a middle, and a lower deck.

"For, behold, I shall bring a flood of water to cover the earth and destroy from under the heavens all flesh that has a breath of life in it: everything on earth will perish. But I shall keep a covenant with you, and you will come into the ark with your sons, your wife, and your sons' wives. From all life, from all flesh, bring two of each kind, male and female, to live with you in the ark. Take with you every kind of food that is eaten and store it as food for you and the animals. Take seven pairs of every clean animal, male and female. And of every unclean animal take one pair, male and female. Take also seven pairs of the birds of the sky, male and female, so that the seed may be kept alive on the face of the earth. For in seven days I shall bring rain to the earth for forty days and forty nights. I shall obliterate from the face of the earth every living creature I have made."

And Noah did all that the Lord commanded him to do.

Noah was six hundred years old when the waters of the flood covered the earth. When the waters of the flood rose, Noah and his sons and his wife and the wives of his sons went into the ark.

The clean animals, the unclean animals, the birds, and all that crawled over the ground went with Noah, two by two, male and female, into the ark, as God had commanded. The springs of the deep burst forth, the floodgates of the heavens were opened, and the rain fell upon the earth forty days and forty nights.

Everything on earth that had in its mouth the breath of the spirit of life died. Only Noah and those who were with him in the ark survived. The waters surged over the earth for a hundred and fifty days.

God remembered Noah and all the beasts and animals that were with him in the ark. He made a wind blow over the earth, and the waters subsided. The springs of the deep and the floodgates of the heavens were sealed, and so the rain ceased. The waters receded from the earth and continued to recede, so that after another hundred and fifty days they had abated. The ark came to a rest in the Ararat Mountains. The waters continued to abate until the peaks of the mountains could be seen.

After forty days had gone by, Noah opened a window and released a raven. Then he sent out a dove to see whether the water had receded from the surface of the land. But it returned to the ark, for water still covered the face of the earth.

Noah waited another seven days and once again sent out the dove. This time the dove returned to him toward evening with a freshly picked olive leaf in its beak. Noah knew that the waters had receded. He waited another seven days and sent out the dove once again. This time it did not return.

In the six hundred and first year of Noah's life, on the first day of the first month, Noah opened up the ark's hatch and saw that the surface of the ground was beginning to dry. By the twenty-seventh day of the second month the earth was completely dry.

And God spoke to Noah, saying, "Go forth from the ark, you and your wife and your sons and their wives. Take with you every living creature—the birds, the beasts, and the creatures that crawl over the earth—so that they may be fruitful and multiply."

Noah built an altar to the Lord and made a burnt offering from one of every clean animal and every clean bird. When the Lord smelled the pleasant odor, He said to Himself, "Never again shall I curse the ground because of humanity, for the inclination of the human being is evil from his youth. And never again shall I strike down all life, as I have done. As long as the earth endures, seed-time and harvest, cold and heat, summer and winter, day and night will never cease."

God's Covenant with Abraham

GENESIS 17:1–27

Despite its apparent simplicity, this is one of the most astounding of all Jewish tales. In a way, all Jewish stories are based on this story. For this is the story of the establishment of a reciprocal relationship between God and Abram and his descendants—for the sake of all humanity. Because it is a covenant of life with the One who is the origin of life, the sign of the covenant is placed upon the organ of life. Thus the announcement of the covenant includes the announcement of the birth of a child into the world: the covenant with God is the covenant of this birth. The Talmud says that Abraham was not whole until he bore this sign, and, indeed, it is true: the wholeness of the human being lies in his covenantal relation to God.

Abram was ninety-nine years old when the Lord appeared to him and said, "I am God Almighty. Walk before Me and be without blemish, for I shall make My covenant between Me and you and shall greatly increase your numbers. No longer will you be called Abram, but your name will be Abraham, for I have made you a father of many nations. Kings will come forth from you. And I shall keep the covenant between us and your descendants after you as an eternal covenant throughout the generations. To you and to your children I shall give the land where you now dwell as a stranger. The whole land of Canaan will be for you an everlasting heritage, and I shall be a God unto all your children."

Then God said unto Abraham, "As for your part, every male among you must be circumcised. The flesh of your foreskin is to be circumcised, and this will serve as the sign of the covenant be-tween Me and you. From generation to generation every male

BIBLICAL TALES ॐ 31

among you will be circumcised when he is eight days old, whether he is born within your household or is among those purchased from an outsider. The soul of any male who is not circumcised shall be cut off from his people, for he has broken My covenant."

And God said to Abraham, "Your wife Sarai will no longer be call Sarai, for her name will be Sarah. I shall bless her, so that she will bear you a son. I shall bless her, so that she will become the mother of entire nations; kings will come forth from her."

Abraham fell upon his face and laughed, saying to himself, "Can a man of a hundred years have children? Can Sarah, at the age of ninety, bear a child?"

God replied, "Your wife Sarah will give birth to a son whom you will call Isaac. I shall keep My covenant with him as an eternal covenant for the sake of his descendants after him. I shall also bless Ishmael, the son borne to you by your servant Hagar. He will be exceedingly fruitful and greatly multiply his numbers. He will be the father of twelve princes, and I shall make him into a great nation. But My covenant I shall keep with Isaac, whom Sarah will bear to you at this time next year." When He finished speaking, God rose up from Abraham.

Abraham took his son Ishmael, all those born within his household, and all those purchased with money—every male in his household—and circumcised the flesh of their foreskins on the very day that God had spoken to him. Abraham was ninety-nine years old when he was circumcised and his son Ishmael thirteen.

Sodom and Gomorrah
GENESIS 18:16–19:29

The story of Sodom and Gomorrah is the precedent for one of the most important and most humanitarian of Jewish traditions, namely that a person may say anything to God—even engage in an argument with Him— if he does so in the interests of human life. It is God's memory of a man's—Abraham's—argument with Him for the sake of others that leads Him to spare the lives of Lot and his family. And it is a man's argument with God for the sake of others that is the sign of his righteousness. Neither God's memory nor the man's argument is possible without the covenant between them. For the covenant is made not just for the sake of God or Abraham but for the sake of all who recognize the sanctity of a single human life. As for Lot, we see his righteousness in his care for the strangers who visit his city. But what shall we say about his offer to hand his daughters over to the mob in order to save the strangers?

Two of the strangers who had visited Abraham's tent rose up and turned their gaze toward Sodom. Abraham went with them to send them on their way.

And the Lord said to Himself, "Shall I hide from Abraham what I am about to do? After all, Abraham is to become a great and mighty nation, and through him all the nations of the world will be blessed. For I have chosen him, that he may command his children and his household after him to follow in the path of the Lord through charity and justice. Then will I bring him all that I have promised him."

God said to Abraham, "The cry rising up against Sodom is so great and their sin so grave, that I shall descend upon it to see whether they have indeed acted according to this outcry that has come to Me. And if not, I shall know."

Abraham drew closer to God and said, "Will You really wipe out the innocent along with the guilty? What if there are fifty innocent people in the city? Would You still destroy it, rather than spare the place for the sake of the fifty good people there? Far be it from You to act in such a manner, to kill the innocent along with the guilty, allowing the righteous the same fate as the wicked! Far be it from You! Will the Judge of the world not act justly?"

And the Lord said, "If I find fifty righteous people in Sodom, I shall spare the entire area for their sake."

Abraham continued to argue with God: "I, who am but dust and ashes, have already presumed too much to speak before my Lord. But what if there are five fewer than the fifty righteous people? Would You destroy the whole city for want of these five?"

"I shall not destroy it if I find forty-five there," He said.

"What if there are forty?"

"For the sake of forty, I shall not do it."

"Let my Lord not be angry, but I must speak. What if there are thirty?"

"If I find thirty, I shall not do it."

"I know I have said too much before my Lord, but what if there are twenty?"

"I shall not destroy the city for the sake of those twenty."

"Let my Lord not be angry, but I must speak just once more: what if there are ten?"

"For the sake of ten I shall not destroy it."

Having finished speaking with Abraham, the Lord left, and Abraham returned home.

It was evening when the two angels arrived at Sodom, and Lot was sitting at the city gate. When Lot saw them, he rose to greet them, bowing his face to the ground. Said Lot, "Please, my lords, turn aside to my house. Spend the night there, and wash your feet. Then you can rise early in the morning and be on your way."

"No," they replied. "We shall spend the night outside."

But Lot persisted, until finally they went with him to his house. He made a feast for them and baked flatbread, and they ate.

Before they could retire for the night the men of Sodom—young and old, all of them—surrounded the house. They called out to Lot, saying, "Where are the strangers who came to you this night? Send them out, that we may know them!"

Lot went out to them, shutting the door behind him. He said, "My brothers, do not do such an evil thing! Look, I have two daughters who have never known a man. Let me bring them out to you, and you can do with them as you please. But leave these men alone, for they have come under my roof."

"Out of our way!" they shouted. "This fellow came to us a stranger, and now he pretends to judge us! Out of our way, or else you'll get it worse than they do!"

They pressed hard against Lot and tried to break down his door. The strangers in his house drew Lot back inside and closed the door. They struck the men who were standing at the doorway with blindness, both young and old, and the men grew weary from groping for the door.

Then the strangers said to Lot, "Who else do you have here? A son-in-law? Sons of your own? Daughters? If you have anyone anywhere in the city, remove them from this place. We are about to utterly destroy it, for the outcry that has reached the Lord is great."

Lot went out and spoke to the men who were betrothed to his daughters. "Get up!" he cried. "Get out of this place. For the Lord is about to destroy the city!" But they took it as a joke.

Dawn was breaking, and the two angels urged Lot. "Go!" they said. "Take your wife and your two daughters! Or else you will be consumed because of the city's iniquity!"

When Lot hesitated, the strangers took him, his wife, and his two daughters by the hand, led them out of the city, and left them at the city's outskirts. Thus the Lord showed them mercy. Once they had led them out, the angels said, "Run for your lives! Do not look back or stop anywhere in the valley. Flee to the hills, lest you be consumed!"

Lot said to them, "Oh, Lord, no! Your servant has found favor in your eyes, and you have shown me great kindness by saving my life. But I shall never make it to the hills. The disaster will overtake me, and I shall die! Please, there is a small city nearby, insignificant, where refuge may be found. Let me flee there, so that my life might be saved!"

The angel of the Lord said to him, "I shall do this thing for you as well: I shall not destroy the city you speak of. But hurry! Flee there, for I can do nothing until you arrive!"

The sun had risen by the time Lot arrived in the small city. And from out of the heavens the Lord rained down fire and brimstone on Sodom and Gomorrah. He overturned those cities and all that was in the valley, all the inhabitants and everything that grew up from the ground. But from behind him Lot's wife looked back upon the destruction, and she was turned into a pillar of salt.

Abraham rose up early in the morning and hurried back to the place where he had stood before the Lord. Staring at Sodom and Gomorrah and the whole of the valley, he could see only thick smoke rising up from the earth, like the smoke of a furnace. When God destroyed the cities of the valley, He remembered Abraham. And so when He overturned the cities where Lot had lived, He allowed Lot to escape the destruction.

The Binding of Isaac

GENESIS 22:1–19

This brief tale is one of the most harrowing in all of Scripture. Abraham, a man known for his righteousness, is asked to offer up to God the life of his son, and by his own hand. The tale is as disturbing for its silence as it is for its words. We are told nothing, for example, of the three days during which Abraham traveled to Moriah with the son he would sacrifice at his side. And what must those three nights have been like? Not only is Abraham to make murder into an act pleasing to God, but he must cling to the promise of the covenant with God, which included the promise of a nation to be born to Isaac. What the binding of Isaac teaches, perhaps, is that while human life may be insignificant before God, it takes on an infinite value when God returns and thereby sanctifies it. Thus only God can demand a life absolutely, and only God can absolutely forbid the taking of it. Perhaps that is why Moriah, and not Sinai, became the Temple Mount.

God decided to test Abraham, and called, "Abraham!"

Abraham said, "Here I am!"

"Take your son, your only son Isaac, whom you love, and set off to the place called Moriah. There, on a mountain that I shall point out to you, offer him up as a burnt offering."

Abraham rose early in the morning and saddled his ass. Along with Isaac he took two of his young servants. He cut wood for the sacrifice and then set out for the place God had named.

On the third day Abraham looked up and saw the place from a distance. He said to the two young servants, "You stay here with the donkey. The boy and I will go up there to worship, and then we shall return to you."

Abraham took the wood for the sacrifice and placed it upon the shoulders of his son Isaac. Then he took the fire for the offering and the knife for the slaughter, and the two of them set out together.

Isaac said to his father Abraham, "Father?"

"Here I am, my son."

"We have the fire and the wood for the offering, but where is the lamb?"

Abraham answered, "God will provide a lamb for the offering, my son."

The two of them went on together. When they finally arrived at the place designated by God, Abraham built an altar and laid the wood upon it. Then he bound up his son Isaac and set him on the wood. Finally Abraham reached out his hand and seized the knife to slaughter his son.

An angel of the Lord called out to him from heaven, saying, "Abraham!"

And he said, "Here I am!"

"Do not lay your hand on the boy. Do not harm him in any way. Now I know that you fear God, for you have not withheld even your only son from Me."

Then Abraham looked up and saw a ram caught in a thicket by its horns. He took the ram and offered it up as a burnt offering instead of his son. Abraham called the place "The Lord will see." Thus it is said, "On the Mount of the Lord, He will be seen."

The angel of the Lord called to Abraham from the heavens a second time, saying, "The Lord declares, 'By My Being I swear that, because you have done this and have not withheld your only son, I shall bless you greatly and multiply your descendants as the stars of the sky and the sand of the sea. Your children will seize the gates of their enemies, and all the nations of the world will be blessed through your children. For you have heeded My voice.'"

Abraham returned to his young servants, and together they set out for Beersheba. And Abraham dwelled in Beersheba.

Jacob Wrestles with God
GENESIS 32:4–32

How did the children of Abraham come to be called Israel? And what does it mean to be called Israel? This story answers those questions. It takes place on the eve of Jacob's reconciliation with his brother Esau, the one who would have received Isaac's blessing, had Jacob not won his father's blessing by deception. Jacob seeks this reconciliation with his brother, so that he may return home. The story tells us what must transpire when anyone undertakes a movement of return and a reconciliation with his fellow human being. For such a movement is a movement toward life, and in order to undertake it, a person must wrestle with the origin and essence of life itself. Thus Jacob wrestles with the divine image in which he is created and which is his essence: He wrestles with himself, and he and all the world are changed forever.

As Jacob made his return to the land of his birth, he sent messengers ahead of him, to seek out his brother Esau.

"Tell my brother," he instructed them, "that during my stay with my father-in-law Laban I have acquired cattle, donkeys, sheep, and slaves. Tell him that I send him these words to gain favor in his eyes."

The messengers went out, but soon they returned and reported that Esau himself was headed toward Jacob and his camp.

"And he has four hundred men with him," they added.

Fearing that Esau meant to avenge and attack him, Jacob divided his camp into two groups.

"If my brother attacks one group," he said, "then at least the other will be saved."

After praying to God for deliverance from the hand of Esau, Jacob decided to send a tribute of cattle, sheep, goats, and donkeys to his brother.

After entrusting the tribute to his servants, he instructed them, saying, "When my brother Esau finds you and asks who owns all of this, tell him that it belongs to me and that I offer it to him as a tribute."

The servants set out ahead of Jacob and left him with his wives, his sons, and all his possessions. That night—in the middle of the night—Jacob rose up, gathered together his wives and sons and all his possessions, and sent them across the Jabbok River.

Thus Jacob was left in solitude. And a man appeared and wrestled with him until the breaking of the dawn. When the stranger saw that he could not overcome him, he touched the hollow of Jacob's thigh, and Jacob's thigh was thrown out of joint as he wrestled with him.

Then the man said to him, "Let me go! The dawn is breaking!"

But Jacob said, "I shall not release you, until you bless me."

"What is your name?"

"Jacob."

And he replied, "No longer will your name be Jacob, but you will be called Israel. For you have struggled with God and man and have prevailed."

"Tell me, please, your own name," Jacob asked the man.

"Why do you ask my name?" answered the stranger, and he blessed Jacob.

And Jacob called the place where he had wrestled Peniel: "For I have seen God face to face, and my soul yet lives."

The sun had risen upon him as he departed from Peniel. He was limping because of his thigh.

Joseph and the Wife of Potiphar

GENESIS 39:1–41:43

In one of the greatest stories about strength of character, Joseph repeatedly says yes to what is holy and no to what the world often permits—adultery. His clinging to holiness is all the more remarkable, for Joseph comes to Potiphar after having suffered betrayal at the hands of his brothers, an ordeal that might have embittered a lesser man. Joseph's wisdom and faith lie in three things: his regard for the sanctity of marriage, his loyalty to one who has shown him kindness, and his fear of God. Even when he is falsely accused, he remains silent and trusts in God rather than malign the wife of his benefactor. This courage and devotion is what places Joseph among the righteous.

One of Pharaoh's officers, an Egyptian captain of the guard named Potiphar, purchased Joseph from a band of Ishmaelites. The Lord was with Joseph and made him very successful, so that soon he was working in his master's house. Potiphar could see that the Lord was with Joseph and that everything prospered that came from his hands. Thus Joseph gained favor in Potiphar's sight and became his personal servant. Potiphar appointed him overseer of his entire household and put him in charge of all that he owned, and the

Lord's blessing continued to fall upon all that Potiphar had, both in the house and in the field. He turned everything over to Joseph and had no care for anything except the bread that he ate.

Joseph grew to be handsome and well built, and after a time his master's wife turned her gaze on him. "Come lie with me," she said to Joseph.

But he refused and said to his master's wife, "My master takes no thought for what I do in his house. He trusts me with everything he owns. No one in the household is more powerful than I. He has not withheld anything from me, except yourself, for you are his wife. How, then, could I commit such an evil? It would be a sin against God!"

Day after day she approached Joseph, but he paid her no heed. He would neither lie with her nor spend time in her presence.

But one day, when Joseph went into the house to do his work, none of the servants of the house was there. The woman grabbed him by his coat and pleaded with him, "Come lie with me!" But he ran away from her and fled from the house, leaving his coat in her hands.

When she saw that she had his coat, she called for her servants and said to them, "Look! My husband has brought us a Hebrew to mock us! He tried to rape me, but I cried out! When he heard me scream, he ran and left his coat here with me!"

She kept the coat beside her until Joseph's master returned home, and she told him the same story. "That Hebrew slave that you brought to us came in here to insult me! When I screamed, he ran off and left his coat here with me!"

When Potiphar heard his wife's words, he was furious. He had Joseph arrested and thrown into the dungeon, where the king's prisoners were held.

Just as Joseph had won favor in the eyes of Potiphar, he soon found favor with the prison warden. The warden placed Joseph in charge of the prisoners, and Joseph came to know each of them well. Among the prisoners were the wine steward and the baker from the court of the Egyptian king. One night the steward and the baker each had a dream, but neither could understand the meaning of his dream. The two of them went to Joseph and asked him if he could interpret their strange visions.

"In my dream," the steward began, "I saw three vines full of grapes. I took the grapes and squeezed them into the king's cup. Then I placed the cup into the hands of the king."

"The three branches are three days," Joseph explained to the steward. "In three days the king will release you, and you shall place the cup in his hands, just as you did before. When you see the king, please remember me."

"Oh, I shall, I shall!" the steward promised, overjoyed at the favorable interpretation of his dream.

"In my dream," the baker put in, also hoping for good fortune, "I was carrying three baskets full of bread and baked goods on my head. But birds came and ate the bread from the baskets."

"Your three baskets," Joseph told him, "are also three days. After three days, however, you will be hanged, and the birds will eat your flesh."

And so it came to pass just as Joseph had said: the steward returned to the court of the Egyptian king, and the baker was hanged. But the steward did not remember Joseph.

Two years went by, and the Egyptian king had two very strange dreams. In the first dream he saw seven fat and healthy cows emerge from the Nile and graze in the marsh. After them came seven lean and sickly cows, who promptly devoured the seven healthy ones. Likewise, in the second dream the king saw seven large ears of grain growing on a single stalk. Behind them grew a stalk with seven thin ears, which soon ate up the seven good ears of grain.

Seeing that the king was very concerned about the meaning of the dreams, the steward remembered Joseph. The steward told the king about Joseph and the dreams he had interpreted. Immediately the king had Joseph taken from the prison and brought to his court.

After relating to Joseph the details of his dreams, the king asked, "What could be the meaning of these visions?"

"The seven healthy cows and the seven good ears of grain," Joseph explained, "are seven years of good harvests. But those seven prosperous years will be followed by seven years of famine: that is the meaning of the sickly cows and the thin ears of grain. You must seek out a man of wisdom to guide Egypt through these years, so that the people will not be destroyed by the famine."

"Since God has revealed to you the meaning of these dreams," the king said to Joseph, "there is no other to whom God has granted the wisdom to guide Egypt through the times of plenty and of famine that lie ahead. Therefore I place you in charge of all of Egypt."

And so Joseph ascended from the prison dungeon to the highest position in all of Egypt, second only to the king himself.

The Burning Bush

EXODUS 3:1–4:17

Moses, the greatest of all the prophets, led the Israelites out of Egypt to receive the revelation at Sinai. He is called by God, and it is only to him that God reveals His Holy Name. God does not speak to Moses until he first moves toward the bush. Like most prophets, Moses is reluctant to take on the task of liberation, a task that, from every rational standpoint, seems impossible. Even if it were possible, Moses deems himself unworthy, which makes him all the more appropriate for the job. Uninterested in his own power and glory, Moses became the most powerful man in Egypt for the glory of God.

Moses was tending the sheep of his father-in-law Jethro, the priest of Midian. Having led the flock to the edge of the desert, Moses came to the mountain of God at Horeb. The angel of the Lord appeared to him from out of a flame that burned in the midst of a bush. Moses looked and saw that, even though the bush was burning, it was not consumed. And Moses said, "I must go and examine this wonder: the bush is aflame, and yet it does not burn!"

When the Lord saw Moses approaching, He called out to him from the midst of the bush, "Moses! Moses!"

Moses answered, "Here I am!"

"Do not come any closer. Remove your shoes from your feet, for the place on which you stand is holy ground." Then He said, "I am the God of your father, the God of Abraham, the God of Isaac, and the God of Jacob."

And Moses hid his face, for he was afraid to look upon God.

The Lord said, "I have seen the affliction of My people in Egypt, and I have heard their outcry under their taskmasters. I know their suffering, and I have come down to deliver them from the hand of Egypt. I shall raise them up from that land and bring them to a good and spacious land flowing with milk and honey, the land of the Canaanites, Hittites, Amorites, Perizzites, Hivites, and Jebusites. Even now the cry of the children of Israel comes to Me. And I see the oppression that the Egyptians inflict upon them. Come, then, I am sending you to Pharaoh to bring My people, the children of Israel, out of Egypt."

But Moses said to God, "Who am I, that I could possibly go to Pharaoh and take the children of Israel out of Egypt?"

"I shall be with you," He replied. "And you may take this to be a sign that I have sent you: when you have brought the people out of Egypt, you will come to serve God on this mountain."

Said Moses, "If I go to the Israelites and tell them, 'The God of your fathers has sent me to you,' they will surely ask me His name. What shall I say to them?"

"I Will Be Who I Will Be," God answered Moses. "Tell them, 'I Will Be has sent me.' Say to them, 'The Lord, the God of your fathers, the God of Abraham, the God of Isaac, and the God of Jacob, has sent me to you.' This is My eternal name, and this is how I am to be remembered throughout the generations.

"Go and gather together the elders of Israel and say to them, 'The God of Abraham, Isaac, and Jacob has appeared to me, saying, "I have seen what you have suffered in Egypt. I promise you that I shall bring you out of the affliction of Egypt to the land of the Canaanites, Hittites, Amorites, Perizzites, Hivites, and Jebusites, to a land flowing with milk and honey."'

"They will heed your words, and you and the elders of Israel will go to the king of Egypt. You will tell him, 'The Lord, the God of the Hebrews, has revealed Himself to us. We ask that you please allow us to journey three days into the desert, where we shall offer sacrifices to the Lord, our God.'

"I know already that the king will not allow you to go, unless he is forced by a mighty hand. Therefore I shall stretch forth My hand and strike Egypt with wonders that I shall perform in the land. Then Pharaoh will let you go. And I shall give the people favor in the eyes of the Egyptians, so that when you leave, you will not leave empty-handed. Each woman will borrow from her neighbor or from the woman she lives with items of silver and gold, as well as articles of clothing. You will put them on your sons and daughters and thus drain Egypt of its wealth."

Moses answered and said, "But they will not believe me, neither will they listen to me. They will say, 'The Lord did not appear unto you.'"

"What is that in your hand?" asked the Lord.

"A staff."

"Throw it on the ground."

Moses threw it to the ground. It turned into a snake, and Moses ran from it. Then God said, "Reach down and take it by the tail." Moses reached down and took it by the tail. And in his hand the serpent changed back into a staff.

"Thus shall they believe that the Lord, the God of their fathers, the God of Abraham, Isaac, and Jacob, has indeed appeared unto you."

Then the Lord said to him, "Place your hand inside your robe, on your chest."

Moses did so and then removed his hand from his chest; it was leprous and white as snow.

"Place your hand inside your robe again, on your chest."

Moses did so and then removed his hand from his chest; his skin was restored, like the rest of his flesh.

"If they pay no heed to the first sign and do not believe you, they will believe the second. And if they fail to believe both signs and pay you no heed, then take some water from the Nile and pour it out on the ground. There the water will turn into blood."

But Moses said to God, "Oh, my Lord, I am not now nor have I ever been an eloquent man. I am slow of speech and heavy of tongue."

The Lord answered, "Who has given man a mouth? Who makes a person deaf or mute? Who gives him sight or strikes him blind? Is it not I, the Lord? Go, then! I shall teach you what to say."

"I beg you, my Lord, please send another!"

Then the Lord grew angry with Moses, saying, "Is not Aaron

the Levite your brother? I know that he is an eloquent man. He is coming out to meet you, and when he sees you his heart will rejoice. You will speak to him and place the words in his mouth. Then I shall be with you and with him and teach you both what to do. He will speak to the people for you. To you he will be as a mouth, and to him you will be as a judge. Take this staff in your hand; with it you will make the signs."

The Angel of Death Passes Over
EXODUS 12:1–42

The story of the first Passover is the foundation for all tales of liberation. The Israelites are liberated not just from the forced labor of Egypt but from the self-serving struggle for power and possessions that is at the root of idolatry. This liberation from idolatry comes not by their own hand but by the hand of the Holy One, blessed be He. Serving God, the Israelites are set free. Humanity itself is transformed forever. For freedom lies not in doing whatever one is inclined to do but in the realization of what one must do, for the sake of God and humanity. Only with this realization do we escape the Angel of Death who passes over us.

The Lord said to Moses and Aaron in the land of Egypt, "This month will be the beginning of all months, the first month of the year. Speak to the whole community of Israel and tell them that on the tenth day of this month every man must take a lamb for his household. If he cannot afford a lamb, he and his neighbor may purchase one together. The lamb must be without blemish, a male one year old. It may be taken from the sheep or from the goats and is to be kept until the fourteenth day of the month. On the afternoon of that day the whole community of Israel will slaughter the lambs. Then they must take the blood of the lambs and smear it on the doorposts and the lintels of the houses in which they will eat the lambs. The meat is to be roasted over a fire and eaten that night with unleavened bread and bitter herbs. Anything left over must be burned. You must eat it in haste, with your belt around your waist, your shoes on your feet, and your staff in your hand. This is the Passover offering to the Lord.

"For on that night I shall pass through Egypt and strike all the firstborn of Egypt, both man and beast, and upon all the gods of Egypt I shall execute judgment: I am the Lord. The blood will be a sign on the house where you are staying. When I see the blood, I shall pass over you, so that no mortal plague will befall you when I strike Egypt.

"This day is to be a day of remembrance for you. This is a law for all time, and you must observe it as a festival unto the Lord throughout the generations to come. You must eat matzo for seven days. Upon the first day your homes must be clean of all leaven. Anyone who eats leaven from the first day until the seventh will have his soul cut off from Israel. The first day is to be a holy day and the seventh day is to be a holy day. On these days no work is to be done, except the work required for everyone to eat."

Moses then summoned the elders of Israel and said to them, "Select lambs for your families, so that you may slaughter them for Passover. Take a bunch of hyssop and dip it into the blood gathered in a basin. Then touch the lintel above the door and the two doorposts with the blood from the basin. None of you is to go out of the house until morning. For the Lord will pass through the land to strike Egypt. When He sees the blood on the lintel and the doorposts, He will pass over, so that destruction will not enter your homes.

"You and your children must keep this service forever. Your children may ask, 'What does this service mean to you?' You must answer, 'It is the Passover sacrifice to the Lord. For He passed over the homes of the Israelites in Egypt and spared them when He struck the Egyptians.'"

The Israelites bowed down and worshiped, and they did exactly what the Lord and Moses and Aaron had commanded them to do.

At midnight the Lord struck down all the firstborn of Egypt, from the firstborn of the Pharaoh on his throne to the firstborn of the prisoner in the dungeon, as well as the firstborn of all the animals. Pharaoh rose up in the night with all his servants and with all the rest of Egypt. There was a great outcry in the land, for nowhere was there a house in which somebody had not died. And in the night Pharaoh sent for Moses and Aaron. "Go!" he said. "Go away from my people, you and the Israelites! Go! Serve the Lord as you said you would. Take your sheep and your cattle, but go! And bless me!"

The Egyptians urged the people to hurry away from their land, saying, "We are all dead men!" So the Israelites took their dough before it had time to rise, wrapped it in their robes, and put it on their shoulders. They also asked the Egyptians for gold and silver and articles of clothing, as Moses had said to do, for the Lord had given the people favor in the sight of the Egyptians. Thus they drained Egypt of its wealth.

Numbering about six hundred thousand men on foot, plus women and children, the people of Israel traveled from Rameses to Succoth, along with their sheep, cattle, and other livestock. The Israelites baked the dough they had brought with them into matzo cakes, for they had been driven out of Egypt and had no time to prepare anything else. This night remains a vigil unto the Lord, kept by the people of Israel throughout all generations.

The Revelation at Sinai

EXODUS 19:10–20:18

The revelation at Sinai marks the greatest moment in Jewish history—indeed, in the history of all humanity. It is the moment when the Lord God, Creator of heaven and earth, entered into the midst of His creation and sanctified it. This revelation of the Divinity consummates the liberation of humanity from the greedy pursuit of mammon to the embrace of the holy, from the despair of isolation to the joy of relation, from the meaningless to the meaningful. The ten utterances inscribed on the two tablets fall into two categories. The first five pertain to the relation of human being to God and the second five outline the relation of human being to human being. Spoken, according to the Talmud, in a single utterance, the two are of a piece. Each imparts meaning to the other, and both impart meaning to life.

The Lord said to Moses, "Go to the people and sanctify them to-day and tomorrow. Have them wash their clothing, so that they may be ready on the third day, for on that day the Lord will descend upon Mount Sinai in the sight of all the people. Tell them not to go up the mountain or near its perimeter, for anyone who touches the mountain will die. When the shofar sounds with a long blast, then they may come up the mountain."

Moses went down from the mountain to sanctify the people, and they washed their clothing. He said to them, "Prepare yourselves for the third day and have no sexual relations."

On the morning of the third day there was thunder and lightning, and a heavy cloud rested upon the mountain. There was a loud shofar blast that made all the people in the camp tremble. Moses led the people out of the camp to meet God, and they gathered at the foot of the mountain.

Mount Sinai was covered with smoke, for the Lord had descended upon it in fire. The smoke rose up from it like smoke from a furnace, and the whole mountain shook violently. As the blast of the shofar grew louder and louder, Moses spoke, and God answered him with a voice. The Lord descended to the summit of Mount Sinai and called Moses to ascend the mountain.

The Lord said to Moses, "Go down and warn the people that they must not cross the boundary to gaze upon the Lord, lest they perish. The priests, too, who approach the Lord must sanctify themselves, lest the Lord strike them down."

Moses went down to the people and warned them not to come too close to the mountain. Then God spoke these words, saying, "I am the Lord your God, who brought you forth from the land of Egypt, out of the house of slavery. You shall have no other gods before Me. No gods shall you carve into a graven image or likeness of anything in heaven above or the earth below or in the water beneath the land. Neither bow down to them nor worship them, for I the Lord your God am a jealous God, visiting the iniquity of the fathers upon the third and fourth generations of those who despise Me. As for those who love Me and keep My commandments, I shall love them for thousands of generations.

"Do not take the name of the Lord your God in vain. For the Lord will not allow anyone taking His name in vain to go unpunished.

"Remember the Sabbath to keep it holy. Six days you shall labor and do all your work. But the seventh day is a Sabbath unto the Lord your God. Do no work on that day, neither you nor your son, your daughter, your slave, your maid, nor your animals, nor the stranger dwelling within your gates. During the six days of the week the Lord made the heavens and the earth and the sea and all that is in them, but on the seventh day He rested. Therefore the Lord blessed the Sabbath day and made it holy.

"Honor your father and your mother, that you may live long in the land that the Lord your God gives you.

"Do not commit murder.

"Do not commit adultery.

"Do not steal.

"Do not bear false witness against your neighbor.

"Do not envy your neighbor's house. Do not covet your neighbor's wife, his slave, his maid, his ox, his ass, or anything else that belongs to him."

When the Israelites saw the lightning and the smoking mountain, and when they heard the thunder and the blast of the shofar, they trembled, grew afraid, and drew back. They said to Moses, "You speak to us, and we shall listen. But do not let God speak to us any longer, for if He does, we shall die."

"Do not be afraid," replied Moses to the people. "God has come to test you, so that you will fear Him, and you will not sin."

And the people stood far back as Moses entered into the heavy darkness where God was.

Balaam and Balak

NUMBERS 22:4–24:25

Not only did God reveal Himself at Sinai, but in this tale we see that He reveals Himself to all. As the sages have taught, the Torah was given at Sinai and not in the Promised Land so that the Jews would not be so conceited as to think it was theirs alone nor other nations so complacent as to suppose that it did not apply to them. Balaam is not an Israelite, yet he

declares that he must do whatever the Lord commands—in this lies his
freedom. A servant of God, he is free from all other servitude.

Balak, son of Tzippor and king of Moab, sent his messengers to
the land of Pethor on the Euphrates River, to Balaam, son of Beor.
They were to summon him, saying, "A people has come out of
Egypt, so numerous that they cover the earth. They are camped
across from me and are too powerful for me. Please come and curse
this people for me, that I may drive them out of the land. For I
know that whomever you bless is blessed and whomever you curse
is cursed." Thus the elders of Moab and of Midian, with magical
artifacts in hand, went to Balaam with Balak's message.

"Stay here for the night," Balaam replied to them. "When the
Lord speaks to me, I shall have an answer for you."

God appeared to Balaam and said, "Who are these men that
have come to you?"

Balaam answered, "Balak, son of Tzippor and king of Moab, has
sent me a message: 'A people covering the face of the earth has
come out of Egypt. Come and curse them for me, so that I may do
battle against them and drive them out of the land.'"

But God told Balaam, "Neither go with them nor curse these
people, for they are blessed."

So Balaam rose in the morning and said to Balak's emissaries,
"Go home! The Lord refuses to allow me to come with you."

The Moabite emissaries returned to Balak and told him Balaam's
reply. So Balak sent another delegation, larger than the first and
higher in rank. They went to Balaam and gave him Balak's message, which was, "Do not refuse to come to me, for I shall bestow
upon you great honor and shall do anything you say. But please
come and curse these people for me."

Balaam answered the servants of Balak, saying, "Even if Balak
should offer me a palace full of gold and silver, I would do nothing
large or small to transgress the word of the Lord my God. Nevertheless, stay the night. Then I shall know what God would say to
me."

That night God appeared to Balaam and said, "Go with these
men, but do only what I tell you to do."

The next morning Balaam rose, saddled his ass, and went with the Moabite emissaries. But God grew angry, and the angel of the Lord stood in the road to oppose him. When the ass saw the angel of the Lord standing with sword in hand, she turned off into a field. Balaam drove the ass back onto the road. Then the angel of the Lord stood in a narrow path leading through a vineyard, with a wall on either side. When the ass saw the angel of the Lord, she moved over to the side, crushing Balaam's foot against the wall; Balaam beat her again. Then the angel of the Lord went on ahead and stood in a narrow place, where there was no room to turn to the right or to the left. When the ass saw the angel of the Lord, she lay down, and Balaam took a stick and beat her again.

Then the Lord opened the mouth of the ass, and she said, "What have I done to you to make you beat me these three times?"

"You have mocked me!" he shouted. "If I had a sword in my hand, I would kill you!"

The ass answered Balaam, saying, "Am I not your ass, who has borne you all your life? Have I ever wronged you?"

"No," Balaam replied.

And the Lord opened Balaam's eyes, so that he could see the angel standing in the road, sword in hand. And Balaam bowed down and fell to his face.

The angel of the Lord said to him, "Why have you beaten your ass these three times? I have come to you because your mission is abhorrent to me. Each time the ass saw me, she turned aside. Had she not done so, I would have killed you and spared her."

Said Balaam to the angel of the Lord, "I have sinned, for I did not know that you were standing in the road in front of me. If what I do is an evil, I shall turn back."

But the angel of the Lord responded, "Go with these men, but do not say anything except what I tell you to say." And so Balaam continued on with Balak's emissaries.

When Balaam arrived in Moab, Balak took him to the upper altars of Baal, where he could see the Israelites. Balaam ordered Balak to prepare seven altars for the sacrifice of seven bulls and seven rams, and the two of them made a burnt offering of each animal. Then Balaam went off to a desolate peak. There the Lord placed words in Balaam's mouth and said, "Go back to Balak and tell him what I have said to you."

When Balaam return to Balak, he uttered the Lord's words, say-ing, "Balak, King of Moab, has summoned me from Aram, from the mountains of the east, to curse Jacob and denounce Israel. But how can I curse those whom God has not cursed? How can I denounce those whom He has not denounced? From the heights I behold them, these people who dwell alone, without counting themselves among the other nations. Who can count the dust of Jacob or num-ber even a fourth part of Israel? May I die the death of the just, but let my death be as theirs!"

Hearing this, Balak said, "What have you done to me? I brought you here to curse my enemies, but you have done nothing but offer them your blessing!"

Balaam replied, "I can say nothing except what the Lord puts into my mouth."

Then Balak took Balaam to another height, from which they could see the Israelites. There too they offered up sacrifices, and once again Balaam went off to seek a vision. God appeared to Balaam and sent him back to Balak as an oracle.

Balaam cried out, "God is not a man that He should speak lies, nor the son of man that He should repent. Does He say one thing and do another? Does He speak without fulfilling what He has said? He has offered His blessing, and I cannot do otherwise. He perceives no falsehood in Jacob and no despair in Israel. The Lord their God is with them. He has brought them out of Egypt, and they are as the horns of an ox. No occult art or divination can prevail against Israel. They rise up like a lion that does not lie down until it has devoured its prey."

Said Balak to Balaam, "If you cannot curse them, then at least do not bless them!"

And Balaam replied, "Did I not tell you, 'All that the Lord says, I must do'?"

Nevertheless Balak took Balaam to yet another height. But this time, after they had made their burnt offerings, Balaam turned his face toward the desert, where he saw Israel dwelling in peace. And the Spirit of God was upon him, and he said, "How good are your tents, O Jacob, and your tabernacles, O Israel! They stretch out like gardens along a river, like aloes and cedars that the Lord has planted along the waters. God has brought them out of Egypt, and they are as the horns of an ox that will consume His enemies. Israel crouches like a great lion; who would dare to rouse him? Those who bless you are blessed, and those who curse you are cursed."

Balak became enraged at Balaam and cried, "I brought you here to curse my enemies, but you have blessed them three times! Get out of here! Quick! I promised you honor, but the Lord will not allow it!"

Balaam answered, "I told your messengers that even if you should give me a palace of gold and silver, I would do nothing to transgress the word of the Lord. I shall return to my people now, but first I shall tell you what this nation has in store for your people in the last days."

Balaam then prophesied: "A star shall come forth out of Jacob and a staff shall rise up from Israel to crush all the princes of Moab and to devastate the sons of Seth. Edom will be occupied and Seir destroyed, but Israel will triumph. Rising up from Jacob will be one who will annihilate even those who escape the city."

And finally Balaam cried out, "Alas! Who will remain alive after God's devastation? Ships will set sail from Kittim to afflict Assyria and Eber, but they too will ultimately come to ruin."

Then Balaam rose up and returned home. Balak went on his way.

Samson and Delilah

JUDGES 16:4–30

Samson is one of the most famous of all the Nazirites, that is, those among the Israelites who vowed to refrain from wine, touching a corpse, and cutting their hair. Samson's long hair is a symbol of his tie to God, and his great strength derives not from his hair but from that link to the Holy One. Those who would subdue Samson are those who would subdue the power of God through him. But even though the Nazirite himself may die, God will not be subdued.

Samson fell in love with a woman named Delilah. But the lords of his enemies, the Philistines, came to her and said, "Seduce him and find out the secret of his great strength, so that we may overpower him, bind him, and subdue him. If you do this, each of us will give you eleven hundred pieces of silver."

Agreeing to this, Delilah said to Samson, "Tell me, please, what is the secret of your great strength? How might someone bind you and subdue you?"

Samson told her, "If I were to be bound with seven fresh bowstrings that have not been dried, then I would grow weak and become like any other man."

So the lords of the Philistines got seven fresh bowstrings that had not been dried, and Delilah bound him with them, while several men were lying in wait in her room. She shouted to him, "Samson! The Philistines are upon you!" But he snapped the bowstrings like straw near a fire, so the secret of his strength remained hidden.

Then Delilah said to Samson, "You have mocked me and lied to me! Tell me, please, how you might be bound."

And he told her, "If I were to be bound with new ropes that have not been used, then I would grow weak and become like any other man."

So Delilah took new ropes, tied him up with them, and cried, "Samson! The Philistines are upon you!" Once again there were several men lying in wait in her room, but Samson snapped the ropes from his arms as if they were bits of thread.

Then Delilah said to Samson, "So far you have done nothing but mock me and tell me lies! How might you really be bound?"

"If you," said Samson, "were to weave together the seven locks of my hair and then tie them with a pin, then I would grow weak and become like any other man."

And so, as he slept, Delilah took the seven locks of Samson's hair, wove them together with a web, and tied them fast with a pin. Then she shouted, "Samson! The Philistines are upon you!" But when he awoke, he simply pulled the pin from his hair.

Then Delilah implored him, saying, "How can you tell me you love me when your heart is not mine? Three times you have mocked me and have refused to tell me the secret of your great strength." Day after day she pressured him with her words, until his soul was sick to death. Finally he told her the secret of his heart, saying, "A razor has never touched my hair, for I have been a Nazirite unto God since my birth. If my hair should be shorn, then my strength would leave me, and I would grow weak."

When Delilah realized that he had revealed to her the secret of his heart, she summoned the lords of the Philistines and said to them, "Come now, quickly, for he has revealed to me his secret."

The lords of the Philistines came to her with the money they had promised. Having enticed Samson to fall asleep on her knees, she called for her servant, and he shaved off the seven locks of Samson's hair. Then she began to taunt him, for she saw that his great strength had left him.

"Samson!" she cried. "The Philistines are upon you!" As on the previous occasions, Samson awoke thinking that he would rise up and shake himself free of his bonds. For he did not realize that the Lord had left him. The Philistines seized him and gouged out his eyes. They took him to Gaza, bound him in chains of bronze, and forced him to work in the prison mill. But his hair began to grow again.

One day the lords of the Philistines gathered together to rejoice and offer a great sacrifice to their god Dagon, saying, "Our god has delivered our enemy Samson into our hands!" When the people saw Samson, they praised their god, crying out, "Our god has delivered into our hands the ravager of our land, who has slain so many of us!" They grew excited and shouted, "Bring out Samson, so that we can taunt him!" So Samson was led out of the prison and chained between two pillars so the people could have their sport.

As he stood there, he said to a boy who was holding his hand, "Please let me lean against the pillars on which the house stands."

The house was full of men and women, and all the lords of the Philistines were there. On the roof stood some three thousand men and women, who looked on as they made fun of Samson. Then Samson cried out to the Lord, saying, "O Lord God, remember me, please, and give me strength this one time, so that I might be avenged against the Philistines for just one of my eyes!"

Samson took hold of the two middle pillars upon which the house rested, leaning his weight against them, his right hand on one and his left hand on the other and cried, "Let me die with the

Philistines!" Then he lowered himself with all his might, and the house came tumbling down upon the lords and all those who were in it. Thus the dead whom Samson slew upon his death were more numerous than all he had slain during his life.

Mother of the Messiah

FROM THE BOOK OF RUTH

The story of the great-grandmother of King David, from whose house the Messiah will be born into the world, The Book of Ruth is also the story of a proselyte—of one who chooses to become a Jew. By her example, Ruth demonstrates to all Jews that those who count themselves among the chosen people must also be choosing people; God summons us to choose loyalty over indifference, responsibility over frivolity, and life over death. Ruth embodies what the Messiah will come to teach us: a devotion to God expressed through a devotion to our fellow human being.

In the time of the judges, when famine ravaged the land, a man of Bethlehem named Elimelech took his wife Naomi and their two sons, Mahlon and Chilion, to the country of Moab. Soon after their arrival, however, Elimelech died, leaving behind his wife and sons. Before long Naomi's sons took Moabite wives, one named Orpah and the other Ruth. They lived in Moab for some ten years, until Mahlon and Chilion also passed away.

Bereft of her husband and sons, Naomi decided to return to her homeland, having heard that the Lord had remembered His people and the famine was over. Her two daughters-in-law set out with her, but she urged them, "Go, return to your mothers. May the Lord treat you as kindly as you have treated the dead and me. And may both of you find husbands and a new home." Then she kissed them.

"We want to stay with you and return with you to your people," Ruth and Orpah cried.

But Naomi answered, "No, you must turn back, my daughters. Why should you go with me? Are there yet sons in my womb who may become your husbands? Turn back, my daughters, and go your own way, for I am too old to marry. Even if I should marry this night and bear sons into the world, could you wait until they were grown? No, my daughters. I am terribly sorry, for your sake, that the hand of the Lord has moved against me."

Still they wept, and Orpah offered Naomi a parting kiss. But Ruth continued to cling to her.

"You see," Naomi said to her, "your sister-in-law has gone back to her people and her gods. You should go too."

But Ruth replied, "Please do not ask me to leave you. Where you go, I shall go; where you dwell, I shall dwell. Your people will be my people and your God, my God. Where you die, I shall die, and there shall I be buried. May the Lord do all this and more for me, even if death should take you from me."

Naomi saw that Ruth was determined to go with her and said no more.

They arrived in Bethlehem at the time of the harvest. Among Naomi's relatives from the family of Elimelech was a wealthy man named Boaz. Ruth said to Naomi, "Let me go to Boaz's fields and glean, so that I might find favor in his sight."

And Naomi answered, "Go, my daughter."

So Ruth set out to glean in the fields. When Boaz caught sight of her, he asked his servant in charge of the reaping, "Who is this woman?" The servant answered, "It is the Moabite maiden who came back with Naomi. She has worked from early this morning without a moment's rest."

Boaz approached Ruth and told her, "Listen, my daughter, do all of your gleaning in this field, and not in another. I have forbidden these men to bother you. And when you are thirsty, go over and drink from the water the men have drawn."

Ruth bowed to the ground and said, "Why have I, a foreigner, found favor in your eyes, that you should show me such kindness?"

Boaz explained, "I know of everything you have done for your mother-in-law since the death of your husband, how you left your mother and father and people to come to a strange place. May the Lord, God of Israel, under whose wings you have taken refuge, be gracious to you for all you have done."

"You, my lord," she answered, "have been gracious unto me, for you have spoken to me and shown me kindness, even though I am not one of your maidservants."

When it was time for the midday meal Boaz invited Ruth to eat with him. And when it was time to return to work, he told his men to allow Ruth to glean even among the sheaves. And so she gleaned until evening and every day thereafter, until the end of the harvest.

Naomi rejoiced in the kindness that Boaz had shown to Ruth and urged her to keep close to him, saying, "Is Boaz not our kinsman? Have you not gleaned with his maidservants?" When the harvest came to an end, Naomi decided that it was time for her to find a home for Ruth, and Boaz naturally came to mind. She told Ruth, "Wash and anoint yourself, and put on your finest clothes. Go down to the threshing floor, but do not let Boaz see you until he has finished eating and drinking. When you see him lie down, go uncover his feet and lie down with him. Then he will tell you what to do."

Ruth did exactly as Naomi had said. She went to the threshing floor, waited for Boaz to lie down to sleep, and then laid herself at his feet. At midnight he awoke, startled, and asked, "Who are you?"

"I am Ruth," she replied, "your maidservant. Spread your cloak over me, for you are my next of kin."

And he said, "May the Lord bless you, my daughter, for this kindness is greater than the first, as you have not chased after young men, rich or poor. I shall do as you ask, for everyone knows that you are a woman of valor. It is true that I am a close relative, but there is one who is closer. If he is willing to do his part as the next of kin, then very well; if not, then as the Lord lives, I shall do the part of the next of kin. Now lie down here until morning."

The next day Boaz sought out Ruth's next of kin and explained to him, "Naomi is selling the portion of land that belonged to our kinsman Elimelech. But the man who buys it will also marry her daughter-in-law, the Moabite widow of Naomi's dead son, so that the name of the dead might be restored to his inheritance."

The kinsman replied, "I cannot redeem this property, for if I do, I might jeopardize my own inheritance. You may take my right of redemption if you wish."

Boaz then went to the elders and declared, "Witness this day that I have purchased from Naomi all that belonged to Elimelech and her sons, Chilion and Mahlon. And with this purchase I take the Moabite Ruth to be my wife, so that the name of the dead may not be cut off from his brothers."

And the people answered, "We are witnesses. May the Lord make the woman coming into your house as Rachel and Leah, who together raised up the house of Israel. May you prosper in Ephrath and be renowned in Bethlehem. May your house be like the house of Perez, whom Tamar bore to Judah, for the children that the Lord will give you through this young woman."

So Boaz took Ruth to be his wife, and she bore him a son. And Naomi nursed the child, who was named Obed. He became the father of Jesse, who was the father of David.

David and Goliath
1 SAMUEL 17:19–54

Here is a story about the connection between faith and courage. While few of us may face the likes of Goliath, many of us face what seem to be insurmountable problems. The young David teaches us that even though faith may come in small packages, it is capable of overcoming the greatest of difficulties. Very often we are daunted not so much by our lack of courage as by our lack of faith. Faith is among the first things of life, and after it comes courage.

King Saul and all the men of Israel had gathered in the valley of Elah to do battle with the Philistines. That morning David rose up early and left his sheep in the care of another. As his father Jesse had commanded him, he gathered provisions to bring to his older brothers, soldiers in Saul's army, and set out. When David arrived at Saul's camp, the hosts were preparing for battle and shouting out the war cry. David left his parcels with the baggage keeper and rushed out to join the ranks.

He greeted his brothers, and as he was speaking to them, the Philistine champion from Gath, Goliath, stepped out from the ranks of the Philistines. He stood six cubits and a span high, and his armor weighed five thousand shekels of bronze. The shaft of his spear was like a weaver's beam, and the head of his spear weighed six hundred shekels of iron.

"Why do you line up for battle?" Goliath cried. "I am a Philistine, and you are the servants of Saul. Choose a man from your ranks and have him come out to meet me. If he kills me, then we shall be your servants. But if I kill him, then all of you will come and serve us."

All of the men of Israel fled at the sight of Goliath, saying, "Have you seen him? Surely the king will greatly reward the one who kills him and give him his daughter to marry."

"Who is this uncircumcised Philistine," David asked, "that he should defy the armies of the living God?"

David's older brother Eliab heard what he said and grew angry with him. "Why have you left the sheep in the wilderness to come down here?" he asked. "I know what you are thinking and the wickedness in your heart; you have come to watch the battle."

David replied, "What have I done now? All I spoke were words."

Now the words that David spoke were repeated to Saul, who sent for David. The lad said to the king, "Let no man's heart grow faint because of Goliath. Your servant will go out to fight the Philistine."

Saul answered, "You cannot stand up to this Philistine and fight him. You are just a boy, and he has been a warrior from his youth."

But David said to Saul, "I used to keep sheep for my father. Whenever a lion or a bear came to take sheep from the flock, I would go after him and strike him and thus deliver the sheep from his mouth. And if he rose up against me, I would take him by the beard and kill him. Your servant has killed lions and bears. This uncircumcised Philistine will be like one of them, for he has defied the armies of the living God. The Lord, who delivered me from the claws of the lion and the claws of the bear, will deliver me from the hand of this Philistine."

So Saul said to David, "Go! And the Lord be with you!"

Saul outfitted David in his armor, with a helmet of bronze and a coat of mail. David fastened his sword over the armor, but when he tried to walk, he was unable to, for he was not used to the armor. So he said to Saul, "I cannot wear this," and removed the armor. He took his staff, selected five smooth stones from a stream nearby, and put them into his bag. Then, his sling in hand, he approached the Philistine.

The Philistine came out and went toward David with his shield-bearer in front of him. When he saw David, he had nothing but contempt for the fair lad. Said Goliath, "Am I a dog, that you come after me with sticks?" Then, cursing David in the name of his gods, the Philistine said, "Come to me, and I shall feed your flesh to the birds of the air and the beasts of the field!"

David replied, "You come to me with a sword and a spear, but I come to you in the name of the Lord of hosts, the God of the armies of Israel, whom you have defied. The Lord will deliver you this day into my hands, for I shall strike you down and cut off your head! This day I shall feed the bodies of the Philistines to the birds of the air and the beasts of the earth, so that all will know that there is a God in Israel!"

Then Goliath came toward David, and David ran out to meet him. He took a stone from his bag, placed it in his sling, and hurled it toward the Philistine. It struck Goliath on the forehead, sinking into it, and he fell on his face to the ground.

Thus David prevailed over the Philistine with but a sling and a stone. He went over to the Goliath, took his sword from him, and cut off his head. When the Philistines saw that their champion lay dead, they fled. The men of Judah and Israel rose up with a shout and chased them as far as Gath and the gates of Ekron, and then they plundered their camp. David took the head of Goliath and brought it up to Jerusalem.

The Prophet and the King

2 SAMUEL 11:2–12:15

One of the most fundamental of all Jewish teachings is that no man, not even a king, is above the law of God. In this story David, King of Israel, violates one of the most sacred of all human relationships: that between husband and wife. Even an Israelite king cannot betray another man, though the one betrayed be a lowly Hittite and a servant to the king. As it some-

times happens, the violation of the marriage here leads to murder and ends in the death of a child. When marriage is no longer sacred, neither is human life. And when human life is no longer sacred, children die. Holy matrimony is the highest expression of our relation to the Holy One, who sanctifies life and brings children into the world.

Late one afternoon, when King David arose from his couch, he saw from his roof a woman bathing, and she was very beautiful. He asked a servant who she was, and the servant told him, "She is Bathsheba, daughter of Eliam, wife of Uriah the Hittite."

David sent for her, and she came to him. He lay with her, and she was with child.

Upon discovering that she was pregnant, David sent for Uriah the Hittite. Uriah came to him, and David asked how the people were doing and how the war was going. Then he said to Uriah, "Go down to your house and wash your feet." The king offered him a present, and Uriah left of the house. He did not go home, however, but slept at the King's door with all the servants of his lord.

When David found out that Uriah had not gone home, he said to him, "Have you not returned from a long journey? Why did you not go down to your house?"

Uriah answered, "The ark, along with Israel and Judah, all dwell in tabernacles. My lord Joab and the servants of my lord are camped in the open field. Shall I then go to my house and lie with my wife? As you live, and by the life of your soul, I shall do no such thing."

"Remain here today," David replied. "And tomorrow you may go."

So Uriah stayed in Jerusalem that day and the next. David invited him to eat and drink, until he was drunk. In the evening Uriah went out to lie down with the servants of his lord. But he did not go down to his house.

The next morning David wrote a letter to his commander Joab and sent it with Uriah. The letter said, "Place Uriah in the front line of the fiercest fighting, and then withdraw from him, so that he may be struck down and die."

As Joab besieged a city, he ordered Uriah to the front along with other brave men. The men of the city came out and fought with Joab's army, and several of David's servants fell. Joab then sent word to David, telling him all the news of the battle. He instructed the messenger, saying, "If the King should grow angry and ask about all the dead, say to him, 'Your servant Uriah the Hittite is dead too.'"

The messenger did just as Joab told him to do and said all that he was told to say. David instructed him, "Go back to Joab and tell him not to let this matter trouble him. For the sword devours now one and then the other. Tell him to strengthen his attack on the city. And tell him that we support him."

When Uriah's wife heard that her husband was dead, she went into mourning for him. And when the period of mourning was over, David sent for her and brought her into his house. She became his wife and bore him a son.

But the thing David had done displeased the Lord. The Lord sent the prophet Nathan to David. Nathan said to him, "There were once two men who lived in a city, one quite rich and the other very poor. The rich man owned many flocks and herds, while the poor man had nothing but a single little ewe lamb. He raised the lamb with care, and it grew up with him and his children. It would eat from his food and drink from his cup, and he would hold it to his breast as though it were his daughter. Now a traveler happened to visit the rich man, but the rich man was unwilling to butcher one of his own flock to feed the wayfarer. So he took the lamb that belonged to the poor man and served it to his guest."

Hearing the tale, David grew very angry. "The man who has done this deserves to die! He should restore the lamb four times over for doing this and for having no pity!"

Nathan said to David, "You are the man. The Lord, God of Israel, says, 'I anointed you king of Israel and delivered you out of the hand of Saul. I brought you into your master's house and gave you all his wives, along with the houses of Israel and Judah. If you believed this to be insufficient, I would add still more. Why, then, do you show contempt for My word, doing what is evil in My sight? You have struck down Uriah the Hittite with a sword and have taken his wife to be your own. Now the sword will not depart from your house. Evil will rise up within your own walls. I shall take your wives and offer them to your neighbor, and he will lie with them in broad daylight. What you did secretly, I shall do before all of Israel."

"I have sinned against the Lord," said David.

Nathan answered, "The Lord has forgiven your sin; you will not die. But because this deed is abhorrent to Him, the child born to you will die."

The Wisest of Men
1 KINGS 3:4–28

What might a man ask for, if he could be granted anything? If he were wise, as Solomon was wise, he would ask for the ability to discern between good and evil, for the sake of the lives around him, that he might walk in the ways of God. One sign of this wisdom would be insight into a mother's heart, for to know the secret of a mother's love is to know the secret of all that is precious in the sight of God.

One day King Solomon went to Gibeon to offer up a thousand burnt offerings. When he fell asleep that night, the Lord appeared to him in a dream and said, "Ask for anything that I may give you."

Solomon replied, "You have shown great kindness to your servant David, my father, for he was a man of faith and righteousness. You have continued to show him this kindness by allowing his son to sit upon his throne even now, having made your servant king after my father. But I am very young and do not understand how to conduct myself in the simplest of matters. Now Your servant stands in the midst of Your chosen people, whose number is so great it cannot be reckoned. Grant Your servant the wisdom to discern between good and evil, so that he may govern this multitude. For who, indeed, could govern such a great people?"

The Lord was pleased by Solomon's request and answered, "Because you have asked for the wisdom to do what is right, and not for a long life or riches or the deaths of your enemies, I now grant what you have asked for. Behold, I bestow upon you a wise and discerning heart, like none before you and none after you. To that

I shall add what you have not asked for: riches and honors as no other king has enjoyed. If you follow in My ways, keeping to My commandments, as your father did, I shall give you long life as well."

When Solomon awoke, he went to Jerusalem and stood before the Ark of the covenant, where he offered up sacrifices and peace offerings, and he made a feast for all his servants.

One day two harlots came before him with an infant. One of them said, "O my lord, this woman and I live in the same house, where I gave birth to this child. Three days after my delivery, she too had a baby. We were all alone in the house. Now one night this woman's infant died, for she lay upon him in her sleep. In the middle of the night, as I slept, she took my son from beside me and placed her dead son next to me. When I rose in the morning to nurse my little one, I found that he was dead. But when I looked at him more closely, I realized that he was not mine."

At that the other woman broke in, saying, "It isn't true! The baby who is alive is mine, and the dead child is yours!"

The first woman replied, "No! The dead baby is yours, and the one still alive is mine!"

King Solomon spoke. "One of you declares, 'This is my son, who is alive, and the dead one is yours!' And the other insists, 'No, your son is dead, and mine is alive!'" Ordering his servant to bring him a sword, Solomon told the servant, "Take the sword and divide the living child in half. Give one part to the first woman and the other part to the second."

Then the mother of the living child, whose heart ached with pity for him, cried out, "O my lord, give her the child, and do not kill him!"

But the other woman said, "Divide it! The child will be neither mine nor yours!"

Ruled King Solomon, "Give the babe to the first woman. She is his mother."

Hearing his judgment, all of Israel was in awe of the King, for they perceived in him the wisdom of God to render justice.

Chariot of Fire

2 KINGS 2:1–18

One of the most mysterious Jewish stories ever told, this tale describes how the prophet Elijah did not die but ascended to the heavens in a chariot of fire to await the time when he would return to this world and proclaim the coming of the Messiah. Elijah passed his mantle on to Elisha, who began his life as a prophet with the frustration that confronts nearly all the prophets: when he spoke, he was not believed.

As the time drew near when the Lord was to take Elijah up to heaven in a whirlwind, the prophet and his disciple Elisha were walking from Gilgal. Elijah said to Elisha, "Please stay here, for the Lord is sending me to Bethel." But Elisha replied, "As the Lord lives and as you yourself are alive, I shall not leave your side."

So together they went to Bethel. The prophets who lived in Bethel came out to greet Elisha and told him, "Do you know that today the Lord will take your master from you?" Elisha answered, "Yes, I know. But hold your peace."

Elijah then said to him, "Elisha, please stay here, for the Lord is sending me to Jericho." But Elisha replied, "As the Lord lives and as you yourself are alive, I shall not leave your side."

So together they went on to Jericho. There the local prophets came up to Elisha and said, "Do you know that today the Lord will take your master from you?" Elisha answered, "Yes, I know. But hold your peace."

Elijah then said to him, "Elisha, please stay here, for the Lord is sending me to the Jordan." But Elisha replied, "As the Lord lives and as you yourself are alive, I shall not leave your side."

So the two of them continued on together, and fifty men from the brotherhood of the prophets went with them. As Elijah and Elisha stood beside the Jordan, the men of the brotherhood kept at a distance. Then Elijah took off his mantle and struck the waters of the Jordan. The waters parted for them, so that he and Elisha could walk over dry ground to the other side.

After they had crossed over, Elijah said to Elisha, "Ask of me what I may do for you before I am taken away."

Elisha answered, "Please allow me to inherit a double share of your spirit."

"You ask a hard thing," Elijah replied. "And yet, if you see me as I am being taken away from you, it shall be so. If not, then you will not receive what you ask for."

As they continued on and talked, a chariot of fire with horses of fire appeared and separated them. Elijah ascended to heaven in the whirlwind. When Elisha saw this, he cried out, "My father, my father! The chariot of Israel and its steeds!" And he saw his master no more.

Elisha then took hold of his clothes and tore them in two. He picked up the mantle that had fallen from Elijah's shoulders and went back to the banks of the Jordan. There he took Elijah's mantle and struck the water, saying, "Where is the Lord, the God of Elijah?" And when he struck the river, the waters parted, so that he could cross over.

When the brotherhood of the prophets saw him from a distance, they declared, "The spirit of Elijah rests upon Elisha!" They went out to meet him, bowed to the ground, and said, "Behold, there are fifty strong men among your servants. Let them go to look for your master. Perhaps the spirit of the Lord has taken him up and set him on some mountain top or cast him into some valley." But Elisha answered, "Send no one."

Yet they pressured him so much that finally he gave in and said, "Go ahead and send them."

Thus they sent out fifty men, and for three days they searched everywhere for Elijah but did not find him. At last they returned to Jericho, where Elisha was staying, and he said to them, "I told you not to go looking for him."

A Child Returned to Life

2 KINGS 4:8–37

The true mission of a prophet, demonstrated symbolically in this story, is to return life to the world where, it seems, there should be no life. Elisha returns a dead child to life by pressing his own body against the body of the child. Just so, the prophets summoned Israel to return to God and therefore to life not just through their admonitions but by living God's words and commandments in the nation's midst. The spirit of life that the prophet Elijah imparted to Elisha is here imparted to the child. According to the Zohar, a mystical commentary on the Bible, the child whom Elisha returned to life was none other than the prophet Habakkuk.

Whenever Elisha used to pass through the town of Shunem, he visited a wealthy woman who would give him food. His visits became so frequent that the woman finally said to her husband, "Let us prepare a small room up on the roof for him, with a bed, a table, a lamp, and a chair, so that whenever he comes to us he can stay there. For I believe that this man is a holy man of God."

One day when Elisha was visiting the woman and her husband, he retired to the room they had prepared for him. He said to his servant Gehazi, "Bring the Shunammite woman to me."

When she came to him, he said, "You have gone to all this trouble for us, so tell me, what can we do for you? May we speak to the king on your behalf or have a word with the commander of the army?"

"I dwell among my own people," she replied.

"What, then, may we do for her?" Elisha asked Gehazi.

"Well, she has no son, and her husband is old," said Gehazi.

Elisha turned back to the woman, "At this time next year you will hold a son in your arms."

"O, my lord," she answered, "how can that be? Please, do not deceive your servant."

But the woman conceived and gave birth to a son, as Elisha said she would. The child grew, but one day he went out to his father among the reapers, complaining, "Oh, my head, my head!"

"Take him to his mother," his father ordered a servant. The servant picked up the lad, took him to his mother, and placed him on her lap. There he sat until midday. And at midday he died. His mother carried him upstairs and placed him on the bed where the man of God slept. When she went out, she shut the door behind her.

Then she called to her husband and said, "Bring a servant and an ass to me, quickly, so that I may go to the man of God and bring him back here."

"Why are you going to him now?" he asked. "It is neither the Sabbath nor the new moon."

"Never mind," she answered.

She saddled the ass and said to her servant, "Urge the beast on, and do not slow down until I tell you to." So she rode, until she came to the man of God at Mount Carmel.

When the man of God saw her, he said to Gehazi, "Look, it is the Shunammite woman. Go out to greet her and ask if all is well with her and her husband and child."

When Gehazi asked, she told him all was well. But when she approached the man of God on the mountain, she fell to the ground and took hold of his feet. Gehazi started to push her away, but Elisha said, "Leave her alone, for she is terribly distressed. But the Lord has hidden her trouble from me, and I do not know what it can be."

"Did I ask my lord for a son?" she said. "Did I ask you not to deceive me?"

Elisha told Gehazi, "Pack your bags, take my staff, and go with her. If you meet anyone along the way, do not stop to greet him, and if anyone greets you, do not return the greeting. When you get there, lay my staff upon the face of the child."

But the child's mother said to Elisha, "As the Lord lives and as you yourself are alive, I shall not leave your side." So Elisha went with her, while Gehazi hurried on ahead of them. When Gehazi arrived at the woman's home, he laid the staff upon the face of the child, but there was no sound or sign of life. Then he went back to meet Elisha and told him, "The child has not awakened."

When Elisha arrived at the house, he saw the child lying dead on the bed. He closed the door and prayed to the Lord. Then he went over to the child and lay down on top of him, pressing his mouth against the child's mouth, his eyes against the child's eyes, and his hands against the child's hands. As he lay upon the child, the child's body grew warm. Then Elisha got up, walked about the house, and returned to lay himself on the child once more. Seven times he did this, and the seventh time the child suddenly sneezed and opened his eyes.

Elisha summoned the Shunammite woman and said, "Here, take your son." She fell to his feet and bowed to the ground. Then she lifted up her son and left.

The Salvation of a Nation

FROM THE BOOK OF ESTHER

It is not its discourse on the God of Abraham, Isaac, and Jacob—indeed, God is not mentioned in the tale—that makes this story great, but its concern with the deliverance of a community from death. According to the Jewish tradition, however, to take such an interest in the well-being of a community is to take an interest in God. Esther and Mordecai demonstrate their piety not by paying lip service to God but by saving lives. This is the truest service to God and the most profound utterance of His Name. And this is what is celebrated when the tale is told each year at Purim, the festival that commemorates these events.

During the time of the Babylonian exile, Ahasuerus, King of Persia, gave a lavish feast for all the people, great and small, who lived in his capital city of Susa. The feast lasted for seven days, and on the seventh day the king ordered the lovely Queen Vashti to be brought before the merrymakers, so that he might parade her beauty before them. But when the queen refused to comply with his command, the king became furious. He consulted his counselors, who told him that he should offer her position to one who was more worthy than she, lest the wives of every man in the kingdom lose respect for their husbands. The king ordered that all the beautiful young virgins of the land be brought to him, so that he might select a queen to take the place of the rebellious Vashti.

Now in Susa there lived a Jew named Mordecai. A righteous man who had been carried away from Jerusalem into exile, Mordecai brought up as his own the orphaned daughter of his uncle. She was called Hadassah, or Esther, and was a maiden of rare beauty. So, when the maidens of the land were brought to the palace, Esther was chosen for one of the most honored positions in the king's harem. Mordecai visited the palace every day to see how Esther fared. When she was finally brought before King Ahasuerus, the king fell in love with her and chose her to wear Vashti's crown.

Mordecai continued to visit the palace. One day he happened to overhear two of the king's eunuchs plotting to take their master's life. Immediately he went to Queen Esther with the information, and she hurried to the king. The two men were hanged, the life of Ahasuerus was spared, and all was recorded in the Book of Chronicles.

After these events transpired, King Ahasuerus promoted Haman the Agagite to chief minister. In his arrogance Haman required that everybody must bow down to him. But the righteous Mordecai refused. Haman was so enraged by this that he plotted to destroy all the Jews of the kingdom.

Haman went to King Ahasuerus and said, "There is a certain people scattered throughout your provinces, who live by different laws and do not pay heed to the laws of the king, so that it does not profit the king to tolerate their existence. Therefore, if it please the king, let it be decreed that they be destroyed." Letters were sent to all the provinces of the kingdom with orders to kill all the Jews—young and old, women and children.

When Mordecai found out about the plot to annihilate his people, he tore his clothes, put on sackcloth and ashes, and went about the city raising a loud and bitter cry. To warn Esther of the danger, he sent word to her, saying, "Do not suppose that you will escape the death awaiting all the Jews simply because you sit in the king's palace. But it is not by chance that you have been made queen."

Esther sent a message in reply to Mordecai that read, "Gather all the Jews of Susa. Tell them to fast for three days and three nights, as I and my maids shall fast. Then I shall go to the King, even though it may cost me my life."

On the third day of her fast Esther donned her royal robes and went to Ahasuerus.

"What is your request, my queen?" asked the king. "Name it and it shall be yours, even unto the half of my kingdom."

Esther answered, "If it please the king, have Haman come to a dinner that I will prepare for you."

When Haman received the invitation to attend a dinner with Esther and the king, he was overjoyed. The only thing that threatened to spoil his merriment was the sight of Mordecai at the king's gate. Therefore Haman ordered a gallows to be built, so that Mordecai might be hanged.

That night the king could not sleep. He ordered the Book of Chronicles to be brought to him and the memorable deeds of his realm read to him from it. Listening to the tales of his rule as king, Ahasuerus was reminded of Mordecai. "What honors have been bestowed upon Mordecai for his great service?" he asked.

"Nothing has been done for him, Sire," was the servant's reply.

Just at that moment Haman was brought before the king, who asked him, "What should be done for the man whom the king wishes to honor?"

Thinking Ahasuerus spoke of him, Haman answered, "Let the man be dressed in the royal robes of the King, and let a crown be placed upon his head. Let a noble prince conduct the man about the city on horseback, proclaiming, 'Thus shall it be done for the man whom the king delights to honor.'"

Haman's suggestion pleased Ahasuerus, and he ordered Haman to array Mordecai and lead him through the city. Although Haman was very much vexed by having to comply with such an order, his spirits rose a bit when he attended the feast that Esther had prepared for him and the king. As they sat and drank their wine, Ahasuerus turned to Esther and said, "What is your request, my queen? Name it, and it shall be yours, even unto the half of my kingdom."

Queen Esther replied, "If it please the king, let my life be spared at my petition and my people at my request. For it has been decreed that my people and I are to be destroyed, slain, and annihilated."

The king was shocked and asked, "Who is the man that dares to do this thing?"

"It is your enemy, the wicked Haman!" Esther declared.

Enraged, the king rose and went into his garden. But the evil Haman stayed, fell on Esther's couch, and begged her for his miserable life. As the king returned to the banquet hall, he saw Haman on Esther's couch and said to himself, "Will this man assault the queen, and in my own house?" Turning to one of his attendants, he ordered, "Take the gallows that Haman has prepared for Mordecai and hang him!"

All the wealth that Haman owned Ahasuerus gave to Queen Esther, and he decreed that the Jews be allowed to defend themselves against their enemies. Thus, on the day that those who hated the Jews had hoped to destroy them, they were themselves destroyed. Mordecai the Jew came to be second only to the king in honor and power, and he was loved by all his brethren. For he sought only the well-being of his people and peace for everyone in the kingdom.

The Affliction of a Righteous Man
FROM THE BOOK OF JOB

After Abraham descended from Mount Moriah, he did not speak again with God. According to one tradition, the man who took his place in humanity's ongoing argument with God was Job. The question that Job poses is perhaps even more ancient than the tale itself: if God is good, just, and almighty, then why do the righteous suffer so? While the tale ends without an answer, the importance of the question lies not in its resolution but in the truth that God's justice and goodness are what make the question meaningful. Even after God rebukes Job for his moment of rebellion, He declares, "My servant Job has spoken rightly." Why? Because it pleases God that Job would ask, as he does, in the name of the very righteousness and justice that God demands of all His creatures.

One day the angels of God presented themselves to the Lord. The Lord turned to the one called Satan and asked, "Where have you come from?"

"From walking the earth," he replied.

"Have you noticed my servant Job?" asked the Lord. "There is none like him. He is a righteous man, blameless, who fears God and shuns evil."

"Of course," Satan answered. "You have blessed him in every way. But if You should lay Your hand upon him, he will curse You to Your face."

"We shall see," said God. "All he has is in your power, all except his life."

Soon after that one of Job's servants came to him and said, "The Sabeans have fallen upon your oxen and asses and have taken them away. They killed your servants, and I alone have escaped."

No sooner had he spoken than another servant came and reported, "A fire came down from heaven and consumed your sheep and the servants who were with them. I alone have escaped."

And even as he spoke, a third servant came and said, "The Chaldeans have raided your camels and killed your servants. I alone have escaped."

Finally a fourth servant ran to Job and told him, "Your sons and daughters were eating and drinking in their oldest brother's house, when a wind rose up and destroyed the house, killing them all. I alone have escaped."

Upon hearing all of this, Job tore his clothes, shaved his head, and fell to the ground to worship God, saying, "Naked I came from my mother's womb, and naked shall I return. The Lord gave, and the Lord has taken away. Blessed be the Name of the Lord."

When God pointed out to Satan that His servant persisted in his righteousness, Satan replied, "Skin for skin! A man will give up anything to save his own life. But if You strike him in his flesh and bone, he will curse You to Your face."

The Lord said to Satan, "He is in your power. Only spare his life."

So Satan afflicted Job with boils and sores from head to toe. Seeing the condition he was in, Job's wife said to him, "Why do you cling to your empty integrity like this? Better to curse God and die!"

But Job answered, "Shall we receive only good from the hand of God, and not evil as well?"

Job had three friends named Eliphaz, Bildad, and Zophar. Upon hearing of his misfortune, they came to him and sat in silence with him for seven days. At the end of the seven days Job cried out and cursed the day he was born, blaming God for allowing people born under foreboding omens to remain alive and suffer unjustly.

But Eliphaz answered him, saying, "Was there ever anyone among the innocent who perished unjustly, or among the sowers of iniquity who did not reap the same? In the dead of night terror once came over me, and from the depths of silence I heard a voice ask, 'Can a mortal man be righteous before God or a mere man stand pure before his Maker?' Man is born for trouble, and God frustrates the devices of the clever. Blessed is the man whom God reproves, for He who wounds also heals. If it seems that He acts unjustly it is not because He is unjust but because we cannot fathom His ways."

And Job answered, "Oh, that my anger were weighed and my misfortune laid in the balances, for now it would be heavier than the sand of the seas! If only God would crush me and be done with it! Show me where I have gone wrong, and I shall be silent. Those who go down to Sheol do not come up. Therefore I shall not hold my tongue. If I, who am so small, should sin, what harm can it do to You, O Lord, who are so great? My suffering far exceeds my transgression!"

Then Bildad spoke and said, "If you seek God and are pure and upright, then He will show you His favor. But surely your children have sinned. Remember the teachings of our fathers: can papyrus grow where there is no marsh? God will not reject a blameless man. Repent and you will find forgiveness."

"What you say may be so," Job replied, "but how is a man to contend with God? How can I hope to answer Him? Even if I were innocent, my own mouth would condemn me. The earth is given into the hands of the wicked, and He covers the faces of its judges. For if it is not His doing, then whose is it? And if it is His doing, then where is His justice? I would say to God, 'Do not condemn me, but tell me why You raise Your hand against me. It is You who have made me, and now would You destroy me? If I sin, You mark me for doom. If I am righteous, I cannot raise my head, for I am disgraced. Why did You bring me forth from the womb? Would that I had died before any eye had seen me!'"

Hearing Job's words, Zophar said, "You claim to be innocent before God, but what He exacts from you is even less than your guilt deserves! Can you fathom the depths of the Almighty? If you set your heart aright, you will stretch out your hands to Him, and He will heal you of your misery."

Job answered Zophar, saying, "You are no wiser than I. I have been a righteous man, and now I am a laughingstock, while the tents of thieves are at peace! And all of this has come from the hand of the Lord. I have seen Him deprive the elders of their insight and nations of their strength. Nevertheless, I would speak to the Almighty and argue my case with God. As for you, your proverbs are like ashes, and your pretense is like clay. O Lord, why do You hide Your face from me and count me as an enemy? If a man dies, will he live again? No man can prevail against You. He grows old, and You send him to his fate. He knows nothing of his sons' honors. And all he feels is the pain of his own body."

Job and his friends continued to argue. Eliphaz, Bildad, and Zophar persisted in their efforts to convince Job that there was no mortal without sin and that God's just punishment was visited upon the wicked. Job continued to maintain that his life had been made unjustly miserable and that he had done nothing to merit this suffering. Insisting that the wicked prosper while the righteous suffer, he maintained his argument that God was either indifferent or unjust. Yet he longed for an audience with the Lord.

Throughout these disputations a young man named Elihu had stood by listening to the arguments of Job and his three friends until finally he could no longer hold his tongue. Addressing Job, he said, "You claim to be pure and free of transgression, saying, 'A man derives no profit from taking delight in God.' But far be it from God that He should do anything wicked or unjust! The more you speak, the more you add rebellion to your sin. God does not hear an empty cry nor does He take note of it. Rather than keep the wicked alive, He confers upon the afflicted their right and delivers them by their very affliction. He opens their ears so that they may be taught and thus return from their iniquity. Listen to the thundering of His voice and humbly consider His works of wonder! For He is great in power and justice and will do no violence to the righteous."

Then the Lord answered Job from out of a whirlwind, saying, "Who is this that darkens counsel with words void of wisdom? Answer Me: Were you there when I laid the foundations of the earth? Have you given the dawn its shining or walked the depths of the sea? Do you know the place where the light resides or where the darkness dwells? Can you know the ordinances of the heavens or establish their rule on earth? Do you provide the lion with his prey or the horse with his strength? Is it by your command that the hawk soars or that the eagle makes his nest on high? And will you then condemn Me, that you might be justified?"

Humbled, Job answered, "What shall I say to You? I have spoken once but will speak no more. For I have uttered what I did not understand and spoken of things too wondrous to know. Therefore I despise myself and repent in dust and ashes."

Then the Lord turned to Eliphaz and said, "My wrath is kindled against you and your friends, for you have not spoken rightly, as my servant Job has. Therefore you must take seven bulls and seven rams and sacrifice them as burnt offerings. My servant Job will pray for you."

After Job had prayed for his friends, his family and all who knew him came to his house and comforted him for his suffering. The Lord restored to him twice as much as he had before, beginning with sheep and camels, oxen and asses. He also gave Job seven sons and three daughters, and in all the land there were no women as beautiful as the daughters of Job. After all this had come to pass Job lived a hundred and forty years and lived to see his children and his children's children unto the fourth generation. And then Job died an old man full of days.

Jeremiah's Scroll

JEREMIAH 36:1–32

This story tells of one of the major trials that the prophet Jeremiah endured: the assault on his words. It is a trial common in one way or another to all of the prophets, faced as they are with the task of sustaining the word of the Lord, restoring meaning, and thereby restoring the relationship between humanity and God. Many writers, upon finding that their words have gone up in flames, might succumb to despair, but not Jeremiah. Instead, he writes another scroll, this time including the tale of the burning of the first scroll. He thus teaches us that rewriting is more important than writing. And the story teaches us that burning a book will not destroy the word of God.

In the fourth year of the reign of Jehoiakim, son of Josiah, this word from the Lord came to Jeremiah: "Take a scroll and write upon it all the words I have spoken to you concerning Israel and Judah and all the nations, from the time I first spoke to you, when Josiah was king, until now. The House of Judah will hear the of the destruction that I intend to bring to them and, so hearing, perhaps they will abandon their evil ways. Then I may forgive them for their iniquity and their sin." So Jeremiah called Baruch, the son of Neriah, and Baruch wrote upon a scroll all that Jeremiah dictated to him.

Then Jeremiah gave Baruch these instructions: "Because I am banned from entering the House of the Lord, you must go in my stead. On the day of the fast, in the hearing of all, you are to read from the scroll the words of the Lord that I have dictated to you. Read them so that all the men of Judah may hear them. Perhaps then they will offers prayers of forgiveness to the Lord and turn from their evil ways. Great is the anger and the wrath that the Lord will bring upon these people." In the ninth month of the fifth year of the reign of Jehoiakim, Baruch completed all that Jeremiah had commanded him to do.

Now Micaiah, the son of Gemariah, heard all the words of the Lord read from the scroll and went to the secretary's chamber in the king's house. Gathered there were all the princes of Judah, and Micaiah told them the words that Baruch had read in the hearing of the people. After listening to Micaiah, the princes sent Jehudi, son of Nethaniah, to Baruch with a message, saying, "Come to us and bring the scroll that you read in the hearing of all the people." When Baruch arrived with the scroll, they told him to sit down and read it. When they had heard all the words it contained, they turned to one another in fear. "We must report all of this to the king," they told Baruch. "Tell us, how did you happen to write this? Did someone dictate it to you?"

Baruch replied, "Jeremiah dictated to me all the words that I have written upon the scroll."

"Then you and Jeremiah must go into hiding," the princes warned him, "and let no one know where you are."

After placing the scroll in the care of the secretary Elishama, the princes reported all the words they had heard to the king, who sent for the scroll and ordered Jehudi to read it to him. Now it was winter, and the king was sitting next to a fire burning in a brazier. As Jehudi read the scroll to him, the king cut three or four columns from it at a time and threw them into the fire, until the entire scroll was consumed in flames. Although they heard every word of the scroll, neither the king nor his servants grew afraid. Several of the princes of Judah urged him not the burn the scroll, but he would not listen to them. He ordered that Jeremiah and Baruch be seized and brought to him, but the Lord kept them safe in hiding.

After the king had burned the scroll, the word of the Lord came to Jeremiah once again: "Take another scroll and write upon it all the words that were in the first scroll, which Jehoiakim, King of Judah, has burned. As for Jehoiakim, you shall say, 'Thus says the Lord: You have burned the scroll, asking why it was written that the King of Babylon would surely come and destroy this land and cut it off from man and beast. Therefore, says the Lord, Jehoiakim, King of Judah, will not sit upon the throne of David, but his dead body will be cast out into the heat of the day and the frost of the night. I shall punish him and his offspring and all of his servants for their iniquity. I shall bring upon him and the people of Jerusalem and all the inhabitants of Judah the destruction I have pronounced against them, for they would not heed My words.'"

Thus Jeremiah took another scroll and gave it to the scribe Baruch. He dictated to Baruch all the words of the scroll that King

Jehoiakim had burned. And he added to those words many that were similar to them.

In the Furnace of Babylon

DANIEL 3:1–30

The essence of exile is idolatry, while deliverance from exile comes through faith. Although the three men in this tale lived during the Babylonian Exile, they did not live in servitude. Demonstrating not only a confidence in the Lord but a willingness to die for their faith, they are free from the power of their oppressor. These three men teach their oppressor not by words but by their example the truth of their faith. And by teaching them that truth, they reveal to him the presence of a fourth—the presence of the angel of God—in the midst of the flames.

During the days of exile King Nebuchadnezzar fashioned an image of gold sixty cubits tall and erected it on the plain of Dura in Babylon. All the officials throughout his kingdom were ordered to attend the dedication of the idol. As they stood before the golden image, the herald proclaimed to them, "Men of all peoples, nations, and languages! Upon hearing the sound of the horn, pipe, lyre, triangle, harp, bagpipe, or any other musical instrument, you are commanded to bow down and worship the golden image that King Nebuchadnezzar has set up on the plain of Dura! Whosoever does not bow down to the image will immediately be cast into a burning furnace of flames." So whenever the people heard the sound of musical instruments, they bowed down and worshiped the golden image that King Nebuchadnezzar had made.

Now some Chaldeans who hated the Jews took advantage of the occasion and brought malicious accusations against them. They went to King Nebuchadnezzar and said, "O King, may you live forever! You have decreed that anyone who hears the sound of the horn, pipe, lyre, triangle, harp, bagpipe, or any other musical instrument must bow down and worship the golden image, and that whosoever does not bow down to the image will immediately be cast into a burning furnace of flames. We know of certain Jews whom you have appointed over the affairs of Babylon. Their names are Shadrach, Meshach, and Abednego. These men, O King, ignore your decree: they refuse to bow down to your gods or worship the golden image that you have erected."

Nebuchadnezzar became furious and ordered that Shadrach, Meshach, and Abednego be brought before him. "Is it true," he said to them, "that you refuse to bow down to my gods or worship the golden image? If you are prepared now to bow down and worship the image that I have fashioned, all will be well with you. But if you refuse to worship the image, you will immediately be cast into the furnace. What god then will deliver you from my hand?"

Shadrach, Meshach, and Abednego answered, "O Nebuchadnezzar, we have no need to reply to you in this matter. If it should be His will, the God whom we serve will be able to deliver us from the burning furnace of flames. And if it is not His will, then you, O King, will know that we shall not bow down to your gods or worship the golden image that you have set up in the plain of Dura."

Hearing their reply, Nebuchadnezzar became even more enraged and ordered the furnace to be heated to a temperature seven times hotter than it had ever been. He selected the strongest men from his army and ordered them to bind Shadrach, Meshach, and Abednego and cast them into the flames. So the Jews were bound with their mantles, their tunics, their hats, and other garments and cast into the furnace. And because the furnace had been heated seven times hotter than it had ever been, the men from the army who had bound Shadrach, Meshach, and Abednego perished along the edge of it.

Once the Jews had been taken away, King Nebuchadnezzar rose up with his counselors and hurried to the furnace to see whether they had been consumed. But when he looked into the flames he was astonished. "Did we not have three men bound and cast into the flames?" he asked his counselors.

"We did, O King."

"But I now see four men unbound, walking unharmed in the midst of the flames. And the fourth among them has the appearance of one of the sons of the gods!"

Nebuchadnezzar approached the door of the furnace and

shouted, "Shadrach, Meshach, and Abednego, servants of the God Most High, come forth!"

Shadrach, Meshach, and Abednego came out of the flames. The officials and counselors of the king saw that the flames had no power over the bodies of the three men. The hair on their heads and the mantles they wore were not singed; there was not even the smell of fire about them.

Finding them unscathed, Nebuchadnezzar cried out, "Blessed be the God of Shadrach, Meshach, and Abednego, who has sent His angel to deliver His servants for their faith in Him, reducing to naught the command of the king! For they have yielded up their bodies rather than bow down and worship any god but their own God. Hear therefore my decree: anyone of any people, nation, or language who utters a word against the God of Shadrach, Meshach, and Abednego shall be torn limb from limb and his house shall be reduced to rubble. For there is no other god who can bring salvation such as this."

And Shadrach, Meshach, and Abednego won the favor of the King of Babylon.

Daniel in the Den of Lions
DANIEL 6:1–28

While this story bears certain similarities to the preceding one, there are some important differences. For example, the attitude of Darius is quite different from that of Nebuchadnezzar. Darius is a man who learns something about the power of words and about the need to be careful with words. On a more symbolic level, when Shadrach, Meshach, and Abednego stood in the flames of the furnace, they were in their element. For, as it is written, "the Lord God is a consuming fire" (Deuteronomy 4:24), and, like the Torah itself, the passionate faith that comes from Him is as a fire. When Daniel walks among the beasts in the den of lions, however, this may suggest his walking among vicious men whom idolatry has reduced to beasts. Yet his faith brings to the lions the peace that comes from God, so that they do not harm him.

In the time of the Babylonian exile there was a Jew named Daniel whom King Darius favored. Filled with a wondrous spirit, Daniel proved himself superior to all those around him, and the king made plans to entrust him with the whole of his kingdom. So the other ministers and satraps of the realm grew jealous of Daniel and looked for some means of removing him from his position. But they could find no complaint against him or any fault within him, for he was completely faithful to the king. So they came up with a devious plan. The only way to incur the disfavor of the king toward Daniel would be to bring Daniel into some conflict with the law of his God.

The ministers and satraps formed a delegation and went to the king. "O King Darius," they said, "may you live forever! We are all in agreement that you should establish an ordinance and issue a decree declaring that for the next thirty days, whoever brings a petition to anyone, god or man, other than you, O King, shall be cast into the den of lions. Sign this document and issue this decree at once, O King, in keeping with the law of the Medes and the Persians, which cannot be revoked." King Darius signed the document and issued the decree.

When Daniel heard that the document had been signed, he retired to his house, whose upper-chamber windows faced Jerusalem. There, as always, he went down on his knees three times each day to pray and give thanks to his God. One day the men who plotted against him went to see Daniel, knowing that they would find him in prayer and supplication before God. Having confirmed that Daniel so prayed, they immediately went to the king and said, "O King, did you not decree that for the next thirty days whoever makes a petition to anyone, god or man, other than you will be cast into the den of lions?"

"So it has been decreed and so it stands," answered the king, "in keeping with the law of the Medes and the Persians, which cannot be revoked."

"Well, the exile from Judah named Daniel pays you no heed, O King, and ignores the decree you signed, for he makes his petition to his God three times each day."

When the king heard these words he was deeply distressed, and until the sun went down he thought and thought, seeking some way to save Daniel. But the men who opposed Daniel persisted and declared to the king, "Know, O King, that according to the law of the Medes and the Persians, no ordinance or decree that the King has signed may be altered."

Having no choice in the matter, Darius issued an order that Daniel be seized and cast into the lions' den. Darius said to Daniel, "May the God whom you serve so faithfully deliver you!" Then a stone was placed over the entrance to the lions' den, and the king sealed it with his own signet and with the signet of his noblemen, so that nothing could alter Daniel's fate. The king spent that night in his palace fasting. He refused to see any of his concubines, and sleep would not come to him.

At daybreak the king rose up and hurried to the den of lions. As he neared the pit he cried out in anguish, "O Daniel, has the living God, whom you serve so faithfully, been able to deliver you from the lions?"

And Daniel answered, "O King, may you live forever! My God sent His angel and closed up the mouths of the lions. They have done me no harm, seeing that I stand blameless before the Lord. Nor have I have committed any wrong against you, O King."

The king was overjoyed and ordered that Daniel be taken out of the lions' den. Then he ordered that the men who had accused Daniel be arrested and cast into the den of lions, along with their wives and children. No sooner did they reach the bottom of the pit than the lions seized them and crushed their bones to bits.

After these events King Darius wrote to all the inhabitants of his kingdom: "Peace be with you always! I decree that throughout my royal empire men shall tremble with fear before the God of Daniel. For He is the true living God, who endures forever. His kingdom will never be destroyed, and His dominion over the earth will endure unto the end of all things. He saves and sets free, working signs and wonders in heaven and earth. For He has delivered Daniel from the jaws of the lions."

Daniel prospered under the reign of Darius and the reign of Cyrus the Persian after him.

The Story of Jonah

FROM THE BOOK OF JONAH

The Book of Jonah is read in the synagogue on Yom Kippur, the Day of Atonement. It teaches us that responsibility is not something we choose but something for which we are chosen. It teaches us about the need to repent not just for sins against God but for sins against our fellow human beings. Indeed, the two relations are of a piece: the return to God entails a return to a fundamental responsibility for the welfare of our neighbors. Therefore Jonah learns that where there is repentance, there must be forgiveness, even if the prophet has declared God's wrath—even if God's forgiveness should be an embarrassment to the prophet.

The Lord spoke to Jonah, son of Amitai, saying, "Rise up and go to the great city of Nineveh and cry out against it, for the wickedness of its people has become known to Me." Jonah, however, did not do as the Lord commanded him. Instead he set out to flee from God to the distant city of Tarshish. So he went down to Joppa and paid his fare for passage on a ship bound for Tarshish.

The Lord unleashed a violent wind upon the sea, so that the ship was about to break up, and the sailors were terrified. They threw their cargo overboard, and each of them cried out to his god. Jonah, however, was fast asleep below deck. The ship's captain went down to him and shouted, "How can you sleep? Get up and call out to your God! Perhaps He will save us!"

The sailors said to one another, "Let's cast lots, so that we might find out who is to blame for this." They cast lots, and the deciding one fell to Jonah. "Tell us," they said to him, "what you are doing here. Where are you from? Who is your people?"

"I am a Hebrew," Jonah replied. "I worship the Lord, God of heaven, who made the sea and the land. But now I am caught fleeing from His presence."

Hearing this, the men grew frightened and said, "What have you done? How can we make the waters grow calm?"

"Take me," Jonah answered, "and throw me into the sea. For I know it is because of me that this storm has come upon you."

At first the sailors did not want to do what Jonah had said, so they tried to row the ship to shore, but in vain. The harder they rowed, the more violent the storm became. Finally, they decided to do what Jonah had told them and cried out to God, saying, "We beg You, O Lord, do not let us perish on account of this man's life! Let no innocent blood be on our hands!" They took Jonah and threw him into the sea. Then the sea grew calm, and the sailors offered sacrifices to the Lord.

When Jonah was in the midst of the waters, the Lord sent a great fish to swallow him up. Jonah remained in the belly of the fish for three days and three nights. And from the bowels of the fish Jonah prayed to God: "I cried out to the Lord in my distress, and He answered me. From the belly of Sheol I cried, and You have heard my voice. For You hurled me into the waters, and I was engulfed in the flood. Cast from Your presence, I wondered whether I might ever again behold Your Holy Temple. The waves closed over me, and the abyss wrapped itself around me. I descended into the deep, down to a place beneath the earth. But You, O Lord my God, lifted up my life from the pit. For when my soul grew faint, I remembered the Lord, and my prayer came to You in Your Holy Temple. Those who bow to idols worship in vain. And so, in a voice filled with thanksgiving, I shall offer my sacrifice to You. For salvation comes from the Lord."

Having heard Jonah's prayer, the Lord commanded the fish to vomit him out onto the land. The Lord spoke to Jonah a second time, saying, "Rise up and go to Nineveh. Preach to them the message I have given you." And so Jonah went to Nineveh, as the Lord had commanded him.

When Jonah arrived at the great city, he cried out to the people, warning them, "In forty days Nineveh will be destroyed!" The people of the city believed this word from God, and they declared a fast to be held throughout the city and put on sackcloth, from the greatest of them to the least. When the words of Jonah reached the king of Nineveh, he too put on sackcloth and covered himself with ashes.

"By the decree of the king and his ministers," he proclaimed, "let no morsel of food or water pass the lips of man or beast, herd or flock. Let all be covered with sackcloth and cry out to God. Let everyone renounce his evil ways and shun the violence of his hands.

Perhaps God will then repent of His anger and spare us, that we may not perish." When God saw the repentance of the people of Nineveh, His anger abated. And the city was saved.

Jonah, however, grew angry and said to the Lord, "I thought this would happen before I ever left my country. That is why I tried to flee to Tarshish. For I know that You are a merciful God, slow to anger, abounding in love, and quick to forgive. Therefore, O Lord, take my life from me, for there is no point in my living."

"Is your anger truly justified?" the Lord asked him.

Jonah left Nineveh and sat down to watch what would become of the city. The Lord God made a plant grow, which gave Jonah shade against the heat of the day. But at dawn the next morning, God made a worm attack the plant, causing it to wither. Then He stirred up a wind from the east, and the hot sun beat down on Jonah's head, until he grew faint and longed for death.

"Is your anger over the plant truly justified?" God asked him.

"Yes," he replied. "I am angry enough to die."

And the Lord said, "You have pity for the plant, which you did not care for or cause to grow. Should I not, then, have pity on Nineveh, where more than a hundred and twenty thousand people live, to say nothing of all the animals?"

The Light Returned from Darkness

FROM 1 MACCABEES 1–4

This story recounts the events that are commemorated by Hanukkah, the Festival of Lights. According to tradition, when the Temple was rededicated after being defiled, there was only enough oil for the menorah, the candelabrum, to burn for a single day, against all reason. This light is the light of the Holy, the light that came into being upon the first utterance of creation and sanctified all creation. Through Bible study, service to God, and deeds of loving kindness, human beings exemplify this light. Without this light life has no meaning or value. For this is the light that opposes material power with spiritual truth, imparting to all life its sanctity and significance, its center and direction.

In the days when Antiochus Epiphanes ruled over the land of Judah, there arose among the Israelites a group of renegades who abandoned the teachings and the covenant of their fathers to embrace the practices of the pagans. Seeing his authority so established, Antiochus marched on Jerusalem. There he desecrated the Temple, removing from it the golden altar and the menorah, along with the table for the loaves of offering, the cups, the vessels, the censers, and all the Temple's treasures. The city was pillaged, and women and children were taken captive. Throughout the land people went into mourning, and all the House of Jacob fell into shame and despair.

Having laid waste to the Holy City, the king declared that all the people in the land of Judah were to bow down to idols and profane the Sabbath. They were ordered to forsake the Torah and revoke all the observances of the Law, to leave their sons uncircumcised and to partake of unclean animals. Anyone who failed to obey the orders of the king would be executed. There were some among the Jews who obeyed, but others went into hiding and sought places of refuge. Many in Israel stood firm in the covenant of their fathers, even though it meant death.

During that dreadful time there lived a priest named Mattathias. When he encountered the blasphemies being committed throughout the land, he lamented having lived to witness the desecration of the Temple and the devastation of the people. One day the emissaries of the king entered the town of Modein, where Mattathias lived with his five sons. "You are a respected and influential leader in this town," they said to him, "with sons and brothers to support you. Be the first to comply with the orders of the king, and you will be honored among the friends of the king."

Mattathias replied in a loud voice, "My sons, my brothers, and I follow the covenant of our fathers, and not the orders of the king. We shall never forsake the Holy Torah and its commandments."

As he spoke, a Jew came forward to offer the pagan sacrifices, in keeping with the orders of the king, and Mattathias flew into a rage. He fell upon the Jew and killed him, along with the emissaries of the King. He marched through the town, shouting, "Let everyone who would embrace the Torah and the covenant of our fathers come out and follow me!" And then he and his sons fled to the hills.

Soon after this incident, the king learned about a group of Jews who had gone into the desert to continue their life of observance and righteousness. He sent his soldiers after them, and on the following Sabbath the soldiers killed the company of the faithful, who refused to fight and thereby profane the Sabbath. When the news of their deaths reached Mattathias, he mourned for them, but he realized that if their example were followed, the Jews would soon be wiped off the face of the earth. Thus he determined to fight the pagans, even if it meant fighting on the Sabbath. Refugees from the persecution rallied to his side, and they fought back, until they began to wrest the Torah out of the hands of those who would destroy it.

Now Mattathias was advanced in years, and as his days drew to a close, he passed on his command to his son Judah. Judah raised a formidable force of believers to fight for the cause of his father. When Seron, commander of the Syrian troops, heard of this he said, "I will make a great name for myself and win the favor of the king if I take up arms against Judah." So he launched a mighty campaign against the Israelites, vastly outnumbering them. Nevertheless, Judah and his men bravely met the Syrian forces and vanquished them.

This greatly infuriated Antiochus, who gathered his army and hired other armies to wage war against Judah and the Israelites and utterly destroy them. Although Judah and the Israelites were daunted by the armies gathering against them, they took heart and opened up the Book of the Law, offering prayers to God, that He might come to their aid. Camped near the town of Emmaus, Judah addressed his men, saying, "Do not be afraid of their numbers. Remember how our ancestors were delivered from the Egyptians at the Red Sea. Let us now beseech God to remember His covenant with our ancestors and destroy the armies that are upon us."

That day Judah and his men fought the enemies of Israel and won the first of many victories, until at last they were able to ascend Mount Zion. But when they reached the sanctuary, they found that it had been turned into a wilderness. The altar had been desecrated, the gates burned down, and vegetation had grown over the courts. Judah immediately appointed priests who had been faithful in their observance of the Torah and told them to purify the sanctuary. The priests erected a new altar of unhewn stones, as the Torah prescribed. They made new sacred vessels and brought them into the Temple, along with censers and the table.

On the twenty-fifth day of the month of Kislev the priests rose at dawn and made sacrifices on the new altar, and all the people bowed down to worship in joy and thanksgiving for eight days. Judah, his brothers, and all of Israel decreed that these days of the dedication of the altar should be celebrated each year in the proper season with rejoicing and gladness. And so it has been celebrated, from those days until now.

A Mother and Her Seven Sons

2 MACCABEES 7:1–42

*This is a tale about martyrdom—*Kiddush Hashem, *which means "sanctification of the Name." The martyr declares that unless we have something to die for, we have nothing to live for, and if we have nothing to live for, our lives are empty of all meaning. With his blood the martyr sanctifies the Holy Name in an absolute affirmation of the life sanctified by God. Martyrdom, then, is not only for the sake of the Holy One but also for the sake of the human life that God makes holy. It is an intimate and ultimate joining with the Creator that imparts depth and dearness to all of creation. Tradition identifies the courageous mother in this tale as Hannah.*

During the rule of the tyrant Antiochus Epiphanes a Jewish mother and her seven sons were arrested for refusing to renounce the faith of their fathers and eat the flesh of a pig. When they were brought before the king, the eldest of the sons stepped forward and declared, "We are prepared to die rather than violate the laws of our ancestors!"

Hearing his words of defiance, the enraged king ordered pans and cauldrons to be heated over a fire. As soon as they glowed red-hot, he ordered the son's tongue cut out of his mouth, his head scalped, and his limbs chopped off while his mother and brothers looked on. Then, as the young man lay with the faint breath of life still on his lips, he was placed in a large pan and fried alive over the fire.

"The Lord God is watching," the mother and his brothers encouraged one another, as the smoke from the pan drifted over them. "Surely He will take pity on us, as it is said in the song of Moses."

Then the murderers seized a second brother. They stripped the skin from his head, hair and all, and demanded, "Will you eat the flesh of the pig, before your body is tortured limb by limb?"

In the language of his ancestors he replied, "Never!"

So he too suffered the fate of his brother, crying out with his last breath, "You may take our lives, but the King of the world will raise us up to live again, for we die for the sake of His Torah!"

When they seized a third son, he bravely put out his tongue for them and extended his hands, saying, "God gave me these limbs. For the sake of His Torah I offer them up, and from Him I shall receive them again." The king and his attendants were astonished by the young man's show of courage in the face of terrible suffering, yet they dealt him the same death.

The fourth son was taken next, and as he neared his end he declared, "We make the better choice, to meet death at the hands of men while relying on God's promise that we shall be raised from the dead. But for you there can be no resurrection, no new life."

When they began torturing the fifth son, he turned to the king and said, "You may have power over mortals and think you can act as you please. But do not think that God has deserted our people. Soon you will see His power and His might leveled against you and your nation."

After him the sixth son was murdered, and as he died he cried out, "We are suffering for our own sins against God, and not because of your power. Do not think that you will go unpunished for waging this war against God."

Antiochus tried a different tactic with the seventh son, promising him riches and happiness if he would abandon the traditions of his ancestors. When the youth would not heed the king's promises, the king appealed to the mother. She agreed to try to persuade her son, but, instead, said to him in the language of her ancestors, "I beg you, my son, to have pity on your mother and consider all that is in heaven and earth, knowing that God created them. Have no fear of this murderer but prove yourself worthy of your brothers and welcome death. Then on the day of God's great mercy I shall receive you back, along with your brothers."

No sooner did his mother finish speaking than the last son declared to the King, "What are you waiting for? I shall never renounce the Torah given to our ancestors through Moses. You, who plot every evil against the Hebrews and prove yourself to be the bloodiest of villains, will not escape the hand of God. My brothers have endured a few moments of pain and now drink from the spring of life everlasting. Therefore I too surrender my body and my life for the sake of my fathers. And I pray that with my death all may come to affirm that our Lord alone is God and that the wrath of the Almighty may come to an end." And so he too went bravely to his end.

Perhaps greater than the suffering of the seven sons was the suffering of their mother. For in a single day she saw all seven tortured to death. And yet, in the language of their ancestors, she spoke words of courage to each of them, saying, "It was not I who endowed you with the breath of life or formed you into men. It was the Creator, who ordains the birth of every human being and presides over the origin of all things, and who in the end will return to you the breath of life. For He has seen that you have more regard for His Torah than for your own life."

And, after suffering the horror of witnessing the cruel murder of her seven sons, the mother too was put to death.

Talmudic Tales

MOST OF THE SELECTIONS PRESENTED are from the Babylonian Talmud; the Babylonian Talmud is made up of sixty-three tractates. One selection is from the Jerusalem Talmud; two are from the Tosefta, a collection of teachings and commentaries from the Talmudic sages that were not included in the Talmud. As the years passed after the destruction of the Second Temple, when it appeared that the Temple would not be rebuilt in the near future, the Rabbis determined that a new center of Jewish religious life must be constructed if the teachings of the Torah and its traditions were to endure. Under the leadership of Rabbi Yehudah ha-Nasi, the Rabbis set about editing the primary body of teachings known as the Mishnah, as well as the commentary on the Mishnah known as the *gemara*. Together these form the Talmud, the oral law. The Talmud was compiled between the second and seventh centuries. The aim of the Talmudic sages was not just the explication of Jewish law or the interpretation of biblical teachings but the penetration of the mysteries of the Holy One Himself. These Talmudic tales, much more than quaint and curious anecdotes about the sages, are about the avenues through which the Holy enters into the world.

The Rabbi's Last Blessing

BERACHOT 28B

No human being can stand innocently before God, yet every human being stands eternally before God—that is the message conveyed in this story about the last hours in the life of Rabbi Yochanan ben Zakkai. Rabbi Yochanan is one of the central figures in the Talmud. After the destruction of the Second Temple, he reestablished the Sanhedrin in Yavneh, making Yavneh the new center of Jewish life and learning. As Rabbi Yochanan reminds his disciples in the last blessing he confers upon them, one must forgo a superficial concern for social fashion and public opinion: there is Another whose opinion alone truly matters.

When he was advanced in years, Rabban Yochanan ben Zakkai fell mortally ill. Hearing of this, his disciples decided to visit their ailing teacher. They arrived at the rabbi's home and were shown to the room where he lay dying. When they went in to see him, the sick man took one look at them and began to weep.

Surprised at their teacher's tears and hardly able to withhold their own, the disciples said, "O Lamp of Israel, pillar of God's right hand, mighty hammer! Tell us, please, why do you weep?"

He replied, "If I were being taken this day before a human king—who breathes now but tomorrow who will lie in a grave, whose anger with me would not last forever, who may imprison me for a time but not for all eternity, who indeed may send me to my death but not to death everlasting, and whom I might persuade with words or bribe with money—even then I might be brought to tears.

"But, you see, the One I go to is the Almighty King of kings, the Holy One, blessed be He, without whom there is no life and whose life endures for all eternity. The anger He may direct at me is an everlasting anger, and if He imprisons me, it is an eternal imprisonment. If He puts me to death, it is a death without end, and there is no persuading Him with words or bribing Him with money. Don't you understand? When two paths stretch out before me, one leading to Paradise, the other to Hell, and I do not know which is mine, do I not have cause to weep? Surely you can see that? Have I taught you nothing?"

The rabbi, his eyes red from weeping, fell silent and stared at his disciples. Would they indeed understand the tears he had shed? Finally they broke the silence and said to him, "Master, bless us."

At that moment the rabbi saw the opportunity to convey to them what troubled him. And so, without hesitation, he conferred upon them this blessing: "May it be God's will that the fear of heaven will be upon you as much as your fear of flesh and blood."

Having expected something more elaborate and much more profound, the disciples looked at one another, rather puzzled, and said, "Is that all?"

Answered their teacher, "You think it such an easy and simple matter? Oh, if only you could attain so much! When a man acts not according to the will of God but according to his own will and commits a transgression, what does he say to himself? He says, 'I hope no one will see me. I hope no one will find out.' But know that there is One who always sees, whose eyes never close. He knows the innermost secrets of your heart, and He always finds you out. When you stand before Him, He will ask you about what He already knows—and what you have yet to confess, perhaps even to yourself. Let His question be my last blessing."

The Fox and the Fish

BERACHOT 61B

In this parable told by Rabbi Akiva, one of the greatest of the Talmudic sages, we receive a lesson about what sustains life and the importance of remaining in that element, even when death is all around. For a Jew, that element is the Torah. On many occasions throughout history Jews have been tempted to exchange the Torah for something that appears to be more attractive and more conducive to the so-called good life. But, as Rabbi Akiva teaches, when making such a trade, we give up the very thing that makes our lives possible.

Soon after the destruction of the Second Temple, during a time of terrible persecution at the hands of the Romans, the Roman government issued a decree forbidding Jews to study the Torah, teach the Torah, or follow its commandments. The Romans knew that to the Jews the Torah was the Tree of Life and that without the Torah the Jews would not endure in the world.

Despite the evil decree of the Romans, however, Rabbi Akiva continued to study, teach, and observe the commandments of the Torah. One day his friend Pappus ben Yehudah happened to find the rabbi holding a public gathering and openly discussing the Torah. Fearing the consequences of such an action, he said to him, "Akiva, you know what the Romans have decreed, and you know the cruelty of which they are capable. Are you not afraid of what they might do to you?"

Rabbi Akiva answered, "If I am afraid of the Romans, there is One before whom I am even more afraid. For He has entrusted to us His Torah, without which we have no life. Therefore it is far more dangerous to abandon the Torah than to adhere to it, despite the decree of the Romans. Let me explain.

"Once a fox went for a walk alongside a river. There he came upon a school of fish that were frantically swimming about, fleeing from one place to another. 'What are you fleeing from?' the fox asked them.

"'We are fleeing from the nets that the fishermen have cast into the river,' they replied.

"'Why don't you come up onto the land?' the fox suggested.

'Then you will escape the fishermen's nets. You can live with me and adopt my ways, just as both of our ancestors once lived together. You will be safe.'

"Said the fish to the fox, 'We thought you were supposed to be the most clever of all animals. How, then, can you speak such foolishness? If we are afraid here in the water, in the element that sustains us, how much more should we fear on the land, in the element where we would die?'

"So it is with us," said the rabbi to his friend. "We may live in peril as we study, teach, and follow the Torah. But as it is written in the Torah, 'this is thy life and the length of thy days.' If we should abandon that which contains the sum of our life, where would we be then? Where would we turn when evil was upon us?"

With All Thy Soul

BERACHOT 61B

In the Talmud this remarkable tale of Rabbi Akiva's martyrdom follows immediately after the parable of the fox and the fish. What does it mean to live up to the truth of the Torah? What does it mean to declare that human blessedness lies in bearing witness to that truth? What does it mean to find happiness in that truth? For Rabbi Akiva happiness lies neither in an Epicurean life of comfort and ease, nor in a stoic life of disregard for the flesh. It lies, rather, in the Sanctification of the Holy Name, body and soul. For the very heavens declare Akiva to be happy.

The Roman emperor Hadrian issued a decree in the Land of Israel prohibiting the study, teaching, and practice of the Torah on pain of torture and death. But there was one who feared God more than he feared men: Rabbi Akiva, who persisted in publicly expounding the Torah and openly defying the Roman order. So the Romans arrested him and cast him into prison to await his terrible fate.

Rabbi Akiva's friend Pappus ben Yehudah was also arrested and was imprisoned in the cell next to him. Upon discovering the rabbi in the adjoining cell, Pappus cried out, "Happy are you, Rabbi Akiva! For you have at least been arrested for your devotion to the Torah.

But woe to Pappus! I have been imprisoned as a result of my involvement in idle and meaningless affairs."

Before long the Roman guards came for Rabbi Akiva. It was the hour designated for the recitation of the Shema. Rabbi Akiva could not let the hour pass without saying his prayers. As the torturers mutilated his aged flesh with iron rakes, he raised his cry to heaven and began shouting, "*Shema Yisrael!* Hear, O Israel!"

Now thanks either to the cruelty of the Romans or to their mercy —who can say which?—the rabbi's disciples were allowed to come and be with him in his last hour. But when they heard their teacher cry out the prayer in the midst of being tortured, they pleaded with him, saying, "Master, even to this point? Will you sing your praises of God even as you endure this terrible torture?"

"All of my life I have been haunted by the commandment that you are to love the Lord God 'with all your soul,'" Rabbi Akiva replied. "Do you understand what this all means? It means that you are to love Him even if He takes your very soul. Realizing this, I wondered: When shall I ever be blessed with the chance to fulfill this commandment? Now I have been so blessed. Shall I fail, then, to fulfill what I have longed to fulfill?"

So he continued his prayer: "*Adonai Eloheinu, Adonai Echad!* The Lord our God, the Lord is One!" As the word *Echad* came from his lips, he drew it out, until the last breath issued from his body.

At the very moment when he breathed his last, the Holy Word vibrating on his breath, a Voice resounded from Heaven, proclaiming, "Happy are you, Akiva! For your soul has departed from this world with the word *Echad!*"

It is said that when the ministering angels had witnessed the cruel death visited upon the rabbi, they gathered about the Holy One, blessed be He, and asked, "Is this to be the reward for one so faithfully devoted to Thy Torah? Surely he should have been delivered by Your hand from the hands of these murderers. They should have died so, not he!"

"They already have their portion in this life," the Lord answered the angels.

And a Voice resounded from Heaven, proclaiming, "Happy are you, Akiva! For you are destined for a portion of life in the World to Come!"

King David and the Angel of Death
SHABBAT 30A–30B

Like many Talmudic tales, this story is about the definitive connection between the Torah and life. Every human being, from pauper to king, is subject to death. Just so, every human being, from pauper to king, finds his life in Torah, and not in wealth or worldly accomplishments. The Torah is the Tree of Life eternal, and as long as we are in its power, we are free from the power of death.

Singing his praise of God in what was to become the thirty-ninth Psalm, King David wrote, "Lord, make known to me my end and the measure of my days, so that I may know how frail I am." As these words came from his hand, David cried out to the Holy One, blessed be He, "Sovereign of the Universe! Reveal to me, I implore You, when my end will come."

God answered him, saying, "Surely you know that, according to My decree, no creature of flesh and blood may know the time of his death."

But the servant of the Lord, King David, persisted, beseeching Him, "I plead with You, O King of kings, show me when I shall cease to be!"

At last the Lord took pity on him and said, "You will die on the Sabbath."

"If it may be Your will, O Lord," David replied, "please let me die on the first day of the week, so that I can be immediately prepared for burial."

"I cannot allow that," God answered him. "For on that Sabbath day the reign of your son Solomon will come due, and the reign of one king may not overlap the reign of another, even by a hair's breadth."

"Then let it be Your will," David said, "that I die on the eve of the Sabbath."

But God replied, "One day less of your life on earth would mean one day less of your Torah study. Know that a single day of your engagement with the holy task of learning is more dear to Me than the thousand burnt offerings that your son Solomon will offer up on the altar in the Temple that he is to build."

Now it was David's custom to spend each Sabbath day studying the Torah. Finally there came the Sabbath on which his soul was to be laid to rest. At the appointed hour the Angel of Death stole his way into David's home. But because the words of Torah were continually rising up from the mouth of the king, the angel had no power over him. And so the angel waited impatiently, wondering what to do, until at last he devised a plan.

The angel slipped out of David's room and went into the royal garden next to the king's house. There he climbed up a tree and made a curious rustling sound in its branches. David heard the odd noise, and, with the words of the Torah still on his lips, he went out to see what it could be. Once in the garden, he noticed that the sound was coming from somewhere up in the tree. Deciding to look more closely, he took a ladder to climb into the tree and find out what it could be.

That was just what the Angel of Death had plotted. As David ascended the ladder, the angel caused it to break under him. When David fell to the ground, he ceased reciting the teachings of the Torah, and his soul finally found its rest.

Slow to Anger

SHABBAT 30B–31A

Because the path to God leads through the lovingkindness that we show our fellow human beings, the rabbis teach us to be slow to anger. For anger, it is said, robs our face of its human image, and when we lose our human image, we lose our presence before God. Among the rabbis most known for compassion is Rabbi Hillel. In this tale about Rabbi Hillel we see the importance not only of being slow to anger but of offering a teaching in the place of anger.

It was the custom of our rabbis to teach their disciples that a man should always be patient and compassionate, as Rabbi Hillel was, and not short of temper, as Rabbi Shammai was known to be. With this teaching they would call to mind the time when two men made a wager with one another to see which of them could move Rabbi Hillel to anger. For Rabbi Hillel was known to be long suffering and slow to anger.

The first of the men declared, "I know exactly how to make Hillel lose his temper." And he set off to visit the rabbi.

It was the eve of the Sabbath, and, in preparation, the rabbi was busy washing himself. The man bent on angering him went up to Hillel's door and, using no title of respect, rudely shouted, "Hey! Is Hillel here? Where is he? I'm looking for Hillel."

Instead of ignoring or chastising the man, Rabbi Hillel left off with his bathing, calmly put on his robe, and went out to greet his guest. "What may I do for you, my son?" he asked.

"I have a question for you," the man replied.

"Then please ask, my son."

Thinking the rabbi would lose his patience over a ridiculous and insolent question, the man said, "Tell me, why are the heads of Babylonians like you so round?"

The rabbi did not grow angry. Instead, he replied, "You have asked a very important question, my son. You see, the heads of Babylonians are round because they have no skillful midwives. And few tasks are as important as the task of a midwife."

Frustrated by Hillel's patience, the man left and reflected on other ways of moving the rabbi to anger. Soon he returned to Hillel's house, went to the door, and, again, most disrespectfully, shouted, "Hey! Is Hillel here? Where is he? I'm looking for Hillel."

Once again Hillel left his bath, put on a robe, and went to greet his visitor. "Please," he said to him, "how may I help you, my son?"

"I want you to answer a question for me," the man demanded.

"Go ahead and ask, my son."

"Tell me, why are the Palmyreans so bleary-eyed?"

The rabbi did not grow angry. Instead, he answered, "You have asked a very important question, my son. The Palmyreans live in the wilderness of the Syrian desert. Their lives are very hard, and the wind is always blowing sand into their eyes."

Again the man was frustrated by Hillel's patience, so he left to reflect further on ways of arousing the rabbi's anger. He returned once more to Hillel's house, went up to the door, and, as rudely as ever, yelled, "Hey! Is Hillel here? Where is he? I'm looking for Hillel."

A third time the rabbi left his bath, put on his robe, and patiently went out to greet his guest. "In what way may I help you, my son?" he asked.

"I have a question for you," said the man.

"Then please feel free to ask, my son."

And for the third time, convinced that the rabbi's patience must be wearing thin, the man asked, "Why are the feet of the Africans so wide?"

But Hillel did not grow angry. Instead, he said, "You have asked a very important question, my son. The feet of the Africans are wide because they live among watery marshes. It is very important for a man to be able to stand in the places where he would dwell."

"I see," said the man, as he continued to think of ways to anger the rabbi. "I have many questions for you," he added. "But I think that you may become angry if I persist in asking them."

At that, and still dressed in his robe, Rabbi Hillel sat down before the man and said, "Please ask all the questions you want."

"Are you truly Hillel," the man asked, "the one they call the Prince and the Patriarch of Israel?"

"I am."

"If that is so," the man retorted, "may there be no other like you in all of Israel."

"Why do you say that, my son?" the rabbi wondered.

"Because on your account," the man complained, "I have lost four hundred zuz."

"Be careful about your moods, my son," the rabbi cautioned him. "The fact that I have not grown angry with you may be worth your four hundred zuz. And even if it should cost you another four hundred, I still would not lose my temper. For the price of anger far exceeds any amount of money."

God, Satan, and the Law of Moses

SHABBAT 89A

Like life itself, the Torah comes into the possession only of those who offer it to others. The vessel of God's truth and teaching, the Torah comes to life in its transmission from mouth to mouth. Therefore, to live by the Torah is to live in dialogue with our fellow human beings. Moses exemplified that dialogical relationship. Satan, on the other hand, would possess the Torah as his own, not to offer a responsive word to another but to have the last word and thereby condemn (which is the meaning of his name) rather than embrace humanity.

After he had delivered the Israelites from the bondage of Egypt with the help of God, Moses led them to Mount Sinai. There Moses ascended the heights to receive from God the revelation that he was to offer to all of Israel. When God had finished speaking the words He wanted to speak, Moses descended from the mountain, bearing the Torah that the Holy One, blessed be He, had entrusted to him, eager to offer the great treasure to the people of Israel.

All the while, however, Satan had stood by, awaiting the opportunity to lay claim to the Torah and make it his own. When he saw Moses leave the presence of the Lord, he approached the Holy One and said, "Sovereign of the Universe, please tell me, where is the Torah?"

"I have given it to the earth," the Lord answered him.

Satan descended to the earth, approach it and asked, "Where is the Torah?"

But the earth replied, "God alone traces the path of the wisdom you seek, for He sees all things, even unto the ends of the earth. Go, then, and look to the ends of the earth, where the land meets the sea."

Satan descended from the earth to the sea. Standing upon its shore, he asked the sea, "Where is the Torah?"

"The wisdom you seek is not to be found here," the sea answered him. "But since the eye of God penetrates into the depths of the abyss, perhaps you should seek it within the deep."

Heeding the words of the sea, Satan descended further still, into the fathoms of the deep, and asked, "Where is the Torah?"

The deep replied, "It is not in me. Nor is it to be found in all the seas. Even death and destruction can say no more than, 'We have heard a rumor of it.'"

In despair Satan returned to God and said, "Sovereign of the Universe! I have searched the world over and can find the Torah nowhere on the earth, around the seas, or in their innermost depths."

"Go, then," God answered him, "and seek out the son of Amram."

Hearing these words, Satan took heart, hastened off to Moses, and said, "Tell me, son of Amram, where is the Torah that the Holy One, blessed be He, entrusted to you?"

But Moses replied, "Who am I, that the Lord God should give me something so precious as His Torah?"

Hearing Moses reply, God reproached him, saying, "Moses, would you be a liar?"

"Sovereign of the Universe!" said Moses. "You have entrusted the treasure of Your Torah to me. Should I be so bold as to keep it only for myself? Surely it was not intended for me alone but for all the children of Israel."

The Holy One, blessed be He, replied, "Moses, because you have humbled yourself and have set above yourself the Torah and the children of Israel for whom it is intended, My teaching will be called by your name."

So it is written in the words of the prophet Malachi, "Remember the Torah of My servant Moses."

Hillel the Elder
and the House of Learning
YOMA 35B

Hillel the Elder was one of the great sages of the Talmud. His commitment to learning robs us of all our excuses for failing to study Torah. Two other sages, Shemayah and Avtalyon, recognized the importance of such commitment. Having been shown compassion by Shemayah and Avtalyon,

Hillel became noted for his compassion, and, more often than not, his rulings on various points of Jewish law came to hold sway over the rulings of Rabbi Shammai. Indeed, it was from the descendants of Hillel that the heads of the Sanhedrin were selected.

When our teacher Hillel the Elder was a young man, he was very poor indeed. Although he labored from dawn to dusk, he earned only a few pennies each day. Half of what he earned he would spend on food for his family, for he was a devoted husband and father. The other half he would take to the house of learning, for he was also devoted to the Torah. There, each day, he would offer his pennies to the man who stood guard at the door, so that he might gain entrance into the place where the wisdom of the sages could be heard.

One winter's day, however Hillel was unable to find any work, and so he was left without money. Nevertheless, he went to the house of learning and implored the guard to allow him to enter. The guard stood firm and refused him, but Hillel would not be turned away. Despite the cold that was setting in toward the end of the day, he climbed up to the roof and crawled over to the window that served as a skylight for those engaged in study in the room below. There he listened carefully to the teachings of the Torah that came from the mouths of the sages, Shemayah and Avtalyon. He listened so intently that he did not notice the snow beginning to fall, so completely that he lost all sense of time, until he finally fell asleep on the skylight.

With the first light of the next morning, which was the Sabbath morning, Shemayah and Avtalyon entered the house of learning to study Torah. Before they could begin, however, Shemayah looked around and said, "Brother Avtalyon, every morning there is plenty of light in the house of learning, but today it is dark. Could it be so cloudy outside?"

At that they looked up toward the skylight and saw the figure of a man in the window. Wondering who it could be, they went up to the roof and found Hillel covered with snow. Immediately they realized that he had been there the whole night and had come to hear the teachings of the Torah.

"This man," they declared, "deserves to have the Sabbath profaned for his sake, so devoted is he to the words of the Torah."

So the two sages carried Hillel down from the roof and into the house of study. They gave him a warm bath and placed him next to the fire. There the three of them occupied themselves with the wisdom of the Torah, to which Hillel had demonstrated his devotion.

When a poor man stands before the heavenly court and says that he could not study Torah because he was too busy earning his sustenance, he is asked, "Were you poorer than Hillel?" And the story of Hillel the Elder is repeated on high.

Shimon the Just
and the Conqueror Alexander
YOMA 69A

While most tales from the Bible deal with God's involvement in the affairs of humanity, this tale from the Talmud is about humanity's involvement in the affairs of God. Just when it appeared that Israel was doomed to destruction, Alexander the Great (356–323 BCE) turns the course of human events to favor God's people. Throughout his conquests Alexander had been guided by a vision of Shimon the Just, the high priest of the Israelites, and so he chose to favor those who were devoted to God. For this was a sign, Alexander surmised, that God had favored him: God's truth may do more than a general's power to save a city.

In the days of Alexander the Great the Samaritans plotted to destroy the Temple in Jerusalem and erect their own temple on Mount Gerizim. In order to further their diabolical design, they went out to greet the conqueror just as he was entering the Holy Land. Offering themselves up as his allies, they convinced him that he should allow them to march on Jerusalem and lay waste to the holy Temple. Without having yet laid eyes on the holy city, the Macedonian granted their request.

Before the Samaritans could execute their plan, however, news of what had taken place reached the ears of Shimon the Just, high priest of the holy Temple. Wasting no time, he robed himself in his priestly garments and set out to meet Alexander. Flanked by torch bearers,

Shimon walked all night long, until at last, with the first light of the dawn, he and his companions reached the town of Antipatris. There they found Alexander in the company of the Samaritans who were preparing to attack the holy city and destroy the Temple.

At first Alexander did not see Shimon the Just. And so he asked the torch bearers who preceded the high priest, "Who are you?"

"We are the children of Israel," they replied, "servants of the Most High God."

"If you are the children of Israel," Alexander asked, "then who are these Samaritans?"

"We'll tell you who they are," answered the torch bearers. "They are Jews who are plotting to rebel against you."

At that moment, wondering whether he should destroy them all, Alexander caught sight of Shimon the Just. Suddenly he was transfixed and transformed. He face stricken with awe, the conqueror of the world descended from his carriage, walked over to Shimon, and bowed down to the ground before the high priest. His officers, counselors, and even the Samaritans surrounding him cried out, "How can a great king like you humble yourself before this wretched Jew?"

"It is his image," Alexander answered, "that has arisen before my eyes each time I have gone into battle and won." Then, turning to Shimon the Just, the conqueror asked, "What have you come for?"

"Is it possible," Shimon replied, "that you have allowed these idolaters, worshipers of the stars, to deceive you? For they plot to destroy the House in which prayers are said for you and your kingdom."

"Tell me, then, who these people are," Alexander replied.

"They are Samaritans," said Shimon, "the enemies of the God to whom we offer our prayers."

"Take them," Alexander ordered. "I place them in your hands."

Hearing these words, Shimon the Just and his companions seized the Samaritans, pierced their heels with an awl, and tied them to the horses they had intended to ride in their attack on Jerusalem. The horses dragged the Samaritans over thorns and thistles all the way to Mount Gerizim. There the Israelites plowed the ground under and planted it with vetch, just as the Samaritans had plotted to do with the holy Temple and the Temple Mount. Alexander left the Israelites in peace.

The Renegades of Babylon

BETZA 32B

This Talmudic tale offers a response to an age-old question of Jewish inquiry: What does it mean to be a Jew? It demonstrates that the word Jew designates something more that a biological category or even a religious category. A Jew is one who possesses the qualities of modesty, generosity, and lovingkindness. A Jew is one who engages in a certain action and engenders a certain relation to his fellow human being. Those Jews who fail to treat their fellow human being with kindness betray not only the other person—they betray who and what they are.

Long ago, during the days of the Babylonian exile, a certain Shabtai ben Marinus fell on hard times and was in need of help, not for himself but for the care of his family. But wherever he turned for assistance, he was refused, until he was all but overcome with despair. Finally, he heard it said that a community of Jews lived to the east, in Babylon, and a ray of hope entered his soul. For he knew that the Jews were renowned for their modesty, generosity, and above all, their lovingkindness.

And so, his joy renewed, Shabtai ben Marinus set out to seek help from that Jewish community, thinking, "At last someone will come to my aid. My wife and children will hunger no more. And laughter will take the place of their tears."

After many days of hard travel, sustained only by his confidence in the kindness he would find, Shabtai ben Marinus came at last to the Jewish community in Babylon. Immediately he went to the home of one of the community's most prominent members. There he knocked on the door and submitted his plea for assistance.

The head of the household answered him with a curt "No" and turned him away without so much as offering the supplicant a morsel of food.

Shabtai ben Marinus continued undaunted. He went on to another house, but there too he was turned away, hungry and empty-handed. Puzzled but still clinging to his trust in the Jews, he went to another house: the same refusal. Then on to another and another, only to meet again and again with the same indifference, the same disregard, the same cruelty. Finally, dishearteningly, Shabtai ben Marinus gave up his last hope and set off for his homeland.

And as he journeyed, he reflected to himself, "Clearly, I have been misinformed. This cannot be a community of Jews but a counterfeit bunch passing themselves off as Jews. We have been taught from days of old that whoever treats his fellow human being with lovingkindness is surely of the children of our father Abraham. And whoever shows no mercy toward his fellow human being surely is not of the children of our father Abraham. No, these renegades who call themselves Jews must be the descendants of the mixed multitude that went out from Egypt. Nothing else can explain the way they treated me."

Lulianus and Pappus

TA'ANIT 18B

Sadly, many Jewish tales are tales of persecution and martyrdom. Sometimes, as in the story of Daniel and the lions, they end happily. Other times, as in the tale of Rabbi Akiva's death, they end tragically. This story about the death of Lulianus and Pappus at the hands of Trajan (who, according to some sources was actually Trajan's general Lusius Quietus, who was executed by Trajan) falls into the latter category. The greatness of these tales, however, lies not so much in their outcome as in their affirmation of the Holy One Himself. For it is a willingness to die in sanctification of His Name that enables us to live a life rooted in sanctity.

In the days of the Roman persecutions, when it was a capital crime to study and observe the teachings of the Torah, Lulianus and his brother Pappus were arrested in Laodicea. Immediately sentenced to death, the two were brought before the Roman Trajan, who was himself to serve as their executioner. In his cruelty, however, the Roman did not deem it enough simply to execute the two brothers for their devotion to God and their refusal to worship idols. He was determined first to taunt them and test their faith, thereby breaking their spirit.

His face distorted into a sneer, Trajan said to them, "If you are of the people of Hananiah, Mishael, and Azariah—the three who refused to bow down to Nebuchadnezzar's idol and were cast into the burning furnace—then let your God show Himself and deliver you from my hands, just as He delivered them from the hands of Nebuchadnezzar."

But Lulianus and Pappus were not swayed by the Roman's words, and they refused to tempt God simply to prove their own worth. So they answered their executioner, saying, "Hananiah, Mishael, and Azariah were men pure of heart and perfect in their righteousness. Therefore they deserved the miracle that God performed for them when they emerged from the furnace unscathed. Nebuchadnezzar, too, was a king worthy of the miracle, for he was able to recognize the hand of the true God when he saw it at work. But you, Trajan, are a common, vulgar, and evil man, utterly without any merit that might lead God to bring about a miracle through the work of your unworthy hands. As for the two of us, we have knowingly brought our fate upon ourselves and do not merit the consideration that God showed to Hananiah, Mishael, and Azariah. So you see, it must be the will of the Omnipresent that our time has come to die, if not by your hand, then by one of the many other means He has at His disposal. For He has created lions, bears, and many other beasts of prey that could attack us at any time."

"If that is so," Trajan demanded, "then why has He seen fit to deliver you into my hands, and not into the claws of one of these beasts?"

"He has delivered us into your hands," they replied, "so that at a time soon to come He may exact punishment of you for spilling our blood. For you yourself are no better than a beast of prey."

Enraged at these words, and despite their warning, Trajan took up a sword and killed the two brothers Lulianus and Pappus. Hardly having time to wipe their blood from his hands, Trajan caught sight of two men approaching him with clubs in their hands. They had been dispatched from Rome with orders to split his skull.

Who Will Have a Share?
TA'ANIT 22A

While no mortal who walks the earth knows who has a share in the World to Come, the prophet Elijah, who was taken up to heaven in a chariot of fire, is privy to such information. He is said to have appeared to certain sages and personalities of the Talmud. In this tale Elijah points out to a rabbi men who, by most human standards, appear to be unlikely candidates for salvation in God's kingdom—men who might seem to be frivolous and certainly not renowned for their piety. One merits a place in the World to Come by maintaining the sanctity of the relationship between men and women, two others by bringing laughter into people's lives. What they have in common is the peace that they offer to those around them. Thus they may find peace in the next world.

Rabbi Beroka Hoza'ah used to frequent the market in Be Lapat, the capital city of Khuzistan. For there the prophet Elijah would sometimes appear to him, often in the disguise of a beggar. But the rabbi's vision was so astute that he could spot the prophet at a glance.

One day, as the two of them walked together through the marketplace, Rabbi Beroka asked Elijah, "Do you see anyone here who has a share in the World to Come?"

Elijah scanned the faces of the people around him, reading in each one of them the fate that awaited him or her. Then he replied, "No, none of these has a share in the World to Come."

But just as he uttered these words, he caught sight of a man who looked as though he were a Gentile. For the man wore black shoes, after the manner of Gentiles, and had no fringes on his garments, as the Jews do. A smile came over the prophet's face, and he declared, "That man has a share in the World to Come."

Surprised at the prophet's pronouncement upon one who seemed so unlikely for such an honor, Rabbi Beroka ran after the man to question him. When he finally caught up with him, the rabbi said, "Please, sir, tell me, what is your occupation?"

The man was taken aback by the question, and looked around, as if he were afraid of being seen with the Jew. "Go away," he told the rabbi. "But come back tomorrow, and we shall speak then."

Seeing the man's agitation, Rabbi Beroka did as he asked. The next day he returned to the marketplace and searched for the man who looked like a Gentile but seemed somehow to be a Jew. At last he found the stranger and asked again, "What is your occupation?"

"I am a jailer."

"A jailer?" the rabbi repeated, wondering how it might be that a jailer could have a share in the World to Come. "What exactly are your duties?"

"I see to it that the men and the women in the jail stay away from one another," he explained. "Each night I place my bed between them, so that they may not succumb to the temptations of sin. Whenever I see a Jewish girl upon whom the Gentiles have cast their eyes, I stand between her and the ones who would take her, even at the risk of my own life. Once it happened that a Jewish girl betrothed to be married caught the attention of a group of Persians. I suspected what was in their wicked hearts. So I took some red wine, stained her skirts with it, and told them that she was unclean. For I knew that they would not touch a menstruating woman."

"I see," said the rabbi, now understanding why this man had a share in the World to Come. "You are clearly a child of Abraham. But tell me: why do you wear black shoes, after the manner of the Gentiles, and walk about with no fringes on your garments?"

"My work requires that I constantly move among the Gentiles," the man answered. "I wear these shoes and walk without fringes so that they may not suspect that I am a Jew whenever a decree against the Jews is handed down. Because I am in constant contact with the Gentiles, I often hear of such decrees before the Jews become aware of them. As soon as I have such information, I go to the rabbis, so that they may pray to God and have the decree annulled."

Rabbi Beroka nodded his approval and asked further, "When I saw you yesterday and asked about your occupation, why did you tell me to go away and come back today?"

"An order against the Jews had just been issued," the jailer explained, "so I could not be seen with you. I was on my way to the rabbis. I told them about the decree, and they prayed to God for its annulment. Thanks to their prayers, it has been annulled."

"You are truly blessed," said the rabbi and went his way.

The next day Rabbi Beroka once again walked through the market with Elijah. "Do you see anyone here today who has a share in the World to Come?" the rabbi asked Elijah.

Elijah looked around and noticed two men who were passing by. "These two have a share in the World to Come," he declared.

Thinking once more that the two whom the prophet had pointed out seemed an unlikely pair, Rabbi Beroka walked up to them and said, "Pardon me, but may I ask, what is your occupation?"

"We are jesters," they replied.

"Jesters?" the rabbi repeated, wondering how mere jest might win for a person a share in the World to Come.

"That's right," they said. "We delight in cheering people up whenever they seem depressed. And if we should see two people quarreling, we bring them laughter and thus make peace between them."

Hearing this, Rabbi Beroka smiled to himself and thought, "Yes, the prophet has spoken well."

Choni the Circle Drawer
TA'ANIT 23A

The mark of righteousness, as it is often understood in the Jewish tradition, is exemplified in this tale of a man who engages in a dispute with God, exposing himself to God's wrath, not for his own sake but for the sake of the community. One may wonder why he had to pray so many times to make himself clear to the Holy One, blessed be He. Perhaps it is because God so enjoyed the man's prayers that He did not want to cut them short. It is pleasing to God when even one person speaks out in behalf of many.

One year during the time of the Second Temple, nearly the whole month of Adar went by without a single drop of rain. Fearing for their crops, the people sent a message to a man named Choni—the Circle Drawer, as he was soon to be called—and asked him to please implore God to send rain, lest there be no food. For Choni was known to have the ear of the Holy One, blessed be He.

Immediately Choni set about praying for rain. But despite the intensity of his prayers, not a cloud appeared in the sky. Seeing that his prayers were insufficient, he resolved to offer himself. So he drew a circle in the dry earth, stood at its center, and cried out, "Master of the Universe! Your children have turned to me in their hour of desperation because they believe that I am a member of Your household and thus have Your ear. But since You have ignored my prayers, I swear by Your Holy Name that I shall not move from this circle, until You have mercy upon Your children and bring them rain!"

At that moment a few drops of rain began to fall from the sky. But it was far too little to even dampen the parched earth. So Choni's disciples said to him, "We came to you for the sake of the people, that you might save us all from death. The rain has come, yet it is so little that it seems God has sent it for no other reason than to release you from your oath."

Suspecting that they were right, Choni raised his hands toward the heavens and declared, "All-knowing Master of the Universe, I have not prayed for this sprinkling but for a rain that will fill the cisterns, ditches, and caves. Until it comes, I shall not budge from this circle!"

With those words the rain began to fall more and more heavily. It came down in sheets, with every drop as large as the opening of a barrel. The rain was so severe that Choni's disciples grew afraid and said, "We came to you for the sake of the people, so that you might save us all from death. But this rain is so heavy that we fear God has sent it to destroy the world!"

Sharing their alarm, Choni turned once more to the Holy One and shouted, "O Lord, Master of the Universe! Knowing all, You know that I have prayed not for this rain of destruction but for the rain of benevolence, bounty, and blessing!"

Finally, the rain fell in a normal manner. Yet it continued to fall until the Jews of Jerusalem were forced to seek shelter on the Temple Mount. As the waters rose, Choni's disciples beseeched him yet again, saying, "Master, please, just as you prayed for the rain to come, pray now for it to end!"

"Tradition teaches us," Choni replied, "that we may not pray on account of an excess of good. Nevertheless, bring me a bullock that we may sacrifice it as an offering of thanksgiving."

Immediately his disciples obeyed him and brought him an un-blemished bullock for the thanksgiving sacrifice. Laying both hands upon the animal, Choni raised up his prayer to God, saying, "Master of the Universe! Your people, the children of Israel, whom You brought forth from the bondage of Egypt, can endure neither an excess of good nor an excess of punishment. When You were angry with them, they could not endure the drought. Nor could they en-dure it when You showered upon them an excess of the goodness of rain. May it be Your will that the rain cease and relief come to the land."

No sooner did these words come from Choni's mouth than a wind rose up and dispersed the clouds from the sky. The warm sun came out, and the people went into their fields to gather mush-rooms and truffles.

Before long, word of Choni's persistent prayers reached Shimon ben Shetach. He responded to the news by sending a message to the circle drawer that said, "If it were not for the fact that you are Choni the Circle Drawer, I would have excommunicated you. If this time of famine had been like the time of famine that ravished the land in the days of Elijah—the one in whose care the keys to the rains were placed—would not the Name of Heaven have been profaned through your attempts to force God's hand? But what am I to do with you, when you act so contemptuously before the Omnipresent and He nevertheless grants your request, as a father would grant the request of his persistent son? You are like the boy who says, 'Father, bathe me in warm water. Now wash me in cold water. Give me nuts and almonds, peaches and pomegranates,' and his father grants his every wish. Surely King Solomon spoke of you when he said in his Proverbs, 'Let your father and mother be glad, and let her that bore you rejoice!'"

And because with his prayers Choni the Circle Drawer deliv-ered a generation humiliated by its sin, Shimon ben Shetach sent him his blessing, and not his ban.

The Old Man and the Carob Tree

TA'ANIT 23A

Gratitude and responsibility are two of the most important links between God and humanity: gratitude for the labor of those who have lived before us and thanks to whom we have life, and responsibility for those who are yet unborn and whose lives are entrusted to our care. These are the things that situate us in time, and when that relationship is lost, our time is lost. That is why in this tale Choni prays for death when he lives beyond his time.

"Is it possible for a man to sleep continuously for seventy years?" Choni wondered to himself, as he was traveling one day. "And if it were so, how interesting it would be thus to see into the future!"

Just then he happened upon an old man hard at work planting a carob tree. Perplexed that such an old man would work so hard to plant such a young tree, he asked, "How long will it take this tree to bear fruit?"

"Seventy years," the old man replied.

"Do you really believe that you will live another seventy years," Choni asked, "so that you may see it bear fruit?"

"When I came into the world," the old man answered, "I found carob trees already growing and bearing fruit, planted by my fathers before me. Therefore I too plant carob trees so that they may grow here."

After traveling a bit further, Choni sat down to have a meal and reflect on what the old man had said to him. Soon a deep sleep overcame him, and a rocky formation enclosed him, so that he was hidden from sight. He slept and he slept and continued to sleep until seventy years had gone by. Then he awoke and crawled out from behind the rocks that had served as his shelter. Somewhat confused, he started back in the direction from which he had come seventy years earlier, not realizing how long he had been asleep.

Soon he came to the carob tree, surprised to find that it was fully grown. A man was gathering fruit from its branches.

"Could it be . . . ?" Choni wondered fearfully. "Are you the man who planted this tree?"

"No," the man replied. "I am his grandson."

"Then it is true!" Choni exclaimed. "I have slept for seventy years!" At that Choni returned to the home that he had called his own to search for his son, who now would be an old man himself. But he arrived only to find strangers living in his house. Nevertheless, in his desperation he asked, "Is the son of Choni the Circle Drawer still alive?"

"His son is no more," the people told him. "But his grandson is still alive."

Saddened to hear that his son had died, Choni tried to convince them, "I myself am Choni the Circle Drawer! And this is my home!" They did not believe him.

Having no home, but knowing that he could always find a place in the house of study, Choni went there to seek out the scholars. When he arrived he found them engaged in a dispute, and his heart was filled with hope when he heard his name mentioned.

"The law is as clear to us," the scholars declared, "as it was in the days of Choni the Circle Drawer. For whenever he came to the house of study he would settle any difficulty that arose."

Hearing these words, Choni cried out, "I am he! I am Choni the Circle Drawer!"

The scholars did not believe him and took him for some crank. So lonely and hurt was the circle drawer that he prayed for death. And his prayer was answered.

Said the Babylonian sage Rava, "Thus we have the saying: Either companionship or death."

The Wisdom of Abba Chilkiah

TA'ANIT 23A–23B

The story of Choni's grandson, Abba Chilkiah, teaches that not all things are evident to scholars. Perhaps even more important is a point that is made in another tractate of the Talmud: "Blessing is found in a man's home only on account of his wife" (Bava Metzia 59a). Like the rain that begins to fall in one spot and then spreads throughout the land, the blessing that begins in just one man's home may spread throughout the community.

Long ago, whenever the world was in need of rain, the sages would send word to Abba Chilkiah, grandson of Choni the Circle Drawer, asking that he pray for rain. Like his grandfather before him, Abba Chilkiah would honor their request, and his prayers would be granted.

On one occasion, when the land was especially parched from drought, the rabbis sent two scholars to personally seek out Abba Chilkiah and plead with him to pray for rain. They came to his house and asked for him, but he was not there. Recalling that Abba Chilkiah worked for his bread, they went to the fields outside of town to look for him. Sure enough, they found him hard at work with a hoe. Pleased to have come to him at last, the scholars extended their greeting to Abba Chilkiah. But he said nothing in reply. The scholars were puzzled by his failure to answer, but they waited patiently and respectfully for Abba Chilkiah to acknowledge them. And as they waited, he worked.

Before long evening approached, and Abba Chilkiah gathered up some wood and his hoe. The wood and the hoe he placed on one shoulder, and over the other he threw his cloak. Then he set out for his home with the two scholars following behind him. All the way home he walked barefoot, except when he came to a stream. Then he would put on his shoes, cross the stream, and take them off again. Whenever he came to a patch of thorns or thistles, he would lift up his garments so that they would not get caught. As he neared the city, his wife, beautifully dressed, came out to greet him. Upon reaching his home, his wife entered first, followed by Abba Chilkiah, and then the two scholars.

Once inside, Abba Chilkiah sat down to a modest meal that his wife had prepared for him. The scholars wondered why he did not invite them to join him, but still they said nothing. Abba Chilkiah shared his meal with his two sons, offering the older son one portion and the younger son two.

When the meal was finished, he said to his wife, "I know that these scholars have come to ask me to pray for rain. Come with me, then, to the roof, and we shall offer our supplication to God. Perhaps the Holy One, blessed be He, will have mercy and the rain will come, without any credit due to us."

The two scholars followed Abba Chilkiah to the roof, where he took up a position in one corner, while his wife stood in another. As soon as the prayer came to his lips, clouds began to form over the place where his wife stood, and it began to rain.

When they all had returned inside, Abba Chilkiah finally spoke to the two scholars.

"Why have you come here?" he asked them, just to be sure that he had guessed rightly.

"We came to implore you to pray for rain," they replied.

At that Abba Chilkiah exclaimed, "Blessed be God, who has deemed that you no longer be dependent on Abba Chilkiah! For this rain has come not due to my merit but by the mercy of God."

"We believe, sir," they said, "that the rain has indeed come on your account. But we do not understand the meaning of the mysterious way you have acted. Why, for example, did you ignore us when we greeted you?"

"I hired out my labor to work the whole day," he explained, "and I said that I would not relax on the job."

"What about the wood?" they asked. "Why did you carry it on one shoulder and your cloak on the other?"

"The cloak was borrowed," said Abba Chilkiah, "and I borrowed it for only one purpose—to wear and not to shoulder wood."

"What about your shoes?" they wanted to know. "Why did you walk barefoot, except when you came to a stream, and then put on your shoes?"

"When I walked along the road," he answered, "I could see where my foot would fall. But when I crossed the stream, I could not see."

"And why did you lift up your garments when you came to a patch of thorns and thistles?"

"This body of mine," he said, "heals itself when it is torn. But my clothes do not."

"And your wife?" they asked. "Why did she come out to greet you so beautifully dressed?"

"It was so that I might not cast my eyes on any other woman."

"And when we came to your house," they persisted, "why did she enter first, with you following, leaving us to enter last?"

"That was because I did not know what sort of men you are, and I wanted to be sure to protect her."

"What about the meal? Why did you not invite us to eat with you?"

"Forgive me," Abba Chilkiah replied, "but I had only enough for my children."

"And when you shared it with your sons, why did you give only one portion to the elder son and two portions to the younger one?"

"My elder son studies in the synagogue all day and takes a meal there. But my younger son is at home all day and waits until this meal to eat."

"And the clouds?" they inquired. "Why did they first appear where your wife stood, and only afterward over the corner where you were?"

Said Abba Chilkiah, "Because a wife stays at home and offers bread to the poor, which they can enjoy at once. I merely give them money, which they cannot enjoy at once. Therefore she is closer to God than I am." Then, after of moment of further reflection, he remarked, "Or perhaps it may have to do with certain thieves in our neighborhood. I prayed that they might die, but she prayed that they might repent. And they repented, for her prayers were more righteous than mine."

Hearing this, the two scholars rejoiced. For they had found not only the rain they sought but a wisdom as precious as the rain.

Ptolemy and the Translators

MEGILLAH 9A–9B

From ancient times the integrity of the Holy Tongue has been a principle central to Jewish thought. According to tradition, Hebrew is the language that came from the mouth of God Himself when He offered His Torah to Moses. Therefore it is the language Jews use when offering their prayers to God and to which they adhere when reading the Torah—not because God understands no other language but because it is the language that rises up toward God. Jews believe that the sanctity of the Holy Tongue must be retained in order to distinguish between the holy and the profane. This Talmudic tale is about a divine measure taken to preserve that distinction even when the Holy Tongue was translated into an alien language.

The Egyptian monarch Ptolemy Philadelphus gathered together seventy-two elders from the people of Israel and placed each of them in a separate room. None of them knew that the king had summoned the others, nor did any of them know why the king had called upon them.

Once he had them all quartered, the king went to each of them and said, "I would like you to translate the Torah of your teacher Moses into Greek."

Knowing that it was a very dangerous matter to disobey the king, each of the elders set about the task of translating the Holy Word into the Greek tongue. But in order to preserve the integrity of the translation, God prompted the elders, so that each of them, in isolation from the others, wrote precisely the same translation of the Scripture: "In the beginning God created. . . ," "Come let Me descend and confound their tongues. . . ," "Which the Lord thy God distributed to give light to all nations. . . ," and so on. Thus the Holy Tongue was preserved according to its consistency, if not according to its letter.

And instead of writing "the hare," each of them wrote, "the beast with small legs." For the name of Ptolemy's wife meant "hare," and God preserved the elders from arousing the wrath of the king for making fun of his wife.

Four Who Entered the Garden
CHAGIGAH 14B

This is a tale about the dangers encountered by those who would penetrate the deepest mysteries of God and His Creation. The garden is a metaphor for that realm in which the mystic seeks a union with God. Rashi identifies it as heaven. Rabbi Chananel maintains that it is a vision, and not a place. However it is interpreted, one thing is clear: only those who are most righteous, who are most deeply versed in the mysteries of the Torah, and whose faith is complete can hope to draw nigh unto the Face of God and return unscathed.

Four sages determined that they would enter into the Garden of the Divine Mysteries. They were Ben Azzai, Ben Zoma, Elisha ben Abuyah, and Rabbi Akiva.

As they made their preparations, Rabbi Akiva warned his comrades, "When you approach the stones of pure marble in the palace of the Holy One, blessed be He, do not be afraid, even though they may look like a wall of water ready to engulf you. Do not cry out, 'Water! Water!' For it is written, 'He that speaks falsehood will not be established before My eyes.' Therefore, if you would draw nigh unto God, you must do so in truth and in faith. Do you understand? In truth and in faith!"

Having spoken these words, Rabbi Akiva spoke no more. He and the other sages proceeded. When Ben Azzai entered into the holy realm, however, the vision of God's palace was too much for him. As he drew near the pillars of white, he was convinced that he was about to drown. But before he could shout, "Water! Water!" he perished. Thus in the Scriptures it is written, "Precious in the sight of the Lord is the death of His saints."

After Ben Azzai came Ben Zoma. But he too failed to heed the warning of Rabbi Akiva. Confusing the pure marble for water, he fell into a state of absolute confusion and went mad. Thus in the Scriptures it is written, "Have you found honey? Eat only as much as you need, lest you be filled to overflowing and vomit it up."

Then came Elisha ben Abuyah, who also believed the deception of his eyes rather than the truth of Akiva's words. Unlike his comrades, however, he succumbed neither to death nor to madness but fell prey to a fate far worse: he lost his faith—which he, perhaps, never had, since it is through faith that the eyes behold marble instead of water—and became an apostate. Forever thereafter he was known as Acher, the alien Other.

Rabbi Akiva, so great was his faith, entered the garden without mistaking the pure marble for water. He alone entered in peace and departed in peace. For Rabbi Akiva alone entered in truth and in faith.

The Need of Another

NEDARIM 50A

Wisdom and righteousness lie in serving the needs of others. Here the prophet Elijah dons his favorite disguise in order to seek out the righteous and the wise. And he finds both in Rabbi Akiva. The combination of understanding and action that distinguishes Akiva is what goes into the making of a great scholar. And the devotion of Akiva's wife, truly a woman of valor, leads Akiva to set out on the path toward greatness.

When the daughter of the wealthy Kalba Savua agreed to marry a penniless shepherd named Akiva, her father vowed that she would not receive one cent of his riches. Their discussion about the matter was heated, as one might expect, but she never wavered in her love for the shepherd, which far exceeded her interest in her father's wealth. Thus, after the appropriate time of betrothal had passed, she bade farewell to her father and married the young Akiva.

The newlyweds lived in poverty. So severe was their need that they did not even have a bed to sleep on, only a pile of straw. Each morning when he awoke, Akiva would pick the straw from his hair. The only thing that marred his happiness was that he could not buy precious gifts for his beautiful wife.

"If only I could afford it," he said to her, "I would buy you a golden brooch with the image of Jerusalem engraved upon it."

"If I had wanted gold," she replied, "I would have stayed with my father. Even with this bed of straw, your love makes me far richer than all the gold of Solomon could."

One day the prophet Elijah came to their house disguised as a beggar. This was the prophet's favorite disguise, for a man's righteousness can always be determined by his treatment of others who are in need.

"Please," he cried out as he knocked at the couple's door, "could you spare me a bit of straw? My wife is going to give birth, you see, and I have nothing for her to lie on."

"Of course," replied Akiva, opening his home to the stranger. "Here. Take all you need."

Filled with gratitude and gladness, the prophet offered his thanks, took an armload of straw, and left.

"You see," remarked Akiva to his wife after the beggar had gone, "there are those whose need is much greater than ours. For there goes a man who lacks even straw."

His wife rejoiced in her husband's act of kindness. Like the prophet Elijah, she could see that she was married to a righteous man. Therefore she said to him, "Go and become a scholar." For she knew that the wisdom of the sages lies in their performance of deeds of lovingkindness.

"But I am an ignorant man," he replied. "It would take me years to become a scholar. And who would look after you?"

"God will look after me," she answered. "Go and become a scholar."

That very day Akiva set out for Yavneh, where he spent the next twelve years studying under Rabbi Eliezer and Rabbi Yehoshua. Thus began the scholarly life of one of Israel's greatest sages.

Joseph's Coffin

SOTAH 13A–13B

Memory is central to Jewish thought and tradition. It is our link to the patriarchs and the prophets, to the rabbis and the sages, thanks to whom we have not only the Torah but life itself. In this tale the Israelites bear the bones of their father Joseph into the wilderness along with the tablets that they received at Sinai. It is the memory signified by the bones of Joseph, who lived by everything contained in the Ark of the Torah, that opens up for the Israelites the presence of God signified by the tablets in the ark.

When the hour of liberation was at hand for the Israelites of Egypt, our teacher Moses did not concern himself with the spoils of Egypt. No, instead of worrying about his own gain, he remembered his obligation to carry the bones of Joseph out of the land of bondage and into the land of the promise. Although he did not know the secret of where Joseph's remains were buried, he recalled having heard it said that Serah, the daughter of Asher, knew. And so he went to her and said, "Serah, the time of our liberation is at hand. Can you tell me where the coffin of our father Joseph lies buried, so that we may carry it with us to the Promised Land?"

"Yes, I know," she answered. "But it will be impossible to retrieve it."

"Why impossible?"

"Because the Egyptians fashioned a coffin of iron for him," she explained, "and laid him in it. Then they took the coffin and placed it in the Nile, so that the waters that nourished their fields would be blessed. For they knew that Joseph brought many blessings to Egypt, and they wanted to keep him near forever. I am afraid that you will never be able to retrieve it from the river."

Moses was not daunted by these words but immediately fetched several men to serve as bearers for Joseph's coffin and set out for the banks of the Nile. For he knew the power of the Most High to overcome all obstacles.

When he reached the edge of the waters, Moses cried out, "Joseph, Joseph! The time for the liberation of your children has come, as the Holy One, blessed be He, promised it would when He declared, 'I shall deliver you.' Know that we have remembered the oath you imposed upon our fathers when you asked them to swear that they would take you out of this land and return you to the land of your birth. Therefore show yourself, so that we may honor the oath. Otherwise we shall deem ourselves free of the promise our fathers made to you."

No sooner did Moses finish speaking than the coffin of Joseph floated up to the surface of the waters and over to the bank where he and the bearers stood. They took it upon their shoulders and went to prepare for the liberation from Egypt. They carried it with them all the way to Mount Sinai. And from Mount Sinai they bore it, alongside the Ark of the Covenant that contained the tablets of the Torah, all the way to the Promised Land.

Thus year after year, as the Israelites made their way through the wilderness, they took with them one ark containing the bones of Joseph and another containing the Shechinah, the Divine Presence of God. Each time they encountered travelers along the way, the strangers would ask them, "What is contained in these two arks that you bear?"

The Israelites would reply, "One contains the bones of the dead, and the other is a vessel of the Shechinah."

"Is it your custom," they would ask further, "to bear the dead alongside the Shechinah?"

"The one whose remains lie in this ark," the Israelites told them, "fulfilled all that is contained in the other."

And so the wayfarers realized the wisdom of the Israelites. For the Israelites knew that, if their liberation was to be complete, they must bear with them the memory of the dead in their pursuit of the future.

From Yerushalayim to Yavneh

GITTIN 56A–56B

During the time of the Roman siege of Jerusalem, when the Holy City was about to fall, a sage feigned death to save a remnant from destruction. The center of learning was moved from Jerusalem (Yerushalayim) to Yavneh, making it possible for the truth and light of the Torah to endure and for God's Presence to continue to dwell in the land, even in the midst of terrible persecutions.

In the days when the Roman general Vespasian besieged the Holy City of Jerusalem, there lived in the city three men of great piety and wealth. One was named Nakdimon ben Gorion, for whose sake, it was said, the sun shone. Another was named Ben Kalba Savua, a man who was known for his generous hospitality. And the third was a righteous man named Ben Tsitsit Hakeset, so called because his *tsitsit*, the fringes on his garments, were so long that they draped the cushions upon which he sat.

As the siege continued, the city's food supplies began to dwindle, and the people grew afraid. Nakdimon ben Gorion assured them: "Do be afraid. I shall offer up all of my wealth to keep you in wheat and barley."

To this offer Ben Kalba Savua added, "Fear not. For I shall see to it that you have plenty of wine, oil, and salt."

"And I," Ben Tsitsit Hakeset put in, "shall keep you in wood."

So, thanks to the generosity of these pious men, the people of Jerusalem stored away provisions to last them for more than twenty years.

Nevertheless, in order to prevent undue bloodshed and avoid the destruction of the Holy City, the rabbis of Jerusalem urged the people to go out and make peace with the Romans. Among the most powerful groups in the city, however, were the Zealots, who refused to allow anyone to approach the Romans with offers of peace.

"Let us go out and fight them," they cried, "and either drive them out of the land or die like men."

"Their might and their numbers are too great," the rabbis answered the Zealots. "You will never succeed but will only bring death upon all."

"Then so be it," the Zealots replied. And they burned the stores of wheat and barley, casting the city into a terrible famine.

Now Abba Sirka, the leader of the Zealots, was the nephew of one of Israel's greatest sages, Rabbi Yochanan ben Zakkai. Fearing for the lives of the Jews on the brink of starvation, the rabbi sent a message to his nephew that read, "Come immediately. I would have a word with you in private."

When Abba Sirka arrived at the rabbi's home his uncle asked him sternly, "How long do you plan to carry on this way? Is it your intention to starve us to death?"

"There is nothing I can do," Abba Sirka replied. "If I should utter a word of objection, the Zealots would kill me."

"Then you must devise some means for me to get past the city walls," said the rabbi. "Once outside, I may be able to go to the Romans and save at least a remnant of the people."

After giving his uncle's request a few moments of thought, Abba Sirka instructed him, "Pretend to be deathly ill, and let everyone, especially the Zealots, come to ask about you. Take some foul-smelling meat and hide it next to you, so that when they approach you they will think you are dead. Then have your disciples come to carry you away, but let no one else near you. For they may notice that you are still light and suspect some trick, since they know very well that a living soul is lighter than a corpse."

Rabbi Yochanan listened carefully to everything his nephew told him and did exactly as he had said. When his disciples came to carry him out of his house, Rabbi Eliezer took one side of the bier and Rabbi Yehoshua bore the other. As they were leaving Yochanan ben Zakkai's house, some of the Zealots started to shove a lance through the rabbi's body, but Rabbi Eliezer stopped them.

"Would you have the Romans declare," he asked, "that we have pierced our Master?"

Others were about to push the body off the bier, when Rabbi Yehoshua said to them, "Shall the Romans have cause to accuse us of casting our teacher to the ground?"

The Zealots finally opened up the city's gate for them, so that they could bury the sage.

Rabbi Yochanan ben Zakkai lost no time making his way to the Roman camp. As soon as he caught sight of the general Vespasian, he cried, "Peace be unto you, O King, peace be unto you, O King!"

To which Vespasian replied, "Your life is forfeit, Jew, on two counts. First because you have addressed me as king when I am not a king. And second because, believing me to be a king, you did not come to me before now."

"Oh, but sire," said the rabbi, "you must be a king, for if you were not a king Jerusalem would never be delivered into your hands. And I have not come to you before now because the Zealots in the city would not allow it."

Just at that moment a messenger from Rome arrived in the camp and shouted, "All rise! For the emperor is dead, and the leaders of Rome have declared that you, Vespasian, are to be his successor!"

Hearing these words, Vespasian turned to the rabbi and said, "You are wise indeed. I must leave for Rome immediately, but I shall send another to take my place here. Meanwhile I shall grant you a request."

"All I ask, sire," answered the rabbi, "is that you allow me to go with our sages, including the scholars of the school of Rabbi Gamliel, to dwell in peace in the city of Yavneh."

Vespasian agreed.

And so the new emperor departed to his new seat of power, and

Rabbi Yochanan, along with the wisest men of Israel, set out for their new seat of learning. Yavneh became renowned as a center from which the light of Torah emanated into the world.

"My Children Have Defeated Me!"

BAVA METZIA 59A–59B

There is a saying in the Jewish tradition, God likes to be defeated by His children, which is exemplified by this Talmudic tale. Here, indeed, we are taught several lessons. First, the authority of Halachah, or Jewish law, does not lie with a single individual. Second, miracles that contravene the laws of nature are not proof of an individual's claim to authority. Third, the Torah is not hidden away in heaven but belongs to all the children of Israel. And finally, the God of Abraham, Isaac, and Jacob listens to the arguments of his children and may be swayed by them.

The sages who bequeathed to us the wisdom of the Talmud once were engaged in an argument over those cooking utensils that might be rendered unclean. When the discussion turned to the issue of cleanliness as it pertained to ovens, Rabbi Eliezer declared that if an oven is made of distinct pieces, with sand separating one tile from another, it is clean.

"Since each piece of the oven is not itself a utensil," he reasoned, "the sand between them prevents the whole structure from being viewed as a single utensil."

The other sages, however, insisted that no, such an oven is unclean. "The outer coating of mortar," Rabbi Yehudah maintained in the name of Rabbi Shemuel, "unifies the pieces into a whole. Therefore it is liable to uncleanness."

Now Rabbi Eliezer was not used to any disagreement with his rulings, and the scholars' reaction disturbed him. Determined to convince them that his view was the correct one, he mustered every conceivable argument to support his pronouncement on the law. But still the rabbis were not swayed. Finally, deciding to summon all his powers of persuasion, he cried out, "If the law is as I have ruled it to be, then let this carob tree prove it!"

At that the carob tree growing on the spot where they sat up-rooted itself, moved a hundred cubits away—some say four hun-dred cubits—and planted itself back into the ground. But the sages simply shook their heads, unimpressed, and replied, "The move-ments of a carob tree are no proof of the law."

Growing more frustrated, Rabbi Eliezer shouted, "Very well! If my ruling is in keeping with the law, let this stream of water prove it!"

With these words the stream of water that ran by the place where they sat reversed its course and began to flow uphill. Even this did not convince the scholars who simply retorted, "The flow of a stream of water is no proof of the law."

Driven to the end of his patience, Rabbi Eliezer finally rose up and shouted, "If I am correct in my ruling on the law, let the walls of the schoolhouse prove it!"

Whereupon the walls of the schoolhouse that stood nearby be-gan to lean, until it looked as though they would fall in. At that moment Rabbi Yehoshua intervened and cried out to the walls, "When scholars are engaged in halachic disputes, you have no right to interfere!"

Thanks to the honor that was Rabbi Yehoshua's due, the walls leaned no further and did not fall. But because Rabbi Eliezer was due honor of his own, they did not stand upright either. (For many years, they leaned slightly to one side.)

Rabbi Yehoshua's intervention, however, did not discourage Rabbi Eliezer. One last time he shouted, "If the ruling I have pro-nounced is in keeping with the law, then let Heaven itself offer proof!"

A Voice cried out from on high, "Why do you engage in this dispute with Rabbi Eliezer? For you know that in all matters the law is in agreement with his rulings!"

But Rabbi Yehoshua exclaimed, "The Torah is not in Heaven, as it is written in the Torah itself! It was entrusted to us, the children of Israel, at Sinai. Therefore we do not heed the Heavenly Voice."

With that the dispute came to an end. Not long afterward the prophet Elijah appeared to Rabbi Natan, who asked him, "What did the Holy One, blessed be He, do in that hour when Rabbi

Yehoshua raised his voice to the heavens?"

Elijah smiled and answered, "He laughed with joy, all the while repeating, 'My children have defeated Me! My children have defeated Me!' For nothing pleases Him more than those who argue with Him for the sake of His Torah."

Why Elijah Failed to Appear

BAVA METZIA 85B

Once the prophet Elijah failed to attend a meeting of the rabbis. The reason? To be sure that the Messiah would not come before his time. In explaining his reason, we are given an interesting look at the afterlife. There, it seems, we do not go to rest but, like Adam working in the garden of Eden, we engage in the task of study and prayer. Finally, it is worth noting the suggestion in this story that even Elijah, the one who did not die but ascended to heaven in a chariot of fire, is fallible and subject to the chastisement of Heaven. If his punishment seems excessive, it is precisely because he excels in his righteousness.

The prophet Elijah frequented the gatherings of the rabbis at the academy of Rabbi Yehudah ha-Nasi, compiler of the Mishnah, the sage known simply as Rabbi. One day, at the time of the New Moon, Rabbi waited and waited for the prophet to show up, but in vain. Rabbi was worried. After all, the prophet was known for his punctuality. If anyone knew the importance of being in the right place at the right time, it was Elijah. And the coming of the New Moon was a time of renewal of life, a time when he was most needed. What could have become of him?

The next day, however, just before the morning prayers, Elijah did show up. Rabbi asked him, "Why did you not come to us yesterday?"

"The patriarchs delayed me," he explained. "You see, I had to awaken our father Abraham early in the morning and see to it that he washed his hands for his prayers. After he finished with his morning prayers, I laid him back to rest again. Next I had to awaken his son Isaac. He too washed his hands and said his prayers and then was returned to his rest. Finally I had to do the same with Jacob. They take up my time, those patriarchs."

"But why did you not awaken all three of them together?" Rabbi wanted to know. "Then you could have joined us."

"I was afraid," Elijah explained, "that if they were all to pray together, they would force the Messiah to come before his appointed hour."

"I see," said Rabbi. "And are there any among the living who compare to the patriarchs, whose prayers might bring the Messiah before his time?"

"There are," Elijah answered. "Rabbi Chiyya and his sons."

Hearing this, Rabbi proclaimed a fast and called Rabbi Chiyya and his sons to the stand where the Torah scrolls were read and the prayers were conducted. "You will lead the prayers today," Rabbi told them. The morning service began.

When they came to the Amidah prayer and Rabbi Chiyya cried out, "He causes the wind to blow," a wind rose up around the academy. And when he uttered the words, "He causes the rain to fall," rain descended to the earth. But just as he was about to exclaim, "He quickens the dead," all the universe trembled. And he fell silent.

At that moment the Holy One, blessed be He, asked His angels, "Who has revealed our secret, that Rabbi Chiyya's prayers are so powerful?"

The angels replied, "Elijah."

The prophet was immediately brought before the heavenly hosts. There he was subjected to sixty flaming lashes for having endangered the universe. Having borne the anger of God, he assumed the form of a flaming bear and descended once more to Rabbi's academy. There he entered and in his fearsome disguise dispersed the rabbis.

The Angels Rebuked

SANHEDRIN 39B

This brief tale reminds us that every human being, friend or foe, Jew or Gentile, is a child of God and a descendant of Adam. Each person is essentially related to all people. Why is the Hebrew word for face, panim, *plural? Because every human being has two faces: his own and the face of Adam, the face of humanity itself. Therefore the death of any single human being diminishes the humanity of all—even the death of an enemy.*

When the Israelites gathered on the beach of the Sea of Reeds, they feared that their exodus from Egypt had come to an end. Pharaoh's army was in hot pursuit, and it seemed that, if he could not enslave them, he was determined to destroy them. Indeed, the order to annihilate the Israelites was not a difficult one for the Egyptian soldiers and charioteers to follow: the Egyptians had paid a terrible price so that Israel might be set free. Only hours before they set out to overtake the liberated slaves of Egypt, the Angel of Death had passed through the land to claim the firstborn of every household.

As the Egyptian army approached the sea, they could hear the howl of a great wind and the rush of the waters. When they arrived at the shore they were stricken with wonder: the sea had parted, and the hosts of Israelites were making their way over dry land where the waters had been.

The Egyptians remained undaunted. At the order of their commanders, the soldiers and charioteers set out down the path cleared by the parting of the sea, more determined than ever to bring death to the people who, they believed, had brought death to them. Faster and faster they rode, the wind that held the waters at bay roaring in their ears. But when they saw the last of the Israelites emerge on the other side, no longer did they hear the wind. The only sound they heard, the last sound they heard, was the sound of the waters that rushed over them and drowned them.

They did not hear the song of Moses, as he sang praise to God for His deliverance of the Hebrews. Did they hear the song of the angels praising God for destroying those who were bent on destroying God's chosen? Perhaps they heard God rebuke the angels, saying, "My children are drowning, and yet you utter song before Me!"

The Torah Is Fire

AVODAH ZARAH 18A

According to the teaching of Rabbi Shimon ben Lakish in the Midrash on the Song of Songs, the scroll that God gave to Moses was made of black fire written on white fire. "The scroll was itself fire," said Resh Lakish, "hewn from fire, completely formed of fire, and given in fire." Perhaps Resh Lakish derived this teaching from an example set by a sage who was martyred over a century earlier at the hands of the Romans: Rabbi Chanina ben Teradyon. Indeed, the teaching that issued from the rabbi's example was powerful enough to lead his executioner to join him in death. Like God Himself, the Torah is a consuming fire that will not be consumed, and those who make themselves part of the Torah do not succumb to the fires that are forged by human hands, though they be consumed.

In the days when the Roman authorities ruled over Caesarea and their cruel prohibition against studying the Torah was in force, there lived a sage named Rabbi Chanina ben Teradyon. Fearing heaven more than he feared humanity, Rabbi Chanina refused to bow to the injunction against learning and living by the Torah. Despite the threat of death, he continued to teach and to study, for he knew that without the Torah there is no life.

One day the Roman authorities found him in the midst of a public assembly. With his daughter at his side, he held the Torah scrolls to his heart and spoke to those gathered around him about the teachings of Moses. The Romans decided to make an example of the rabbi. They arrested him immediately and wrapped him in the scrolls of the Holy Word that he had held dearly in his arms. Once he was wound in the Torah, they ordered bundles of dry branches piled around the rabbi. Then they set fire to the fagots, and, before the flames could rise too high, they soaked pieces of wool in water and placed them on Chanina's chest, so that he would not enjoy the release of death too quickly.

Seeing what had befallen her father, Rabbi Chanina's daughter cried out in tears, "Oh, father, woe that I should have lived to witness this!"

"Do not weep for me, my child," he said to her. "The One who sees to the care of the Torah will see to my care."

"Oh, Father," she wept, "my tears are not only for you but for the Torah that is to be burned with you."

"You needn't shed tears for the Torah, little one," he answered. "For the Torah is fire. And fire cannot burn fire."

As the flames began to rise, the disciples who had gathered around called out, "Rabbi, what do you see?"

"I see the parchment consumed in the fire," he replied. "But the letters. . . the letters are ascending on high!"

"Rabbi!" they shouted to their teacher. "Open your mouth and breathe in the flames, so that you may put an end to this terrible suffering!"

"Let the Holy One who gave me my soul take it from me," he said. "But let no man do injury to himself."

Beholding this scene and hearing these words, the executioner who had set fire to the sage was overcome by the truth and testimony before him. He cried out, "Rabbi, if I should take away the tufts of wool over your chest, will you take me with you into the World to Come?"

"Yes," was the rabbi's reply.

"Swear it!" the executioner cried in desperation.

"I swear," answered the rabbi.

The executioner quickly reached up into the flames and removed the water-soaked wool from the rabbi's chest. Within seconds the sage expired, and the executioner threw himself into the flames.

At that moment all who were there heard a Voice from on high, declaring, "Rabbi Chanina ben Teradyon and the executioner have found a place in the World to Come!"

When, more than a century later, Rabbi Yehudah ha-Nasi heard the tale of Rabbi Chanina's martyrdom he wept and said, "Truly there are those who earn eternal life in a single hour, while others must labor for many years!"

A Good Heart

AVOT 2:9

God's favorite dwelling place, tradition teaches us, is the human heart. It is said that the sum of the Torah lies in the heart, for the Torah begins with the letter beit and ends with the letter lamed, the two letters that spell lev *or "heart." Therefore the Torah commands us to lay its words and its truth upon our heart (Deuteronomy 6:6), so that it may become the center from which all good emanates into the world.*

One day Rabbi Yochanan ben Zakkai gathered his disciples around him and said to them, "I have a very important task for you. I want you to go out into the world and search out the ways of men to see what is truly good in humanity. Then return to me and tell me what you have found."

As always, the disciples obeyed their teacher. They walked among people of every class and occupation, every background and lot in life. After a time, when each believed that he had found what was truly good in people, they returned to the rabbi to report what they had learned.

"So tell me," said Rabbi Yochanan, first addressing Rabbi Eliezer. "What have you found to be truly good?"

"A good eye," Eliezer replied. "For those who have a good eye have an eye for the suffering of others. So they are led to be generous."

"Well said," the teacher nodded. "And you, Rabbi Yehoshua, what have you found to be truly good?"

"A good friend," he answered. "A man should not only cultivate a good friend but should himself be a good friend. That is how life takes on value. For a friend has no price and is more precious than gold."

"You too have spoken well," the rabbi answered. Then, turning to Rabbi Yose, he asked, "What have you learned?"

"I have learned," said Yose, "that a good neighbor is truly good. A man cannot live in isolation from others but needs company in order to be truly good. It is from a good neighbor that we learn how to be a good neighbor."

"We all may learn from what you have learned," Rabbi Yochanan commented. "But I wonder what Rabbi Shimon has found to be truly good."

"I have found that the person who looks ahead and attends to the consequences of his actions is truly good," said Rabbi Shimon. "Our deeds create angels for good or for evil, and the angels we create go out into the world to do good or evil. Thus our every move, our every thought, disturbs all the universe and affects human lives."

"What you say is profound," said Rabbi Yochanan. "Listen well, all of you, to Rabbi Shimon. But we have not yet heard from Rabbi Eleazar."

The disciples and their teacher turned to Rabbi Eleazar, prepared to listen to his discourse on what is truly good in humanity. But all he said was: "A good heart is truly good."

At this their teacher smiled and declared, "I prefer the words of Eleazar ben Arach to all of your words combined. In his words are contained your words. A good heart sees rightly and seeks out other human beings, loving our neighbor, as the Torah commands us. And a good heart looks not only ahead but also above, loving God, as the Torah also commands us. Yes, Rabbi Eleazar has spoken well."

Keeping the Deep at Bay
MAKKOT 11A

Just as the Torah is not one text among many in the world, the Temple is not one structure among others. Like the Divine Name, both are unique in their capacity to signify the presence of the Holy One in the world. And, like the Divine Name, both keep at bay the chaos and the void that Creation itself opposes, as long as even a remnant of the Temple remains. This story tells us what threatens the world and what keeps that threat at bay. It tells us that all the world rests on the Divine Name and the Torah that it symbolizes. And it tells us that without the actions of a righteous human being, the world would be turned over to the deep.

In order to prepare the way for his son Solomon to raise up the holy Temple, King David set about digging the foundations for the structure from which light would emanate into the world. As he was digging, however, the waters of the deep came surging up from beneath the earth's surface. Immediately King David realized that the water threatened to flood all the earth and that he must act quickly to keep it at bay.

Knowing that the Torah alone could overcome the powers of the abyss, he cried out to his counselors, "What does the law tell us about writing the Divine Name on a shard and throwing it into the deep?"

Ordinarily it was forbidden to inscribe the Name on a shard. His counselors knew this as well as he did and so were afraid to answer, despite the rising waters.

David grew impatient and exclaimed, "Whoever knows anything about this matter and remains silent, may he suffocate!"

Hearing this, Achitophel reasoned to himself, "In a case where harmony must be restored between a husband and wife, the Torah says, 'Let My Name be inscribed in a scroll, rather than be blotted out by water.' If the Name may be inscribed for the sake of harmony between husband and wife, then surely it may be written in order to deliver the world."

Having thus reasoned, the king's advisor shouted, "Yes, it is allowed!"

Without wasting another second, David took a shard, inscribed upon it the four letters of the Divine Name, and cast it upon the face of the deep. No sooner did the Name touch the surface of the waters than they receded to their own region. In fact, they receded so rapidly that David grew afraid: perhaps the earth would be made completely dry and wither away. Thereupon he composed the fifteen Psalms known as the "Song of Ascents."

So there, where the Name of the Holy One, blessed be He, keeps the deep at bay, the holy Temple was erected.

But the tale does not end here. Tradition teaches us that our moral conduct influences the shard's ability to keep the deep at bay. Whenever we harm our neighbor in any way, the Divine Name is erased from the shard, and the waters begin to rise. Therefore God has appointed the angel Yazriel to keep watch over the shard. The angel has in his possession seventy engraving tools, and each time the shard is erased, he engraves upon it once again the letters of the Holy Name. If you put your ear to the earth and listen very carefully, you can hear the angel carving away, keeping the deep at bay.

Moses and Akiva
MENACHOT 29B

Even after Moses' death, he engaged God in various arguments concerning the Torah and humanity. Here the prophet to whom God gave the Torah speaks on behalf of the sage who expounded it. What is disturbing about this tale is God's insistence that Moses be silent. Moses' question about the fate of Rabbi Akiva is a question that lurks in the hearts of all of us. God's reply that Moses should remain silent makes all the more painful the silence of God Himself. Yet He does not remain altogether silent, for He speaks, albeit in mysterious ways, through tales like this one.

When Moses breathed his last and ascended to heaven, he found the Holy One laboring over the Torah that He had given to Moses. Wondering what God could possibly be adding to the truth that He had revealed, Moses came closer to see what He was writing. When he looked, he found that God was attaching crowns to the letters.

Summoning his courage, Moses asked, "O Lord of the Universe, can there be anything lacking in Your Holy Torah that You must make these additions?"

In His infinite patience, the Lord answered, "At the end of many generations there will rise up the wisest of the sages, Akiva ben Yosef. He will examine every stroke of My hand, every line of My Law, and will penetrate its secrets for the sake of all."

"Lord of the Universe," said Moses, "please allow me to see this wise and righteous man."

"Turn around," God replied, "and you will behold him."

Moses turned around and saw that eight rows of scholars were seated before Rabbi Akiva. They were listening to their master and answering him, struggling to understand every detail of the Torah. Moses took a seat behind them and tried to follow their words. What they said was completely strange to him, and, failing to understand their arguments, he soon grew anxious.

At one point, however, the disciples challenged their master, asking him, "Whence do you know this?"

Akiva replied, "It is a law given unto Moses at Sinai."

At that Moses was reassured, convinced of the wisdom and holiness of Rabbi Akiva. In fact, he was convinced that Akiva's insights exceeded his own, so he rose up and returned to the Holy One, blessed be He.

"Lord of the Universe," he said to God, "how is it that You have such a man in Your service, and yet You chose to give Your Torah to the likes of me?"

Instead of answering Moses' question, God simply said, "Be silent: I have decreed it to be so."

"Very well," Moses replied. "But, Lord of the Universe, since You have revealed to me the Torah expounded by this righteous sage, please show me the reward he is to reap for his efforts."

"Turn around," God answered, "and you will behold his reward."

Moses turned. Much to his astonishment, he witnessed not a sublime reward conferred upon the rabbi but the terrible death by torture that the Romans would inflict upon him. Overcome with compassion and agony, he saw Akiva's flesh torn to bits and weighed out on scales in the market place.

Unable to hold his tongue, Moses turned to God and cried out, "Lord of the Universe, how can such a great sage who offers the world such profound teachings meet with such a horrible end?"

God did not answer Moses' question but sternly said, "Be silent: I have decreed it to be so."

And, fearing to ask further, Moses fell silent.

When Abraham Stood in the Temple

MENACHOT 53B

*When Abraham walked the earth he demonstrated his righteousness by
arguing with God over the fate of the people of Sodom and Gomorrah. Like
Moses, Abraham continued to speak to God in behalf of humanity even
after he had ceased to walk this earth. This teaches us that the righteous
continue with their life's work even after they have departed this world. It is
thanks to the testimony and the argument of our fathers that we are returned to life whenever death threatens.*

When the Babylonians were about to destroy the Temple, the Holy
One, blessed be He, gazed down from on high and saw our father
Abraham standing at the Temple altar. Said He, "Why have you,
my beloved, come to stand in My house?"

"I have come," Abraham replied, "because I am concerned about
the fate of my children. Where are they? Why is the Temple
empty?"

"Your children have sinned," God explained. "They bowed to
the idols of the world and have done violence unto one another.
Therefore I have sent them into exile."

"Perhaps," said Abraham, "they sinned in error, without realizing what they were doing. After all, they are but flesh and blood."

"No," replied the Lord, "Israel has been as a harlot who goes
looking for sin. She has turned herself over completely to the flesh
and has forgotten the image of the Holy Spirit in which she was
created."

"Then perhaps," Abraham persisted, "there were only a few who
went astray, and not the many. Surely You would not punish the
innocent with the guilty!"

"I wish it were so," God answered. "But the harlot has committed lewd acts with many. Far too many."

"And yet," Abraham continued, "You might have remembered
the covenant of circumcision, as You did in the days of our en-
slavement in Egypt. Without Your memory of the covenant, their
memory is like the wind."

"But," God retorted, "they tried to forget the covenant with attempts to hide and undo their circumcision, in order to walk after the gods of the Gentiles."

Still Abraham would not be turned away. "Perhaps if You had given them just a little more time, they would have repented and returned to You. After all, the sum of all time is Yours."

"Am I to rejoice in their wickedness?" God replied. "And you, Abraham, what joy can you find in this?"

At that Abraham fell into despair, lowered his head into his hands, and wept bitterly. "O Lord of the Universe," he cried aloud, "Heaven forbid that they should be without hope!"

At that moment a Voice resounded from the very heights of the heavens, declaring, "The Lord has said that Israel is like a leafy olive tree, fair and abounding in fruit!"

Abraham understood and was comforted. Just as the olive tree produces it best fruit only at the end of the season, so would Israel return from her exile and flourish at the end of time. Some say God was comforted, too.

Beware of What You Ask For

CHULLIN 60A

What do we ask for when we pray? We ask for wisdom, forgiveness, healing, and the like. We do not ask for things, and we give thanks for the profound blessings we have received. We do not ask God to prove Himself by giving us things. He may respond not by refusing such prayers but by granting them.

Emperor Hadrian's daughter once approached Rabbi Yehoshua ben Chananiah to ridicule the God of the Jews. Supposing that she might trick Rabbi Yehoshua by showing him that his God was nothing, she said to him, "In the psalms of your King David it says that your God 'lays the beams of His upper chambers in the waters.' I take it, then, that He is a carpenter."

Refusing to be drawn into an argument about such a foolish view of God, Rabbi Yehoshua replied simply, "As you say, if that is how you would understand Him."

"Ask Him to make a spool for me," she commanded the rabbi. "And we shall see whether He is indeed a carpenter."

Without responding to her blasphemy, the rabbi did as she commanded him and prayed to God, asking Him to make a spool for the emperor's daughter.

Immediately the woman was stricken with leprosy, and as was customary in Rome, her father had her removed to the city square where she was given a spool with which to wind thread. There people would see her, take pity on her, and pray for her recovery.

After the Emperor's daughter had spent a few days with her spool in the city square, Rabbi Yehoshua happened to pass by. He saw her winding her thread, and remarked, "My God has given you a beautiful spool."

"Indeed!" she cried. "I beg you, please, ask your God to take back what He has given me!"

But Rabbi Yehoshua explained, "Once our God has granted a request, He never takes it back."

How the Merchants of Death Were Made to Choose Life
ME'ILAH 17A

In the Torah God enjoins us to choose life (Deuteronomy 30:19). One of the ways we choose life is by sanctifying a place in time where the Holy One may step into His creation. Therefore, in keeping with God's commandment, we remember and observe the Sabbath. A husband and wife become partners of the Creator in the act of creating life. Thus conjugal relations are sanctified through laws of ritual purity. In this Talmudic tale we see how the Romans tried to eliminate the Jews by destroying their relationship with God, and we see how one wise Jew was able to annul the Romans' evil decree.

Once the wicked Roman governor of Judea issued a decree forbidding the Jews to observe the Sabbath or to circumcise their children and requiring Jewish men to have conjugal relations with menstruant women. For the governor knew that by imposing these things he could eradicate Jewish life.

Among the Jews, however, there was a certain Rabbi Reuven ben Istroboli, who was as wise as he was brave. He cut his hair, shaved his beard, and began to dress in the Roman manner, so that he might associate with the rulers of the land. So clever was he, that he soon found his way into the governor's inner circle of friends, and before long he had the ear of the governor himself.

"Sire," he approached the ruler one day, "tell me, if a man has an enemy, does he wish him to be poor or to be rich?"

"Why, to be poor, of course," the governor answered.

"Then why do you prohibit the Jews from resting on the Sabbath?" asked the rabbi in his Roman disguise. "For this added day of work will raise them up from their poverty."

"Then let them do no work on the Seventh Day," the governor declared, "so that they may continue in their impoverishment."

And so the decree forbidding the observance of the Sabbath was revoked.

Then the rabbi said to the governor, "Tell me, sire, if a man has an enemy, does he want him to be weak in body or strong?"

"He certainly wants him to be weak," the governor replied.

"Then I shall tell you how to make the bodies of these Jews weak," said the rabbi. "Require them to circumcise their children when the infants are eight days old."

"Yes," the governor nodded, "I think you have something there. Henceforth the Jews are to circumcise their male children at the age of eight days!"

And so the decree forbidding circumcision was overturned.

Finally, the rabbi sought to fool the governor into forbidding Jewish men from having conjugal relations with menstruant women, saying, "Tell me, sire, if a man has an enemy, does he want his enemy to increase or decrease?"

"You know yourself," said the governor. "He wants his enemy to decrease."

"Well," the clever rabbi continued, "I know a way to keep these Jews from multiplying so rapidly: forbid them from having intercourse with menstruant women."

"Ah, you are indeed wise, my friend," the governor nodded. "Let it be so."

Thus, thanks to a rabbi who was not afraid to take on the appearance of a Roman, the evil decrees were annulled.

How the Wise Men Answered Alexander

TAMID 32A

The courage of the sages is as remarkable as their wisdom. They did not allow themselves to be blinded by a fear of human authority but, as this tale illustrates, remained faithful to the authority of God.

Once the conqueror Alexander had entered the Land of Israel, he decided to test the sages to see whether they were, indeed, as wise as they were said to be. "I want you all to answer me truthfully," Alexander began, "and have no fear for your lives. Tell me, please, who is called wise?"

"He who can see what will come to pass," they told him. "For the wise know where they are and where they have been according to where they are going."

"Then who is called mighty?" Alexander continued.

"He is mighty," they answered, "who can subdue his evil inclination. For a man cannot rule a world if he cannot rule himself."

"Who, then, is a rich man?" the conqueror asked.

"One who rejoices in what God has given him," they replied. "For it is better to want what you have than to have what you want. And he who wants more is forever in want."

Impressed by their reply, Alexander put to them yet another question: "What must a man do in order to have life?"

"He must offer up his life," they declared to him, "to the study of Torah, prayer, and acts of lovingkindness. For to have life is to impart life to others."

"And if a man wants to kill himself?" Alexander pressed the matter. "What then should he do?"

"If he would kill himself," they answered, "then he should try to engage in every selfish or sensual indulgence. For to consume life is to be consumed."

"How should a man go about making himself popular?"

"He should renounce all sovereignty and authority over others," the sages told Alexander. "For he is loved who is a servant to his fellow human being."

Now this reply disturbed Alexander, who was known for his authority over all the world. Therefore, thinking to divide the sages against one another, he asked, "Which among you is the wisest?"

"We are all equally wise," they answered him, "since we have all agreed on the answers we have given you."

Realizing that he could not trick them, the mighty conqueror finally asked, "Why do you resist me?"

"We do not resist you," they explained, "but the Satan who is acting through you. For he has been given power over you, so that you might test us."

"Are you not afraid that I will have you all killed?" Alexander pretended to threaten them.

"You will do us no harm," they replied, "for in bringing us here together, you have promised us safe conduct, and it would be unfitting for a king to go back on his word."

Very much pleased with these last words, Alexander dressed the sages in purple, placed gold chains around their necks, and sent them on their way. He was convinced of the wisdom and the holiness of the people of Israel.

The Arrest of Rabbi Eliezer
TOSEFTA SHECHITAT CHULLIN 2:24

This tale is from the Tosefta, a body of rabbinical teachings that were not included in the Mishnah or the Talmud. In it Rabbi Eliezer perceives the hand of God at work even in the acts of the Romans, so that when he is arrested by them, he knows there is a good reason for it.

There was a time when the Romans persecuted a new Jewish sect whose members were known as Christians more than they persecuted the Jews. Rabbi Eliezer was arrested for his involvement in Christian affairs. The rabbi would have understood it if he had been charged with teaching Torah, but to be arrested for taking up with the Christians was incomprehensible to him.

The Romans wasted no time bringing the rabbi to court. There the magistrate asked him, "How is it that an elder of your standing should become involved with this renegade sect?" For even the Roman magistrate knew of Rabbi Eliezer's reputation as a student of the Torah.

"I place my trust in the Judge," Rabbi Eliezer answered.

The magistrate did not realize that the rabbi was speaking of God, the Judge of judges, but thought the rabbi was speaking of him.

"Since you place such trust in me," the Roman judge replied, "this is my ruling. Clearly it is impossible that this gray head should err in matters such as those that pertain to the Christians. Therefore I find you to be innocent of all charges. Go. You are free."

Nevertheless, when Rabbi Eliezer departed from the court, he remained troubled over having been arrested for any involvement with the Christians. He knew that God had brought him to such a pass for a good reason, but what that reason might be he could not fathom.

Hearing of the rabbi's distress, his disciples came to him and offered him all the words of comfort they could think of. But the rabbi would not be comforted: there had to be a reason for his arrest.

Finally Rabbi Akiva spoke. "Rabbi Eliezer, may I please say something to you that might ease your distress?"

"You may," replied the rabbi.

"Could it be," said Akiva, "that on some occasion one of the Christians might have said something to you about their teachings that pleased you?"

Rabbi Eliezer thought carefully for a moment and said, "Oh, yes! How could I have forgotten? I was once strolling through the camp at Sepphoris, when I happened to meet a man who related to me one of the teachings of the Christians. And, I must confess, it did please me.

"That is why I was arrested—not for my involvement with the Christians but for having transgressed one of the teachings of the Torah. For there we are told, 'Keep far away from the harlot and do not go near the door of her house.' But, like a man passing by the harlot's door, I was tempted by the words of that Christian."

Thus we learn that we must always flee from that which is disreputable or has even the appearance of being disreputable. The Judge is forever looking on.

The Ammonite Proselyte

TOSEFTA YADAYIM 2:17

The Jews were the first ancient people to adopt the notion of conversion. Understanding their chosenness to mean being chosen to bear witness to the chosenness of all, the Jews welcomed any human being who had resolved to enter into the covenant of Abraham and become one of those who were chosen for this testimony. Thus it was the Moabite Ruth—from a "cursed" people—who became the mother of the House of David, from which the Messiah will arise. This tale from the Tosefta deals with just such an issue. In it we find that even those who are deemed outcasts—a Moabite or an Ammonite—can enter into the company of the children of Abraham. For they are already the children of God.

One day when the rabbis were gathered before the house of study, an Ammonite proselyte by the name of Yehudah approached them. Longing to join the company of sages in prayer and study, he asked, "Please, may I be allowed to enter the congregation?"

Without hesitation Rabbi Gamliel, who had a great love for the Torah, told him, "No, you are prohibited from entering."

Without hesitation Rabbi Yehoshua, who had a great love for those who loved the Torah, declared, "Yes, you are permitted to enter."

Immediately a discussion ensued. Rabbi Gamliel turned to Rabbi Yehoshua and insisted, "In the Torah given to us by Moses it is written: 'An Ammonite or Moabite is not to enter into the assembly of the Lord even unto the tenth generation.' Have you forgotten that this man is an Ammonite or the teaching that forbids him entry into this assembly?"

"I have forgotten neither," Rabbi Yehoshua replied. "Nor have I forgotten what the prophet Isaiah teaches us: 'I have removed the bonds that bind the people and have plundered their treasures; and I have brought low those who sit on thrones.' Surely you have not forgotten, that Ammon and Moab no longer sit on their thrones. For Sennacherib, king of the Assyrians, has long since risen up to confound all the nations that inhabited the land."

"What you say is true," said Rabbi Gamliel. "But I know the teachings of the prophets as well as you do. And I remind you of the words of Jeremiah: 'After these things have come to pass, I shall return from captivity the children of Ammon.' Have they not, then, been returned?"

"Some have been returned," Rabbi Yehoshua conceded, "but, as with the children of our Father Abraham, many have not. Remember what the prophet Amos tells us: 'I shall raise up from captivity My people Israel and the House of Yehudah, says the Lord.' Just as many among the people of Israel remain in exile, so do many among the Ammonites and Moabites."

To this point Rabbi Gamliel offered no response but remained silent.

The Ammonite proselyte known as Yehudah listened intently to the rabbis' dispute, eager more to abide by their decision than to enter the congregation. For as much as he loved the Torah, he loved the wisdom of the rabbis who studied it. When it seemed that the two sages had nothing more to add to their arguments, he asked them, "What shall I do?"

And they said to him, "You have heard the ruling of the elder. Please, join us, you may enter the congregation."

Midrashic Tales

The word *midrash* means "searching." It is a method of seeking deeper levels of understanding the Torah, often by means of storytelling, which is a form of teaching and testimony. The body of texts that makes up the Midrash was composed between the fifth and thirteenth centuries. Midrashic tales and commentary, however, continue even today, as modern sages and scholars continue to wrestle not only with the words of Scripture but with the silence between the words.

Midrashic tales serve to fill in the gaps, exploring the motivations of the characters and the implications of their actions as presented in the Bible, as well as in the Talmud. In the tale of Abraham's binding of Isaac, for example, the Midrash tells us that God sent an angel to stop Abraham because He was too embarrassed to face Abraham Himself. The aim of the Midrashic tales collected here is not merely to entertain but to provide insight into Scriptural matters that are as urgent as they are elusive. In addition, Midrashic tales provide continuity between incidents that belong to ancient times and developments that appear in later times, such as the destruction of the Second Temple and doctrines concerning an afterlife. While it may seem that the rabbis who compiled these tales were amending the Scriptures, it is their view that the Torah is eternally contemporary and that it contains hidden meanings relevant to any given time. What unfolds in these Midrashic tales, therefore, is a process of renewal and a vision of the eternal that lie at the heart of Jewish life. Through the Midrash the silence that characterizes much of Scripture begins to speak. As we attend to that silence, we are made into storytellers.

Why Cain and Abel Quarreled

GENESIS RABBAH 22:7

When God gave Moses the Ten Commandments at Mount Sinai, they were inscribed on two tablets. Why two? One explanation is that the first five commandments pertain to the relationship between God and human beings (adam la-Makom), while the second five pertain to the relationship of one human being to another (adam l'adam). The first commandment on the second tablet is "Thou shalt not murder," since this is the most fundamental rule of human relations. Indeed, to come face to face with another human being is to encounter this commandment. And yet the first transgression between human and human was murder. And it was a brother's murder of his brother: we kill what resembles us. This tale from the Midrash considers why one brother might kill another. And in it we may see why other brothers kill each other.

The first of the earth's offspring born to man and woman, Cain and Abel had all the world before them and all that was in it. But Cain and Abel were men, and for men, being in the world is not always enough: men suppose that they must possess the world and thus enter into a deadly confusion between being and having. Hence they were named Cain, which means "acquisition," and Abel, which means "vanity," suggesting the vanity of acquisition.

Each driven by his longing to possess, the two of them approached one another, saying, "Come, let us divide up the possessions of the earth."

After a heated discussion concerning who would own what, they begrudgingly agreed that Cain would take possession of the land, while Abel would own all movable property. However, this division of property led not to peace but only made for further arguments.

"You are standing on my land!" Cain declared to his brother.

"And what you are wearing is mine!" Abel retorted.

"Get off my land," Cain shouted. "Now!"

"Not until you strip yourself bare!" Abel replied.

In the heat of their quarrel over their possessions, Cain rose up against his brother Abel and killed him.

According to Rabbi Yehoshua of Siknin, however, it did not happen quite that way. To be sure, Cain and Abel longed to possess the property of the world. But they managed to come to an agreement, whereby each would own a portion of the land and each would possess a share of movable property. But that was just the beginning of their disagreement.

No sooner did they divide up the land, than did Cain declare to Abel, "The Temple must be erected on my share of the earth, so that God will favor my children over yours!"

"No!" Abel replied, his anger mounting. "The Temple must be built on my share of the land! For mine is the true way of worshiping God!"

Having divided up the wealth of the earth, they fought over whose path to God was the proper one. Those who wanted to possess the earth wanted to posses the favor of Heaven as well. In the heat of their argument over who was holier Cain rose up against his brother, and in the name of the God who forbids murder, killed him.

Yehudah, however, maintains that Cain killed his brother for another motive, one perhaps even more base and certainly more common. You see, when Eve gave birth to Abel, she gave birth to Abel's twin sister.

Both of the brothers lusted after this woman, and each wanted to take her to be his wife.

"She is mine," Cain insisted. "I am the firstborn, and it is my right to be the first to take a wife."

"No!" Abel refused. "She was born with me, and so I shall have her!"

Thus they argued over who would take the woman to be his own, until, in a fit of jealousy, Cain rose up and killed his brother Abel.

Why do men kill one another? For the vanity of property, in a betrayal of their religion, and for the possession of a woman that they cannot possess.

The Death of Cain

ECCLESIASTES RABBAH 6:2

In this elaboration on the life and death of Cain, the Midrash considers the life of a wanderer. In this case the wanderer is not a man who seeks a home but one whose wandering in the world reflects the exile of a soul that has cut itself off from the life of humanity through the act of murder. Cain's punishment for taking the life of his brother Abel was to live a life steeped in death, until at last death overtakes all of humanity in the Flood. For all of humanity had come to resemble Cain.

Having taken the life of his brother Abel, Cain was punished by being cast into an exile. Wandering in the land of Nod, a land whose name means "wandering," Cain built a city to protect himself, which he populated by bearing a hundred children. Yet the city itself came to express the very epitome of his exile. Surrounded by the walls he had erected, he became most estranged from the life that he had brought into the world.

No longer one who tilled the earth and harvested its fruits, Cain became a merchant who had only one aim in life: to acquire more. He was possessed by the idea of possession. To Cain, more was better, but it was never enough. The more he had, the more he wanted—he was beggared by his abundance. He loved things and used people, not the other way around, so that he came to resemble the lifeless things with which he sought to surround himself. And he would commit any act of violence to increase his accumulation of things. He exemplified a generation steeped in violence. Indeed, he was among the leaders of that generation and one who mocked a righteous man called Noah.

When the rains came, Cain persisted in his efforts to increase his wealth. The waters rose around him, but still he schemed to add to his fortune, ignoring the pleas of his hundred children, who by now had realized their fate. As the waters continued to rise, Cain continued to clamber after more and more, until at last he and all the wealth he had accumulated were swept away by the deluge.

The Idol Atop the Tower

FROM GENESIS RABBAH 38:6–10

The Tower of Babel signifies the human lust for power. From on high God ordains and sanctifies all of creation. Indeed, when God undertook Creation, He created the heavens before He created the earth, so that all who dwell upon the earth might derive their meaning from on high, and not from the vanity of a power struggle. In this story we see how men struggle with God in an attempt to appropriate the dimension of height that signifies the realm of the divine. But humanity cannot undertake such a struggle without losing its meaning and its sanctity to the power that it seeks.

After the great Flood there appeared a man named Nimrod. He was the grandson of Ham, son of Noah, and was the first to amass power, setting himself up as ruler over Babel, Erech, and Accad, all cities built in Babylonia. He was a tyrant and ruled with a terrible might, wielding power over every word and every deed of every person in his kingdom. His craving for power was infinite, and he longed to rule over the Infinite One Himself. Therefore he determined to fashion with his hands a god to take the place of the God who had fashioned humanity. And he resolved to place this idol in the heights of God's heavenly abode. The heavens would be his.

"Let us make us a name!" he declared, and he meant: Let us make an idol. "Let us raise up a tower," he ordered, and he meant: let us usurp the throne of God. For atop the tower he intended to place an idol holding a sword with which to do battle against the Holy One.

The people of Babylonia set about raising up the Tower of Babel. But when God is replaced by the graven image of a mere thing, those who are created in the image of God are reduced to mere things. If a brick dropped off the tower and shattered when it fell to the ground below, the air was filled with a great wailing and gnashing of teeth. But when a man slipped and fell to his death, none of his neighbors even noticed. Already the idol intended to wage war with God was taking its toll on human life.

In order to confound this terrible deed, God decided to confuse the tongues of those who had not a word of kindness or compassion for others. The people of Babylonia were destroyed by the words of their own lips—as happens even today.

One would say to his fellow worker, "Bring me a bucket of water," whereupon his comrade would hand him a bucket of earth. The one who had asked for the water would then strike his fellow and split his skull.

Another worker would say to his fellow, "Bring me a spade," whereupon his comrade would hand him an axe. The one who had asked for a spade would then take the axe and split his fellow's skull.

Those who were created in the image of the living God took on the image of the dead idol and dealt out death to one another. Hence those who set out to assail the heavens were scattered over the face of the earth. A third of the tower that was to have reached the heavens sank deep into the earth, and a third of it was reduced to ashes. The other third remained standing. Even from atop the third that remained, the palm trees below looked like grasshoppers. But the people who built it were nowhere to be seen.

The Death of Abram's Brother

GENESIS RABBAH 38:13

The Midrashic account of the death of Abram's brother Haran teaches us as much about Abram as it does about his brother. Here we discover Abram's opposition to idolatry from the time of his childhood. We also learn about the depth of Abram's faith, which led to his becoming Abraham, as well as about the nature of faith itself. Just as we see that Abram will not compromise his faith even under threat of death, so we see that genuine faith cannot be imitated. Faith is not reducible to gestures, deeds, or even words, but is an internal presence invisible to the eye. To confuse faith with a nod of the head is not only false—it is deadly.

In the days when Nimrod ruled over the land of Babylonia there lived a man named Terach. So afraid was Terach of the tyrant Nimrod that not only did he abide by the ruler's every decree, but he became a party to the idolatry that Nimrod imposed upon the people. Terach made his living by fashioning idols from clay and selling them to the people of Babylonia.

Now Terach had two sons: one named Haran, the other Abram. Of the two, it seems, Terach favored Abram, for Abram was a lad of unusual talents and intelligence. It was Abram whom Terach hoped to bring into the business of making and selling idols, and Abram was often to be found working at his father's side in the idol shop.

From time to time, Abram's father would leave the shop in his son's care. One day a man came into the store to purchase one of the graven figures. As Abram watched the customer gaze adoringly upon an idol, Abram was struck by an idea—or a question.

"Excuse me, sir," Abram said to him, "but how old are you, if I may ask?"

"Why I'm fifty years old," the gentleman replied, puzzled by the lad's question.

"Then how is it, sir," asked Abram, "that one who is fifty years old can bring himself to worship an object no older than a day?"

The man grew ashamed at the thought and did not know how to answer. Without saying a word he put back the idol he held in his hands and hurried out of the store.

Abram said nothing to his father about the incident, but he was haunted by his own question and by the man's embarrassment. Soon Abram's bewilderment turned into understanding, and Abram knew he must somehow act on his realization.

The next time he was left alone in the shop, a woman came into the store carrying a bowl of flour.

"Please," she said, gesturing to the idols that filled the shop, "I'm in a rush. So would you take this flour and offer it to them?" She handed Abram the flour and went on her way.

"Yes," the thought occurred to the lad as he gazed at the bowl of flour. "I have just the offering for them." At that Abram took a stick and smashed all the idols but one, the largest one. Then he placed the stick in the hands of the remaining idol and awaited his father's return.

He did not have long to wait. When Terach entered the shop, he was horrified at the sight of the broken idols that littered the floor.

"What have you done?" he shouted at his son. "Have you lost your mind?"

"I cannot hide the truth from you, father," Abram answered. "While you were out a woman came in with a bowl of flour. She asked that I offer it to the idols and then left. I was about to make the offering, when one idol exclaimed, 'Let me be the first to eat!' Hearing this, another insisted, 'No, I must be the first!' Just when it looked as though all of them would break out in an argument, the largest idol rose up, took a stick, and broke the rest. Then he took the flour for himself."

"Are you mocking me, boy?" his father cried. "Do you take me for a fool? They have no speech or understanding!"

"Father, please," Abram replied, "let your ears hear what your mouth is saying. The true God, the living God, the Creator of Heaven and earth, is invisible, eternal, and above all flesh. It is He alone whom we should worship."

But Terach would not hear these words. He feared Nimrod more than he feared God, so much so that he seized his son and denounced him to the king. Just to be sure that Haran, Abram's brother, would not fall prey to the same folly, Terach took him along as well.

Nimrod had Abram brought before him to be judged. Next to the place of judgment stood a pit of raging flames, and Nimrod was certain that it would be enough to frighten the lad into repentance.

"Your father," said the king, "claims that you have destroyed the images that are sacred to us. It this true?"

"It is true that I have broken some pieces of clay," Abram answered. "But I have broken nothing sacred. The living God, Creator of heaven and earth, alone is sacred. Nothing has its being except by Him."

Invoking the idols that he adored, the wicked king replied, "Then fire must be worthy of our worship, since our idols of clay are hardened by the fire. Indeed, we worship these flames that rise up beside you."

"If you think fire is a thing to be worshiped," said Abram, "then perhaps you had better worship water, since water extinguishes fire."

"If you would have us worship water," Nimrod retorted, "then better to worship the clouds that bear the water."

To which Abram replied, "If you invoke the clouds, then better to worship the winds that disperse them. And if you worship the winds, then you may well decide to worship mere human beings for withstanding the wind."

Finally running out of patience, Nimrod cried, "Enough of these word games! We worship fire and fire alone. And to show you the might of the fire that we worship, I shall have you cast into these flames this instant. Let the God whom you claim to adore save you if He can."

All the while Abram's brother Haran stood by listening to the exchange between Abram and the king. He continued to look on, as Abram was led to the pit of flames.

"If my brother Abram should emerge from the flames unharmed," thought Haran to himself, "then I shall declare that I share his belief. But if the flames consume him, then I shall say that Nimrod spoke rightly."

Nimrod's guards took Abram and cast him into the pit. The flames rose up higher than ever, but just when it seemed that Abram would be lost, he climbed out of the pit unscathed.

The king watched all of this very carefully. He saw the amazement on the faces of everyone around him, including Haran. Turning to Abram's brother, he asked, "Whose belief do you follow? Your brother's or mine?"

"I follow the belief of Abram," Haran declared.

Immediately Nimrod ordered that Haran be seized and thrown into the pit of flames. No sooner was Haran cast into the fire than his inward parts were consumed by the flames, and he died in the presence of his father Terach and his brother Abram. Faith will not be imitated. And a father's idolatry always takes its toll on his children.

Abraham and Samael

GENESIS RABBAH 56:4

When God asked Abraham to offer up his beloved son Isaac in sacrifice, the patriarch did not have the luxury of acting hastily. No, he had to journey for three days—and for three nights—to the place called Moriah. In this tale from the Midrash we see that these three days, more than all the centuries, set Abraham at a distance from the world in which we live. During these three days he had to struggle with what the world would deem unthinkable and abominable. To Abraham, the temptation that might turn him away from doing God's will was precisely the sense of justice for which he was known. And the evil angel Samael knew it.

When his three-day journey finally came to an end, Abraham lifted up his eyes to the mountain that stood before him. No one can guess where he found the courage, no one can imagine the look in his eyes as he gazed upon Mount Moriah, the place that God had designated for the sacrifice of his beloved son Isaac.

Would he come face to face with God on the summit of those heights? More dizzying than the mountain that rose above him was the prospect of peering down into the eyes of his child bound to the altar. Perhaps that was where he would behold the face of God: in the face of his son Isaac. Would he be able to raise the knife in that moment when the eyes of his boy would meet his? And what of Sarah, who had borne him the child of his old age? How could he look upon her face? What could he say to her? How, indeed, could he ever return from this place beyond the horizons of the earth?

As Abraham climbed up the mountain—or perhaps it was during the night before, when he lay next to the sleeping child—an apparition appeared before him, blocking his way to the place of sacrifice. It looked enough like him to be his brother. But it was not his brother. It was the angel of darkness and death, Samael.

The wicked angel spoke to Abraham, and for an instant he had the patriarch's ear. "What is the meaning of this, old man? Have you gone mad? Does the life of this child, the beloved child of your old age, mean nothing to you? Turn back while you still can!

It cannot be God who asks this horror of you but some devil! Remember God's promise that you will be the father of a nation. Go back, lest you take away that promise!"

"I will not turn back," Abraham declared to the angel. "Even this I will do, if God commands it."

"And what if He should put to you a test more terrible than this?" Samael persisted. "If God can demand this of a man, there is nothing He cannot demand."

And the Patriarch replied, "Just so. I will not weary of God's behest."

Yet Samael tempted him further, saying, "You know what He will say to you tomorrow, don't you? He will confront you with this insanity, with this horror. He will say to you, 'Murderer! You are guilty of taking the life of the son I promised you, the one who is to become the father of My chosen!'"

"Still I am content with doing God's will," said Abraham.

Realizing that he could not turn Abraham aside, Samael appeared unto Isaac, hoping to tempt him into refusing the word of God.

"You pitiful child of an unhappy mother!" he cried. "Don't you realize where your father is taking you? Can't you see what he is about to do? He intends to kill you!"

"My fate comes from God," Isaac answered the wicked angel. "And I accept the deeds of my father."

"Would you have your mother, then, give to the outcast Ishmael all the fine tunics she has made for you? For her sake, turn back!" urged the angel.

When Isaac did not answer, Samael thought that he may have snared him. And, indeed, the angel may have planted a thought in the boy's mind. For at that Isaac spoke to Abraham, saying, "My father, my father, we have the fire and the wood, but where is the offering for the sacrifice?"

Hearing these words, Abraham muttered an imprecation under his breath: "May the one who incited the boy to speak be drowned!" And with all the love of a father he answered his son: "Do not worry, my child. God Himself will provide the lamb." Then, after a moment of hesitation, the old man added, "If He fails to do so, then you, my son, . . . you shall serve as the offering to God."

Much to the dismay of Samael, Isaac said nothing in reply to

Abraham's utterance but took his father by the hand and proceeded up the mountain.

The Blinding of Isaac

GENESIS RABBAH 65:10

In these tales from the Midrash we find the notion that even a person's infirmities may be understood to arise from the compassion of heaven. In one instance the explanation of Isaac's blindness entails a vision that was more than the angels could behold; in the other it entails a vision that was more than Isaac—or God—could behold. Both explanations connect the binding of Isaac with his blinding. In both cases the blinding vision contains an understanding of truth and sanctity that does not meet the eyes but is accessible only through the soul.

So great was the faith of Abraham that when Isaac was bound to the altar atop Mount Moriah, he was not overcome by the plea for compassion that filled his son's eyes. The boy was silent, but his eyes cried out for mercy. Yet Abraham somehow managed to raise the hand that held the knife over the child. The boy's eyes followed the knife as it rose above him, and, looking beyond the knife, he turned his eyes to the heavens. At that moment the angels caught sight of the child's eyes filled with longing and agony.

But the angels did not have the faith of Abraham. For at the sight of Isaac's torment, tears began to flow from their eyes. They wept and wept, until their tears rained down from heaven and filled the child's eyes. The tears of the angels left their mark on the child. For in his old age he went blind. Having seen what took place on Mount Moriah, he saw the world in a different light: he saw the world as the angels see it.

But perhaps it was not the tears of the angels that blinded the lad. According to another tradition, when Isaac lifted up his eyes toward the heavens, he caught sight of the Shechinah—God's feminine aspect and indwelling Presence—in all her glory, a vision that is permitted no one. Isaac's beholding the Shechinah may be compared to the case of a king who once saw a friend walking with his son in a garden outside the palace. As the father and son walked past, the king saw the boy gaze into the window at him. The king regarded this as an act of great disrespect, for no one was allowed to cast his eyes directly upon the king. Indeed, such effrontery was punishable by death.

"If I take the boy and have him executed," the king said to himself, "it would cause my friend great suffering. Instead of doing that, therefore, I shall order the boy's windows to be sealed shut for gazing through my window."

So it happened that when Isaac was found to be gazing through the windows of heaven and staring at the Shechinah, the Holy One, blessed be He, declared, "If I slay him now, I shall bring terrible suffering to My friend Abraham. Instead, I decree that the boy's eyes should grow dim in his old age."

Thus Isaac was delivered from death, saved by his father's faith and friendship in God. Indeed, had he been slain, his death might have been construed as a punishment, and not as a sacrifice. But as soon as God remembered His friendship with Abraham, He sent an angel to stay the patriarch's hand.

Satan's Slaying of Sarah
GENESIS TANCHUMA, VAYIRAH 23

After the account of Abraham's binding of Isaac in the twenty-second chapter of Genesis, we are told in the opening lines of chapter twenty-three that Sarah has passed away. How did she die? This tale from the Midrash Tanchuma—a collection of tales and commentary on the Torah, so named because Rabbi Tanchuma bar Abba is frequently mentioned in it—fills in the details surrounding the matriarch's death. It tells us that, from the standpoint of a mother's love, a father's trial of faith may appear to be horror and madness. It also tells us that Satan may prey on us precisely through the ones we love.

When God ordered Abraham to offer up his son Isaac as a sacrifice, the aged patriarch spoke not a word to anyone, not even to his beloved wife Sarah. For he feared that she would not understand. Who, indeed, could understand him? How could he make himself understood? What was he to say to her? "I am going to kill our son"? "God requires the life of our child"? No. Abraham wanted to spare his wife the temptation of turning away from God and refusing Him such an offering. Or was it that he wanted to spare himself the agony of revealing what to all eyes must appear to be madness?

Isaac was no longer a child but a man of thirty-seven on the day he ascended Mount Moriah with his father. When he asked his father about the lamb for sacrifice, he already suspected what was in Abraham's heart. He knew that he could overcome the old man at any moment, but Isaac's faith was equal to the faith of his father. He was indeed his father's son. So when the moment of terrible sacrifice had arrived, he laid himself upon the altar and allowed himself to be bound tight.

Abraham feared that he might falter at the sight of his beloved Isaac bound for sacrifice. After all, had Satan not appeared to him on the way to the mountain? Had the Evil One not challenged him, saying, "Have you gone insane? You are about to murder the child of your old age!" And yet, in spite of Satan's temptations, Isaac's faith strengthened his father's resolve. Abraham raised the knife over his child.

But Satan is not one to give up so easily. Just as Abraham was about to bring the knife down upon Isaac, Satan seized the old man's hand and forced him to drop the knife. Even in this terrible instant, however, Abraham could not ignore the word of God. He bent over and picked up the knife to go through with the ordeal.

As he held the knife high, a voice from the heaven commanded him, "Do not lift your hand against your son!"

Thus Abraham defeated the Evil One, and, thanks to the faith of father and son, Isaac was spared. So great is the evil of Satan, however, that he sought one more means of devastating Abraham. At the very instant when the heavenly voice stayed the hand of Abraham, Satan assumed the form of Isaac and appeared before Sarah.

While she did not know where Abraham had taken Isaac or why the two of them had set out on their journey, Sarah knew that

Abraham had left with their child three days earlier. And so, taking fright at her son's ghostly apparition, she asked, "What has your father done to you, my child?"

Satan answered, "My father has taken me, the child of your old age, and laid me upon an altar in a place called Mount Moriah. There he raised a knife over me to slaughter me as an offering to God!"

Hearing these words, Sarah screamed out in agony—as no mother had cried before. And with her outcry, her soul left her.

A Daughter's Wisdom

EXODUS RABBAH 1:1

The Talmud teaches us that those who are wise can learn from everyone, even from children. The wise are good listeners, and in this tale Amram listened well to the wisdom of his daughter Miriam. Indeed, were it not for her wisdom, according to this story, Moses would not have been born. Thanks to a daughter's wisdom, therefore, Moses came into the world, and through Moses, the Torah.

In the days when the Israelites were slaves in Egypt, they endured one harsh decree after another. But the most terrible was the order from Pharaoh declaring that all male children born to the Israelites be cast into the Nile. Not only did the wicked king of Egypt determine to bring death to a whole people, but he decided to enlist the midwives of Israel as his accomplices. He gathered the midwives together and ordered them to deliver all the male babies born to the Hebrews into the hands of the Egyptians.

Among the midwives summoned to Pharaoh was a woman named Yocheved and her five-year-old daughter Miriam. Now Miriam was possessed of wisdom and skills that far exceeded her age, and she helped her mother with the delivery of the Israelite children. Whenever an infant was born, she would take the babe and put a drop of wine on the child's lips, while Yocheved attended to the little one's mother. The baby would smile and make bubbles with the wine, and so Miriam was nicknamed Puah, for the baby's bubbles. Yocheved, for her part, was known to be so highly skilled as a midwife that all of the children she delivered came out looking beautiful. She was nicknamed Shifrah, for the beauty she imparted.

The Torah tells us that Shifrah and Puah refused to abide by Pharaoh's decree. When the mother and daughter stood before Pharaoh with the other midwives and heard his evil edict, the bold little Miriam cried out, "Woe unto this man when God comes to exact His retribution!"

At first, shocked by these words, Pharaoh rose up to kill the impudent child. But her mother, who knew how to soothe anger with her voice, pacified the king, saying, "Would one so great as Pharaoh take notice of one so small? She is a mere child, unworthy of the anger of the king, and knows nothing of what she is saying."

Appeased by the child's mother, Pharaoh nodded and with a wave of his hand sent the midwives away. No more of his royal time would he squander on these Hebrew women.

Yocheved took Miriam and hurried home to inform her husband Amram of the terrible order that had come down from the King. Amram was the head of the Sanhedrin, the council of Jewish elders that ruled their fellow Israelites, and his decision regarding Pharaoh's decree that would affect the entire community of Israel.

After much thought, he handed down his ruling: "If this evil king is determined to slay our infant sons, then we shall have no more children: husbands are to cease lying with their wives."

When Miriam heard her father's words, she realized at once that such a measure would amount to playing into the hands of the wicked Egyptian king. "Father, forgive me for questioning your decision," she said to Amram, "but your decree is more severe than the one that Pharaoh would impose upon us. For Pharaoh's decree concerns only the male children, but your decree falls upon males and females alike. The only way to live under Pharaoh is to live in spite of him and trust in God. Pharaoh is an evil man, and it may well be that God will not allow the fulfillment of his decree. But you are a righteous man, and it is certain that God will join His will to yours in the rulings that you hand down."

Hearing these words, Amram thanked God for having given

him such a wise daughter. Wasting no time, he reversed his ruling, and lay with his wife. Unto them was born a son, the one called Moses.

Moses the Stutterer
EXODUS RABBAH 1:26

When God spoke to Moses from the burning bush and ordered him to bring the Israelites out of Egypt, Moses was reluctant to undertake the task, saying that he was "slow of speech and of tongue." This remark traditionally is understood to indicate that Moses was a stutterer. And yet, when it is God's will, even a stutterer may become a spokesman. This tale from the Midrash explains how Moses came by his speech defect. Heaven may intervene in our lives to bring us an infirmity essential to performing the mission that God has placed before us.

Pharaoh's daughter Bitiah was stricken with leprosy. Each day she would go down to the Nile with her servants and bathe in the river's soothing waters. One day, as she was bathing, she spied a basket floating along the bank of the river, and when she looked to see what it might contain, she found a Hebrew infant, a male child who, according to her father's decree, should have been slain at birth. Bitiah reached into the basket and removed the infant, so that she might turn him over to her father. But as soon as she touched the child, her leprosy was cured. Realizing that the baby had come to her from God, Bitiah adopted him as her own. And because she had drawn him forth from the waters, she named him Moses.

Now the child's sister Miriam had been watching over him all along. When she saw Pharaoh's daughter embrace the little one and heard her declare that he was to be hers, she stepped forward and said that she knew a woman who could nurse the baby. Pleased to hear this, Bitiah ordered her to bring the woman into her household. Thus it happened that Moses' mother Yocheved was able to nurse her infant. For two years she nursed her baby boy, and he quickly grew to be a healthy and handsome child.

Bitiah loved the little boy who had cured her as if he were her very own son. She never allowed him to stray from the palace and would hug him and kiss him at every opportunity. He was such a beautiful child that everyone in Pharaoh's court came to see him. Indeed, they could not take their eyes off him and delighted in watching him play with Bitiah for hours on end.

Pharaoh, too, loved the little one, no less than his daughter did. He would take the child and bounce him on his knee, all the while offering him a grandfather's loving embrace. In the midst of his laughter and play, Moses would take the crown from Pharaoh's head and place it on his own head.

While the magicians of Pharaoh's court delighted in the child, they grew suspicious of him when they saw him take the crown from Pharaoh's head and place it on his own. "Do you think it wise, O Pharaoh, to allow this child to take your crown from you?" they asked. "We fear that it may be an omen of a time when he will unseat you and assume your power. Indeed, we have a prophecy that one day a man may rise up to unseat you from your throne. Perhaps the one you bounce upon your lap will grow up to be that man."

Some of Pharaoh's counselors, in fact, advised him to take no chances and slay the child.

But among those counselors was the Midianite Jethro, the man who would one day become Moses' father-in-law. He appealed to the love that Pharaoh had for the boy, saying, "Sire, would you kill the child that your daughter has made her own? He is hardly more than a babe, and this is nothing more than the play of an innocent boy. But if you would have your mind put at ease, test him. Bring in a gold vessel and a glowing coal and place them before him. If the child reaches for the gold, then you will know that he is ambitious and may be a threat to your power. Then you can slay him. But if he reaches for the hot coal, you will know that he has no sense and is no threat to you."

Pharaoh deemed Jethro's advice to be sound, and he ordered a gold vessel and a red-hot coal placed before the child Moses. The boy delighted in the sight of the shiny things and started to reach for the gold. Just at that instant the angel Gabriel appeared, invisible to all but Moses, and turned the child's hand aside. Guided by the angel, Moses took the glowing coal in his hand and put it to his mouth. The ember burned his tongue, and thereafter Moses was slow of speech and of tongue. But the angel had seen to it that his life was spared to do the work of God.

The Appeasement of Samael

EXODUS RABBAH 21:7

Intended to explain one of the more puzzling books of Scripture, this tale from the Midrash elucidates the story of Job, who was afflicted by Satan. Since Job was known to be a righteous man, why would God permit Samael—Satan—to bring suffering upon him without good reason. Here we are offered the reason: so that the people of Israel could be brought out of Egypt. The righteous, then, do not suffer for nothing. They suffer so that others might be saved. Indeed, that is part of their righteousness: they value the lives of other human beings above their own, even if it means bringing suffering upon themselves.

When the Israelites departed from Egypt and stood at the edge of the Sea of Reeds, the wicked angel Samael came before God to level accusations against His chosen, so that God would not allow their liberation. For their liberation lay in God's revelation, and Samael sought to keep that revelation from the world.

"Lord of the Universe!" cried Samael. "When these Israelites lived in the land of Egypt, they were known to have worshiped idols. And just look at how they have robbed the Egyptians of their gold and silver! Why do You now prepare to divide the sea for these thieves and idolaters? They merit none of Your compassion!"

"It is not based on their merit that I have brought them out of Egypt," God answered, "but because of My covenant with their fathers. As I created the world with love, so I liberate My children with love."

What did God do? He acted like a shepherd leading his flock across a river, when suddenly a wolf appears, ready to attack the sheep. Knowing just how to deal with such beasts of prey, the shepherd takes a large goat and throws it to the wolf. Says the shepherd to himself, "Let the wolf struggle with this powerful goat until I have led my flock safely across the river. Then I shall return and deliver the goat from the wolf."

Among Pharaoh's counselors was a righteous man named Job. Having realized early on that the Israelites were the chosen of God, he had advised Pharaoh to let them go. Like the shepherd who set the goat before the wolf, God knew the strength of this righteous man and turned him over to the wicked Samael.

"While the angel is occupied with My servant Job," said God, "the children of Israel will be able to cross the sea in safety. Once they are on the other side, I shall return and deliver Job from the hands of the accusing angel."

When Samael took hold of the righteous man, Job realized what had taken place. He cried out, "The Lord God has given me over to the hands of Satan, so that Israel might emerge from its trial free of guilt. Blessed be the Name of the Lord!"

At that moment God informed Moses, "Behold, I have given My servant Job over to Satan, so that you may declare to the children of Israel that they are to set out across the sea. Know, then, that your liberation comes not only by My grace but by the strength of a good man."

Thus it was thanks not only to the compassion of God but to the righteousness of Job that the children of Israel were delivered from the armies of Pharaoh and from the hands of the evil Samael.

The Golden Calf

PIRKE DE RABBI ELIEZER, 62B.11

This tale brings to bear two aspects of the Holy One—and of our teacher Moses: judgment and mercy. God needs the cooperation of Moses to exact judgment, as well as the intercession of Moses to show mercy. Each character in the story needs the other to be who he is in the face of the worst of all transgressions: idolatry. We are taught that to commit idolatry is to break all 613 of the commandments contained in the Torah. Acting as though they possess a life of their own, the letters of the Torah fly back to heaven in

*the face of idolatry. But in a manifestation of God's mercy, Moses buries the
retribution of heaven in the earth and lies next to it, so that he may protect
his people from it.*

When Moses received the Torah from God and was about to carry
the tablets down from Mount Sinai, the Lord informed him, "Your
people Israel have forgotten the wonders that I performed for them
when I brought them out of Egypt and led them across the Sea of
Reeds. They have fashioned a golden calf and are bowing down
to it at this very moment. Go to them and put a stop to this abomi-
nation!"

Fearing the anger of the Lord, Moses said to Him, "Sovereign of
all worlds! Before the people of Israel had fallen into this sin, You
referred to them as Your people. But now that they have succumbed
to this idolatry, You speak as if they were mine alone. Do You
forget what You have written in the Torah, declaring them to be
Your people?"

Without waiting for a reply, Moses turned and hurried down
the mountain. It was not on his feet that he ran. The two tablets
that he held under his arms carried not only their own weight but
his weight as well: Those who bear the Torah are borne by it. But
when the letters on the tablets caught sight of the golden calf and
the Israelites dancing around it, they fled in horror at the spec-
tacle. As the letters returned to Heaven, the tablets grew unbear-
ably heavy in Moses arms, and he cast them to the ground, where
they broke to bits.

Immediately Moses rushed to Aaron and demanded, "What have
you done to this people, that they have fallen into such a hideous
wantonness?"

"When I saw that they were about to kill Hur," Aaron explained,
"for objecting to their folly, I grew afraid and went along with it,
hoping you would return before they could finish making the hor-
rid idol. I tried to stall them by demanding that they bring their
jewelry and melt it down. But to no avail. You can see, however,
that not all of them have committed this terrible act. The sons of
Levi, our brothers, have refused to have any part of it."

Cried Moses in a loud voice, "Whoever would embrace the Lord
God and reject this lifeless idol, let him come to me now!"

All the sons of Levi gathered around Moses, who ordered them to take the idol and grind it into dust. All who had taken part in the idolatry were then forced to drink water mixed with the dust of the idol. The lips and bones of those who had worshiped the golden calf turned into gold, and they were slain by the tribe of Levi. At the end, three thousand lay dead. Though he was saddened to the core of his being, Moses deemed this retribution to be sufficient.

But God did not think it was sufficient. In His divine rage He threatened to destroy all of the Israelites and summoned five angels to carry out this heinous task. Their names were Wrath, Anger, Temper, Destruction, and Glow of Ire. But Moses had heard God make the terrible threat, and he hastened to the cave of Machpelah, where the patriarchs lay buried. There he called out to Abraham, Isaac, and Jacob to intercede in behalf of Israel.

"Fathers of our fathers!" he cried. "If you truly have a portion in the World to Come, rise up before me now! Go to the Creator of heaven and earth and plead for us! For behold, in this very hour the God of the covenant is preparing His chosen for slaughter!"

Hearing our teacher's plea, Abraham, Isaac, and Jacob rose up. With the patriarchs at his side, Moses addressed the Holy One, blessed be He, saying, "Sovereign of all worlds! Did You not swear to these our forefathers that You would increase their seed to be like the stars of the heavens and the sand of the seas? Would You now break Your covenant with them?"

Thanks to the merit of the three patriarchs, three of the angels—Wrath, Anger, and Temper—were prevented from doing any harm to Israel. But Destruction and Glow of Ire remained. Realizing the threat that was still hanging over the children of Israel, Moses raised up his voice to God: "Sovereign of all the universe! For the sake of the covenant and Your Holy Name, please remove from Israel the angel called Destruction!"

Thanks to the merit of Moses and His remembrance of the covenant, God withdrew the angel Destruction from the Israelites. But one more angel, the most fearsome of all, remained. "Sovereign of the universe!" pleaded Moses. "For the sake of the covenant and Your awesome Holy Name, I pray that You please hold back from Israel the angel called Glow of Ire!"

This time, however, Moses did not wait for God's reply. Instead he took up a spade and began digging a hole in the ground. Frantically and tirelessly he dug until he had excavated enough earth for the foundation of a building. Then he seized the angel known as Glow of Ire, cast him into the hole, and buried him there. After that, every time Israel would slip into sin, Glow of Ire would rise from his massive grave to consume the children of Abraham. And every time he rose Moses would pronounce the Name of God to send the angel back into the ground that imprisoned him.

So pleased was the Holy One, blessed be He, with Moses' efforts to save the children of Israel that when Moses died God buried him next to Glow of Ire.

Each time that Israel falls into sin, the dreaded angel opens up its grave and rises to destroy the chosen of God. But as soon as it catches sight of the place where Moses is buried, it returns to the ground. Thanks to the love and the labor of a single man, the people of Israel are saved.

Sureties for the Torah

MIDRASH ON PSALMS 8:4

According to an ancient teaching, every word we utter, every deed we do, creates an angel of good or an angel of evil. The angels we create go out into the world. Some of them return to us or to our loved ones, bringing them either good or evil, according to our deeds. Therefore the lives of those both near and far are placed in the balance through every move we make: the consequences of our every action extend far beyond our field of vision. As this Midrash explains, the lives of those most dear to us—our children—are at stake.

The people of Israel, whom the Lord had liberated from the bondage of Egypt, were gathered around Mount Sinai to receive the Torah. The moment of Revelation had come, and the Israelites were prepared. But the Holy One hesitated. There was nothing He desired more than to entrust His chosen with the dearest of

His treasures, but for an instant He was afraid of what might become of that treasure, afraid for His Torah, afraid for the Israelites, afraid for all creation.

God said to the Israelites, "Holding you most dear, I am about to offer you what is most dear to Me. But you must give Me sureties that you will live by the Torah that you are about to receive."

The people of Israel did not know at first what they could offer up to God that would be a surety for such a gift. What comes from God is infinitely precious, and they had nothing to compare to it. But then it occurred to them: it was thanks to God's memory of the covenant He had made with Abraham, Isaac, and Jacob that He had brought them out of Egypt to receive the Torah. And so in a single voice they shouted, "Behold, the patriarchs will be sureties for us!"

"I cannot accept your offer," God replied, "for the patriarchs themselves are indebted to Me for the very covenant that they have received from Me. Would that they were able to stand as sureties for their own persons!"

The Israelites were like the man in the parable who went to a king and asked to borrow money from him.

"Bring me a surety," the king told him, "and you will have all the money you desire."

The man departed and returned with a friend, who was himself in debt to the King, saying, "Sire, my friend will stand as a surety for me."

"This one you have brought me," said the king, "already owes me for all that I have done for him. If only he could stand as a surety for himself!"

Just so, the Holy One, blessed be He, declared to the people of Israel, "You bring Me the Patriarchs as sureties against whom I already hold many pledges! Bring Me sureties who are not already in My debt!"

Hearing this, the people were at a complete loss as to what they might offer as sureties for the Torah. If Abraham, renowned for his wisdom and righteousness, could not stand as surety, then who could, they wondered?

Finally, in desperation they turned to God and asked, "Who in the world is not indebted to You?"

God answered in a single word: "Infants."

Immediately the people of Israel realized that only those little ones, who were uncorrupted and infinitely dear, could serve as sureties for the Torah. So they gathered together the babes who suckled at their mothers' breasts, along with all the pregnant women among them. As they stood in the presence of God, the bellies of those who were with child turned as transparent as glass, so that the embryos in their wombs could see God and speak with Him.

Asked the Holy One, "Will you agree to stand as sureties for your mothers and fathers, so that it they fail to live by the Torah, your lives will be forfeited because of them?"

While their parents trembled at these words, the babies answered in a single, angelic voice, "Yes, we agree."

The Holy One, blessed be He, began to speak the words of the Torah. To every utterance from the Mount they replied, "Yes."

When God said, "I am the Lord thy God," they answered, "Yes."

When God said, "Thou shalt have no other gods before Me," they answered, "Yes."

And so, offering themselves up as sureties for the Torah and for the sake of their mothers and fathers, the infants and the embryos cried, "Yes," each time God said, "Thou shalt," and "No" each time Him declared, "Thou shalt not."

When God finished speaking the words of the Torah, He proclaimed, "Out of your mouths, My little ones, have I given the Torah to the people of Israel and to all the world! As they live by it, so shall you live! And as you live, so shall the world remain alive!"

Why Moses Was Not Buried in the Holy Land

DEUTERONOMY RABBAH 2:8–9

The Hasidic master Rabbi Zusia once said, "When I stand before the Celestial Tribunal, I shall not be asked, 'Why weren't you Abraham?' or 'Why weren't you Moses?' I shall be asked, 'Why weren't you Zusia?'" Moses confronts a similar question in this combination of tales about his burial, which teaches us that our task in life is to become who we are. We must engage the task to which we have been summoned and bear the testimony that we are called upon to bear. When we try to pass ourselves off as something that we are not, we betray both ourselves and the One who has given us life.

At the end of many years of trial and ordeal, Moses stood atop a mountain and gazed upon the Promised Land, where the Israelites were to settle after their wandering in the wilderness. At no time during all those years in the desert was his longing for the land so great as it was at that moment, yet Moses knew that as he gazed upon the land, he faced the hour of his death—and that he was not to be allowed entry into the land.

Turning to God, Moses cried out, "O Lord, Master of the Universe, why may I not enter into the land of Your promise? Is it because I maligned Your children by calling them rebels? If so, then surely You recall that You referred to them as such before I did."

"True," God replied. "But that is not the reason."

"Could it be," Moses continued, "that you refuse me because I tried to refuse You when You called to me from the burning bush and commanded me to bring the Israelites out of Egypt? If so, then I beg You to recall the time when You Yourself were about to destroy the Israelites over the incident of the golden calf. Recall that it was I who interceded on their behalf, so that You might spare them. As You repented of Your decision to destroy them, surely You know that I have repented of my efforts to resist delivering them."

"Yes," God said, "we have both repented of certain things. But that is not the reason."

"Then why," Moses persisted, "having made me great do You now degrade me in this manner? I have been true to You in my labor to bring the living into the land along with the dead. For You know that I saw to it that Joseph's remains were brought out of Egypt along with the Israelites. Even as the Israelites were plundering the land of its gold and silver, I myself took up Joseph's coffin. And now You are about to allow the people to bear his bones into the land. If I may not live to walk on that sacred earth, then at least allow my bones to be brought into the land and laid to rest along with the bones of Joseph."

"I am sorry, Moses," God answered, "I cannot do that. And I shall tell you why. He who acknowledged his native land is to be buried in the land, but he who did not acknowledge his native land is not to be buried there. In all the years that Joseph dwelled in the land of Egypt, never once did he deny that he was a Hebrew. But you, Moses, when you fled from Egypt and went to the land of Midian, you tried to pass yourself off as an Egyptian. You stood by when Tsiporah, your future wife, declared to her father Jethro, 'An Egyptian came to our aid.' That is why you will neither walk the sacred earth nor be buried in it."

Hearing this, Moses fell silent. At last he understood the wisdom of the Holy One in refusing him even a place of burial in the Promised Land.

"There is another reason," God continued, "one tied to your merit, and not to your shortcomings. If you are buried here, outside of the land, along with those who have died in the wilderness, then at the time of the resurrection they may enter the Land for your sake, when you enter the land."

"I am not sure I understand what You mean," Moses replied.

"There was once a man," explained God, "who dropped a handful of bronze coins in a dark place. He thought to himself, 'If I call out to my companions to bring me a light, no one will pay me any heed, since these coins are of so little value.'

"Wondering what to do, he finally decided that he would toss a gold coin down where he had dropped the bronze coins. Then he called out to his companions, 'Please bring me a light, for I have dropped a gold coin here.'

"Immediately his companions brought him a light. As soon as he had retrieved his gold coin, he said to his friends, 'Please wait a moment while I pick up the rest of my coins.' And so because of one gold coin he was able to gather up the rest of his smaller coins.

"You see, Moses, if you are buried in the wilderness, when I come at the time of the resurrection to take you up into the Promised Land, I shall gather together all of those who died in the wilderness. You will be at their head. Even in death they are entrusted to your care. You were summoned to take them all from the place of bondage to the place of liberation. And so you shall."

Why God Buried Moses

DEUTERONOMY RABBAH 11:7

Central to the Jewish liturgy and the Jewish tradition is the memory of those who have lived before us and by whose labor our own lives have been made possible. Our acknowledgment of the sanctity of their lives is a large part of what makes our own lives sacred. Attending to the dead is one of the most holy tasks in Judaism. The example set by the Holy One in His burial of Moses reveals why the chevrah kaddisha, the burial society, is one of the most esteemed Jewish communal offices.

When the time had come for their liberation from Egypt, the Israelites busied themselves with gathering gold and silver from the Egyptians. Indeed, they had been told to despoil the land, and they engaged in this task with great zeal.

Moses, however, understood that he had a more important task: to find Joseph's coffin and take his remains out of Egypt for burial in the promised land. At the time of his death, Joseph had obtained from the Israelites a promise that on the day of their return to the land of the patriarchs they would bear with them his remains and bury him in the sacred earth promised to Israel by God. Remembering this oath, Moses worked tirelessly for three days and three nights, looking everywhere in the city for the coffin that he knew he had to find.

After three days of ceaseless searching, Moses grew weary and sat down to rest for a moment. As he sat, a woman named Segulah happened by and noticed that he appeared to be exhausted from all of his efforts.

Concerned for his condition, she asked, "My lord Moses, you look so tired! Is there anything I can do to help you?"

"For three days and three nights," he explained, " I have been wandering through the city searching for Joseph's coffin, but I cannot find it anywhere."

At that Segulah smiled and said to him, "I know where our father Joseph lies buried. Come with me, and I'll show you."

Pleased that God had sent him such a kind woman, Moses rose up and followed her through the Egyptian city all the way to the river Nile.

Pointing to the waters from the bank of the river, she declared, "This is the burial site of Joseph's coffin. You see, the wicked magicians and astrologers of Pharaoh's court knew of the vow the people had made to Joseph. When Joseph passed away the magicians and astrologers buried him in a coffin of iron weighing five hundred talents and cast it into the river. They were able to assure Pharaoh that the people of Israel would never leave the land of Egypt. They knew the Israelites would not betray their word."

But the faith of Moses was so great that he was undaunted by Segulah's words. From the river's edge he sent his cry over the waters, saying, "Joseph, Joseph! You urged the children of Israel to give you their promise that they would take your bones out of Egypt, saying that God would remember them if they remembered you. Now the hour of our redemption is at hand. Honor God, then, from on high, as you honored Him when you walked the earth. Take your good deeds to Him and intercede with your Creator. Rise up from the depths of the river, so that we may bear your coffin into the promised land!"

Immediately the waters of the Nile began to churn, and Joseph's coffin rose up from its depths like a stick rising to the river's surface. It floated over to the shore where Moses stood, and Moses dragged it from the water by the strength of his own hands. Bearing the coffin on his shoulders, Moses then turned to go and lead the children out of their bondage in Egypt. While the Israelites were gathering the Egyptians' gold and silver to despoil the land, Moses busied himself with the service and duty we owe to our ancestors.

When Moses came to the end of his days, God remembered the care with which Moses had borne Joseph's remains out of Egypt. "Moses, Moses!" He declared to His servant. "You may believe that you did a small thing in taking Joseph's coffin out of Egypt. But I say that this act of kindness shown to the dead is a great thing. Because you placed this service to the dead above amassing gold and silver, I Myself shall attend to your burial."

And so, when he died, the Holy One Himself buried our teacher Moses.

David Asks for Madness

MIDRASH ON PSALMS 34:1

God has His reasons for creating all things, including those things we might suppose we should shun. God's reason's are not human reasons, and His ordering of the world cannot always be fathomed according to humanity's sense of a rational order. God's design even may include the madness that undermines rational thought. As David discovers, our cunning sometimes serves us best when it is lost. If the world could not endure without madmen, as Maimonides once suggested, perhaps we all need a touch of madness once in a while in order to endure.

One day, not long after he had slain Goliath, David sat and composed songs of praise to God. As he raised his voice in melody, he surveyed all that God had created and declared, "Everything You have made, O Lord, You have made beautiful. And yet more beautiful than anything that meets the eye is wisdom. It is our means of knowing You, and it is Your means of loving us." David sang a song in praise of wisdom.

Suddenly, however, a disturbing thought entered his mind. What of the madness that seems to be the contrary of all wisdom? Can it be that God has made all things in wisdom and has made them well, except for madness?

David turned to the Holy One, blessed be He, crying, "Master of the universe, tell me, please. When a madman runs about the marketplace and rends his clothes, or when children follow after him and mock him, can this be beautiful in Your eyes?"

"You raise up a cry against madness, do you?" God asked. "By your very life, you will be in need of madness one day. Know that in his hour of need, a man may be seized and even saved by the very thing he despises. The hour will come when you will long for and pray for madness before I give you even an ounce of it."

"How can this be?" David wondered to himself. "I do not understand."

The Israelites had come to regard David as their greatest hero. David began to fear King Saul's jealousy, so he rose up to set off to see Achish, King of the Philistines. Along the way the Holy One, blessed be He, stopped him and said, "David, why do you leave your own people to go to Achish? Only yesterday you killed the giant Goliath. His blood is not yet dry on the sword that you took from his hand and with which you chopped off his head. And here you set out for Achish, whose bodyguard is Goliath's brother, a man who surely has vengeance in his heart."

Nevertheless David continued onward, for he was more afraid of Saul than he was of the Philistines. When the Philistines saw him approaching, they said to Goliath's brother, "Behold. David, the one who killed your brother Goliath, is coming to see Achish." Then, turning to their king, they cried out, "Let us kill this Hebrew who has slain our brother!"

Achish replied, "Was it not in a fair fight that Goliath fell to David? If Goliath had slain this one who has slain him, would it not have been a fair fight? Need I remind you of what Goliath himself declared unto David, that if the Hebrew should kill him, we would all become the servants of Israel?"

"If that is so," they replied to the King, "rise up from your throne and offer it to David, so that we may all become the servants of the Israelites!"

But Achish was loathe to relinquish his throne and considered what he might do next.

Witnessing this, David grew afraid for his life, and a prayer came to his lips: "Master of the Universe, I beseech You to hear my prayer in this my hour of need!"

"What is it that you ask?" God answered him.

Said David, "I beg You to give me a touch of the madness You have created in Your wisdom, so that the Philistines might have pity on me!"

"Did I not tell you," God reminded him, "that a man may be seized and saved by the thing he despises? And now you ask Me for madness!"

Hearing the Philistines plotting his death, David cried out to the Lord, "Am I then doomed to die by the hands of the godless, whom I have fought for the sake of Your people and Your holy Name?"

Having raised this cry unto God, David's demeanor suddenly changed into that of a madman. Screaming and babbling, he took a piece of chalk and wrote on the doors of the house of Achish, "The king of the Philistines owes me one hundred thousand, and his wife owes me fifty thousand."

Convinced that he was touched by the gods, the Philistines grew afraid of David and did not harm him. Realizing that by his madness his life was spared, David inwardly rejoiced and secretly declared unto the Holy One, blessed be He, "How very good is the madness that You have created, O Lord!"

The Shechinah in Exile

LAMENTATIONS RABBAH 1:6

The Talmud teaches us that the world is sustained by the breath of little children engaged in the study of Torah. Why? Because on their precious breath vibrates the breath of the Shechinah, the Indwelling Presence of God in the world. Without children we are without God's presence. Without God's presence, we are without meaning. As we care for our children, so we care for the presence of the Most Dear in the world. The Infinite comes in small packages. It comes not only in the children we hold dear but also in tales about children such as this one.

When the holy city of Jerusalem was under siege at the hands of the Babylonians, the affliction of Israel was terrible indeed. Neighbor turned against neighbor, and the most prominent men of Israel turned their backs on their brothers. Therefore the Holy One, blessed be He, turned His face from all of Israel. For, as Rabbi Azaryah teaches, when Israel does not abide by the will of the Omnipresent, they weaken, if one may say so, the power of Him who is above all creation. Likewise, when they live by His will, they add strength to the heavenly powers. The sages say: God is the shadow of man.

The Temple was made not only of stones but of the will of the Holy One. When we do not follow His will, those who are most holy in our lives—our children—suffer. It is through our children that the heavenly powers manifest themselves. It is thanks to our children that the heavens receive our prayers. How do we follow the will of the Holy One? By attending to our children, whose lives are at stake in our observance of God's Torah.

It happened, therefore, that when the soldiers of Babylon came and took away the members of the Sanhedrin, the great court housed in the Temple, the exile of those sages was a terrible blow to all of Israel. No longer did the halls of the Temple echo with the interpretations of the law and commentaries on the Torah. The Shechinah, nonetheless, continued to abide in the Land.

Next the Babylonians seized the Temple singers, who ceaselessly uttered God's praise, and sent them into exile. That, too, was a terrible blow to Israel, for the songs sung to God in joy and thanksgiving—the two means of drawing nigh unto the Lord—were heard no more in the Temple. Nevertheless, the Shechinah continued to dwell in the land.

Then came the most terrible blow of all, the blow that truly announced the destruction of the truth of the Temple. For next the Babylonians came and took the children into exile. No more were lips unsullied by sin heard to utter words of Torah and offer to God prayers that only they can offer. And so, when the children of Israel were sent into exile, the Shechinah went into exile with them.

The Two Jewels

MIDRASH ON PROVERBS 30:10

Rabbi Meir was one of the most prominent Talmudic sages of the second century. A student of Rabbi Akiva, Rabbi Meir came from a family of Roman proselytes and was instrumental in laying the foundations for the Mishnah. Rabbi Meir's wife Berurya, daughter of the martyred Rabbi Chanina ben Teradyon, was equally exalted for her great wisdom. Though their wisdom is severely put to the test in this tale, their faith in God never wavers.

In keeping with his custom, Rabbi Meir spent several days one summer in the house of study in Tiberias. But with the approach of the

Sabbath, he set out for home to be with his wife and his two sons, who were two and three years old. One of the primary aims of his Torah study was to add depth to the embrace he offered his family. And one of the primary aims of the Sabbath was to offer them that embrace.

The hour was late when he arrived home, but since it was summer, the sun had not yet set. Very often during the summer months the little ones would fall asleep before the coming of the Sabbath, so the rabbi supposed that he would have to wait until the next morning to see his beloved children.

He was not surprised when his wife Berurya was alone as she greeted him with a loving smile. She set the table for the two of them with braided loaves of challah and the cup of wine for the kiddush prayer. She lit the candles to usher in the Sabbath bride, as the Sabbath is often called, and the rabbi recited the kiddush. After that he sang to his wife the song *Eishet Chayil*, "A Woman of Valor," said the blessing over the bread, and began the Sabbath meal.

Rejoicing in God's bounty, they sanctified the holy day of rest. One thing, however, struck the rabbi as peculiar: his wife's unusual silence. Although he wondered what might be troubling her, he said nothing but also ate in an uneasy silence.

"She will speak when she is ready to speak," he told himself. And when they had finished their meal, the two of them retired for the night.

Early the next morning, after her husband had finished his prayers, Berurya asked him, "May I have a word with you, my husband?"

"At last," he thought, "she will tell me what has been on her mind." And he said to her, "What is it, my love?"

"Sometime ago—not so very long ago, it seems now—two precious jewels were placed in my keep. The jewels had a value beyond all reckoning, and I took the greatest possible care to keep them safe. Yesterday, before you arrived home for the Sabbath, the one who entrusted them to me came to claim them. I did not want to part with them, but I knew they were his. I knew I had to offer them up in good faith, in good cheer even."

"You have acted rightly," the rabbi told his wife. "Whatever is placed in our care must always be returned to its owner in good faith and good cheer."

"I knew you would say as much," she replied.

"But tell me," said the rabbi, "where are our two little ones? Is it not time that they were up and about?"

Berurya said nothing but led her husband by the hand to the room where their sons slept.

The rabbi was puzzled by what she had said, but as they approached their sons' room his bewilderment turned to dread. When they entered the chamber and he saw the toddlers lying still and cold in their beds, he realized the terrible truth behind his wife's question about the jewels. He wept bitter tears.

"I did not know what to do," Berurya told him, her hand on his heaving shoulders. "I was afraid to disturb your joy in the Sabbath. But you yourself said that we must return what has been placed in our care, and we must do it in good faith and cheer. God entrusted us for a time with the care of these two priceless jewels. But He has come to claim what belongs to Him."

"My own teaching comes back to me," said the rabbi between his sobs. "For I have taught that if we weep and mourn too much over the loss of a loved one, our grief may become a murmuring against the will of the Holy One, blessed be He. We must add our voices to the voice of Job and declare, 'The Lord gave, and the Lord has taken away: Blessed be the Name of the Lord.' We must. . . we must. . ."

And yet their tears would not heed his words.

The Stag and the Goats

NUMBERS RABBAH 8:2

In ancient cultures, a person could not choose to leave the tribe or nation of his birth, nor could others choose to enter it. Judaism, however, insists upon the sanctity of all human beings and allows room for any believer to enter into its fold. This tale from the Midrash emphasizes not only that outsiders should be welcomed into the community of Israel but that

*those who choose to take upon themselves the task and the testimony of
Israel have a very special place in the tradition.*

"I love those who love Me," God declares. And those who love
God are counted among the righteous. Why does God love the
righteous? Because their worth is determined not by heritage, nor
by power or possession, but by Torah study, prayer, and deeds of
lovingkindness.

What about the priests and the Levites, you will ask, those whose
service to God is determined by their fathers? A man cannot become a priest by his own choosing but is an heir to that office. Nor
can one join the ranks of the Levites whose father is not a Levite.
Are they not dear to God?

Indeed they are. But more dear are the righteous, and even a
Gentile may be counted among the righteous. Those who love
God are not the heirs of that love but come to love God according
to their own resolve and their own merit. That is why the Holy
One, blessed be He, loves them above all. Most dear to Him are
those who as proselytes come forward to choose God in the midst
of His having chosen them.

A king once had a flock of goats. Each morning the flock would
go out into the fields and graze on the king's lush grass. And each
evening they would return to the care and protection of the king.

One day a stag happened upon the king's goats while they were
out in the fields. Drawn by their beauty and by the care the king
provided them, the stag joined the flock and grazed with them. At
the end of the day he remained with them and returned with them
to the courtyard of the king. The stag grew to love the goats and
remained with them day after day.

"A certain stag has joined the flock," the chief shepherd finally
informed the king. "He grazes with them in the fields every day,
and every evening he comes in with them. What shall we do about
him? Shall we chase him back into the forest?"

The king was moved by this stag, who could roam wherever he
wished but had chosen to remain with the flock. He went out into
the fields with the shepherds and looked upon the stag with great
affection.

"Let him have the finest pasture," the king ordered the shepherds. "Let him graze anywhere he likes in my fields. No one is to lay a hand on him or mistreat him, but all are to take good care of him. When he comes in with the flock at the end of the day, see to it that he has a cool drink of water."

The king loved the stag more and more with each passing day. Every day he watched over the stag and cautioned his servants to treat him well.

One day his servants said to him, "Sire, you possess so many he-goats, so many lambs, and so many kids, and yet you have never directed us as to how we should care for them. But each day you instruct us on how to attend to the stag. Why such an interest in him?"

The king explained, "The goats of my flock have no choice as to their lot. Each morning they must go out to my fields, and they must return in the fold each night. Stags, however, dwell in the forest and are free to roam the entire world. It is not their nature to live with my flock. Shall we not, then, regard with great merit this stag who has left behind the forest, where he can do as he likes, and has chosen instead to abide in the courtyard of the king?"

So it is with the proselyte. He has left his family and his father's house—indeed, he has left behind his people—and has chosen to dwell among us, to share with us our burdens and responsibilities, our testimony and truth. Therefore God accords the proselyte a special place in His heart and has commanded Israel to take great care in their treatment of him. Beloved are the proselytes, for Scripture in every instance compares them to the children of Israel, who are God's chosen.

Kabbalistic Tales

THE BODY OF JEWISH MYSTICAL TEXTS known as the Kabbalah, a term that means "tradition," dates from the twelfth and thirteenth centuries. Some of tales in this section come from the twelfth-century texts written by a group of mystics known as the Iyyun Circle, or the Circle of Contemplation, who lived in southern France. One tale has been selected from the Bahir, a kabbalistic text first published around 1176 by the Provence school of Kabbalists. Most of the tales in this section, however, are taken from the best-known and most extensive text of the Kabbalah, the Zohar, which was written by the Spanish mystic Mosheh de Leon (1250–1305).

Jewish mystics sought an intimate knowledge of God beyond the boundaries of strictly rational thought, searching both within themselves and in the realm of nature. Believing that all the world had come from the hand of God and reverberates with His divine speech, the mystics pursued this intimate knowledge of God's word through techniques of prayer and meditation. These tales themselves may be viewed as akin to the prayers that draw not only the mystics closer to the Holy One, blessed be He, but anyone who seeks to attend to His Voice.

Relating and receiving these kabbalistic tales is a means of penetrating the secret side, the sacred side, of all things, both within us and beyond us. They open up connections between life and meaning, without which we have neither.

God's Back

FROM THE IYYUN CIRCLE

According to the Jewish tradition, when Moses received the Torah at Sinai,
he received not only the written Torah but the oral Torah—the Talmud—
as well. It is also said, however, that Moses later received the mystery
underlying all of Torah. This came about when he asked to behold God's
face (Exodus 33:13). Although God would not allow Moses to see His
face, He did show him His back. What did Moses see? According to the
Talmud, he saw the knot of the tefillin, the phylacteries, tied in back of
God's head, so that even here God shows Himself in the mode of command-
ment. But this tale from the Iyyun Circle offers an additional response to
that question.

After Moses had received the Torah at Sinai and offered it to the
people of Israel, his longing to penetrate every mystery of the divine was greater than ever, so he turned to God one day and asked,
"O Lord, Sovereign of the Universe, please show me Your ways."
  Knowing that no man can fathom God's ways and that great
danger lies in any attempt to do so, God answered, "You cannot
see My face. For you have asked about a mystery and a darkness
that go to the very source of My being. The darkness is part of the
realm that preceded the creation of heaven and earth. You cannot
comprehend it. Any effort you make to understand the mystery of
that darkness would result in a misunderstanding. Indeed, should
you try, you would perish. But if you wish, I shall show you My
back. Seeing My back, you may perceive everything that lies below that darkness, everything that proceeds from it, including My
essence, the power of My name, and the radiance of My glory."
  "I beseech You, then," Moses replied, "to show me Your back."
  At that moment, God moved past Moses, holding His hand over
the face of His beloved servant to protect him from the terrible
mystery. But as soon as He had passed by, He revealed to Moses

His awesome back. Suddenly Moses beheld the primeval light of Creation, which is the root and secret of all things. It consisted of two entities, one overflowing with light and the other engulfed in darkness.

Both entities gushed forth through various channels. Sometimes the flow weakens like a small stream that grows smaller and smaller, until it is nothing more than a thread. The thread stretches until it is like tiny droplets scattered over the deep. These drops increase and merge with one another, becoming larger and larger, until a sap pours forth from them. The sap, in turn, increases and congeals. From the coagulated sap issues a kind of foam that floats on the waters and transforms everything into a fluid. And out of the depths of this fluid there arises a great wind, which is known as the Holy Spirit. Thus it is written, "And the spirit of God hovered on the waters." From that spirit arise all the powers, entities, and objects of creation.

Then Moses understood: what transpired at the time of Creation transpires all the time. The primeval light is not buried in the past—it contains the past, the present, and the future. God's back is before us. And on the other side, the side that forever eludes us, is the radiance of His face.

Jeremiah Seeks a Companion

FROM THE IYYUN CIRCLE

This story is very interesting for its suggestion that the prophet Jeremiah was one of the early mystics. Indeed, it opens with Jeremiah's study of the Book of Creation, a mystical text attributed to Adam and whose origin is unknown; the earliest commentaries on the Book of Creation date from the tenth century. The Book of Creation is the basis for the tradition of ecstatic Kabbalah known as the Kabbalah of Names. According to this tradition, it is possible for a person to achieve the ecstasy of moving into God's presence if he knows the secret of the proper combinations of the letters that form the many names of God. Those who are among the initiated may also learn the mystery of how to create a humanlike being, or golem, by gather-

ing together a heap of clay, shaping it into a human form, and uttering certain incantations, which are also made of variations on the divine name. Here God's name is not confined to the tetragrammaton of YHVH but includes other names as well.

The lesson that comes to us from this tale is that those who seek a companion in this realm must maintain their devotion to the realm of the holy. For no one can create his own companion, since God is the creator of all beings. Therefore the oneness of God includes all relationships above and below. Indeed, there is only one relationship, the relationship with God, which we are to express in all other realms of relation.

One day, as the prophet Jeremiah was engaged in the study of the mystical Book of Creation, a heavenly voice resounded from above, saying, "Find yourself a companion."

Understanding this to mean that he was to create for himself a living being, Jeremiah sought out his son Sira to help him in the task. For three years they sat together and studied the Book of Creation in order to learn the secrets of bringing dead matter to life.

After three years of laboring with all the possible combinations of the letters of the alphabet, Jeremiah and his son finally managed to transform a mass of clay into what appeared to be a man. On the creature's forehead were written the words *YHVH Elohim Emet*: "The Lord God is Truth." But the humanoid being took a knife and scraped away the *alef*, the first letter of the word *Emet*, leaving the word *Met*, so that now the inscription on his forehead read, "The Lord God is dead."

Beholding this blasphemy, Jeremiah tore his clothing and cried out, "Why have you taken the *alef* from *emet* to make 'truth' into 'dead?'"

The creature explained. "There was once a learned architect who built many houses, cities, and courts. So skilled was he that no one was able to imitate his style, for no one possessed his knowledge or understanding of structures and designs. One day, however, two arrogant men forced themselves upon him, urging him to teach them the secrets of his craft. For three years they pressured him, until finally he relented and taught the two men the secrets of his designs.

"Once they had learned the secrets of the trade, they began to argue with him over the wisdom of his designs, until they broke away from him and became architects on their own. They charged lower prices for their work, so that soon people went to the new-comers and offered them the commissions that they had once paid to the master architect.

"So, too, has God created you in His image and likeness. But now you have taken over the secret of that image and have created a man, just as He has. Now people may say, 'There is no God in the world other than these two makers of men!'"

Realizing that the creature might be right, Jeremiah implored him, "What can be done to reverse this terrible thing?"

The creature told him, "Take the letters of the alphabet that you have combined and write them backwards on this piece of clay. Only do not meditate, as you did before, on thoughts of honor and restoration. Rather, meditate on the opposite thoughts."

Jeremiah and his son Sira did exactly as the creature told them to do, and the being they had created turned to dust and ashes before their very eyes. Said Jeremiah to his son, "I now realize that these matters must be studied only with the aim of understanding, insofar as it is possible and permissible, the wisdom and the power of God. But a man must never engage in an activity that belongs to God alone."

Then Sira addressed his father, saying, "My lord, I have made a careful study of the esoteric subjects to which we have devoted ourselves. I know that the spirit of the Holy One, blessed be He, is intimately connected to the sound that vibrates on a man's breath. Now I realize that a man must be very careful with every word that comes out of his mouth and understand the difference between what is above and what is below."

"You have spoken well, my son," Jeremiah replied. "Our purpose in delving into the secrets of the name is not to imitate God in the creation of a man-like being, but so that we may become men by assuming within ourselves and in our actions the image of God."

The Truth Is Life

FROM THE BAHIR

The patriarchs Abraham, Isaac, and Jacob are the fathers not only of a people but also of a faith. This tale from the Kabbalah tells us something about the elements that combined to give birth to the Jewish faith. Represented by Abraham, Isaac, and Jacob, they are respectively lovingkindness, fear, and truth: lovingkindness for our fellow human beings, a fear of God and for God, and the divine truth by which we are both judged and redeemed. Each is connected to the other, and all are dimensions of a life steeped in the holy. Without fear and truth, lovingkindness is no more than a whim; without lovingkindness and truth, fear is paralyzing; and without lovingkindness and fear, truth becomes a matter of mere opinion.

Our father Abraham was blessed by God with the performance of acts of lovingkindness. Each time he performed one act of lovingkindness, he was rewarded by being led to perform another act of lovingkindness. Thus he opened his home to the three strangers as he sat recovering from his circumcision. The sign that he had entered into a covenant with God was not only his circumcision but the deeds of lovingkindness that he showed toward all who came to his door. Since life is born into the world through deeds of lovingkindness, the three strangers to whom Abraham opened his home announced to him that he would have a son called Isaac.

Lovingkindness is rooted in a fear of God, which the righteous understand to be fear for our fellow human beings. Therefore the blessing bestowed upon our father Isaac was fear. What did he fear? He feared falling short of his love for God, for he knew that a love for the Infinite One must be infinite. Having lain upon the altar at Moriah, he knew how much God asks of us. And he knew that in our offering to God we are charged with the care of humanity.

Fear, therefore, is a dimension of truth. And so, as the son of Isaac, our father Jacob was blessed with truth. His sons became the fathers of the twelve tribes that stood at Mount Sinai. There the truth with which Jacob was blessed was revealed to all the world.

There the children of his children declared, "We will do and we will hear," when asked if they would live by the truth that is Torah. Like Jacob, they understood that truth lies not in knowing but in following its path. The truth is life.

How God Acquired a Name

FROM THE ZOHAR ON GENESIS, 1B–2A

God's name is tied to His activity as the creator of heaven and earth. In His name there abides a question: Who? Indeed, in the midst of the Hebrew word for "question," she'elah, are the letters alef and lamed of the word el, which means "God": God is in the question. What comes into being at the time of the Creation, then, is not a what but a who. Thus through the question of who is God we address the questions of who we are and who our fellow beings are. Upon such questions all the world is founded.

One day Rabbi Shimon sat by the sea contemplating the verse from the Book of Isaiah: "Lift up your eyes on high and see: who [mi] has created these?" (40:26). Long and hard he reflected on the words, struggling with every fiber of his being to penetrate their meaning and their mystery. But they remained sealed to him.

All the while the prophet Elijah was looking on, as he does whenever a sage engages the holy word. Seeing Rabbi Shimon's plight, Elijah decided to appear to him and raise a question. Asking a question, you see, is one of Elijah's favorite ways of helping.

Approaching the sage, Elijah inquired, "Rabbi, can you tell me, please: what is the meaning of the word *mi*, "who," in the verse 'who has created these?'"

Rabbi Shimon answered, "The *mi* here refers to the heavens and all the heavenly hosts. It refers to the works of the Holy One, blessed be He, the works that we contemplate and that lead us to bless Him. For in blessing Him, we are blessed."

To this Elijah replied, "Rabbi, know that the Holy One harbors a profound mystery, which He has revealed to the sages of the celestial academy. It is this: When the Most Mysterious determined that He would reveal Himself, He first produced a single point, which He then transformed into a divine thought. This thought consisted of innumerable designs, and through it He engraved innumerable images. Issuing from this primal thought was a wondrous structure that harbored a mystical lamp. He engraved the holiest and most mystical of all designs into this lamp, and from the lamp issues the light of all creation.

"Now the foundation of this edifice and the light of the lamp is the *mi*. It is both existent and nonexistent, deeply shrouded in mystery and unknowable by name. That is why it is called *mi*, or "Who." Entering into the act of creation, the *mi* longed to reveal itself and to be called by name. Thus the *mi* clothed itself in garments of splendor and glory and created *eleh*, or 'these.' How then was the name formed? From the union of the *mi* and the *eleh* there emerged the name made of both: *elohim*, which, of course, means 'God.'

"Once *mi* joined *eleh*, the two bonded together for all time. Upon this mystery the entire world is built."

Having brought the sage this insight, Elijah flew up to the heavens and vanished from Shimon's sight. Thus Rabbi Shimon came to know something of the mystery that sustains all creation. It is the mystery of the eternal Who that summons all, even God Himself, into being.

The Man from the Other World

FROM THE ZOHAR ON GENESIS, 5A–7B

The Talmud teaches us that the wise person is one who can learn from all people. The people around us may harbor insights that exceed anything we can imagine, and a stranger's questions may open up to us new horizons of understanding. In this tale the stranger seems to be Rav Hamnuna, the third-century Babylonian sage who was the head of the academy at Sura and who was known for his emphasis on Torah study as the key to the heavenly realm. Just as the stranger may come to us from such realms, so may the questions he raises take us to another world. This story contains several allusions to elements belonging to another, mystical realm, such as the Celestial throne upon which God sits and the Sabbaths associated with that other world. It is a place "on high," as the stranger explains to the rabbis, where a mysterious poor man resides with God in an equally mysterious tower. There the great sages who have passed away continue to gather to study Torah with the Holy One Himself. Most mysterious of all is the stranger himself, who, like the stranger Jacob encountered at Peniel, appears to be now man, now an angel, and finally God Himself.

One day Rabbi Eleazar, son of Rabbi Shimon, was traveling to visit his father-in-law Rabbi Yose. Rabbi Abba joined Eleazer on his journey, as did another man, a stranger to them both, who followed behind them, leading the ass that bore their baggage. The rabbis knew that it was appropriate to speak of Torah whenever two companions came together, so that the presence of God would enter into their midst. Therefore Rabbi Eleazar began by raising a matter concerning the Sabbath.

"The first three days of Creation," he said, "are veiled in great mystery. During that time the activities of the three primordial elements—fire, water, and air—remained undisclosed. From the fourth day onward God revealed the nature of His work, for on that day He created the luminaries of the heavens, by whose light we behold all that God has made. That is why we say that the fourth day symbolizes the fourth leg of the Celestial Throne, from which God judges the world: on that day all things came under the light of the heavens, and the Throne could stand firm. And yet the activities of Creation are not consummated until the seventh day, on the Sabbath. Therefore it would seem that the Celestial Throne could not stand until the seventh day. That is why the Celestial Throne was not put into position until the Sabbath."

The stranger who followed behind the two rabbis listened carefully to these words, and asked, "What does God mean when he commands us to have reverence for His sanctuary?"

"The Celestial Throne," Rabbi Eleazar replied, "stands in the heart of the sanctuary. Therefore our reverence for God's sanctuary is a reverence for the sanctity of the Sabbath."

To which the stranger replied, "Does that mean the Sabbath has no sanctity of its own?"

"That is correct," Rabbi Abba declared.

"If it has no sanctity of its own," the stranger wondered, "then how is it that we are summoned to honor the Sabbath and not just the Most High from whom it derives its sanctity?"

Hearing this question, Rabbi Eleazar advised his friend, "Do not argue with this man. It seems that he is aware of some mystery of which we are ignorant."

Suspecting that the stranger was no ordinary man, the rabbis said, "Speak what you have to say."

So the stranger spoke: "God declared to Moses and the Israelites, 'You must keep My Sabbaths' (Exodus 31:13). Why does He refer to His 'Sabbaths,' in the plural? Because there is a higher Sabbath and a lower Sabbath, which are joined together as one in a realm that is not of this world. But when He created these Sabbaths, He also made the Sabbath that belongs to this world, the one we call 'the Sabbath day,' which is not joined to the other two. Feeling humiliated and isolated, this third Sabbath appealed to God, saying, 'O Lord of the Universe, from the moment You created me, I have been called simply "the Sabbath day." But surely a day must have a night as its companion.'

"Said the Lord, 'O my daughter, you are truly the Sabbath day, and forever shall I call you by that name. But I shall confer upon you a crown more precious than the companion of night that you seek.'

"And God created for the Sabbath a sanctuary that opens on the eve of the Sabbath, as darkness descends. Honoring the Sabbath eve, we enter into God's sanctuary, where the Sabbath is sanctified."

Hearing this, Rabbi Eleazar and Rabbi Abba embraced the stranger and kissed him, saying, "With the profound knowledge that you have shown to us, it cannot be proper for you to follow along behind us. Please tell us, who are you?"

"It is better that you do not ask this question," the stranger answered, "but let us continue on our way and speak further of the Torah."

"If you cannot tell us who you are," the rabbis persisted, "then please explain who assigned you the task of serving as our driver?"

"That too must remain hidden," the stranger told them. "But I can tell you that the One who sent me assigned certain letters of the holy alphabet to accompany me. He ordered the letter *yud*, from which all of creation arose, to accompany me. The *yud* urged the letters *kaf* and *samech*, the letters that support the world, to join me as well, but they refused. And so the *yud* said to me, 'My son, I shall load myself with an abundance of good things and together we shall go into the world bearing our riches.' Thus I travel in this way, the driver of an ass laden with precious things."

"Then, please," the rabbis pleaded with him, "proceed in front of us. It is we who should follow you, not you us."

"No," the stranger declined, "the King has ordained that I follow behind until the time comes for the one who is to ride on the ass to appear."

"Can you at least tell us where you come from" the rabbis wanted to know.

"My dwelling place," he explained, "is a tower suspended on high. In the tower the Holy One, blessed be He, resides, along with a certain poor man."

At this Rabbi Eleazar cried, "Surely you are the son of the most venerable Rav Hamnuna, the one known as the Sacred Lamp, whose wisdom is like the light of the Torah itself! And yet you follow behind us!"

Rabbi Abba begged, "Your name, please, reveal to us your name!"

But the stranger replied by entering into a long discourse on the mysteries of the Torah.

Going from one verse to another, he expounded on the secrets that lay hidden behind the words, between the lines, and in the margins of the holy scrolls. The two rabbis were so overwhelmed, that when the stranger ended his discussion, they prostrated themselves before him. But when they looked up, the stranger was nowhere to be seen. The rabbis collapsed on that very spot and fell to weeping.

Finally Rabbi Abba said, "Surely it is true that where two travelers exchange words of Torah, they are visited by inhabitants of the other world. For it is clear to me that this stranger was none other than the revered Rav Hamnuna, who has come to us from the other world and now has vanished."

The rabbis continued on their journey, until, as the sun was setting, they came to a wooded hill. No sooner had they ascended the hill than they heard the branches of the trees break forth in hymns and a resounding voice cry out above them, "Holy sons of God, you who are the lamps of the house of study, gather yourselves together to study Torah under the guidance of your Master!"

The rabbis had no inkling of who was speaking or to whom. Overcome with fear and trembling, they suddenly fell to the ground. And just as suddenly they rose and hurried on their way. Could the stranger have followed them to that hilltop? Might he not be the master around whom the sages on high, in the heavenly realm, were gathering?

When at last they reached the home of Rabbi Yose, they were filled with joy for having safely arrived after such a strange and awesome journey.

Rabbi Shimon was there too, and he greeted them, saying, "Surely you have traveled a path of heavenly wonders, for I saw the two of you in a vision, and your faces were transfigured!"

Rabbi Eleazar told him the story of how the man from the other world had blessed them with his presence. When he had finished telling the strange tale, Rabbi Shimon fell to his face and saw a vision of Rav Hamnuna uprooting mountains and kindling the lights in the Temple that the Messiah was destined to build. From that moment on Rabbi Shimon gave both Rabbi Eleazar and Rabbi Abba the same name, Peniel, in remembrance of the verse spoken by Jacob when he had wrestled with a stranger in the night: "For I have seen God face to face."

King David's Escape from Geihinnom

FROM THE ZOHAR ON GENESIS, 8A–8B

Jewish texts are relatively silent on the matter of damnation, which makes this story a rather unusual one. Here we catch a glimpse of the angel Duma, who presides over Geihinnom—Hell. This tale suggests that no one, not even the head of the house of the Messiah, is free from judgment; it tells us that God Himself will intervene on behalf of His beloved, provided that His beloved is truly repentant; and finally, it teaches us that no one but God can be certain of whom He counts among His beloved. Therefore, rather than hope for His divine intervention, we should enlist His aid and pursue righteousness.

The angel Duma presides over Geihinnom, with tens of thousands of angels of destruction in his charge. Duma is thoroughly versed in Torah. Those who have defiled the children of Abraham, whose bodies are sanctified by the sign of the covenant, come under the judgment of the Torah that the angel Duma holds over them. The angel has no power, however, to lay a hand upon those who have lived by the Torah's teachings and who have thus preserved all that the sign of the covenant signifies.

Duma likes nothing better than to lay a snare for the righteous. As soon as King David took Bathsheba, the angel declared to God, "O Lord of the Universe! Your Torah forbids a man to lie with his neighbor's wife and commands him to refrain from every act of adultery. Now behold Your servant King David: he has abused the sign of the holy covenant and has taken another man's wife to be his own! Therefore he is mine!"

But God answered, "David is pure, and the sign of the covenant upon his flesh remains undefiled. For at the time of the creation of the world it was revealed before Me that Bathsheba was intended for him."

"It may have been revealed before You," Duma said to Him, "but it was not revealed to him. David sent her husband Uriah to the front lines of battle, knowing that Uriah would be killed and he would be free to take his wife."

"Nevertheless," God replied, "what was done was done lawfully, since every man who goes to war first gives his wife a bill of divorcement."

"Even so," Duma insisted, "David ought to have waited three months for the proper mourning period to be over. Because of his lust for Bathsheba, he did not do this."

God reminded the angel, "That rule applies only where a wife might be pregnant. In this case, however, I know that Uriah never lay with his wife."

"Once again," the angel pleaded, "I must point out that David had no knowledge of whether Uriah lay with his wife. Therefore he should have waited three months. And if he knew, then why did he order Uriah to go home and be with his wife?"

"Truly My servant David was not aware of it," God replied. "And I tell you that he waited not only three months but four, from the seventh of Sivan to the twenty-fourth of Elul. And on the tenth of Tishrei, the Day of Atonement, he was forgiven his sins. He came to Me in repentance."

"Very well," said the judge who presides over Geihinnom. "But You are forgetting one important fact. When the prophet Nathan told David the parable of the rich man who steals the sheep of the poor man, David himself declared that such a man deserves to die. Thus he condemned himself, and my charge against him stands."

"True," God conceded, "these words did come from his mouth. But as soon as he repented and confessed to Me, 'I have sinned against the Lord,' even though he was not truly guilty, you lost all power over him. As for his transgression in sending Uriah to his death, I pronounced punishment upon him, which he suffered immediately."

Realizing that he could not prevail in his arguments with the Lord, Duma returned to Geihinnom.

Now the Holy One had allowed His servant David to listen to His entire conversation with the angel Duma. When their exchange had come to an end, David cried out, "Unless the Lord had come to my aid, my soul would have dwelled in the kingdom of Duma! Blessed be the Name of the Lord!"

David realized that a man must be cautious with his words, lest they lead him to deeds that would defile the sacred sign of the covenant upon his body and turn him over to the judgment of Duma.

The Union of Heaven and Earth

FROM THE ZOHAR ON GENESIS, 30B–31A

The earth longs for the light of the heavens as a bride longs for her groom. This longing for the Most High is a rising up that introduces a dimension of height to our existence on earth. Joined to what is above, what is below takes on meaning. Where do heaven and earth ultimately find their union? In the life of the human being who joins his life to the Holy One by affirming the holiness of other human beings. As the human bears the image of the divine, so does the earth bear the image of the heavens.

The garden of Eden is not a place in this world or of this world, for it existed prior to the creation of heaven and earth. In the beginning, a stream went forth from on high to water the garden of Eden. This stream is the supernal wisdom of God, from which all things were created and by which all things are sustained. The waters of the nourishing stream are gathered from a hidden source, whose mystery very few have fathomed. Out of this hidden source, from which all things flow, there arose two entities, as it is written: the heavens and the earth.

In the beginning the earth and the heavens were one. They came into being together, each clinging to the other, as a husband and wife cling to each other. But when God said, "Let there be light," the heavens took the earth and set it in its proper place between the waters above and the waters below, so Above and Below came into being.

Separated from her beloved, the earth was amazed and dumbfounded. She was overwhelmed by her desire to cleave unto the heavens, for she saw that the heavens were bathed in light, while she was left in the fearsome throes of darkness.

The heavens had compassion for the earth, and their celestial light descended upon her. Receiving the light of the heavens, the earth was sanctified and rose up to stand before the heavens face to face, each in the presence of the other. At that moment the earth was firmly established.

From the right hand of God there then came a new light, and from the left hand of God there issued a new darkness. God sepa-

rated this light and darkness for the same reason that He had separated the heavens and the earth: so that they might be united once
more at a time pleasing to Him. The separation of the light from
the darkness was not an absolute separation. Rather, it was so that
God could bring forth the day from the light and the night from
the darkness. Like the heavens and the earth that draw nigh unto
each other, day and night cling to one another to form a single
creation.

Although it emerged from the side of primordial fire, which is
called "darkness," night has no light of its own, just as the earth has
no meaning of its own. Night remains dark until it is illuminated
by day. Day offers its light to night.

And yet the time will come when the night will be illuminated
of itself, as the psalmist suggests when he says, "The night shines
as day, the darkness is even as the light" (Psalms 134:12), and the
earth will take on the aspect of the heavens, a supernal light unto
itself. At that time there will be a marriage of the heavens and the
earth. And all who dwell below will be instilled with the light of
the beginning that shines from above.

Why the World Was Punished with Water

FROM THE ZOHAR ON GENESIS, 62A

*When we sin, we corrupt all of humanity, and with humanity, all the
earth: creation itself is undermined by our sin. As for the origin of our sin,
it arises when we lose the capacity for making distinctions between what is
above and what is below, as, for example, when we take ourselves to be as
God. When that distinction is lost, meaning collapses. Human life loses all
significance, and human beings lose all value, so that we come to justify
any crime committed against our neighbor. As it often happens in Scripture, the punishment for this crime reflects the nature of the crime itself.*

One day, Rabbi Yitzchak was reflecting on the story of Noah and
the Flood. "The Torah tells us that 'all the earth was corrupt,'" he
thought to himself, "and not just that all men were corrupt. Why

should the earth be corrupt as a result of the actions of men? How, indeed, can human beings corrupt something so vast as the earth?"

Unable to resolve these questions for himself, Rabbi Yitzchak went to his teacher, Rabbi Shimon. There he found Rabbi Yehudah studying with the sage. In fact, the two of them also were examining the story of the Flood. "Tell me," Rabbi Yitzchak asked, "why does the Torah say that all the earth was corrupt, when the corruption lay in the hearts and deeds of men?"

After a moment of reflection, Rabbi Shimon explained, "Because all of humanity is made of the earth. Indeed, the dust from which God created man was gathered from the four corners of the earth. As we treat one another, so we treat the earth that comes from the hand of God. When one human being betrays another, he betrays all of God's creation. Therefore it is written, 'And God saw the earth, and behold it was corrupt, for all flesh had corrupted their way upon the earth.'"

At that point Rabbi Yehudah asked, "Why, then, did the Holy One punish the world with water, and not with some other element, such as fire? Or, if they corrupted the earth, then perhaps mankind should have been punished by the earth and swallowed up in a great earthquake. For we know that the punishment of sin reflects its nature."

"You do well to ask," Rabbi Shimon replied. "But in this case the punishment reflects not only the particular sins of violence against one's neighbor but the essence of sin itself. The failure of mankind to distinguish between what is above and what is below caused the waters from below to unite with the waters from above in a deluge to destroy all of humanity."

"And the heat of passion that leads men to violence?" Rabbi Isaac asked. "For I believe that Rabbi Yehudah did well to raise the matter of fire."

"It is manifested," said Rabbi Shimon, "in the fact that the waters of the Flood were scalding hot and caused their skin to be peeled off. There lies the punishment for violence done in the heat of their passion. All that God did was measure for measure."

Thus the generation of the Flood reaped what they had sown.

Faces Changed by Sin

FROM THE ZOHAR ON GENESIS, 71A

The sages teach us that we bear the image not only of our Creator but also of our actions. When our actions depart from the will of the Divine, we lose our divine image. Such is the message conveyed by this kabbalistic tale: The soul suffers what it inflicts; those who act in a bestial manner take on the image of beasts. When the Talmud enjoins us to present to others a face full of joy and kindness, it is telling us to treat our neighbor with humanity and lovingkindness.

When Adam and Eve were cast out of the garden of Eden, God declared to them, "The fear of you and the dread of you will be upon every beast of the earth." Those creatures who had come to Adam to receive their names and who had been his companions now turned away from him in horror.

Why did the beasts fear the man and woman? Because their faces had been transformed by their sin. Where there had once been the visage of God's love and compassion there were now faces lined with darkness and suspicion. The divine image in which their faces were created was lost in their betrayal of the Divine.

What did the beasts of the earth fear? It was the image of fear itself stamped upon the faces of Adam and Eve. Fear begets fear, and in place of the compassion that their faces had shown for the beasts there was dread. Once the beasts had bowed down before the image of man and woman—in which they had seen the image of the Creator. Now they reacted to them with ferocity, which is the reaction of fear.

And so this teaching is handed down to us: Those who are mindful of their Creator, the Sovereign of the Universe, and who keep themselves from the transgression of the Torah retain in their faces the likeness of the divine. The beasts of the earth bow before them. But when we violate the teachings of the Torah, our faces are transformed into a fear that manifests itself as a fear of the beasts of the earth. And as a fear of our fellow human beings.

Let Us Proceed

FROM THE ZOHAR ON GENESIS, 83A–83B

When a Jew awakens each morning, the first words he utters are Modeh Ani, a prayer of thanks to God for returning his soul to life. As for where our souls return from, that question is answered in this tale from the Zohar. Indeed, when our souls depart from our bodies, they go off to receive tales. These tales are revealed in our dreams, and our dreams are told in our tales. But, as this selection from the Zohar suggests, the tales that come to us in sleep reveal to us something about ourselves, about our very souls. What happens when we are awake, therefore, entails something that happens when we are asleep. Proceeding from sleep to sleep, we proceed from tale to tale, and from life to renewed life.

One day Rabbi Shimon set out on a journey. Traveling with him were his son Rabbi Eleazar, Rabbi Abba, and Rabbi Yehudah. Knowing that it is incumbent upon travelers to exchange their thoughts on the Torah, Rabbi Shimon said, "It is amazing to me that so many people are so indifferent to the teachings of the Torah and the meaning of their own lives!"

"Are you thinking of any particular passage from the Scripture?" Rabbi Abba asked him.

"Yes," Rabbi Shimon replied, "I am. Just now the words of the prophet Isaiah came to me: 'With my soul have I desired Thee in the night.'"

"What do you take these words to mean?" asked Rabbi Yehudah.

"When a man lies down to sleep," Rabbi Shimon began, "his vital essence, his *nefesh* or soul, departs from him, leaving behind only the shell of his body. As his *nefesh* ascends from one level to the next, it encounters a variety of dazzling but unclean spirits. If his *nefesh* is pure, it is able to rise above these spirits without being contaminated by them. If it is not pure, then his vital essence gets trapped by these unclean spirits, which are nothing more than the temptations he encounters throughout the day. A troubled soul wanders at night from one fear to the next, from one apprehension to the next, uncertain of the truth of his life."

"Such a man truly is in a sad state," Rabbi Eleazar commented. "But what becomes of the *nefesh* of the righteous man?"

"When such a man falls asleep," Rabbi Shimon replied, "his soul rises all the way to the gates of the celestial palace. There it yearns with all its might to behold the radiance of the King and to enter into His sanctuary. Abiding along this edge of the World to Come and yearning to draw nigh unto the Holy One, blessed be He, such a soul dwells along the edge of its very origin. The prophet Isaiah declared, 'With my soul have I desired Thee in the night.' Which means: I follow after Thee and refuse to be enticed by false powers."

"What about the words that the prophet utters after these," asked Rabbi Yehudah, "where he says, 'With my spirit within me will I seek Thee early'?"

"You raise an excellent point," said Rabbi Shimon, pleased with his disciple's question. "These words refer to the ruach, to the spirit, which is an aspect of the nefesh. Know, moreover, that there is a third aspect of the soul, one called neshamah, or the higher spirit, to which these first two should cling. When the neshamah dominates the ruach and the nefesh of a man, he is called holy, devoted entirely to God, for the neshamah is the breath of God Himself that He breathed into the first man."

"How, then, are the three related to one another?" Rabbi Abba wanted to know.

Rabbi Shimon explained. "The nefesh sustains the body: it is the part in closest contact with the flesh. When it is sufficiently pure, it becomes the seat of the ruach. And when ruach has sufficiently purified itself, it receives neshamah. Nefesh is like the dark light at the bottom of a candle's flame, like the part of the flame that clings to the wick and exists only through the wick. When the flame is fully kindled, it becomes a throne for the white fire above it. And upon the white flame rests the light that is not fully discerned.

"In the story of Abraham all of this is revealed. When, as Abram, he entered the land, God appeared to him. He built an altar and there received nefesh. As he proceeded further into the Land and journeyed to the south, he received ruach. Finally, he attained the fullness of righteousness and built an altar to the Lord, whereupon he was elevated to neshamah. He was chosen for the covenant with God and became Abraham."

Thus Rabbi Shimon explained how a few words from the prophet

Isaiah contained the tale of Abraham, a tale ridden with the mystery of the soul and the wisdom that it seeks. It is a wisdom that links the movements of the body by day and the journeys of the soul by night.

Realizing all that he had learned from Rabbi Shimon, Rabbi Abba cried out to him, "Who will cause the light of the Torah to shine when you have departed from the world? Happy are those who receive the wisdom of the Torah from your lips!"

To which Rabbi Shimon merely replied, "Let us proceed."

How the World Became Firmly Established
FROM THE ZOHAR ON GENESIS, 86B

Why does the Talmud teach us that to save a single life is to save the entire world? The answer, as this tale suggests, is that the entire world may be sustained by the life of a single righteous person. From the life of a single righteous person may come forth the lives of other righteous people, and through them God is able to enter into the realm of humanity and sustain it. The righteous are the gates by which the Holy One enters and sanctifies His world. When the Creator is barred from entering into His creation— where righteousness is not to be found—the world cannot endure.

In the beginning God summoned the world and all that is in it into being. No sooner had the world appeared than it began to teeter back and forth on the edge of the nothingness that it had overcome.

Said God to His creation, "Why do you rock back and forth so precariously on the edge of the void?"

"Sovereign of the Universe!" the world replied. "How can I do otherwise? I rock to and fro, teetering on the edge of the abyss, because I have no foundation upon which to rest."

"Then you should know," said God to His world, "that I shall raise up in your midst a righteous man who will be called Abraham. He will love Me, and his love for Me is the foundation upon which you may be firmly established."

"I know that his love for You, O Lord," said the world, "might indeed provide a foundation upon which I can rest. But I also know that from Abraham will be born the people of Ishmael and Esau. They will rise up to destroy Your Temple and burn the scrolls of Your Torah. Then I shall tumble into the void from which You have called me forth. For I cannot endure without Your Temple and Your Torah."

God answered the world, saying, "My Temple is sustained and My Torah lives through the righteous who love Me and live according to My teachings. From Abraham there will be born a righteous man called Jacob. From him, in turn, there will rise up twelve tribes of righteous men and women. They are My chosen, and upon My chosen you are firmly established."

Hearing these words, the world rocked no more on the edge of the abyss but rested firmly on its true foundation. And on the foundation of the truth.

Esau's Garments

FROM THE ZOHAR ON GENESIS, 142B

At first glance, the message of this kabbalistic tale seems simple: Clothes do not dignify the man; a man imparts dignity to his clothing. But there is more. The Zohar teaches us that when the Messiah comes, he will recognize the righteous by their odor. Odor is understood to indicate a spirit that issues from the presence of a human being devoted to God. Thus Jacob imparted to his dress a certain air that, even in a state of blindness, his father Isaac could recognize as the mark of sanctity. The smell of righteousness that issues from Jacob is the scent of life that comes into the world from the hand and by the breath of God.

In Nimrod's day there came into his possession the precious garments worn by Adam. Nimrod adored these garments not for their holiness—for God Himself had made them—but for the power they gave him: It was said that anyone who wore the garments would inherit Adam's strength. Thus Nimrod became a "mighty hunter before the Lord," as it is written, because he used these garments as his hunting dress.

Esau, the son of Jacob, had heard of the wondrous hunting clothes that Nimrod possessed and longed to have them as his own. Therefore, when he heard that Nimrod had gone out hunting one day, Esau went out after him and tracked him down. For Esau was a great hunter and an expert at tracking down prey. At the first opportunity he attacked the mighty Nimrod, slew him, and claimed the garments as his own.

When he had removed the clothing from Nimrod's body, Esau took the garments and stored them in his mother Rebecca's apartment. After that, Esau would don the clothing whenever he planned to go hunting, and each time he would return with an impressive kill.

On the day when Isaac was to confer his blessing upon his sons, however, Esau had gone out without the garments. In her efforts to secure Jacob's blessing of the firstborn for her beloved son, Rebecca took Esau's garments and gave them to Jacob, hoping that if he were to wear them, he might deceive Isaac into offering him the blessing intended for Esau. "If Isaac should catch the scent of the fields on these garments," she thought, "he may believe Jacob to be Esau."

Rebecca did not realize, however, that the odor emanating from these clothes was not the odor of the fields but the scent of righteousness that Adam had imparted to these clothes that had come from the hand of God. Isaac did not take Jacob to be Esau—he took him to be the righteous one.

When Esau wore the garments, they emitted no scent. But when Jacob put them on, they were restored to their rightful place on the shoulders of a righteous man, and a sweet odor issued from them. For Jacob had inherited the beauty of Adam, which was the righteousness of Adam, and when he wore Adam's clothes, it was as though they had been returned to their original and rightful owner.

But can it really be that Jacob's beauty equaled that of Adam? We are taught that Adam's heel eclipsed the sun itself. Is it possible to say the same of Jacob?

Adam's beauty was indeed unsurpassed, as he came directly from the hand and mouth of God. After he had sinned, however, both

his beauty and his stature were diminished. And so the beauty of
Jacob rivaled that of Adam.

However, the beauty of both men is but a symbol of their faith
and their holiness. In these respects Jacob was the equal of Adam.
The garments he wore upon his body were but a sign of the Word
inscribed upon his heart. That is why his father Isaac blessed him:
he blessed the one who would be blessed with the name of Israel.

The Foundation Stone

FROM THE ZOHAR ON GENESIS, 231A–231B

*This is a story about the basis of all meaning, all truth, and all there is to
hold dear in life. It is a ground that the void cannot overcome, for from
within it there issues into the world more than the abyss can hold. It is the
center without which there can be no dwelling in the world, for existence
inheres in the song of affirmation that rises up from this center. Therefore
what is here referred to as the Foundation Stone is tied to the Torah itself, a
point made by this kabbalistic tale.*

In the beginning—no, before the beginning—the world could not
come into being, for it had nothing upon which to rest. Therefore
God took a stone unlike any other stone and cast it into the abyss.
The abyss could not swallow the wondrous stone, and it held fast
over the face of the void. From this Foundation Stone the world
issued forth.

The Foundation Stone is situated in the center of the universe,
and upon it rests the center of the world: the Holy of Holies that
harbors the Torah in the heart of the Temple that stands in Jerusalem. Job called it the Cornerstone, for all that exists rests upon it.
The prophet Isaiah knew it as the Stone of Testing, for all are
judged by the truth it upholds. The stone is made of the fire that
purifies, the water that sustains, and the air that animates all life in
the world. Sometimes torrents of water gush forth from the stone
and fill the deep to overflowing, imparting to the very depths the
essence of the stone itself: deep speaks to deep.

The Foundation Stone serves as a sign to the world of the One who sustains all life. When Jacob, who would be called Israel, took a stone and erected it as a sign of God's presence—as a *beit El*, a "house of God"—it symbolized the Foundation Stone itself. By creating a *beit El*, Jacob situated the Foundation Stone both above and below the world. For the world is sustained not only by what is below it but also by what is above it.

From the prophet Zechariah we learn that the stone has seven eyes, each of which looks over each of the seven days of the week. As the seven eyes gaze upon the world, blessings issue from the stone and emanate throughout the world, both from above and from below.

The site where the stone came to rest, the very site of the Holy of Holies, was where the cherubim stood in the beginning. Even now at sunset the beating of their wings can be heard from on high. Indeed, those of us in this realm who listen carefully—who know how to listen—can hear the beating of the cherubim's wings each day at dusk. As soon as the sound of their wings reaches the other angels, they all break into songs of praise, so that God's glory is made manifest above and below. At the second and third watch, all through the night, the cherubim beat their wings, and the angels of Heaven chant their songs.

At dawn the children of Israel take up the song from below, so that the holy Name of God is praised from all sides. During the day the glory of the Holy One rests upon the patriarchs in their heavenly abode. And at night God joins the righteous, who dwell in the garden of Eden, in their study of Torah. Therefore those who stand at their posts day and night, never failing in their Torah study, are among the blessed.

For the Torah is the foundation of the Foundation Stone.

Two Petitions for Rain

FROM THE ZOHAR ON EXODUS, 15A

In Mishnah tractate Avot, also know as Pirke Avot *or* Ethics of the Fathers, *Ben Zoma teaches us that the person who is truly honored is the one who honors his fellow human being; one who is truly righteous acknowledges the righteousness of his fellow human beings, while refusing any acknowledgment of his own righteousness. This tale from the Kabbalah exemplifies the teaching. The rain with which God graces the earth is like the righteousness that He bestows upon His beloved children: both nourish life by assuming the lower position.*

During the years that followed the destruction of the Second Temple, there came a drought that ravaged the land. Rabbi Eleazar ordered his congregation to fast for forty days, so that through their purification of themselves by fasting the land might be purified. During the fast Rabbi Eleazar prayed and pleaded with God to bring rain. But to no avail: after forty days of fasting and prayer, the land was still ridden by drought.

Seeing that the situation had become desperate, Rabbi Akiva gathered the congregation around him and offered up his petition to Heaven. As he spoke the words "Thou who causes the wind to blow," a great wind rose up from the north, and clouds gathered in the sky. When he cried out "And who causes the rain to fall," a heavy rain began to descend from on high, and relief came to the land at last.

The people of the congregation rejoiced in the rains that had come in response to Rabbi Akiva's petition. While he was glad to see relief come to the land, Rabbi Eleazar, however, was disturbed. He was sad and perhaps even a bit angry that God had been so quick to respond to Rabbi Akiva's prayer but had ignored his own. He sat silently amidst the rejoicing crowd.

Gazing into Rabbi Eleazar's eyes, Rabbi Akiva could read what was in his heart. He knew the cause of his comrade's distress, and he knew that he had to say something. He rose before the congregation and declared, "Do not suppose for a moment that our teacher, Rabbi Eleazar, has met with any disfavor from heaven. Indeed, he is closer to God than any of us are. I will explain with a parable.

"Rabbi Eleazar is like a man who is the king's dearest friend and closest companion. Whenever he goes to the king's palace to seek some favor, the king does not grant it at once. Why? Because he loves his friend's devotion and takes such delight in his friend's presence that he says to himself, 'I shall keep him here as long as possible.'

"I, on the other hand, am rather like the king's servant. When his servant goes to the king with a request, the king grants that request immediately. He does not want to be needlessly bothered with the likes of his servant and so quickly gets rid of him. Therefore, when his servant comes around to ask for something, the king declares to his ministers, 'Give this man whatever he wants and send him away from my chamber.'"

Upon hearing the parable related by Rabbi Akiva, Rabbi Eleazar was comforted. He embraced Rabbi Akiva for his righteousness and understood the real reason why God had attended to the prayers of his friend, a reason that both of them had left unspoken.

The City Where No One Dies

FROM THE ZOHAR ON EXODUS, 151B–152A

If there is one question that dominates all Jewish tales and traditions, it is the question of what constitutes the basis of life. Indeed, the ability to respond to this question is the mark of a wisdom that lies at the heart of life. And since at the heart of life we encounter the mystery of death, the matter of how to overcome death finds its way into most religious traditions. The mystical tale before us addresses these questions concerning life and death. It is about the city of Luz, which, according to tradition, was built on the site where Jacob had his dream about the angels ascending and descending a ladder to heaven. Some say that it is the same as the town of Beth El; those who claim that Beth El was in Jerusalem identify Luz and Salem as the two villages that merged to become Jerusalem. Wherever it may have been located, the Kabbalah maintains that there only the forces that sustain life hold sway; there death has no power.

One day Rabbi Shimon told his disciples about an unusual city outside the Holy Land called Luz, where the Angel of Death has no power. Those who live there, no matter how advanced they are in years, do not taste death until they decide to leave the city.

"For despite his awesome powers," said the rabbi, "the dreaded Angel of Destruction is not even permitted to enter the city of Luz."

Why does the Angel of Death have no power over the inhabitants of Luz? After all, does not the whole world lie within his domain? Even in the Holy Land people die. Neither can it be that the city of Luz is situated in a holy place, since no place is so holy as the Holy Land. Nor has the merit of its builder exempted Luz from the power of the Angel of Death, for there have been many builders whose merit far exceeds his.

Rabbi Yitzchak was noted for his ability to offer explanations for the mysteries posed by his teacher Rabbi Shimon. But even Rabbi Yitzchak could find no explanation for Luz being free from the sting of death. "I do not know what to say about this matter," he declared. "Therefore I shall say nothing."

The other disciples, hungering for an explanation of this strange phenomenon, turned to Rabbi Shimon and pleaded with him to tell them why the Angel of Death had no power over this place.

"The Holy One, blessed be He, has forbidden the Destroyer all access to the city of Luz," he told them. "It is His will that no one in that place should ever die. And the building of the city has nothing to do with it: even before the city was erected, those who dwelled on that site, shepherds and nomads, were not subject to death. From the time of the world's creation, Luz was free from the influence of death. For those who would penetrate into the deepest mysteries of God's wisdom, this matter represents the mystery of all mysteries. Listen, and I shall explain.

"When the Holy One, blessed be He, created the world, He used the secret power of the Hebrew letters. All the letters of the alphabet revolved around Him, and from them He took hold of the letters of the Divine Name. Tracing these letters, He set about creating the world.

"The rest of the letters then lined up before Him to take part in the world's creation, according to the various combinations they could form. The Holy One took the letters in all their permutations and fashioned the world in its many aspects. Every letter played its part. Every one, that is, except the letter *tet*. After all the other letters were assigned their role in creation, it was left hanging alone over the place where the city of Luz now stands.

"Now the letter *tet* is the first letter in the word *tov*, which means 'good.' Therefore, just as all that lives is radiant with good, this letter is radiant with the light of life. So God decreed that death should forever turn away from the place over which the tet is situated. Since death turns away from that site, it was named Luz, which means "turns away from." That is why it is a good omen when a man beholds the letter *tet* in his dreams.

"Once He had created the world, the Holy One wanted to see that it was firmly established. So He took a stone and engraved upon it the mystery of the twenty-two letters of the Hebrew alphabet. Then He cast the stone upon the waters of the deep. It drifted from place to place but could find nowhere to rest, until it came to the Holy Land. Once it reached the shores of Israel, the waters continued to carry it upward, into the mountains, until finally it came to rest on the Temple Mount. There the altar was to be established. Having reached the site for which it was intended, the stone sank into the earth to become the foundation for all the world."

"But why," Rabbi Yitzchak wanted to know, "was the Temple not built on the site where the city of Luz stands, since in that place life rules over death?"

"In the city of Luz," Rabbi Shimon explained, "there abides only one letter, while in the Temple we have all the letters of the alphabet, the letters from which the entire universe, both Heaven and earth, came into being. That is why the Holy Land, with the Temple at its center, imparts life to all, both in this world and in the world beyond. But the city of Luz can give life only to those who dwell in this world, and only to those who reside in that city. The purpose of the Temple, you see, was to bring forgiveness for the sins of Israel and thus make it possible for the children of Israel to find a dwelling place in the World to Come.

"Mark this well. The letter *tet* signifies the light of life in all places. That is why it is the first letter in the word *tov*. Whenever the Angel of Destruction encounters this letter, he is put to flight, for he has no power over the light of the good. Opposite the *tet* is the letter *kuf*, which is the first letter in the word *kelalah*, 'curse.' Just as the letter *tet* dominates the city where no one dies, the letter *kuf* dominates the realm of death itself, the place we call Geihinnom."

Rabbi Yitzchak and all those who heard the words of Rabbi Shimon came to understand something of the mystery of Creation, which is the mystery of the Good. They understood what lay behind God's utterance of the words *ki tov*, "it is good," at the time of the Creation: it is the life that death cannot comprehend.

The Innkeeper's Daughter

FROM ZOHAR ON EXODUS, 165B–169A

Light and the lamp from which it issues, like husband and wife, need each other in order to exist. Where the two come together, dwelling comes into being, and the two come together most sublimely in marriage. The Talmud teaches that blessing comes to a man's home only by virtue of his wife. According to the Midrash, the Torah had to be accepted by the House of Jacob, or the women among the Jews, before it could be received by the House of Israel, the men who stood at Sinai. For we need the lamp in order to have the light.

While traveling together, Rabbi Chiyya and Rabbi Yose stopped for the night at an inn. After settling in for the evening, and in keeping with their custom, they rose at midnight to study the Torah.

Now the innkeeper's daughter, a pious woman who was devoted to her guests, heard them stir. She rose up and lit a lamp for the rabbis, but instead of retiring for the night, she tarried for a while, so that, unbeknownst to the rabbis, she might listen to the words of the Torah that came from their lips.

Rabbi Yose began by citing a verse from Solomon's Book of Proverbs: "For the commandment is a lamp and the Torah is a light, and reproofs of instruction are the way of life."

"This teaches us," Rabbi Yose suggested to Rabbi Chiyya, "that those who strive to live by the commandments in this world will have a lamp lit for them in the World to Come. For each commandment that we observe brings light to both worlds. And he who studies the Torah will receive the supernal light, from which the lamp derives its light. Surely a lamp that is not lit has no value, and light cannot shine without a lamp: each has need of the other. Acts of righteousness and lovingkindness, therefore, are necessary for preparing the lamp, and the study of the Torah is necessary to light it. Blessed is he who has both the lamp of lovingkindness and the light of the Torah!"

"Well said," Rabbi Chiyya commented, as he examined the text from Proverbs by the light of the lamp that the innkeeper's daughter had brought them. "But what do you say about the reproofs of instruction that are the way of life?"

Rabbi Yose answered, "Since no one comes into the world perfect, no one can enter into the World to Come unless he receives reproofs and instructions from others, so that he may better avoid evil and embrace good. We have no means of purification except by reproof. Blessed is he who has been reproved for the sake of his soul!"

"Perhaps," Rabbi Chiyya suggested, "the lamp of the commandment is the lamp of David, which is called the oral Torah. The oral Torah is like a lamp that is continually cared for and attended to, so that we may better receive the light from the written Torah. Like the lamp, the oral Torah has no light in itself. All the light that it has, it receives from the written Torah, which is the true source of all illumination."

"Very good." Rabbi Yose nodded his approval of his companion's insight, when he turned and caught sight of the innkeeper's daughter standing behind them. Seeing her there, he gained further insight into the verse they were studying.

"The commandment is a lamp," he declared. "What sort of lamp is it? It is the lamp that belongs to women: it is the lamp of the Sabbath light. Men who are blessed with the opportunity of studying Torah give light to the lamp that is the woman's duty to light. To women belongs the merit of preparing the lamp; without them the world would be left to darkness. To men belongs the study of Torah: it is they who must bring the light to the lamp that women prepare. Therefore both are needed to overcome the darkness of the void. Without one, the other would be lost, and creation would revert to nothingness."

Upon hearing these words, the innkeeper's daughter began to weep. At that moment her father appeared, and, seeing his daughter's tears, he asked why she was crying. When she had explained to him all that she had heard, he too fell to weeping. Rabbi Yose tried to guess why.

"Could it be," he asked the innkeeper, "that your son-in-law, your daughter's husband, is an ignorant man?"

"Alas, yes," replied the innkeeper, "it is so. That is why my daughter and I are forever in tears. Would you believe it? I once saw him jump off a high roof just to be present in the midst of a congregation that was reciting the Kaddish. At the time I said to myself, 'Surely one so devout as to leap from a roof just to be present for the Prayer for the Dead will one day become a great scholar. He would be a wonderful match for my daughter.' On that very day, after the congregation had left, I offered him my daughter's hand in marriage. He was but a youth, and I did not know him very well. Still he seemed to have great potential."

"And now?" Rabbi Chiyya asked.

"Now he does not even know how to recite the Grace after Meals," the innkeeper lamented. "I have even been unable to teach him to say the *Shema* prayer."

"Then perhaps you should consider making a change," Rabbi Yose suggested, "and find another husband for your daughter."

Just then the young man of whom they spoke came into the room and seated himself at the rabbis' feet. Rabbi Yose gazed long upon him. Finally he declared, "Either from this young man or from his descendants the light of the Torah will emanate into the world!"

At this the youth smiled and said, "My masters, may I please be allowed to speak a few words in your presence?"

The rabbis nodded, and he began to expound mysteries of the Torah that neither of the sages had ever before fathomed. At the end of his discourse he saw their amazement, and so he explained, "I am the son of Rav Safra of Babylon, but, sadly, I never knew my father. When I came here to the Holy Land, the land of sages and

wise men, I resolved not to speak words of Torah in anyone's presence for at least two months. Better, I thought, to remain humble
before men such as yourselves and attend for a time to their words
before uttering my own. This very day, at midnight, those two
months came to an end. I have been blessed to have you here in
my father-in-law's inn."

"But how is it," Rabbi Yose asked, "that you are able to penetrate
such mysteries of the Torah but are unable to recite the Grace
after Meals? Can this be true?"

"I can recite the Grace after Meals," the young man answered.
"And I am deeply sorry for having caused my wife and my father-
in-law such grief over supposing that I do not know the prayer. But
until I had fully grasped all of its mysteries, I feared to speak words
that were as yet beyond my comprehension. That is why I have
not consummated our marriage: until this prayer is understood, a
marriage cannot be consummated."

Hearing this, Rabbi Yose and Rabbi Chiyya, the innkeeper and
his daughter, all broke into tears of joy. The rabbis listened to the
young man's insights on the Grace after Meals, and together they
continued to expound upon the Torah throughout the night. When
the sun rose the next morning, the innkeeper invited the villagers
to his inn for a great celebration. It was, indeed, a wedding celebration. For now that the young man had entered into the study
of the Torah, the Supernal Bride had entered the household and
had brought the lamp that now shone with the light of the Torah.

The Entrance of Death
and Demons into the World

FROM THE ZOHAR ON EXODUS, 231A–231B

*The first death, the death of Abel, was not a natural death but a murder,
which suggests that death is something alien to the world, as though it were
forced upon the world from some other realm. The same may be said of evil:
in a creation that God pronounces to be very good, it would seem that evil*

should have no place. This tale from the Kabbalah explains the unnatural means by which death and demons entered the world. It teaches us that when we become accomplices to death and evil, we undermine the foundations of creation itself.

When God gathered the dust of the four corners of the earth and created the first human being, He created a being that was both male and female: male in front and female behind. In order to provide man with a companion who might enable him to overcome the solitude of being, the Holy One separated the woman from the man. Thus two beings came into existence: Adam and Eve. God Himself created a wedding canopy for them and brought the woman unto the man. As they stood face to face before the Divine, they became man and wife, and love was multiplied in the world. With love came new life: Adam and Eve bore children.

But when Adam and Eve disobeyed God, the natural order of creation was undone. The serpent came unto Eve and lay with her. The beast planted within her a venomous seed, and from that seed was born a murderous creature, the one called Cain. Cain rose up and slew his brother Abel. Just as it is the way of the serpent to go into the field and lie in wait for his prey, so Cain went into the field and lay in wait for Abel. There he murdered his brother. Indeed, the ancient books tell us that when Cain fell upon Abel to kill him, Cain bit his brother repeatedly, after the manner of the serpent, until finally Abel's soul departed from his body. Thus was Abel slain, and his body returned to dust. Had Cain not borne the lower, unclean aspect of the serpent, he surely never would have acted toward his brother as he did.

Having seen Abel slain by his brother and Cain sent into exile, Adam despaired of having any children at all; he isolated himself from his wife Eve for one hundred thirty years. During that time, however, unclean female spirits tempted him, and he lay with them. From that unholy union demons were born into the world, those who are known as the "plagues of the children of men."

After those one hundred thirty years had gone by, Adam was once again overcome with longing for his wife Eve, and God brought Eve unto him in all her beauty. Adam joined with her, face to face, and the child called Seth was born in the image and likeness of his father, who in turn bore the image and likeness of God. And so with the birth of Seth man returned to woman, and humanity called upon the name of the Lord.

How God Chose Israel for the Torah

FROM THE ZOHAR ON NUMBERS, 192B–193A

The Torah was given at Sinai, outside of the land of Israel, we are taught, so that the Jews would not be so conceited as to think that it was theirs alone, nor the Gentiles so complacent as to suppose that it did not apply to them. The Torah, belongs to all the peoples of the world. This tale from the Zohar, in fact, suggests that the Torah first was offered to other peoples of the world before it was given to the Jews. But in order to receive the Torah, we must agree to live by it. The Jews had to place God's will above their own self-interest. That was something the other peoples of world would not agree to do.

The people of Israel were not the first to whom God offered His Torah. Indeed, before He approached the children of Isaac and Jacob, He offered His precious teaching to the children of the firstborn of Abraham and Isaac, to the children of Ishmael and Esau. When God descended to Seir, to the land where the children of Esau dwelled, which of the prophets from among them did He summon to receive the Torah? And when God went down to Paran, where the children of Ishmael abided, whom did He choose from among them to be His prophet? From the descendants of Esau He chose Samael, and from the offspring of Ishmael, Rahab.

The Torah came into the world from the mystic head of the King. When it descended down His left arm the Holy One saw that blood born of violence had collected where the left arm was outstretched. Realizing that blood shed in violence does damage to all of creation, He declared, "I must cleanse and purify this arm." However, the only means of purifying the left arm was through the Torah itself.

Thus the Lord God summoned Samael and asked him, "Do you desire My Torah?"

"What is written in it?" Samael wanted to know.

God answered, "Thou shalt not kill."

"Heaven forbid!" Samael cried. "I don't want it! This Torah is Yours, and Yours it shall remain. I shall have no part of it. But if You are seeking a people for whom such a Law is fitting, look to the sons of Jacob."

Samael suggested the Israelites to God in the conviction that they would fail to live by the Torah and would then be wiped off the face of the earth for their transgression. God knew what was in his mind, therefore He declined, saying, "You are the firstborn, and so it is fitting that you should receive My Torah."

"Oh, but I sold my birthright to Jacob and his offspring," Samael protested on behalf of Esau. "Your Torah should go to them."

"Very well," said God. "Since you desire not even a small portion in it, you will have no part of it. But tell Me how I might convince the children of Israel that they should accept My Torah."

Said Samael, "Take a portion of the light that illuminates all the heavens and cast it upon them. For this light is the light of the Torah, and once they are endowed with this light, they will accept Your commandments."

God saw that Samael had wisdom enough to see that the Torah was made of heavenly light, and that was enough to cleanse the blood from the left arm. He then turned to His right arm, which was in the same state. In order to cleanse the right arm, He called out to the Ishmaelite Rahab and said, "Do you desire My Torah?"

"What is written in it?" Rahab wanted to know.

"Thou shalt not commit adultery," God answered.

"Alas," cried the son of Ishmael, "I cannot accept it. For it was given to me to be fruitful and multiply indiscriminately. But two sons came forth from Abraham: Ishmael and Isaac. I beseech You, therefore, to offer Your Torah to the children of Isaac. They are much more suited for it than I."

"But you are the firstborn," God protested. "It is yours by your birthright."

"Then let the birthright I have inherited from Ishmael," said Rahab, "belong to the children of Isaac. Let the light of Your Torah be bestowed upon them."

God agreed to withhold His Torah from Rahab. He then summoned the prophets and the holy ones who had been appointed to lead the other nations of the world. To them, too, He offered His Torah, but they, too, refused. In His divine heart of hearts God rejoiced that He might give His Torah to the Israelites, like a physician with a phial filled with the elixir of life, who longs to keep it for his beloved son.

Said the physician to himself, "If the servants in my house knew that I intended to give this precious gift to my own son, they would grow jealous of him and seek to kill him."

What did the physician do? He took a touch of poison and smeared it around the edge of the phial. Next he summoned his servants and said, "Since you are my faithful servants, I offer you this life-giving drug. Would you care to try it?"

"First let us see what it is," they replied.

No sooner did they take a taste of the drug than they fell ill. "If the doctor gives this drug to his son," they thought to themselves, "the child will surely die, and we shall inherit the master's wealth."

"Master, this wondrous medicine is fit only for your son," they declared to the physician. "We do not deserve such a fine reward for our humble labor. Give it to your beloved child."

Like the wise physician, God knew that if He gave the Torah to Israel without first offering it to the other nations of the world, they would pursue His chosen and seek to kill them for the Torah they had received. In this way the people of Israel inherited God's most precious possession, His Torah, which they shared with the world.

Why the Jews Sway When They Pray

FROM THE ZOHAR ON NUMBERS, 218B–219A

Jews often sway back and forth when they pray. Jewish tradition regards study as a form of prayer, and from ancient times Jews have been known to sway back and forth when they study Torah as well. The usual explanation for this movement is that it is a means of maintaining concentration on the words before them. But the mystics have another explanation, which comes to us through this tale.

Rabbi Abba once related to his son Rabbi Yose a story about his travels with a certain companion.

"We were walking in the heat of the day and, as the sun began to beat down upon us more and more oppressively, we sought out a grove of trees with a pool of water beneath them. Once we reached the trees, we sat down in their shade to rest from the sun's heat. A soothing breeze came up, and the trees began to sway. Gazing upon their branches waving in the wind, I was reminded of Jews at prayer.

"And so I asked my companion, a man of great wisdom, 'Why is it that of all the peoples of the world only the Jews sway back and forth when they are at prayer or engaged in Torah study? Indeed, it is a habit that seems to be part of their nature, as though they cannot keep still, as though they were moved by something greater than themselves.'

"My companion answered, 'Your excellent question reminds me of a profound mystery about which very few people know.'

"At first he said nothing more but appeared to be lost in thought. As I waited for him to speak, I noticed that tears had come to his eyes. I was about to ask what was troubling him, when he said, 'It saddens me to think of all the people who go about like cattle, without any understanding of why they live or how they act.

"'The souls of the children of Israel were hewn from the Holy Lamp, as we are taught in the proverbs of Solomon: "The spirit of man is the lamp of the Lord." Once this lamp has been ignited by the sublime and supernal light of the Torah, it is like the flame that burns on the wick of a candle, forever moving and never ceasing.

"'As soon as a single word of Torah comes to the lips of a Jew, a light is kindled from on high, and he cannot keep still: he sways to and fro like a flame. When the words of the Torah are on his lips, he knows, however vaguely, why we live and die. The souls of heathens, on the other hand, burn as stubble burns, smoldering without a flame. They neither move, nor are they moved, when they engage in prayer or study: they are without the wisdom that sets the soul aflame.'

"After listening to my companion's answer to my question, I was immediately refreshed, as though a flame had been renewed in my soul, and we continued on our journey."

Having listened to his father's story, Rabbi Yose cried, "Surely a great blessing came to you in hearing your companion's words. And blessing has fallen to me for hearing the tale!"

The Selection of a Successor

FROM DIVREI YOSEF

Soon after the expulsion of the Jews from Spain in 1492, a new center of Jewish mysticism was established in Safed (northern Palestine). Among the founders of the new school of mysticism were Rabbi Yosef Karo, author of the famous code of Jewish law known as the Shulchan Aruch (Prepared Table), *and Rabbi Mosheh Cordovero. In this tale from* Divrei Yosef, *(Words of Yosef; 1896 Berlin edition, edited by A. Berliner), we have an account of how a leader was chosen to succeed Rabbi Mosheh after his death in 1570. Rabbi Yitzchak Luria, the Ari, the Lion, was to become the most famous mystic of the sixteenth century.*

At the young age of forty-eight, Rabbi Mosheh Cordovero, leader of the mystics of Safed, lay dying. So sudden was the deadly illness that had befallen him that he did not have time to name his successor. His disciples gathered around his deathbed and begged him to choose the one who would take his place. But the rabbi refused. Instead he declared, "Look for this sign: the one who beholds the pillar of cloud at my funeral is the one you should follow."

With those words he died.

All of Safed was filled with sadness, and every Jew attended Rabbi Mosheh Cordovero's funeral. Among his disciples in the funeral procession was Rabbi Yitzchak Luria, who walked next to Rabbi Yosef Karo, one of the elders of Safed. "Rabbi," said Yitzchak to Yosef, "have you noticed the pillar of cloud that has floated along in front of us ever since we left the synagogue?"

"What pillar of cloud?" asked Rabbi Yosef.

"There!" Rabbi Yitzchak pointed straight ahead.

"I see nothing," Rabbi Yosef shook his head.

Realizing that only he was able to see the pillar of cloud, Rabbi Yitzchak wondered whether it was real. He rushed toward it and, to the amazement of all, suddenly vanished into thin air. No one knew that he had entered the pillar of cloud, since no one could see it. Only a few moments had gone by when, just as suddenly, Rabbi Yitzchak reappeared.

It was not, however, the same Rabbi Yitzchak, for he had been transformed, his face beaming like the face of Moses when he came down from Mount Sinai. Indeed, the cloud that Rabbi Yitzchak had just entered was the same cloud that Moses had entered on Mount Sinai. As the ancient cloud had carried Moses up to heaven, where he received the Torah from the Hand of God, so had it carried off Rabbi Yitzchak. The mysteries revealed to Moses were likewise revealed to Rabbi Yitzchak.

All who were present realized that this was a sign sent to them from the other side of death by their teacher Rabbi Mosheh. Soon after the rabbi's funeral many of the Jews of Safed came to Rabbi Yitzchak and asked to study with him. Although he hesitated at first, he finally agreed to receive them as his disciples. No longer was his holiness hidden.

The Prayer Most Dear

FROM SHAARE HA-EMUNAH

This tale appears in a collection of tales from Rabbi Yitzchak Luria's Safed school of mysticism called Shaare ha-Emunah, The Gates of Faith *(1903 Warsaw edition, edited by N. Dinner). Although Rabbi Luria is a character in the story, it is not a tale about him. Rather, it is about the humility and the passion that are the substance of prayer, the intensity and the longing that infuse the words uttered by one who prays. It is about the truth of all prayer that is beyond all words, the truth of how we draw nigh unto God.*

As the Ari stood in the synagogue of Safed one Yom Kippur, his prayers taking him to the heights of Heaven, an angel appeared at his side. The Ari did not notice the angel until the angel whispered in his ear.

"You think you know how to pray?" the angel asked. "I know of a man whose prayers have penetrated the highest reaches of Heaven. His name is Amos, and he lives in Tiberias. If you want to know what prayers are most precious to the Holy One, you must seek him out."

As soon as Yom Kippur came to a close, the Ari lost no time heeding the words of the angel. He immediately set off for Tiberias to seek out the man whose prayers were most precious to God.

When he reached the city, it was time for the afternoon worship. The Ari said to himself, "I shall go to the house of study, where the men are no doubt holding the Minchah service. Surely the one called Amos will be there."

But the man he sought was not in the house of study.

After concluding his prayers in the study house, the Ari decided to search for the man in the market place. "Perhaps," he thought, "the one I seek is a tradesman and is unable to attend afternoon services."

There too, however, the Ari searched in vain. But one of the merchants told him about a poor farmer by the name of Amos who lived in the mountains on the outskirts of the city.

"Could it be," he asked himself, "that a simple farmer has mastered what the masters themselves cannot?"

The Ari hiked into the mountains and at last came to a house that was no more than a hut. A man answered his knock, and the Ari inquired, "Are you the one called Amos?"

"I am," the man replied. "Please come in."

Happy to have found Amos, the Ari wasted no time and said, "Please, I have come to learn from you the secret of your prayers."

Puzzled and somewhat embarrassed by the Ari's request, the man replied, "But rabbi, I do not know how to pray. I cannot even read, and so the prayer book is closed to me. All I know is how to recite a few letters of the alphabet, from *alef* to *yud*."

The Ari could not believe his ears. Had the angel not declared to him that the prayers of the man in Tiberias named Amos were prayers most precious to God? "Were you in the synagogue on Yom Kippur?" the Ari asked.

"Of course," the man answered. "Where else would I be on Yom Kippur?"

"Did you not pray with the congregation on that day?" the Ari wanted to know.

"I could not pray as they did," the man explained. "But when I saw how beautifully and passionately everyone around me was praying, my heart overflowed with longing. Suddenly, as though they had a life of their own, the letters of the alphabet came to my lips. In the depths of my heart I said, 'Dear God, Lord of the Universe, please take these letters from the lips of an ignorant man and make them into prayers that will rise unto Your ears, as it pleases You, my Lord!' That was the prayer that I repeated over and over, a prayer about praying."

Having heard what the man had said, the Ari realized that God had blessed him by bringing him to this poor farmer. Through this humble man God had revealed to him the secret of the prayer most precious to the Holy One: it is the prayer that rises up from the heart—the true dwelling place of Him who dwells in the highest reaches of heaven.

Blessed is he who knows that within and above are synonyms.

A Year for Each Letter

FROM SHIVCHEI HA-ARI

This tale from Shivchei ha-Ari (In Praise of the Ari; 1905 Jerusalem edition, edited by S. Meinsterl) contains several mystical elements. First, it shows us the powers of Rabbi Yitzchak Luria, the Ari, to peer into one of the deepest mysteries of heaven—the names inscribed in the Book of Life. Second, it shows us the power of prayer to transport a person into the heavenly realm where the Shechinah, the divine presence, dwells. Finally, it shows us that the light of the Shechinah is the light of life itself.

Yom Kippur, the Day of Atonement, had just come to a close, when Rabbi Yitzchak Luria, went to his disciple Rabbi Avraham Beruchim and declared, "Each Yom Kippur the names of those inscribed in the Book of Life for the coming year are revealed to me. Yours is not among them. Unless you do what is necessary to abolish the decree that has come forth from heaven, this will be your last year on earth."

Hearing these words, Rabbi Avraham grew afraid and asked, "What must I do to avert the decree?"

"You must leave for Jerusalem as soon as possible," Rabbi Yitzchak explained. "When you arrive in the city, go to the Western Wall, the last remnant of the holy Temple, and pour out your soul to God. If your prayers are worthy, you will have a vision of the Shechinah. That will be a sign that the decree has been suspended and your name has been inscribed in the Book of Life."

Rabbi Avraham did just as the Ari told him. After fasting for three days and three nights to purify himself for his prayers, he set out from Safed for the holy city. In order to further purify his soul, he chose not to go by donkey or wagon but instead walked the whole way. By the time he reached the gates of Jerusalem, he felt as though he were floating on air.

Once inside the city, he went straight to the Western Wall. As he approached the ancient stones that had heard so many prayers, his lips began to move in prayer. With every word he felt more and more as though his soul were about to leave his body and ascend to heaven. Just when he thought his soul would indeed depart, he saw an old woman dressed in black and deep in mourning emerge from the wall before him.

"It is the Shechinah!" the rabbi gasped to himself. "Oh, how she mourns over the destruction of her Temple and the exile of her children!"

The Shechinah walked toward him, drawing closer and closer, until she walked into him. Suddenly her sadness became his sadness. Suddenly he knew the unfathomable grief of a bride who has lost her groom, of a mother who has lost her child. He fell into a swoon and had a vision.

In his vision he saw the Shechinah once more, this time adorned in a robe of light, more brilliant than the sun at midday. Through the light that beamed from her face he could see the radiance of her joy. She reached out to him, cradled him in her arms, and whispered, "Do not despair, Avraham. My children will be returned to their homeland, and you will enjoy many blessings in the years to come."

Rabbi Avraham awoke from his vision full of the joy of a renewed life and returned to Safed. There he went to Rabbi Yitzchak, who told him, "I see that you have been in the presence of the Shechinah. I see, too, that you will have twenty-two more years of life, one for each letter of the Hebrew alphabet, from which the words of your prayers are made. For the light of the Shechinah emanates from every letter—every letter is an avenue to the Shechinah—and the Shechinah has filled you with her light."

Why We Have Been Created

FROM SEFER HA-CHEZYONOT

This tale is based on an account from a book by Rabbi Chayym Vital, one of the disciples of Rabbi Yitzchak Luria, the Ari, called Sefer ha-Chezyonot *(Book of Visions). It articulates the primary aim of the mystics: to hasten the coming of the Messiah. According to mystical belief, when God brought the light of holiness into being, sparks of that light were gathered into mysterious vessels. When the material world was created, however, the vessels broke, and the sparks of light were lost, so that humanity is now blind to the light of holiness. The task of the mystic is to gather up the sparks hidden in the shells of matter and restore the vessels that hold them. Once the sparks have been gathered and the vessels restored, the Messiah will appear.*

One night during the new moon of the first of the month, Rabbi Yitzchak Luria gathered together a group of his disciples. "Come with me," he told them.

They followed their master into the darkness of the night. Although they had no torch to light the way, a mysterious aura that emanated from the Ari illuminated their path.

"Where could he be taking us?" they wondered.

Before long they arrived at the tomb of Rabbi Shimon bar Yochai, the Talmudic sage who, according to legend, was the author of the

Zohar. As soon as they were standing at the sage's tomb, Rabbi Yitzchak began to rock back and forth in prayer, and his disciples joined him. After a time the Ari ceased praying and fell silent. Just at midnight, he spoke.

"Tonight I reveal to you," he said "the mystery of the shattering of the vessels and the gathering of the sparks. Long before the luminaries of the heavens were created, long before the holy word brought heaven and earth into being, a flame arose from a single point so small as to be invisible. From the depths of that flame sparks of light burst forth and were placed in vessels. Those vessels carried the light, which was the light of holiness, into all the spheres of heaven and earth, like ships bearing a cargo more precious than diamonds. But the light was too much for the vessels. They broke into bits, and the light was scattered throughout the world.

"So you see why we have been created: we must search for the sparks of light, wherever they may be, and raise them to holiness. Once all the sparks of the divine light have been collected, the vessels that once contained them will be restored. On that day we shall rejoice in the coming of the Messiah."

The moment the Ari finished speaking, a star shot across the sky. When his disciples saw the trail that streaked through the heavens, they knew that the words of their teacher had been heard above. They knew that the movement below stirs the movement above. And they knew that another spark had been gathered.

The Lie Told Before the Kabbalah

FROM NIFLAOT MAHARAL

One of Rabbi Yitzchak Luria's famous contemporaries was Rabbi Yehudah Loeb, known as the Maharal (an acronym standing for Our Teacher Rabbi Loeb) of Prague. Taken from a work titled Niflaot Maharal *(Wonders of the Maharal, 1909 Piotrkow edition, edited by Y. Rosenberg), this story reveals the dangers of attempting to study Kabbalah with a lie upon one's lips.*

There was once a count who lived in Prague during the time of Rabbi Yehudah Loeb, the Maharal. The count was obsessed with probing the secrets of heaven and earth. Having heard that the Kabbalah possessed the key to all mysteries, he collected as many volumes of kabbalistic texts as he could. Finally, the day came when he believed he was ready to study them. Knowing that the Maharal was thoroughly versed in the mysteries of the Kabbalah, the count summoned him to his castle.

"I want you to reveal to me the secrets of the Kabbalah," he told the rabbi.

"I cannot do that," the rabbi replied. "There are serious difficulties and great dangers involved, even for a Jew—and especially for one who is not a Jew."

The count, however, was very insistent and resorted to threats. He knew the Maharal would not be intimidated by threats on his own life. So the count simply stated that he would go to the emperor and obtain permission to wipe out the Jews if the Maharal should refuse his request.

"Very well," the Maharal agreed at last.

The count took the Maharal to a secret room that he had prepared just for his study of the Kabbalah. The only light in the room came from a single lamp placed on a small table covered with ancient volumes of kabbalistic lore. Except for the table and the lamp, the room was empty.

"Let us begin," the count declared.

"We cannot begin," the Maharal hesitated, "until I have from you the answer to a question: Are you free of all guilt? Beware how you answer, for any guilt that you bring to the Kabbalah, any transgression unatoned for, could lead you into grave danger."

"I am free of all guilt," the count insisted.

"Are you sure?" the Maharal asked. "A lie would only compound the guilt and put you in even greater danger."

"I tell you I am an innocent man!" the count shouted.

"Then turn around!" the Maharal answered.

The count turned and saw standing before him a young woman with a baby in her arms. His face twisted into a look of horror, and he cried, "No! No! It cannot be!"

"Do you know them?" asked the Maharal.

"It is my sister and her baby boy," the count gasped. "But it cannot be! They are dead!"

"How do you know?" the rabbi pressed the count.

"Because I . . . I . . . "

"Because you murdered them," the rabbi declared. "The child was your own, conceived in incest, and you murdered them both to hide your sin."

At that the count fell into a faint. When the Maharal had revived him, the count vowed that he would never again seek out the secrets of the Kabbalah. But a night did not go by that he did not wake up screaming at the terrifying visions of the sister and child he had murdered. And before long he was a broken man.

Legends
and Folktales

WHAT DISTINGUISHES LEGENDS from folktales, and what do the two have in common? Generally speaking, legends are about a famous figure from a people's past, a hero or a sage who has been part of the development of a people's character and tradition. Folktales, on the other hand, usually deal with common people and often include elements peculiar to the culture of a given region or period in history. Both legends and folktales are the creations of a people—in this case the Jewish people—and not of a specific author. Both may include fantastic or mythic elements, and both generally convey some teaching about what is valued by the culture from which they arise.

Although there has been a proliferation of written literature over the last several centuries, the oral tradition of Jewish legends and folktales has also continued to grow. Indeed, it has greatly influenced the written body of Jewish literature. There is no shortage of anthologies in which various versions of these stories appear, and many Jewish authors have incorporated them into their own work. The growth in the wealth of oral lore over the centuries led to the establishment of the Israel Folktale Archives (IFA) in 1955 by Professor Dov Noy, and several of the folktales in this section can be found in those archives. Today the IFA is located in the Faculty of Humanities at the University of Haifa and contains over twenty thousand folktales from fourteen different ethnic groups. In many cases, the same tales have been told, with slight variations, in several different cultures. The term *Jewish*, then, does not denote an ethnic, geographical, cultural, or racial category. Although they are one in their embrace of the Torah, the Jews are quite varied in their cultural environments and origins.

One thing that distinguishes these legends and folktales as Jewish is their intimate connection to the Jewish religious tradition. The tales of the Jewish people are so intricately interwoven with the teachings of their faith and the writings of their tradition that it is difficult to imagine one without the other. Perhaps this is because the Jewish faith places its accent on living in the world of humanity, and not on the retreat from the world or on aspirations for another world. If study is empty without deeds, among the deeds that complement our study is telling these tales that have so much to do with making a life. For the task of living in the world of humanity is the subject matter most fundamental to Jewish legends and folktales.

How the Second Became the First

The letters of the Hebrew alphabet have an important place in Jewish legends and folklore. The legends surrounding certain letters go back to the very beginning of the Jewish concern with words and their meaning, a concern rooted in the teaching that all things come into being through the word. Indeed, the letters of the alphabet, like the Word of the Holy One, do not belong to created being. They existed prior to the Creation, and they have a life of their own—like this tale that is more than a thousand years old.

Before heaven and earth came into being, in the time before time, the letters of the Hebrew alphabet had an argument over which of them would be the first letter in the Torah, the first in God's act of creation.

"I should be the first," the letter *tet* insisted, "for the word *tov*, meaning 'good,' begins with *tet*."

"No," the letter *shin* argued, "I should be first. After all, I begin the word *Shabbat*, and it is through the *Shabbat*, the Sabbath, that all of Creation is to be sanctified."

"What about me?" the letter *tav* put it. "Without me Torah itself would have no being, since I am the first letter in the word *Torah*."

God listened to each letter's claim to merit; each time He heard a letter's argument, He rejected it. Each time, that is, until the letter *beit* stepped forward.

Without insisting upon any worthiness of its own, the letter *beit*, the second letter of the alphabet, simply reminded the others, "I begin the word *baruch*, which is 'blessed.'"

That was all the Holy One had to hear. Immediately He selected the letter *beit* to be the first letter of His Torah, the letter that is the basis of all Creation.

"Although *beit* comes second in the alphabet," He explained, "it will come first in My creation. For this is the letter that lies at the beginning of all the blessings I shall confer upon humanity and that humanity will offer up to Me. Without these blessings, the world cannot endure."

Thus the Torah begins with the letter *beit*, the first letter of the first word of the Torah: *bereshit*, which means "in the beginning."

Meanwhile one other letter had refrained from all the arguing and remained silent. Indeed, it was the silent letter that begins the alphabet itself, the letter *alef*, which designates the silence of all tongues that form these letters. Pleased with its humility, God turned to the *alef* and declared, "Because you have refrained from all this squabbling over which letter is the most worthy, you shall be placed at the beginning of the Revelation at Sinai, just as the *beit* is to be placed at the beginning of Creation."

And so *alef* is the first letter in God's utterance of *Anochi*, or "I," at Mount Sinai, the first to usher in God's revelation of Himself and His Torah to all of humanity.

From the Tears of Truth

Arising from Ashkenazi, or East European Jewry, this legend is about the creation of the first human being. Since it is about the origin of all human-ity, it is about the substance of all humanity. It deals with the nature of our relation to God and the divine aspect of our being, for each of us comes from the hand of God. And it deals with a human longing that is not only a longing for the truth—it is the longing of the truth; for the truth is not a fact or a datum but a living presence that sanctifies life.

As God prepared to form the first human being on the sixth day of Creation, four angels gathered around Him to serve as godpar-ents: the Angel of Mercy, the Angel of Truth, the Angel of Peace, and the Angel of Justice. Before God could even begin the work of creating a human being, however, the four angels fell into an argu-ment over whether such a being should be created at all.

"This creature may come from the hand of the Holy One," said the Angel of Justice, "but he is to be neither God nor an angel. Therefore he is sure to be imperfect and fall into sin. When that happens, he will have to be destroyed in the name of Justice."

"Perhaps," the Angel of Mercy put it, "but the Infinity of the

Infinite One lies in His infinite mercy and compassion. Therefore
He should proceed with this creation."

The Angel of Peace tried to settle the dispute between Mercy
and Justice, declaring that the very meaning that God imparts to
life rests on the relationship between the two divine attributes of
compassion and judgment. As for the Angel of Truth, he objected
to the creation of man most vehemently of all.

"Many of these human beings," he said, "will live by deception and
die by deception. And those who do not succumb to lies will spend
their lives in suffering, seeking the truth that they can never grasp."

Hearing these words from the Angel of Truth angered God. He
punished the Angel by casting him out of heaven and condemning
him to walk the earth for all eternity. But Mercy, Justice, and Peace
begged God to pardon the Angel.

"Surely heaven cannot endure without Truth!" they cried in a
single voice.

God summoned the Angel of Truth back to heaven, but the
Angel did not return empty-handed. He brought with him a clod
of earth that was soaked with the tears he shed upon being banished from the presence of God. And from that clod soaked with
the tears of truth God created the first human being.

The Story of Adam's Fear

*Creation begins with light, and with light comes truth, meaning, and good-
ness. In times of darkness, we are given over to fear. The first human being,
Adam, was beset by fear. But God answered his trembling by bringing to
him the light that illuminates all of life. That is the light Jews usher into the
world with the lighting of the candles each Sabbath eve.*

Adam came into being on the sixth day of Creation, before the Sabbath came into being. When Adam opened his eyes for the first time,
he saw the light of day and rejoiced in the world that God had pronounced to be very good. But soon he noticed something that made
him tremble with fear: the sun was sinking toward the horizon.

He reached out toward the sun, but, despite his great stature, he could not grasp the luminary to stay its motion. As the fiery disk sank lower and lower in the west, Adam's fear grew greater and greater. Inevitably the sun reached the edge of the earth, and the light slowly faded. When the light diminished to darkness, Adam's fear turned to terror. He was hopelessly lost and horribly alone in a night that, as far as he knew, had no end.

But on this first night of Adam's life came the first Sabbath; with the coming of the Sabbath, God enters into His creation. When God saw that Adam was so terribly afraid, He took pity on the man and led him to find two stones of flint. Adam took the stones and rubbed them together to create fire and light.

Grateful for having received this light from the Creator, Adam cried out, "Blessed be the Creator of the light born of fire!"

Thus fire was a gift given by God to Adam to deliver him from the darkness of night—and to usher in the Sabbath with the kindling of a light.

Abraham and Nimrod

Similar to a story recounted in the Midrash, this tale comes from the legends of the Jews of Ethiopia and dates back to pre-Talmudic times. According to the fifteenth-century rabbi David ben Shelomoh ibn Avi Zimra, the Ethiopian Jews are the descendants of the tribe of Dan, which was sent into exile with the Assyrian invasion of the kingdom of Israel in 722 B.C.E. Some accounts maintain that the Ethiopian Jews are descendants of the children born to Moses after he fled from Egypt, while others claim they are the offspring of King Solomon and the Queen of Sheba. According to yet another legend, the Ethiopian Jews were among the Jews of the Exodus who failed to make it across the Red Sea. In any case, they lived in relative isolation in the hills of Ethiopia, until the Israelis airlifted them out on 26 May 1991 in what was called Operation Solomon. With them there came out of Ethiopia a wealth of legend and folklore.

One day, long ago, the wise men of Canaan approached King Nimrod and declared, "Behold! One called Terach is about to bear a son who will undermine and destroy the ways of the Canaanites!"

Indeed, even as they spoke, a son was born to Terach, whom he named Abraham. But word had come to Terach of the wise men's warning. Fearing for his son's life as well as his own, Terach hid Abraham away in his house for seven years, never allowing him to step outside.

After the seven years passed, Terach let his son go outside one night. The boy looked up in wonder at the moon and the stars and declared, "These will be my lords and masters, and I shall worship them all the days of my life!"

Terach was pleased to hear these words, for it was the way of the Canaanites to worship the luminaries of the heavens. But, as Abraham stood gazing at the sky, he saw the moon sinking toward the horizon and some of the stars descending from sight. When they had disappeared, he said, "Neither the moon nor the stars are worthy of worship, for the darkness is greater than they are."

Hearing such blasphemy from his son's mouth, Terach hid him away once again in his house. A few days later, however, he allowed Abraham to go outside during the day, at noon.

The lad looked up, saw the brilliance of the sun, and was amazed. "This will be my God," he declared, "for it is the brightest of all the heavenly lights."

But, like the moon, the sun set, and the day gave way to night. Therefore Abraham turned to face the east and offered up his prayer, saying, "Neither the sun nor the moon is God but You, O Nameless One, who created both. To You, the Creator of all things, shall I bow down and to no other."

Fearing that his son might utterly fall from the ways of the Canaanites, Terach put him to work in his shop making idols. One day, while his father was away for a short time, Abraham took an ax and smashed all but the largest of the idols. Then he laid the ax next to the earthen figure.

When Terach returned and saw the broken shards of clay littering the floor, he knew immediately what had happened. He turned to Abraham and demanded, "Why have you broken my idols?"

"I didn't do it," the boy answered. "It was this one here, the one with the ax propped up against it. The one that you yourself worship."

"Do you take me for a fool?" his father shouted. "That piece of clay cannot break anything!"

"Then why do you worship it?" Abraham asked. "A man who worships dead things brings death to himself, his parents, and his children."

At that Terach was more afraid than ever that his son would destroy the religion of the Canaanites and that he himself would be blamed for it. So he took the boy to Nimrod and declared, "Your Majesty, my name is Terach, and my son has renounced the idols of our people and broken them to bits! I have brought him to you in the hope that in your mercy you might save him from his folly!"

Hearing the name of Terach, King Nimrod remembered what the wise men had told him years before. Cautiously he turned to the child and said, "Surely this cannot be true, my boy. Come, let's you and I bow down to this idol and worship it together."

But Abraham refused, insisting, "My God is not a piece of clay or anything else that meets the eye but is the Infinite and Invisible One who dwells in heaven, the Creator of the sun and the moon, of the earth and the sky. Indeed, it is He who has appointed you King of Canaan. Were it not His will, you could not rule."

Nimrod grew angry at such impudent words and cried, "Then I shall ascend unto heaven where this god dwells and kill him!"

The king sent for his bow and arrows and climbed atop a huge vulture that he kept on the palace grounds. Riding on the bird's back, he flew up into the clouds. There he found an eagle soaring in the heavens and shot it through with one of his arrows. Before the eagle could fall to the ground, the vulture swooped under it, and Nimrod retrieved the bloody arrow. Then he returned to earth and showed the arrow to Abraham.

"Behold," he boasted, "the blood of your god. I have killed him."

But Abraham would not be duped.

"My God cannot die," he said. "It is He who brings life and death to all."

At that the Canaanite king order a thousand camels and a thousand woodsmen to be sent into the forest to fell a thousand trees. Then, at his command, his servants dug a pit on top of a hill, laid the trees into it, and set the timber on fire.

As the flames rose higher, Nimrod invited the rebellious son of Terach one last time to bow down with him and worship the idol of the Canaanites. But still Abraham refused.

"Do you not understand, foolish boy," the angry King urged him, "that if you persist in your stubbornness, you will be burned to death in these flames?"

"I understand," Abraham answered. "And I refuse."

Abraham was cast into the inferno.

But just at that moment God sent the angel Gabriel into the furnace, where he transformed himself into a massive fountain of water. Immediately the flames were extinguished, and the child called Abraham was saved.

The Hospitality of Abraham

The righteousness for which Abraham was known manifested itself in his concern for his fellow human beings. As we discover in this ancient tale, his capacity to dwell in the Holy Land lay in his ability to make it possible for others to find a dwelling place. The lovingkindness we show to others has an impact on people in times and places completely unknown to us. Thus we may recall the teaching from the mystics that our every deed creates an angel for good or for evil. And the angels we so create go out into the world to work their good or evil. The scope of our responsibility for others, therefore, far exceeds our field of vision.

When Abraham came into the Promised Land, he immediately set about building a house with doors on every side. Why? So that weary travelers coming from every direction could find entry into his home and there enjoy his hospitality. He also planted a beautiful orchard all around his house, so that passersby could find relief in the shade of his trees and nourish themselves with their fruit. Therein lay the happiness of Abraham: providing food and shelter to those in need.

Once Abraham fell ill and could not rise from his bed for several days. Noticing that he had heard no visitors entering his house during that time, he grew concerned and sent for his servant Eliezer.

"Go outside," he ordered Eliezer, "and search the area to see if there are any wayfarers who are in need of a place to stay."

As always, Eliezer did just as his master had asked. But, after searching the vicinity of Abraham's house, he returned and said, "Forgive me, master, but I can find no one to whom you may open your house."

Despite his illness, Abraham was so distressed by this news that he rose from his bed and went out himself to look for someone to whom he might offer his hospitality. He searched everywhere, far and wide, but he too could find no travelers.

Seeing Abraham's eagerness to help those in need and his disappointment over finding no one to serve, God told the angels Michael, Gabriel, and Raphael to disguise themselves as men and go out to meet Abraham. When Abraham saw the three angels, whom he took to be simple folk walking down the road, he was so overjoyed that he ran ahead to greet them.

"Please," he said to them, "come into my home and allow me to provide you with food and rest. You must be exhausted from your travels."

Immediately he became so involved with ministering to their needs that he forgot the suffering and the pain that he had suffered in his illness. Indeed, it seemed that his care for them had cured him.

Once Abraham had attended to the comfort of the angels disguised as men, God appeared to him and said, "Because you have given food and drink to strangers, offering them the shelter and the comfort of your home, I shall do the same for your children. The time will come when they will wander in the wilderness with nothing to drink. In their wanderings I shall provide them with fountains of refreshing water. When the rays of the sun beat down upon them in the desert, I shall place a rain cloud above them to relieve their distress from the heat. When the pain of hunger overtakes them, I shall offer them manna from Heaven, so that they may eat and be satisfied."

Abraham rejoiced in God's words, realizing that, by the grace of the Holy One, his hospitality might extend to his children.

Abraham and the Angel of Death

While every person must die, each must die his own death. This Ethiopian tale about the death of Abraham teaches us that the death we die is determined by how we have lived. Does that mean that the righteous always die a pleasant death? No. It means that for the righteous death becomes part of the task of living, part of the witness they bear. It means that when a life has been devoted to good deeds, the Angel of Death comes to us not as something monstrous but as one bathed in the beauty and light that surround the testimony of our deeds. Our fear of death, then, should have more to do with what we have done than with what awaits us.

When the day of Abraham's death drew nigh, he held a great feast for all the poor, freed all his slaves, and gave away all of his possessions. Seeing these last good deeds of a man who lived his life in goodness, God turned to His angel Michael and said, "The time has come for the soul of My servant Abraham to depart from his body. But do not allow Death to appear to him in a terrifying form or make him tremble at the sight of its awesome image. See to it, rather, that Abraham's hour of death is an hour of good cheer, so that his soul may leave his body without being frightened."

Heeding the word of the Lord, Michael made known to the Angel of Death all that God had told him, as well as all the good deeds that Abraham had performed in his lifetime. Then he sent Death to the patriarch, for the man's hour was at hand.

When the Angel of Death entered Abraham's chamber, he found the old man asleep. Despite the angel's precautions, however, Abraham sensed his presence and awoke from his sleep in a state of agitation. Already he could feel his soul struggling to be released from his body.

As soon as he rose from his bed, he asked the Angel of Death, "Who are you? Tell me, please! From the instant I caught sight of you, I grew frightened in every bone of my body; my soul is struggling to flee. Are you an angel? If so, then I do not behold your glory. For whenever an angel has come to me, I have always been strengthened, my body and soul made glad, and my spirit illuminated. But your presence drains me of life's gladness. My soul is faint, my tongue is weak, and I feel the light of my eyes fading."

Before the Angel could reply, Abraham fell to weeping and cried out in a loud voice to his son Isaac, "Isaac, come here! There is a creature lurking about my chamber, and I am frightened! Old age has weakened my eyes, and I cannot see this stranger! Come, my son, please!"

Isaac immediately ran to his father's room, kissed his wrinkled brow, and said, "What is it, my father? Why do you weep? There is no one here. It is all right."

"O, my son, my beloved son," said Abraham. "If you do not see the one who has come for me, then it must be the Angel of Death, and the hour has come when your father's soul must leave his old body. Soon I shall depart from you, never to return, in keeping with what God wills for every man. Yes, my son, as you say, it is all right."

Hearing his father speak thus, Isaac began to weep, saying, "I am saddened, Father, that you are going to leave me and that I am going to become an orphan. Where shall I ever find anyone like you?"

"Please, my son, no tears," his father replied. "Know that God is with you. He will watch over you until the day of your own departure comes."

At that Abraham returned to his bed, where once again he came face to face with the Angel of Death.

"Please," he said, having grown calm, "tell me for certain who you are and what your name is."

"My name is Death, and I reap the souls of men," the angel answered. "People know me as bitterness and the source of all sorrow. Every soul is ultimately entrusted to my care. I am a terror to men and an affliction to mothers."

"But your form is so beautiful, your face full of light," Abraham said, "not at all full of bitterness and sorrow. Can you be so terrifying to men, having taken a form so beautiful as this?"

"Do not suppose that I come to everyone in such a form," the angel told him. "Only to the righteous do I appear in beauty. To those who sin and do violence to their neighbor I appear in the form of grotesque ugliness. And their souls I devour like a beast."

"But why do you appear to me in such beauty?" asked Abraham, taking no thought for his own righteousness.

"My beauty is yours and yours alone," the angel explained. "I draw nigh unto every man clothed in his deeds. And so I come to you dressed in your righteousness and lovingkindness."

The two of them were silent for a moment. Then the angel said, "Come now. It is time."

The Faith of Nachshon

Those who come to God empty-handed encounter Him as emptiness. In this legend of Nachshon, whose sister Elisheva married Aaron, we find that the one thing we have to offer God is our faith. The tale is an illustration of the teaching that God is the shadow of man. When we move toward God, He moves toward us; when we lose our faith and turn away from Him, God turns away from us. When Moses stood before the burning bush, God did not speak to him until he first moved toward the bush. And when he ascended Mount Sinai to receive the Torah a second time, he had to bring to God tablets he had fashioned with his own hands, so that God could write on them.

When the Israelites came out of Egypt and stood on the shores of the Red Sea with Pharaoh's armies bearing down upon them, they were afraid for their lives.

"What are we to do now?" they cried out to Moses. "Where can we go from here?"

Moses, too, was frightened. But instead of answering the people of Israel, he turned to God and said, "O Lord, Ruler of the Universe, we stand here on the edge of the deep, with no place to turn. Have You brought us here only to be slaughtered?"

In the hearing of all the children of Israel, God answered Moses, "It is in your own power to be delivered from the Egyptian forces. Do not just stand there and cry like helpless children. Cross the sea!"

Moses did not doubt the word of God, but he remained puzzled about what they should do. "Will He, then, part the waters for us?" he wondered.

As Moses stood and pondered, there emerged from the throng a man from the tribe of Judah. His name was Nachshon, and he had heard all that God had said. Moses saw the man coming toward him and thought that Nachshon wanted to offer him some advice. But instead of stopping before Moses, Nachshon walked on toward the sea.

"If the Lord God has told us to cross the sea," he said, "then we must cross the sea."

The fearful crowd looked on as Nachshon drew closer and closer to the waters.

"What is he doing?" they asked one another. "Has he gone mad?"

Paying them no heed, Nachshon went on, until he reached the edge of the waters, the waves breaking against his feet. But the waves did not deter him. He kept going as the water rose higher and higher around his legs.

"Nachshon!" his friends began to shout. "Come back! Are you trying to drown yourself? Think of your family!"

Nachshon ignored their pleas and did not turn back. His eyes set on the horizon, he splashed on. When the water reached his waist, it slowed him down, but it did not stop him. Indeed, it seemed to strengthen his resolve to press on.

Aghast at the folly of this man from the tribe of Judah, the Israelites had all but forgotten the Egyptians who were in pursuit. The Israelites moved closer to the water's edge and yelled for Nachshon to stop. But they would not go past the water's edge for fear that they too might drown.

By now the sea had climbed to Nachshon's chest. He waded farther still, his arms raised above the surface of the water that threatened to drown him with each step. The water rose to his chin, and he gasped for air, but still he lumbered on.

"Nachshon!" the cry of his comrades filled the air.

Just when it seemed certain that he would be swallowed up by the sea, a mighty wind parted the waters. The Israelites followed after the one they had thought to be mad, treading the bottom of the sea made dry by the faith of Nachshon.

The Death of Moses

Death is not a thing of horror to the righteous. Just as the mark of Abraham's righteousness was his concern for the welfare of others, Moses' righteousness shows itself in his loving concern for his family, as this tale from the legends of the Ethiopian Jews illustrates.

As Moses grew older and began to consider that the hour of his death might be growing near, he went to God and said, "O Lord, Sovereign of all Creation, I implore You, by the Holy Name that You have revealed to me to tell me on which day my soul will leave this world."

"You know that no man may know the day or the hour of his death," God answered. "Such things are revealed neither to the prophets nor to the angels. But since you, Moses, are My beloved servant, I shall tell you this much: the Angel of Death will come to claim your soul on a Friday."

Moses offered God his thanks, and every Friday after that he purified himself and donned his burial clothes to prepare for the approach of the Angel of Death. Weeks went by and turned into months, until finally Moses forgot about his preparations for death. One day he ascended Mount Sinai in order to pray to God, but before he could call out God's name, the Angel of Death appeared to him in the form of a young Israelite.

"Peace be upon you, Moses," the angel greeted him.

Right away Moses recognized the voice of the Angel of Death. Taken aback, his speech faltered, his knees shook, and he fell to his face. But no sooner had Moses fallen to the ground than he raised himself up and said, "Tell me truly, who are you? For when you greeted me just now, I swear I have never heard a voice so fearsome."

"Do you really not know me?" the Angel of Death replied. "I am the one who preys upon women and children, old men and young. I raze houses to the ground and build graveyards. As the Lord has ordained, I shall continue my work until the world comes to an end. Know, then, that my name is Suryal, the one known as the Angel of Death."

"I feared as much," said Moses. "But tell me: why have you come here now?"

"Today is Friday," the Angel reminded him. "I have come to claim your soul and take it to God."

Suddenly Moses remembered what God had revealed to him about the day of his death. "By the Holy One who sent you," he pleaded with the angel, "please do not take me just yet, but wait until the third hour of the morning, so that I may go and see my wife and children."

At the moment God said to the angel, "Leave the man alone until his appointed hour arrives."

So the angel left the old man in peace.

When Moses descended from Mount Sinai and was on his way home to his family, he came to a fork in the road. One path led to his wife and children, while the other led to his mother. Knowing that the hour of his death was at hand, he stood at the crossroads and wondered: "Should I take the path that leads home to my wife and children, or should I follow the road to my mother's house? After all, she brought me into the world, and I should bid farewell to her, too."

As he was trying to decide which way to go, he heard a voice from Heaven tell him, "Go first to see your mother."

So Moses went to visit his mother.

When he arrived, he called out, "Mother, please open your door."

Yocheved went to the door to invite him in. As soon as she looked at him, she saw that his face was filled with sorrow and his body was bent low.

"What happened to you, my son?" she asked. "Has some shepherd come and told you that your flocks have been lost?"

"No one calls out to me but God," Moses replied. "And no one frightens me but the Angel of Death."

Suddenly his mother understood and asked, "Can it be that the one who has spoken with God face to face and mouth to mouth will succumb to death?"

"Yes, Mother, it is so," said Moses. "It is God's will that all people, including the prophets, die. I have come to bid you farewell. I ask you to put your foot on my left side, stretch out your arms, and pray to God that He may ease the bitterness of death."

Yocheved did as her son asked. Then he kissed her and went on his way, shedding many tears.

As Yocheved watched her son, she declared, "Let us not believe in the ways of the world, but let us turn our eyes to Heaven to show us the path of truth."

When Moses arrived home, his spirit was faint and his body weak. As soon as his wife, Tsiporah, opened the door to let him in, she saw that he was bent and that his face had grown pale.

"What has happened, my beloved husband?" she asked. "Have your camels been stolen? Has your wealth been plundered?"

"No one calls out to me but God," Moses answered her. "And no one frightens me but the Angel of Death."

Realizing that he was speaking of his death, Tsiporah cried, "Is the one who has the ear of God to die?"

"Yes, my beloved," Moses replied. "As Abraham and all the prophets who lived before me died, so shall death come to me. Tell me, please: where are my children?"

"They are sleeping safely in their beds," she said as tears rose to her eyes.

"Please, bring them to me."

Sobbing with every step, Tsiporah did as her husband asked. After waking their children, she told them, "Come with me to your father to receive his last farewell and his final blessing, for the hour of his death is at hand."

When she stood before Moses with their children at her side, she instructed them, "Look long and hard upon your father, for you are soon to be parted from him forever."

The children fell to great weeping, and Moses wept with them. He took his younger son Eleazar and set him on his right knee. Then he placed his older son Gershom on his left. His voice overflowing with tenderness, Moses pronounced his blessing upon both of them, all the while weeping with such sorrow that Heaven and earth wept with him.

"Why do you weep?" the voice of God suddenly spoke to him. "Is it because you are parting from the earth, or is it because you fear death?"

"The sight of my wife and children moves me to tears," Moses explained. "Tsiporah's father Jethro is dead. My brother Aaron, too, has passed away. With whom, then, shall I leave them, now that I am about to die?"

"When you were born," God said to him, "your mother Yocheved placed you in a basket and cast you upon the waters. I led Tarmut, the daughter of Pharaoh, to find you along the shore of the river and take you into her house as though you were one of her own. I did not forget you then, and I shall not forget your wife and children now. Rise and offer them your kiss. For those who are to take your soul from this world are drawing nigh, and you must go out to meet them."

Heeding God's words, Moses kissed his wife and children farewell and set out from his house. With a faint heart and a pale face he walked, though he knew not where. After a short time he met three young men, who were digging a grave alongside the road.

"May God's peace be upon you," he greeted them.

They returned his greeting.

"Whose grave is this that you are digging?" he asked.

"It is the grave of one who is God's beloved," they replied.

Moses offered, "I shall help you dig."

When they had finished their task of digging, Moses said, "Bring the body of God's beloved, so that we may bury it."

Now the three young men, who were angels that had assumed human forms, told Moses, "We fear that the grave may be too small for the one whom we are to bury. Since he is similar to you in size, would you please lie in the grave, so that we can measure it?"

Moses did as the young men asked and lay down in the grave. There he came face to face with the Angel of Death, who smiled at him, saying, "Peace be upon you, Moses, son of Amram."

"May peace be upon you as well," Moses returned the greeting, now truly at peace.

Thus Moses departed from this world, and the three angels laid him to rest.

Young Solomon Finds the Rightful Heir

There are many legends about the wisdom of Solomon. Most of us are familiar with the story of the two women who approached King Solomon, each arguing that the same child was hers. There the King demonstrated his insight into the relationship between mother and child. In this tale Solomon demonstrates his insight into the relationship between father and son. Indeed, such is the mark of true wisdom: it is an understanding of what a mother and a father and a child are in truth. What is revealing about this legend is the understanding it attributes to Solomon at a very young age, a gift of God that he carried into manhood.

Long ago, during the reign of King David, a certain man of wealth, a good man who cared for his family, sent his grown son on a long journey to attend to a matter of business for him. While his son was away, however, the man died.

Among the servants in the father's household was a slave who was as clever as he was dishonest, as greedy as he was powerful. Threatening the man's widow and daughter with death, he drove them out of their home, seizing all their possessions, the entire inheritance, for himself.

The man's son had been shipwrecked, and many years went by before he was able to return home. Finally he arrived at his father's house, only to discover that the wicked slave had taken possession of all that was rightfully his.

"Where is my father?" the son demanded. "And my mother and sister. What have you done with them?"

"What do you mean your father?" the slave replied. "He was my father, and he has passed away. I am now the master of this house. As for your mother and sister, I don't know what you are talking about. Away with you, you impostor!"

Knowing King David to be a righteous man, the son took his case to him. And, because the king was a just man, he asked the son to bring witnesses to prove his claim on his father's estate. But such witnesses were impossible to find. His mother and sister had been driven away, and the servants of the household were afraid to identify him; the wicked slave had threatened to kill them if they should give him away. In a word, the rightful heir was at a complete loss as to what to do.

The king's young son, Solomon, however, had heard the entire exchange between his father and the petitioner. Finally, he spoke and asked his father if he might be allowed to pursue the matter himself. David recognized a wisdom in his son that exceeded the boy's years and agreed to let him handle the case.

Solomon began by having both men, the slave and the son of the deceased father, brought before him.

"I order each of you," he told them, "to go to the grave of the man whom you both claim to be your father. Dig it up and retrieve one of his bones. Bring the bone back to me and break it before my eyes."

Having no choice in the matter, both men went to the grave. But as soon as they arrived, the true son begged the slave not to disturb his father's resting place. The wicked slave, of course, ignored him and began digging. Before long, and much to the rightful son's outrage, the servant had exhumed the father's body and taken a bone from his remains. Then he hurried back to Solomon with the real son close behind and broke the bone before King David himself.

"You see, young Prince," said the slave, "I have followed your instructions to the letter. Surely this proves that I am the rightful heir."

"What about you?" Solomon turned to the son. "Why have you not done as I ordered you to do?"

"Though it may cost me the sum of my father's wealth," he asserted, "I would never think of disturbing the place where my father has been laid to rest. Better that I should live in poverty for the rest of my life than to even touch a single one of his bones, let alone break it!"

Solomon turned to the king and said, "Is it not clear, Father, which of these men is the true son? A true son would never desecrate his father's remains, as this slave has done. With your permission, I shall see to it that this lying slave returns all the property that belongs to the rightful heir. As for the punishment that is to be dealt to the thieving slave, the true son may decide that."

"It shall be as you say," the King replied to his wise boy.

"As of this moment," Solomon said to the rightful heir, "everything in your father's household, the sum of his inheritance, is yours. What then is to be done with this miserable wretch?"

"My only wish," the son answered, "is that he go to the place where he has banished my mother and my sister. Once they have been returned safely to their home, the slave may have his freedom—on condition that he leave this land forever."

And so it was. The man was reunited with his family, and the wicked slave was exiled from the land. All thanks to the wisdom of a boy who would become the wisest of Israel's kings.

King Solomon's Throne

Legends surrounding the wisest of men—King Solomon—abound. Dating back to at least Talmudic times, this tale is about the throne on which Solomon sat and the judgments he pronounced from it. What is striking about this legend is that it presents the throne not as the seat of power but as the seat of truth. Solomon judged not by his own authority but by the truth of God as it was revealed to the world through the Torah. That is why almost none of the kings who later captured the throne was able to sit upon it, despite the power that they held.

Among the wonders that the Queen of Sheba came to behold in the court of King Solomon was the marvelous throne upon which he sat. It was made of ivory overlaid with the finest gold. At the time of its construction, it is said, a demon flew up to heaven, snatched away a portion of the sapphire footing that lies beneath the divine throne, and placed it under King Solomon's throne.

Six steps led up to Solomon's throne, and twelve golden lions, two on each step, stood guard over it. On each step there was also a pair of different animals, all fashioned from gold. On the first step stood an ox and a lion, as in the visions of Ezekiel; on the second a lamb and a wolf, on the third a leopard and a goat, as in the prophecies of Isaiah; on the fourth there was an eagle and a peacock; on the fifth a falcon and a cock; and on the sixth a hawk and a sparrow.

The throne was outfitted with a mechanical device that transported Solomon automatically up to its seat. As soon as the king set foot on the first step, the ox took him and carried him up to the animal on the next step, and so on up the six steps, until he rested on the throne itself. As he sat court, a dove hovered before him with a Torah scroll in its beak, so that he might contemplate the Word of God while he sat in judgment of humanity.

Because King Solomon's throne was a seat of judgment, it was surrounded by seventy thousand other thrones, upon which there sat the sages, scholars, priests, Levites, and princes of Israel. To the rear of the royal throne were seventy additional thrones for the members of the Sanhedrin. Immediately in front of the King's throne was a smaller throne for Gad and a second one for the prophet Nathan. To Solomon's right sat his mother Bathsheba on her own throne.

When the king ascended the steps to take his seat, his heralds would announce to him the responsibilities with which God had entrusted him as king. Each time Solomon heard one of these injunctions, he would bless and praise the Holy Name of the Lord.

"The King shall not multiply wives unto himself," they cried, as he mounted the first step.

"The King shall not multiply horses unto himself," they declared at the second.

"The King shall not hoard gold and silver for himself," was heard at the third step.

"You shall not pervert justice," was the warning uttered at the fourth step.

"You shall not be partial to anyone," he was told when he came to the fifth.

"You shall take no bribes," was the injunction declared at the sixth step.

And when he was about to take his seat on the royal throne all cried out, "Know before whom you stand!"

The animals of gold that rested on the steps leading up to Solomon's throne were rather unusual. As soon as the process of judgment was underway and witnesses approached the throne, the animals would create such an uproar that all who came near were overcome with fear and trembling. The ox bellowed, and the lion roared; the wolf howled, and the lamb bleated; the leopard snarled, and the goat cried out; the falcon, the peacock, and the sparrow all erupted in their calls. Indeed, the machinery that conveyed Solomon up the steps began to rumble, so that anyone who stood before the king was frightened into speaking the truth.

When King Solomon went to join his ancestors and the Holy Land was divided into two kingdoms, his son Rehoboam presented the famous throne to the pharaoh of Egypt to comfort him for the suffering endured by his widowed daughter. Later the Assyrian ruler Sennacherib laid claim to the throne, but he was forced to surrender it to Hezekiah upon his defeat outside the walls of Jerusalem. After several generations, the throne once again fell into the hands of the Egyptians. Their ruler, King Necho, attempted to ascend the steps of the throne, but he no sooner set foot upon the first step than one of the throne's golden lions attacked him and bit him on the leg. Thereafter he walked with a limp. The same thing happened when King Nebuchadnezzar of Babylon took possession of the throne and attempted to occupy it.

Of all the rulers who seized the throne of Solomon—Persian, Greek, and Roman—none was able to sit where the wise and righteous King Solomon had sat. None, that is, except one: Cyrus the Great was allowed to sit on the throne, for he had allowed the Jews to return from their exile in Babylonia to Jerusalem.

Judge Everyone Favorably

The Talmud teaches that the judgments we mete out to others will be meted out to us; therefore we should be generous in our judgments. Indeed, if one of the characteristics of a Jew is generosity, as the Talmud tells us, then one way in which this generosity shows itself is through the judgments we pronounce upon others. If we are generous in our judgment of others, being slow to condemn and quick to understand, God will be generous in His judgment of us. This tale is based on these teachings from the Talmud.

Once a man from the northern region of Galilee traveled to the south. There he went in search of work and finally hired himself as a laborer, agreeing to work for his employer for a period of three years.

When the period of his hire had come to an end, he went to his employer and said, "May I please have my wages now? I must return to the north, where my family awaits my earnings."

"I am terribly sorry," his employer replied, "but I have no money just now."

"In that case," the man suggested, "perhaps you could give me enough grain to equal the amount that you owe me."

"Forgive me," said his employer, "but I am afraid that I have no grain either."

The laborer proposed that he might be paid in cattle, land, wine, grapes, or fruit. But each time he made his request, the employer simply answered, "I'm sorry, but I have none."

The worker was terribly distressed at hearing this, but he determined that there was nothing he could do. He strapped his meager bag of his belongings to his back and set out for home. There he found that his family was destitute, and he fell into despair over being unable to bring them relief.

A few weeks later who should show up at the worker's door but the employer who had sent him away with nothing. The employer did not come to him empty-handed. With him he had three donkeys laden with food, wine, spices, and fine clothing. In a large purse he carried the three years' wages that he owed to the worker.

The worker invited his former employer into his simple home, and after they had enjoyed a modest meal, the employer asked, "What passed through your mind when I told you that I had no money?"

"Well," the laborer answered, "it occurred to me that you might have come across a great bargain and had spent all the cash you had on hand to acquire it."

"What about when I told you that I had no land to give you?" the employer wanted to know.

"I thought that you might have leased it to someone and therefore could not lay your hands on it," the worker told him. "Or perhaps you had given it to another for his hire."

"And when I told you I had no grain or fruit?" said the employer. "What did you think then?"

"It struck me that perhaps you had not yet been able to pay the tithes on your grain and fruit," the man explained. "Therefore giving me anything you had reaped from the land would have amounted to an offense against God."

"And the wine?" he asked. "The vineyard?"

"I assumed," said the worker, "that you had dedicated all your possessions to the Temple, so that you were not free to offer them to me."

"Then you are truly as righteous as you are insightful," the employer declared. "For everything was just as you supposed, and you have refrained from thinking badly of me. Therefore I am happy to bring to you not only a purse full of gold for your wages, but also these asses laden with food, wine, spices, and fine clothing. Please accept it all as a token of my gratitude for the generosity of your judgments. May the Holy One, blessed be He, judge you as favorably when you stand before the celestial tribunal!"

The Punishment of the Selfish

Similar to the Talmudic tale about Choni the Circle Drawer, this is a story that has its variations in several Middle Eastern traditions, including, for example, the folktales of the Sufis. It is about the difference between offering a gift for the sake of another and offering something for one's own profit. In this story, the man who plants the fig tree demonstrates his care for others by bringing a gift of figs to someone else, even though he had thought that he would never live to see the figs ripen for picking. To be sure, that is the sign of righteousness: to offer something to another without expectation of reward.

There was once an old man who lived in the town of Tiberias. One day he decided that he would go out and plant a fig tree.

"After all," he said to himself, "those who lived before me planted fig trees from which I have eaten. Perhaps others may eat from this tree one day. And who knows? It may turn out that I might live to eat from it myself."

As the old man engaged in the labor of planting the fig tree, Emperor Hadrian happened to be passing by. Impressed by the difficult task taken up by one so advanced in years, the Roman commented to him, "If you had worked so hard in your youth, perhaps you would not have to work so hard in your old age. In any case, surely one as aged as you cannot hope to see this tree bear fruit."

"Your majesty," the old man replied, "I labored in my youth, and so I shall labor in my old age. If it is God's will, perhaps I shall live to see this tree bear fruit, even though I am already a hundred years old."

"Well, if anyone can live as long as that," said the emperor, "I should like to know about it." With those words the emperor went on his way.

It was God's will that the old man live many more years, so that finally he saw the fig tree bear its fruit. Recalling what the emperor had said, he gathered a small basket full of the figs and set out for Hadrian's palace. When the old man was presented to the emperor, the Roman at first did not recognize him.

"God was good enough to allow me to live to see the bearing of this fruit," the old man explained. "I have brought you the best of the tree's figs so that you too may enjoy God's blessing. For we are taught that a blessing is not received until it is shared."

The emperor was so impressed by the old man's kindness that he accepted the figs, had the old man's basket filled with gold, and sent him joyfully on his way.

Next door to the old man there lived a selfish, nosy woman. Always interested in making money and keeping abreast with everyone's business, she knew that the old man had taken a basket of figs to the emperor and had returned home with a basket of gold.

"Ah hah!" she cried when she spied her neighbor's riches. "The emperor is paying a very high price for figs these days!"

Immediately she ordered her husband, who was just as selfish as she was if not just as nosy, to take a huge basket, fill it with figs, and carry it to the emperor.

"The emperor loves figs," she told him, "and will reward you with a basket of gold. At last we shall get what we deserve!"

When her husband arrived at the emperor's court, he declared to the guards, "Please inform His Majesty that I have brought him this basket of figs."

As soon as he received the message, the emperor suspected just what the greedy man was up to. As a punishment for the man's selfishness, the emperor ordered that he be made to stand in front of the palace, where all who passed by would pelt him with his own figs, until the huge basket was emptied. By the end of the day the figs were all gone, and the man was sent home, a little sticky but not too much the worse for wear.

When he arrived, awash in self-pity and fig juice, he informed his selfish wife of what had happened to him. And, in her typical loving tones, she consoled him, saying, "Just be glad that you brought the emperor a basket of figs, and not a basket of coconuts!"

We Find What We Seek

This ancient folktale teaches us that we perceive in the world what we harbor in our hearts. Those whose hearts are filled with goodness gaze upon the world and behold what is good in humanity; those who look upon the world through the eyes of a cynic find only the image of themselves. If we seek a life that is meaningful and overflowing with blessing, we must become the source, and not the recipient, of meaning and blessedness. This comes about precisely when the goodness that sleeps in the depths of our heart awakens in the deeds of our hands. The rabbi in this story is said to be one of the Talmudic sages.

A wealthy rabbi longed to take up residence in a city of righteousness. His children were growing up very rapidly, as children do, and he wanted his family to live in a place that would be good for their souls.

In order to find just the right city, he hired several emissaries and sent them to various places in order to see whether or not they might be places where he and his family would want to live. To each of these investigators the rabbi gave a large sum of money for expenses. He was willing to spend whatever it took in order to dwell among the righteous.

The first man that the rabbi sent forth arrived in the city assigned to him and immediately took a room in a plush and costly inn. Rather than seek out the sages of the city or even meet with its common citizens, he squandered his money on the city's night life. Soon he fell in with a group of shady characters, who ended up stealing his money from him.

Now penniless, the investigator returned to the rabbi and reported, "The city to which you sent me is full of evil. There are thieves and cutthroats everywhere. I tell you, it's a regular Sodom!"

The man denounced the city in such extreme terms that the rabbi wondered whether what he said about it could possibly be true. Therefore he sent a second investigator to explore the same city.

When the rabbi's emissary arrived, he found a very modest room in an equally modest inn and went immediately to the local synagogue. He was a man devoted to God, and it was time for the afternoon prayers. In the synagogue he found numerous people in worship, and after their prayers many of them invited him into their homes.

"Please do me the honor, sir, of sitting at my table," said one.

"Let me offer you a place of comfort to rest from your journey," said another.

"I would like for you to meet my family," offered a third. "One who is new to the city should not have to be alone."

When the man returned to the rabbi to make his report, he declared, "I have found the perfect city for you, Rabbi. It is filled with righteous people who treat strangers with lovingkindness."

While the rabbi was pleased to hear this, he was also rather puzzled over having received such conflicting reports about the same city. Unable to resolve the puzzle, he decided to go to the city and see for himself what was there. Before long he understood.

Upon his return he gathered together the two men he had sent out and said, "I understand now why each of you has returned from the same city with such different impressions of it. It is because one of you is wicked, while the other is good. Those who are wicked seek wickedness, and they inevitably find it. But those who are good seek what is good, and that is what they find. I am in your debt more than you know. For you have taught me that we find not only what we seek—we find what we are. And so there is no need for me to move my family to another city. I need only move my soul closer to the good."

What a Wife Loved Best

One mark of wisdom is the ability to distinguish between the trivial and the important. This capacity is not easily acquired and once acquired, not easily kept. Indeed, most of the things we quarrel about are really of no significance. That is why Jews surround themselves with reminders of what is most precious—with a mezuzah, a kiddush cup, or a menorah, for example. That is why we have folktales like this one that dates back to Talmudic times.

Long ago there was once a husband and wife who quarreled constantly over one thing and another. If they were not arguing about money, they were arguing about work; if it was not his oversight, it was her annoying habits. But it was always something.

Finally they decided that they simply were not suited for one another. The matchmaker who some years earlier had brought them together had made a terrible mistake. So they went to their rabbi and asked him to arrange for a divorce.

The rabbi listened patiently to their complaints. Finally he said to them, "Very well, you shall have your divorce. But unless you can separate on good terms, without anger, I shall have no part in it. Therefore I want you to return home together. When you get there I want you to prepare a fine dinner and invite all your closest friends to eat with you. Come back to me tomorrow, and we shall see to your divorce."

The quarrelsome couple did exactly as the rabbi had told them to do. After all, they were not wicked people who had no regard for their rabbi's advice. They just did not get along with each other, that's all.

That night the meal was prepared, and the husband and wife were surrounded by their dearest friends. Soon their house was filled with good cheer, and everyone's mood was happy indeed. In fact, the man was so overjoyed that, as they were eating their meal, he leaned over to his wife and said, "You know, now that I see all of our dear friends gathered together, good people every one, I realize that we have been blessed to have many happy years together. Sure, there have been times of sorrow, hard times when our burdens seemed heavy. But, thanks to these people, we have had many joyous times as well. So I want you to know that, even though we are separating, there is not a bit of anger in my heart. As a sign of my affection, I want you to have anything you desire from our house, no matter what its value may be. Pick out the thing you love best, and it is yours."

In response to the man's offer his wife gave him a loving smile but said nothing.

The guests, as well as their host, enjoyed their food and drink so much that the festivities lasted until late in the evening. Some friends expressed their thanks to the couple for their hospitality and left. Others, including the wife's husband, finally fell into a sleep of satisfaction at the sumptuous table.

Instead of putting her husband to bed, however, the wife had him taken to her father's home nearby. The next morning, with his wife sitting next to him, the woman's husband awoke somewhat disoriented.

He rubbed the sleep from his eyes, looked around, and asked, "Where am I?"

"Do you not remember what you said to me last night?" she replied. "You told me to take from our house the thing I loved best. Well, I have done just that. I realized that of all the valuables we own, as precious as they may be, I love you more than any of them."

Her husband smiled at her words. "Now I understand why the wise rabbi advised us as he did."

The Value of Confession

There is no repentance without guilt, and, as the Talmud points out, the repentant enter into a nearness to God that the righteous never know. In this folktale we see that one who is basically good and open to repentance is open to becoming better. Through the words of another human being, we may come to hear the words that address us from the depths of our own soul. But in order to hear the voice that speaks from within, we must speak aloud our confession.

There was once a king—some say it was King Solomon—who was renowned for his skill at the game of chess. His favorite opponent was the commander of his army, a highly skilled chess player and an accomplished strategist.

One day, while the king and the commander were involved in a very close game, the king was called away to attend to some urgent business. Now the king's officer lost far more often than he won, and, since the game was so close, he was determined to win this time. In fact, he was so determined to win that he removed one of the king's knights from the chessboard during the king's absence. Sure enough, when the king returned, the officer won the game.

Several days went by, and while the king was sitting at one of the palace windows, he noticed two suspicious characters hanging around the palace grounds. Disguising himself as a vagabond, he went outside to speak to them.

"Ho, comrades!" he called to the two men. "Do you mind if a fellow wayfarer joins you?"

"That depends on who you are and what your business is," they answered as he drew near.

"I am no one in particular," the king replied in his disguise, "and my business is anything that will line my pockets."

Deceived by the king's ragged dress, the two strangers invited him to join them. They explained that they had heard about a vault full of gold and jewels hidden away in the castle and that they intended to find a way to steal the king's treasure.

Hearing this, the king said, "Ah, it is indeed lucky that we have come across one another. You see, I happen to have the keys to the vault. All I needed was a couple of companions like you to help me make off with the gold and jewels. Meet me here at midnight, and I'll take you there. We'll all be rich!"

When the hour struck twelve, the king, still in his disguise, went out to meet the two thieves. He led them into the vault where he kept his treasure. The two men became so engrossed in filling their bags with gold and jewels that the king was able to slip out of the room unnoticed. As soon as he got outside, he slammed the door and locked the two criminals inside.

After changing into his royal dress, the king immediately convened a meeting of his council. Among those who sat on the council was the commanding officer of his army.

"I have called you together," the king explained, "in order to ask your opinion on what should be done with a thief, especially with one who is guilty of stealing from the king."

As soon as he heard these words, the commanding officer became extremely agitated. He was convinced that somehow the king knew of the deception in which he had engaged during their game of chess.

"He has found me out," the officer thought to himself. "The only thing to do is confess my crime, so that I may not add to my sin by denying it."

So the officer cried out, "Forgive me, Sire, I beg you! It's true that I removed one of your knights from the chessboard when we last played. I could never have won the game without that vile deception. Please have mercy on me!"

The king smiled at his officer and said, "My dear friend, I had no idea what you did. I called this meeting to decide the fate of two thieves whom I have locked in my vault. You may be guilty of stealing my knight from the chessboard, but you have shown me that your conscience will never allow you to enjoy any ill-gotten gains. Therefore I see that in your heart you are a good man. I commend your confession. It has won for you my mercy."

To Behold the Light

Like a star that has light only inasmuch as it gives out light, we have only as much life as we impart to others. Such is the teaching that comes to us through this folktale that I have heard from several Polish Jews. It tells us that any substance we may acquire for ourselves lies in our becoming a sign of the substance, of the depth and the dearness, of our fellow human being. A narcissistic life, therefore, is the way of death. Focused only on our own interests, we are beggared by our abundance. For, like Narcissus, when we gaze enthralled only upon the image of ourselves, we end up starving to death.

A very wealthy but miserly man who hoarded every penny he could lay his hands on wanted only one thing in life: more! Never satisfied with what he had, he was blind to the plight of those who had nothing.

In the town where the miser lived was a rabbi known not only for his wisdom but for his lovingkindness. Indeed, he was wise enough to realize that there is no wisdom without lovingkindness. One day the rabbi learned of a family in the community in terrible need of food and medicine who had absolutely no money. After turning to his usual sources for help, he still had not accumulated enough to provide for the poor family, so he went to the miser hoping to convince him to contribute to his fund.

"I'm sorry, Rabbi," the miser replied. "Those people are no concern of mine. I have nothing for them."

The rabbi stared at the man for a moment and then pulled from his coat pocket a mirror. "Here," he said, handing the man the mirror. "Gaze into this and tell me what you see."

The man glanced at it and said, "I see a mirror no different from any other mirror. I see my face. That's all."

"Now," said the rabbi, "come over here and look out the window. What do you see?"

The man stepped up to a window overlooking the street and peered outside. "Nothing unusual out there," he said. "I see men and women going about their business, children playing. There's a couple walking arm in arm. What of it?"

"I'll tell you what of it," answered the rabbi. "When you gaze through this window, through a glass that has nothing to block your vision, you gaze upon life. But when you peer into the mirror, with its back coated in silver, you see nothing but your miserable, miserly self."

"What do you mean?" the man asked, actually showing a sign of interest in what the rabbi had to say.

"Like the window," the rabbi explained, "the mirror is just a piece of glass. But the layer of silver on the back keeps you from seeing past it. Just as this silver coating prevents you from seeing the life on the other side, so has your own silver, your own wealth, blinded you to what is truly dear in life, to life itself."

The man looked down and thought for a moment about what

the rabbi had said. "You are right, Rabbi," he finally spoke. "I have been blinded by something that has no light of its own, something full of unreal images. Now I see the light of life."

Then he looked up at the rabbi and asked, "How much do you need?"

Shalom Bayit—Peace in the Home

This is an old tale that has several variations. Some versions, like this one, feature the Talmudic sage Rabbi Meir as the main character; in others the main character is Aaron, brother of Moses. What is crucial to the tale, however, is not the name of its hero but his wisdom, by which he is willing to suffer humiliation—without feeling humiliated—in order to preserve peace between a husband and wife. In his wisdom and his humility the rabbi understands the profound important of shalom bayit, *peace in the home. For the home is where life is first sanctified. If there is no peace in the home, there is no sanctification of life.*

Rabbi Meir had a great admirer. Every day she would go to listen to his comments on the Torah, and every day she would be enriched by his words.

One day, however, the Rabbi's talk lasted much longer than usual, and the woman did not get home until late in the afternoon. In fact, her husband, a jealous and inconsiderate man, had arrived home before her, and he was very angry with her for failing to greet him and serve him his supper.

"Where have you been?" he demanded, although he knew perfectly well that she had been to the rabbi's talk. "A wife should be home to greet her husband when he returns from a hard day's work."

"Please forgive me," she replied. "You are right, of course. It's just that I attended Rabbi Meir's lecture, and his words were so inspiring that I lost track of the time."

"Since you apparently love being with your Rabbi Meir so much," he yelled at her, "I order you to go back to him this instant. Further, I order you to spit in his face as a payment for his wonderful talk. Don't set foot back in this house until you have done so!"

"But that's impossible!" she pleaded.

"Is it not a wife's duty, according to the law espoused by your rabbi, to do as her husband tells her?" he insisted.

"Yes, but—"

"Then do as I say!" he shouted, and he forced her out of the house.

At a loss, the woman went to the home of one of her good friends, who offered her a place to sleep for the night. The next morning, hoping that her husband had cooled off, she tried to return home. But he was adamant and refused to let her into the house until she had spit in the rabbi's face.

Meanwhile her friend had gone to Rabbi Meir and explained the woman's predicament. Immediately the good rabbi sent for the woman. When she arrived and was presented to him, he pretended to have a speck of dust in his eye.

"I think I have something in my eye," he told her. "Do you know of anything that might help?"

"I'm not sure, Rabbi," she answered, concerned for his discomfort.

"I have heard it said," he replied, "that such a pain can be relieved if a good woman spits into it seven times. Please, would you do me the kindness of spitting into my eye?"

She hesitated, but the rabbi insisted. And so, in the presence of the rabbi's disciples, the woman spit seven times into his eye.

"Thank you," he said to her. "It is much better. Go now, and inform your husband that you have spit in the face of Rabbi Meir, not once, as he ordered, but seven times."

The woman realized what the rabbi had done for her, offered him a thousand thanks, and went home. There she was reunited with her husband, who, having realized the kindness and the wisdom of Rabbi Meir, begged his wife's forgiveness.

After she had left, the rabbi's students turned to him and said, "Master, how could you have permitted such an indignity? It's unthinkable!"

"Don't you see?" he answered in his gentle voice. "Apart from an act of outright cruelty, there can be no indignity in doing something that brings peace between two people."

The Man Who Traded Places with God

The relationship between a husband and a wife can sometimes be difficult, as can the relationship between God and humanity. This East European legend suggests one reason why the relationship between humanity and divinity can be so troubled. Both have their mystery. For man, the mystery is God. For God, the mystery is man. Each has an infinite longing for the other. If Jewish tales are about anything, they are about that longing.

Long, long ago, a man—perhaps it was the first man, yet it could be any man—approached God and said, "We both need to better understand one another. Would You not agree?"

"I do," God answered. "What do you propose?"

"Perhaps," the man suggested, "we could change places with one another. Only for a second, You understand. You will be man, and I shall be God."

God thought for a moment about the man's request. Then He smiled and asked, "Are you not afraid of such a thing?"

"I am not afraid, if You aren't," the man replied.

"Oh, but I am afraid," said God. "Very much afraid—for you. Nevertheless I shall do as you ask."

In the twinkling of an eye God and man exchanged places. The Holy One, blessed be He, became a human being, and the man became God.

A second went by and then two, and God, who was now a man, said, "You asked for a second, and You have had two. It is time to change back."

But the man, who was now God and therefore omnipotent, used His power to refuse. Suddenly neither God nor man was what he appeared to be.

Since that unparalleled hour years have gone by, perhaps centuries. Man's past and God's present—the past for the God who became man and the present for the man who became God—have become too much for either of them to bear. The liberation of one is now inextricably tied to the liberation of the other. And their ancient dialogue has been renewed, charged with despair and dizziness, with anger and frustration, and above all with infinite longing.

The Tailor's Work and the Lord's Work

This Hungarian folktale belongs to the Jewish tradition of arguing with God. Although the tailor in this story does not directly enter into any argument with the Almighty, he does make a comment that questions God's perfection. If there is some humor in his remark, it is because it is a remark that many of us harbor in our hearts. The tale, however, suggests something further: even if we deem God's work to be imperfect, it is no excuse for our own imperfections.

A rabbi was once in need of a new pair of pants. He did not have a lot of money, but, fortunately, he knew of a tailor who was said to do excellent work for reasonable prices, so he paid him a visit.

After the tailor had taken the rabbi's measurements, the rabbi asked him, "When can you have the trousers ready?"

"Well, you know, Rabbi," the tailor answered, "I am very busy right now. But for you I can promise to have them ready in one week. I'll bring them to you then."

Seven days went by, and then an eighth and a ninth. But the tailor still had not shown up with the rabbi's new pants. Finally, three days later than he had promised, the tailor brought the rabbi his new pair of pants.

A bit perturbed over having had to wait so long, the rabbi took the pants and tried them on without saying a word. Sure enough, the tailor had lived up to his reputation: the trousers fit perfectly. Satisfied with the tailor's work and somewhat assuaged, the rabbi paid him.

But before the tailor could leave he said, "Tell me, please, if the Lord took only six days to create heaven and earth, why is it that it took you ten days to make a single pair of pants?"

While the rabbi had spoken jokingly, the tailor looked at him with a very serious expression on his face and said, "Rabbi, just look at these pants. Every stitch is in place, there is not a single defect, and you can see for yourself that they are a perfect fit. Now you tell me: can the same be said of the Lord's work, may His Name be blessed?"

The Miser

Characteristic of the motif of the hidden righteous person, this Russian folktale reminds us that we must be careful in our judgments of others. If we truly possess the qualities of generosity and lovingkindness, then we have no interest in renown. It is the invisible generosity that reflects the invisibility of God. What is done to attract the notice of other people escapes the notice of God. If, on the other hand, God remembers what we forget, He also sees what does not meet the human eye.

In a village much like any other village there lived a rich old Jew who was known to be the most miserly of misers. Not a single resident of the village could recall ever having seen him offer so much as a penny to the poor. If on some rare occasion one of the local beggars should happened to come to his door for alms, he would demand, "Where do you come from?"

"Why I live here in the village," the poor man would reply.

"Then you are a foolish beggar indeed," the old miser would answer. "Everyone in this village knows that I do not dole out a cent to anyone. Be gone!"

Not far from the rich old miser lived another Jew, a shoemaker of very modest means. Contrary to the miser's reputation for greed, the shoemaker was known to be among the most generous of men. Never did he turn away anyone who came to him for alms or aid. To be sure, it seemed that he gave away every nickel he had.

After some years had gone by the wealthy old Jew passed away. Not a tear was shed over his death. At the behest of their rabbi, in fact, the Jews of the village decided that the only place to bury the miser was alongside the cemetery fence. The wealthy old Jew was laid to rest without a funeral procession, without an elegy, and almost without notice. The only one who came to say a prayer at his grave was the shoemaker.

In a few days' time, the old miser was all but forgotten—until, that is, something extraordinary happened.

When the beggars came to the shoemaker's door, he gave them nothing but sadly explained, "I'm very sorry, but I'm afraid I don't have a cent to my name."

When word got around that the shoemaker was no longer able to give alms to the poor, people said to one another, "He's always been so kind and generous, never without something to give. How is it possible that he suddenly has nothing to offer the poor? Has he become as stingy as the old miser?"

In order to clear up the matter, the rabbi sent for the shoemaker and said to him, "You have always been a good man and a great benefactor to those in need. But now you give nothing to the poor. How can this be?"

"I'll tell you how," the shoemaker replied. "Many years ago a very wealthy Jew came to me and placed in my care a large sum of money. He asked me to distribute it among the needy and said that when this money was gone he would bring more. As urgent as his desire to give away his money, however, was his desire to remain anonymous. And so, as a condition of this arrangement, he made me promise never to tell anyone, as long as he was alive, where the money came from. I assured him that I would keep his secret, even though it meant I would be wrongly regarded as a generous man and no one would know of his goodness. But those were his wishes. That wealthy Jew was none other than the 'rich old miser' who has now gone to his grave without a penny. For, with my help, he finally gave away all he had to the poor."

Upon hearing this tale the rabbi gathered together all of the villagers, informed them of what he had learned, and led them to the grave of the "rich old miser." There they said *Kaddish*, the prayer for the dead, for him and begged him to forgive them for having spoken so poorly of him. As soon as he returned home from the cemetery, in fact, the rabbi changed his will to request that he too be buried alongside the fence, next to the grave of the "rich old miser."

To Have and Have Not

A great deal of unhappiness comes from the confusion between being and having. Identifying ourselves with what we have, we turn ourselves over to a world of illusion. Material wealth derives its significance from the imagi-

nary importance we attach to it. When we equate ourselves with our pos-
sessions, we lose our substance. This is the teaching that comes to us through
this tale attributed to the fifteenth-century sage Yitzchak Abravanel.

Two wealthy men wanted to see to it that they would never lose
their riches. Each one of them took his treasure and buried it. One
man buried his gold at the foot of an old tree, while the other
sneaked into his backyard one night and buried his money in his
garden.

Now a thief had been spying on the man who had buried his
wealth under the tree. No sooner had the man packed up his shovel,
than the thief stole his gold. But the wealthy man—who was now
no longer wealthy—knew nothing of the theft. He continued to
believe he was wealthy, happily rubbing elbows with the rich and
powerful and supposing himself to be one of them.

The man who buried his riches in his garden was not known for
his good memory. After a short time had passed, he forgot exactly
where he had buried his gold. Mistakenly supposing he had buried
it under a large rock, he went one day to check on his treasure but
found nothing there.

"I've been robbed!" he cried out in despair, whereas all the while
his wealth was safely buried in his garden.

Thinking himself a poor man bereft of his riches, he lived out
his life in utter misery.

For each man—the wealth of the one and the poverty of the
other, the joy of the one and the despair of the other—life rested
on a complete illusion. Indeed, all that each took himself to be was
no more real than a mirage.

The Silent Confusion of Tongues

*This tale can be found in the Israel Folktale Archives (No. 505) and is
part of the lore that German Jews brought to America during the wave of
their immigration in the nineteenth century. It teaches us that we not only
read the signs by which we communicate, but we also read into them. Our*

understanding of our fellow human beings may tell us as much about our-
selves as it reveals about them. Thus, if we pause to take stock of our own
souls, we may arrive at surprising insights into ourselves and others. And
it may happen that the stake in this understanding is a matter of life and
death.

In a certain city there lived a priest whose heart was full of hatred
toward the Jews. One day he came up with an evil plan. Very pleased
with himself, he summoned the chief rabbi and declared, "It is my
wish to have a debate with a Jew, any Jew of your choosing. The
debate is to be conducted in a sign language of my choosing, and
the Jew you select for the debate must understand every sign that
I make. If no one can be found to take part in the debate, your
entire community will be put to the sword. You have thirty days to
prepare. Now be gone."

The priest's demands sent the rabbi into a terrible state of despair. How could any Jew possibly understand the arbitrary sign
language of the priest? Who would agree to engage in such a debate, with the lives of all hanging in the balance?

In a state of hopelessness, the rabbi informed the community of
the priest's demands and ordered them to fast and pray for God's
deliverance. A week went by and then two, but no one came forward to meet the priest's challenge. Soon the end of the fourth
week approached, and still no Jew could be found who had the
courage to debate the priest.

There was, however, a certain poultry dealer, a good but simple
man, who had been away on business and returned to the city as
the thirty days were coming to an end. While he had no idea of
what had taken place, he noticed that the market was closed and
the streets were empty. When he walked into his house he found
his wife and children shedding tears, immersed in fasting and prayers.

"What on earth has happened here?" he asked, wondering what
could have brought on such a state of affairs.

"We are doomed!" his wife told him. "The evil priest who hates
us all has ordered us to find a Jew to debate him in sign language.
If no one can be found to represent us, we shall all be killed. And if
the one who is sent to the priest fails to understand the signs he
dreams up, then too it will cost us our lives."

"If that's all it is," replied the simple poultry dealer, "I shall go to the rabbi myself and tell him that I am willing to represent the community in this matter."

"What are you saying?" cried his wife. "You are a good man, but you are a simple man. How can you possibly understand the priest's sign language? Don't you realize that the wisest men among us are afraid to take upon themselves such a terrible burden?"

"Then we shall all be killed anyway," said her husband. "There is nothing else to lose."

Off he went to the rabbi. When he arrived at the rabbi's study, he declared, "Rabbi, I shall be the one who goes to meet the wicked priest for this debate in sign language."

"You?!" the rabbi replied, knowing the poultry dealer to be less than intelligent. But by this time the rabbi was so desperate that he was willing to send anyone before the priest, in the hope of somehow averting catastrophe. So he accepted the poultry dealer's offer, saying, "Very well. Thank you, thank you so much! You are truly a good man. May it be the will of the Holy One, blessed be He, that you deliver us from this evil!"

The hour of debate arrived. The poultry dealer was brought before the priest in the presence of a huge gathering of the Christian townspeople. The priest was pleased that the Jews had sent him a simple poultry dealer. He knew that one who came from such humble origins would be no match for him.

"You must understand every one of my signs," the priest explained to him. "If you fail to correctly follow even a single one of them, I shall know that you Jews are an evil and ignorant people. The lives of all of you will be forfeit."

The priest began his silent communication by pointing a finger at the poultry dealer. Carefully reading this sign, the Jew responded by pointing two fingers at the priest. Then the priest reached into his pocket and pulled out a slice of cheddar cheese. The poultry dealer removed an egg from his own pocket. At that the priest took a handful of grain and scattered it across the floor. Without a moment's hesitation, the poultry dealer released a hen from a coop a he had brought along, and the hen ate up all the grain.

"I cannot believe it!" the priest exclaimed at last. "You replied correctly to every question I put to you. I now realize that if such a simple man from among you can understand these signs, you Jews must truly be a wise people and the chosen of God. I have been wrong about you. Please forgive me."

After bestowing upon the poultry dealer many fine gifts, the priest sent him on his way.

Meanwhile everyone in the Jewish community, especially the rabbi, anxiously awaited the news of the dispute in sign language. When they saw the poultry dealer return home, his arms laden with wonderful gifts, they were indeed amazed. With the rabbi at the head of the crowd, they rushed over to greet him.

"What is all this?" they asked. "What happened with the priest?"

"As you can see," he replied, "God has smiled on us. We are saved!"

"But what did the priest ask you?" the rabbi wanted to know. "How did you understand his signs?"

"It was very simple, really," the poultry dealer answered. "First he pointed at me with one finger, which meant that he was going to poke out my eye. I answered by pointing at him with two fingers, to let him know that if he tried that, I would poke out both of his eyes. Next he took out a piece of cheese to show that, while I was hungry, he was the one who had the food. So just to prove to him that I had no need of his charity, I took out an egg. Finally, he threw a handful of grain on the floor. Why, I must admit, I don't know. But I did know that it was feeding time for my hen, and I thought it would be a pity to waste the grain. So I let my hen out of her coop, and she ate up the grain. The next thing I knew, I was walking home with an armload of gifts!"

"Truly God has been merciful!" the rabbi heaved a sigh of relief.

While the rabbi was listening to the poultry dealer, the priest's friends were asking him, "How did it go with the Jew who came to converse with you in sign language? Have you decided to exterminate them?"

"Not at all," the priest answered. "Never have I come across such a wise and holy people. You see, I began by pointing at the Jew with one finger to indicate that there is only one King. He answered by pointing at me with two fingers, declaring that there are in fact two Kings: one in heaven and one on earth—and, of course, he was right. Next I pulled a piece of cheddar cheese from my pocket to ask him, 'Is this cheese made from the milk of a white goat or a black goat?' But the Jew was not easily fooled by such a ploy. In reply to this question, the clever man produced an egg from his pocket, which was to ask, 'Does this egg come from a white hen or a brown hen?' Then I thought I could trick him by changing the subject. So I spread some grain on the floor as a sign that the Jews are spread out all over the world. That wise and humble man, however, released his hen from its coop, and the hen ate up all the grain. Which meant that the Messiah will come to gather the Jews from their exile and return them to the Holy Land. I realized that I had no choice but to acknowledge the man's wisdom and spare his people."

The Lion That Was Kept
Out of the Garden

This Yemenite tale imparts four truths. First, things are not always what they seem to be, even when looked at through the eyes of piety and sagacity. Second, it may require the courage and attention of a whole family to heal the wounds that separate one family member from another. Third, the Torah has the power to change anyone, Jew or Gentile, and bring out the best in that person. And finally, when one person is transformed by the Torah, others are delivered from harm.

Long ago there lived a king who was decent in every respect except one: he loved to have his way with beautiful women. In all his realm not a single attractive woman, Jew or Gentile, was safe from his lust. No sooner would he lay his eyes on one, than he would force her to submit to him.

Not far from the king's palace lived a Jewish sage who was married to one of the most beautiful women in the kingdom. Since he knew very well of the king's passion for women, he would bolt the door to his house each morning before setting out for the house of study.

The king had heard about the sage's beautiful wife, and each morning he would look out the palace window to see whether the rabbi had bolted his door. Each morning the king was disappointed. One day, however, the sage forgot to lock his wife safely inside their house, and the king seized the opportunity to force himself upon her. Without even knocking on the door the king entered the sage's home and demanded that the beautiful woman submit to his lustful desires.

"Very well," she answered, trying to think of a way to stall for time. "Only wait here for a moment, Sire, so that I may go prepare myself for you. While you're waiting, perhaps you would like to read this."

She handed him the Torah. Instead of going to prepare herself for the king, however, the faithful wife slipped out the bedroom window and ran to hide in a neighbor's house.

Meanwhile the king sat poring over the Torah and soon became engrossed in its teachings. Losing all sense of time, he read for an hour, then two, then three. Finally he realized that it was getting late. Without even bothering to look for the sage's wife, he took a bag of gold and left it, along with his rosary, on her bed. Then, because he wanted to continue his reading, he picked up the Book of Torah and left.

The neighbor in whose home she was hiding informed the resourceful wife that the King had gone. As the hour for the midday meal was approaching, the wife immediately went to her kitchen and prepared lunch for her husband and herself. Her husband came home, ate his meal, and then happened to walk into the bedroom. There he found the bag of gold and the king's rosary lying on the bed.

Assuming the worst, he stared hard at his wife and declared through his teeth, "So the king has finally had his way with you!"

"No, I—" she started to protest. But then she thought to herself, "No matter what I say, he will never believe me."

So the poor woman remained silent, imploring him with her loving eyes to have pity on her. But from that day forward the sage neither came to his wife nor spoke to her.

Several months went by, and the faithful wife fell ill. No doctor could be found, and her condition rapidly grew worse, until it seemed that she would soon die. Word was sent to her three brothers, who lived in a nearby town, and they came immediately. When they had gathered around their sister's sickbed, she told them about the king's attempt to force himself on her and how she had managed to avoid him by hiding in a neighbor's house.

"But my husband has lost all trust in me," she muttered in a weak voice. "He will not touch me and no longer utters a word to me."

Hearing this, her brothers went to the sage and insisted that he go with them to see the king. He agreed, and soon all four of them stood before the monarch. Searching for a way to present their case without angering the king, one of the brothers decided to relate to him something of a parable.

"A few years ago," he began his tale, "our father, of blessed memory, passed away. The inheritance that he left us included a house, a vineyard, some fields, and a garden. The three of us who have come to you with this sage are brothers. One of us took the house, another works the vineyard, and the third attends to the fields. But we did not know what to do with the garden, until this wise man here came along. He offered to cultivate the garden, and we signed a contract with him on the condition that he indeed tend to it. For the past several months, however, he has not lived up to the terms of the contract. The land has been left untilled and the ground uncared for. Because he has neglected our precious garden, we ask that he return it to us."

The king listened carefully to all the brother had to say. Then he turned to the sage and asked, "How do you respond to these accusations?"

"What these men say is true," the sage answered. "I have not taken care of the garden over these recent months. Prior to that time, however, I tended the garden most faithfully, according to my duty. But one day, much to my sorrow, I found the footprints of the king's lion in the midst of the garden, and I realized that the lion had made off with the garden's fruit. Indeed, I am afraid that soon the lion will return to the garden and take my life."

Now the king had grown wiser from his reading of the Torah that he had taken from the sage's home. Therefore he understood everything alluded to in the parable he was told, and he knew what had to be done.

"I realize that my lion used to wander about the city to prey on the innocent," the king told the sage and the three brothers. "But you should know that he will wander no more. For I have built up powerful walls to keep him in his den. Know, too, that even though the lion was prowling in your garden, he did not take a single fruit from it or touch a single flower. For the fence surrounding your garden was much too high for him to climb. Therefore he left, taking only a single bunch of grapes, which I shall now return to you."

At that the king pulled the Torah out from under his robes and handed it to the sage, who was overjoyed at the king's words.

With his brothers-in-law trailing behind him, the sage hurried home to his wife and begged her forgiveness for having falsely accused her. He offered her words of kindness and his loving caress. Soon she recovered from her illness, and the two of them lived happily together in a kingdom ruled by a king who had received the light of Torah.

The Sweetest of Melodies

According to the teachings of the Jewish tradition, we may attend to our spiritual needs through prayer and study, but our obligation to our fellow human being is to attend to his physical needs. Are we not to offer others the nourishment of Torah? To be sure. But not when they are hungry or thirsty or sick. Indeed, attending to the material comfort of the other person is the first and most important step in helping him meet his own spiritual needs. Such is the lesson conveyed by this tale from Afghanistan.

Abbas the Great, the renowned Shah of Persia, was a highly intelligent man who delighted in conversing through parables. In order to do that, he surrounded himself with men of wit who could understand his tales. One such man was Merza Zaki, a Jew who was among the wisest of the Shah's ministers.

One day the Shah was holding court, discussing various topics with his council. As they spoke, a question came to him, and he asked, "Who can tell me what is the sweetest of melodies?"

"Oh, Sire," one minister answered, "it is the sound of the flute."

"No," another disagreed. "In my opinion nothing surpasses the beauty of the harp."

"You are both mistaken," a third put in. "The sound most pleasant to the ear is the sound of a violin."

Soon a heated argument ensued. Merza Zaki, however, said nothing but calmly listened to the others.

Several days later Merza Zaki invited the Shah and the ministers of the realm to a banquet in their honor. When they were all seated at the banquet table, his musicians entered the dining hall to entertain the guests. The musicians were among the most talented in the kingdom, and they played beautiful melodies on a variety of instruments. For a brief time the guests enjoyed the music, but soon they noticed that something was missing: there was no food on the table.

Now this was odd indeed, since Merza Zaki was known for the sumptuous food and drink he always served to his dinner guests on such occasions. In the past the table was covered with delicacies of every description. Once his guests had delighted in the first course, it dishes of meat and rice and fine wine followed. This time, however, the table was empty. The musicians played beautifully, but the table was empty. What could Merza Zaki be thinking?

Just as the guests were beginning to grumble among themselves over the absence of food, Merza Zaki ordered his headwaiter to bring in a large pot filled with good food and a tray full of dishes for the guests. When the ministers heard the sound of the clinking dishes, they all breathed a sigh of relief and eagerly waited to be served.

Suddenly Shah Abbas understood exactly what Merza Zaki was up to. Smiling at his host, he declared to the ministers seated around the table, "Merza Zaki has shown us the sweetest of melodies: it is the sound of clinking dishes in the ears of a hungry man!"

The Clever Bedouin

This story from Tunisia is an excellent example of the sense of humor that is to be found in Jewish folklore. Like many humorous tales, it has no heroes, and perhaps the message we are to receive from it lies in the smile it brings.

There was once a very poor but very pious Jew. With the coming of the Sabbath or a holiday he would go to great lengths to properly observe the occasion. One year, however, was especially difficult for him. As the Passover season approached and he saw that his cupboard was bare, he grew more and more worried about how he was going to gather all that he needed for a proper Passover celebration. Then he had an idea.

He went to a rich man and said, "Please, sir, I need your help."

"I have no money for you," the rich man answered before the poor Jew could say another word.

"Oh, but it isn't money I need, sir," the Jew explained. "I was just wondering whether I might borrow your finest donkey for a short while. I promise to have him back by midnight tonight."

"Well," the rich man replied, "as long as it isn't money you're after, I suppose it will be all right. But mind you, I must have the donkey back by midnight." So he let the poor Jew borrow his finest donkey.

The Jew took the donkey to the market, where he announced to every passerby, "Donkey for sale! Donkey for sale! Very good price!"

Before long a clever Bedouin, who had an excellent eye for donkeys, came walking down the street. He could see that the donkey was a fine, strong animal, and he was always eager to take advantage of a bargain. After a few minutes of haggling, he bought the borrowed donkey and took it back to his camp. As for the Jew, he followed the Bedouin from a safe distance.

Soon after nightfall the Jew sneaked into the Bedouin camp, untied the donkey, and took it back to the animal's owner, who was pleased to have his donkey back. Then the Jew went back to the camp, tied himself to the donkey's rope, and waited for sunrise.

Precisely at dawn the Bedouin came out of his tent to admire the fine donkey he had purchased at such an excellent price. To his amazement, however, in the spot where he had tied the donkey he found a man. "Who are you?" he cried, too surprised to recognize the Jew. "What has happened?"

"Alas," the Jew explained, "a sorcerer cast a spell on me and turned me into a donkey. But now, praise be to God, I have changed back into a man."

"I thought there was something strange about you," said the Bedouin as he untied the man. "But I want no sorcery around here. Please, be off."

Happy that his plan had worked, the Jew was able to purchase everything he needed for a sumptuous Passover.

Meanwhile the rich man had decided to take his donkey to the market and put it up for sale. "After all," he said to himself, "I did not miss it when I let the poor Jew borrow the animal, and I can always use a little more money."

The Bedouin, however, missed the donkey very much and went to the market to purchase another one. Soon he spotted a fine looking donkey, and, having an excellent eye for donkeys, the Bedouin immediately recognized it to be the same one had he purchased before. He walked over to the donkey and whispered in its ear, "Ah, my poor man, you've been bewitched again. But let someone else buy you. I'm too clever to be fooled again!"

The Doctor Who Healed a King to Save His People

This Jewish folktale from Libya is one of many tales about the deliverance of the Jewish community from the hands of a wicked king. In this case, however, deliverance comes not when the king is defeated but when, thanks to the wisdom of a Jew, the king is healed. Perhaps it tells us that if we would be delivered from our enemy, we must heal him.

There was once a wicked king who had a blinding hatred for the Jews. In fact, he despised them so much that he decided to wage war against them. Arming his soldiers with the finest bows, swords, and spears, the king led them out to battle. Since the Jews had no weapons, the king was sure they would suffer a swift defeat. The Jews, however, bravely fought back with stones; when they ran out of stones they threw dirt at their attackers.

Some of the dirt that the Jews threw hit the king in the eye and caused him so much pain that he had to break off the fight. His soldiers took him back to the palace, where doctors were summoned to attend to him. They offered various treatments for his eye but to no avail; the king could not stop rubbing it. The more he rubbed his eye, the more swollen and painful it became. Since the doctors were unable to heal him, the wicked king had them put to death and offered a reward to anyone who could relieve him of his suffering.

A Jewish physician known for his wisdom heard about the king's ailment and the offer of a reward. Seeing an opportunity to win the king's favor and possibly save his people, the Jew went to the palace and announced that he could heal the king's eye. Immediately he was taken to the ailing monarch, to whom he declared, "Your Majesty, I am a doctor. If you will undress and allow me to examine you, I am sure I can heal your eye."

"You are a Jew, aren't you?" the king squinted at the man. But before the doctor could answer, the king waved his hand and said, "No matter. Just help me with this eye."

Ready to do anything, the king lost no time disrobing. The Jewish doctor started to take a look at the eye, when he turned his attention to the king's stomach. With a look of concern on his face, he carefully felt the stomach and said, "The trouble with your eye is nothing compared to the problem growing in your stomach."

"What do you mean?" the king asked.

"There's a tapeworm growing inside of you," the Jew explained, "and it is getting bigger every day. If you do not kill it, it will kill you."

The king grew very afraid and asked, "What am I to do?"

"I can help you," the Jew told him, "but only if you carefully follow my instructions."

"Of course, anything!" the king replied.

Pulling a small bottle of oil from his pocket, the doctor continued, "Take this oil and rub a few drops on your stomach every day for a week. By the eighth day the tapeworm will be dead."

The king followed the Jew's instructions very precisely. Unable to think of anything but killing the parasite that threatened to kill him, he forgot all about his eye and stopped rubbing it. Right away the eye began to get better.

On the eighth day the wise physician returned, as ordered, to check on the king. The king undressed, and the Jewish doctor examined him. "Your Majesty," said the Jew, "I am pleased to announce that the tapeworm is dead. By the way, your eye has been healed, too."

The king was so grateful to the Jew whose wisdom had healed him that he gave him a handsome reward and was a friend to the Jews for the rest of his days.

A Father's Wisdom

The wisdom of our parents' advice is not always apparent when they offer it to us. But once we have lived for a while, as our mothers and fathers have, suddenly they seem to be wiser than we had thought. In this Moroccan tale we see not only the wisdom of a father's advice; we also realize that the timing of our action can be as important as the action itself.

A wealthy merchant once had a son who thought of nothing but spending money, chasing women, and generally having a good time. Although the father often tried to guide his son according to the Torah and show him a better way of life, the young man never heeded his father's advice. Not until his father was on his deathbed did the son bother to listen to him. "I owe him at least that much," the young man said to himself as he sat next to his dying father.

"My son," the old man said to him, "I won't scold you anymore for the frivolous life you've chosen. I know now that it is of no use. But I do have three bits of advice for you, and I beg you to listen to what I say."

"Of course, Father," the young man replied, a hint of remorse stirring in his heart.

"First," his father told him, "if you must go drinking in the taverns, never go before two o'clock in the morning."

"No problem," the son said to himself. "That's my favorite time of night."

"Second," his father continued, "if you must chase after women, never go to a woman after ten o'clock in the morning."

"That's easy," thought the son. "It doesn't really matter when I take my pleasure."

"Finally," the old man said, "when you are angry in the evening, do nothing about it until morning."

"More time to think of ways to get even," the son mused. And to the dying man he said, "I'll do just as you say, Father. I promise."

Having received his son's promise to follow his advice, the old merchant died in peace.

By the time the week of mourning had passed, the young man was ready to go to his favorite tavern to take his mind off his sorrow over the loss of his father. Evening came, and he was about to set out for the drinking establishment, when he remembered his promise to his father. After patiently waiting until 2:00 A.M., he went to the tavern only to find his friends sprawled on the floor in a disgustingly drunken state. Realizing that he had often been in the same repulsive condition, the merchant's son was so sickened by the scene that he vowed never to come back.

The next morning the young man rose early with the familiar desire to visit one of his lady friends. Again, however, he remembered what his father had told him and looked at his watch. Since it was not yet ten o'clock, he went to the woman's apartment and knocked on her door. She invited him in and led him to her bedroom, where in the light of day the young man saw her as though for the first time. Without the lipstick, mascara, and makeup that she wore at night, the woman he had thought to be a beauty looked wrinkled, gray, and ugly. Indeed, the young man looked ugly to himself, and he left her apartment never to return.

The merchant's son completely gave up carousing and chasing women, took over his father's business, and soon married a decent woman. A few days after their honeymoon, however, the young man had to set sail on a very long trip for his business. The journey took him nearly two years, and during that time he received no word from home.

One night his ship finally returned to its home port. Since he missed his wife very much, the man decided not to wait until morning and returned home despite the late hour. He was about to open the door to his house, when he heard his wife laughing and speaking to someone. The sounds were coming from her bedroom.

"She has betrayed me!" he thought, overcome with rage. His hand went for his sword, and he was about to break in to kill his wife and her lover, when once more he remembered his father's words of advice and stopped. "Very well, Father," he whispered. "I'll do nothing about my anger tonight. I'll kill them in the morning. Vengeance is a dish best served cold." And he went to spend the night at an inn nearby.

The irate husband rose early the next day and went straight to his house. As soon as he entered the door, he saw that his wife was not alone: there was a baby in her lap just over a year old. "Who is this child?" he demanded.

"This is your son, my husband," she smiled and held the child up. "He was born while you were away. I'm so happy you're—"

"Where does he sleep at night?" her husband interrupted.

"In my bedroom," she answered.

Realizing that he had heard his wife laughing and talking to his son, the man realized the wisdom of his father.

The Most Beautiful Dream

This tale from Turkey has its counterparts in numerous versions throughout the world. While it is told in a humorous vein, it contains the familiar Jewish emphasis on life in this world, and not in a dream world. As for which dream is truly the most beautiful dream, perhaps it is the tale itself. For here three men of three different religions seem to get along fairly well, despite their differences.

So that their money might go farther, a Christian, a Jew, and a Muslim once pooled their funds to share expenses on a trip to Istanbul. When they arrived in the city, they took a room in a modest inn. It was very cold that night, and each of them wanted to sleep in the middle to keep warm. "Clearly it is God's will that I sleep in the middle," the Jew announced to his traveling companions.

"How do you figure that?" the Christian and Muslim wanted to know.

"It is simple," the Jew explained. "You, Ahmed, observe your day of rest on Friday, while you, John, have your holy day on Sunday. Since my Sabbath comes on Saturday, it falls in the middle. Therefore that is my proper place."

The Jew's reasoning made perfect sense to the Christian and the Muslim, and they agreed that he should sleep in the middle.

When they went out the next day the three of them found a gold coin in the street. Since none of them saw it first, they considered how they all might spend it. The Jew listened patiently while his two friends argued over what should be purchased. Finally it was decided that they would buy a delicious cake, for which the Turks were famous.

"After all, we're in Istanbul!" the Christian and the Muslim declared.

"But how shall we divide the cake?" asked the Jew.

Another discussion ensued, until they all agreed that the one who had the most beautiful dream that night would have the cake for himself in the morning. Each would tell his dream to the patrons in a nearby cafe, and they would be the judges.

Night fell, and the three of them went to sleep, each hoping to dream the most beautiful dream. Before long, however, the Jew awoke and was very hungry. "This is silly," he said to himself. "We should all share the cake and eat it now."

He tried to wake his companions, but they were sleeping too soundly. So he helped himself to a small bite of cake and went back to sleep. An hour later he woke up again, more hungry than ever. He tried to wake his friends but again to no avail. Then he had another nibble of the cake. So it went throughout the night. By morning the cake was gone, but the Jew managed to hide the fact that he had eaten it.

When the three of them rose the next day they went straight to the cafe to relate their dreams to the patrons. The Muslim explained to the people all that the travelers had agreed to, and everyone in the cafe was eager to see who had the most beautiful dream.

"In my dream," the Christian went first, "my Lord Jesus came to me and took me to the heaven of heavens. There, in the heart of paradise, he showed me all the Christian saints gathered before God. Is that not a beautiful dream?"

The Muslim went next and said, "I dreamt that the prophet Mohammed took me by the hand and escorted me through the gates of paradise. There he showed me the wonders of heaven. Can there be a more beautiful dream?"

"My dream was nothing like theirs," the Jew told his listeners. "I had no visions of heaven, but in my dream Moses visited this earth and said to me, 'John is in heaven with his beloved Jesus; Ahmed is there too with his master Mohammed. Who knows whether either of them will return from such a beautiful place? So you, Reuven, might as well eat the cake.'"

"Did you eat it?" the patrons asked.

"Of course," the Jew replied. "Do you think I would disobey the teacher and lawgiver Moses?"

Tales of the Hasidim

ASIDISM AROSE in the eighteenth century, when its founder, Yisrael ben Eliezer (1700–1760), appeared on a Jewish scene that was in a state of crisis. The crisis was characterized by tensions between talmudic legalism and Lurianic mysticism that followed in the wake of the Chmielnicki massacres in the Ukraine (1648–1649) and the appearance of the infamous would-be Messiah Shabbetai Tzevi (1626–1676). While Yisrael ben Eliezer—who became known as the Baal Shem Tov (Master of the Good Name) or the Besht—adhered strictly to Jewish law, he expanded Jewish religious life by accentuating the role of joy, love, and fervor in our relation to God and to one another. According to Hasidic teaching, the path to God passes through our fellow human beings.

In no other single movement in Jewish religious life do stories and storytelling play a larger role than in Hasidism. We have little in the way of ideological manifestos or theological tracts from the Hasidic masters. What we do have is a wealth of tales about the masters and their followers. These tales come to us through an oral tradition that has found its way into many different written sources. The most famous compilers of Hasidic tales in recent times are Martin Buber, a philosopher know for his emphasis on the dialogical relationship between human beings, and Holocaust survivor Elie Wiesel. In addition, Nobel Prize Laureate Isaac Bashevis Singer and Abraham Joshua Heschel, one of this century's most prominent spiritual leaders, wrote books about the Baal Shem Tov, and the great scholar of the Talmud, Adin Steinsaltz, has written works on Nachman of Bratslav and Shneur Zalman, the first of the Lubavitcher rebbes. Lesser known but notable scholars who have passed along the tales of the Hasidim include Louis Newman, Meyer Levin, Milton Aron, Harry Rabinowitz, and Louis Jacobs, to name just a few. The stories retold here have been repeated in various forms in a number of works by these and other authors.

The Man Who Recorded
the Words of the Besht

This tale is drawn from the Shivchei ha-Besht *(In Praise of the Besht), one of the earliest collections of legends about the Baal Shem Tov, compiled by his disciple Rabbi Dov Ber, the famous Maggid of Mezeritch (1704–1772). In it we see the Baal Shem's emphasis on the spoken word. A word consigned to the page may be drained of its spirit and contain only the dead flesh of meaning. But a word spoken in tones of lovingkindness can quicken the dead.*

Whenever the Baal Shem Tov would go about discussing matters of Torah and religious life, he would always be accompanied by a group of disciples who listened very carefully to his every utterance. He never wrote down anything himself, but there was a young man among his followers who thought it was very important to record the words of wisdom that came from the mouth of the Besht.

One day the Baal Shem came across a demon walking around with something suspicious tucked under his arm.

"What is that you are carrying?" he demanded of the devil, convinced that what the creature held had to be a snare for trapping the souls of good people.

"Why it is the book that you yourself have written," the demon replied. "Everything contained in it came from your own lips."

Immediately the Baal Shem knew just what had happened: one of his students had been writing down his teachings. He gathered all of his disciples together and asked, "Which of you has been writing down the words that I speak?"

"I am the one you are looking for, Master," one of them declared with pride, and from under his coat he produced a volume of all that he had recorded.

"Please let me see it," said the Baal Shem.

The student handed the manuscript to his teacher, and the Baal

Shem looked at one page, then another, and another. Finally he declared, "These pages contain not a single word that is mine. I said one thing, you heard a second, and then you wrote a third."

Before he could utter a reply, the student realized that the Baal Shem was teaching him yet another lesson: the soul that vibrates on the breath is lost to the imprint on the page.

The Tsaddik Rivka

Holiness sometimes turns up in the most unlikely of places and usually shows itself in very humble ways. In this story from the Shivchei ha-Besht, *about a woman named Rivka, we learn that righteousness not only requires a great deal of charity but a great deal of courage; Rivka would be intimidated by no one—not even the Baal Shem Tov—in her efforts to help those in need.*

During one of his many travels the Baal Shem Tov approached the city of Satnov. As he drew closer to the city, he could see the glow of righteousness that emanated from it, as though the sun itself had settled into its midst: the Baal Shem had an eye for such spiritual lights. When he reached the city's outskirts, a large group of people, who had received word of the Master's visit, came out to meet him.

As they gathered around him, he asked, "Are you aware that a person of great righteousness, a *tsaddik*, lives among you?"

"A *tsaddik*?" they asked, wondering whom he could mean.

"Indeed," the Besht answered. "And it is a woman."

At first they were surprised, but then they realized that the Baal Shem must be referring to Rivka.

"Oh, yes," they said to him. "Surely you mean Rivka, a woman known for her piety and goodness."

"I would like to meet this woman," the Baal Shem told them. "Where can I find her?"

"Oh, don't worry," they all assured him. "She will find you. She goes around asking everyone, even visitors, for donations to help the many poor families that she supports."

Just as the townspeople had predicted, on the following day immediately after the morning prayers the Tsaddik Rivka showed up at the house of study to have a word with the Baal Shem.

Without even bothering to introduce herself, she asked, "Rebbe, please, do you think you could make a donation to the needy families of Satnov?"

"Yes, of course," the Rebbe answered, and he took a coin from his purse and held it out to her.

"I'm sorry, Rebbe," she said to him, looking at the coin in his hand, "but that is not enough. You see, I am collecting for people who are not only hungry but who are sick and need medicine. I know you can do better than that."

"Very well," the Baal Shem replied and offered her a few more coins.

"I'm afraid you do not understand, Rebbe," Rivka stubbornly shook her head. "These people are very poor. They need more than that. I must insist that you donate no less than forty guilders."

"Forty guilders!" cried the Baal Shem, now pretending to be angry. "Who do you think you are? The city treasurer? You should be grateful for anything you can get for these people. I wouldn't be surprised if you were pocketing half the money for yourself!"

Undaunted by the Master's accusation, the Tsaddik Rivka stared him in the eye, held out her hand, and waited for him to give her the forty guilders. Convinced of her courage and perseverance, the Baal Shem gave her the full amount, whereupon the Tsaddik Rivka thanked him and left.

That evening she returned to him with another request.

"How much this time?" the Besht asked, before she could say a word.

"I'm not here for money," she replied. "I'm here for your prayers. Our city's doctor is very ill; I want you to intercede with Heaven, so that he may recover. I insist that you pray for him."

"And I say to you," he told her, "that ever since I arrived in this town I have heard nothing but evil reports about that man and his philandering ways. Why should I pray for such a sinner? If he were to die this very night, the world would be burdened by one less adulterer."

But the Tsaddik Rivka would not be turned away so easily.

"Since you know what the Talmud teaches us about speaking badly of others," she declared to the Rebbe, "you should also know that these evil reports are nothing but hearsay. No one has ever actually caught him in the act. Besides, the doctor may be a learned man of medicine, but he is completely ignorant of our law. I am certain that if he himself realized the gravity of such sinful behavior, he would refrain from even thinking about it. In any case, God is his judge, not you or I."

That was precisely what the Baal Shem had hoped the Tsaddik Rivka would say.

"My good woman," he told her, "the doctor is on his way to recovery even as we speak. Your righteousness has made my prayers unnecessary. The heavenly court had all but sealed his fate; but the generous and merciful words you spoke in his behalf were enough to tip the scales in favor of life. By tomorrow morning the doctor will once again be at work healing the sick."

How to Fast

Hasidism is characterized by rejoicing and a celebration of life; the Hasidic masters generally discouraged the practice of asceticism and mortification of the flesh. The Maggid of Mezeritch, for example, told his followers that they should not be satisfied to eat black bread alone but should try to enjoy the luxury of eating cake as well. "If you think you can manage on black bread alone," he warned them, "then you may come to suppose that your neighbor can manage with a stone." One is, however, permitted to fast under certain conditions. This tale about the Baal Shem tells what those conditions are.

In his youth the Baal Shem Tov was known to have fasted during the six days of the week that separated each Sabbath to the next. Since fasting was not encouraged by the masters, the question sometimes arose: how should one to go about fasting if fasting is necessary for some reason?

The story is told that one Sunday morning the Baal Shem prepared to go off into the forest for six days of prayer and meditation. During such times he would converse with the angels and with Jewish sages of the past. Surrounded by circles of fire, some say, he would study Torah and Talmud with the wise rabbis of old in the highest reaches of heaven.

As he readied himself for the days ahead, the Baal Shem's wife prepared for him a large canteen of water and a sack of six loaves of bread, each one big enough to provide food for an entire day.

"Please take these," she urged him, "so that you won't go hungry or thirsty during your time away from home."

He thanked her and assured her that she need not worry about him. But she insisted that he take the canteen and the bag laden with bread with him. In order to put her mind at peace, he threw the bread over his shoulder, picked up the canteen, and set off.

No one knows exactly where the Baal Shem went or what happened during the time he was away. Perhaps he spent the entire time in the company of angels and sages, encircled by flames of holiness. It is known, however, that on the following Friday the hour of his return home to spend the Sabbath with his wife finally came. When he picked up the sack and started homeward, he was surprised to discover that it still contained the six loaves of bread that his wife had sent with him.

Such fasting is allowed.

When the Deaf See People Dancing

Those who behold the light of the Holy One and hear His voice not only march to a different drummer, they move to a beat that no one else can hear and are often taken to be a bit crazy. When neither revolt nor submission is the answer to the turmoil of life, what remains is a mystical, metaphysical madness. Such madness may, indeed, lie at the beginning of Judaism, as one wonders what Abram's family must have thought when he announced that he was leaving for the Promised Land. Yet he went because he heard what others could not hear. He went because he could not do otherwise. And in that compulsion lay his freedom, as the Hasidim would also discover centuries later.

When the Baal Shem brought his teaching to the Jews of eastern Europe, there were many rabbis who opposed him. Indeed, they feared him because they could not understand his emphasis on joy and fervor, which, they believed, might preclude reverence for the holy law. Some even denounced him for desecrating the Sabbath by encouraging people to let their souls express themselves freely in song and dance.

"This lunatic and the so-called Hasidim who follow him," they declared, "must surely be insane! Have they no reverence, no respect, for Torah study? Do they not know what it means to be serious?"

The Baal Shem Tov knew very well what it meant to be serious. No one was more serious than he in his love for God and humanity. If the others loved the Torah, he loved the people who loved the Torah. And so when his followers asked him why the learned rabbis deemed his teachings to be false, he answered them with a parable.

"There was once a good family," he told them, "who held a great wedding festival. Wanting to spread the joy of this blessing, they invited their friends from all over the village to attend and join in the merriment. In one corner of their large home they set up a place for a group of musicians to play. Soon the entire house was filled with music, dancing, and rejoicing.

"As they were dancing, a deaf man passed by the front window of the house. He could see the people leaping about, whirling around the room, and waving their arms in the air, but he could not see the musicians or hear the music. Thus he declared to himself, 'Look at all that commotion! This must be a house full of madmen!'

"And so the poor man went on his way, unable to take part in the celebration. For he could not hear the music that animated the wedding guests."

Learning to Walk

Sometimes it seems that God is so remote that we will never find our way to Him. Sometimes it seems that He is silent and does not hear our cry. But, as this tale suggests, even when He is far, He is near. Even when He is silent, He is listening.

More than anything, the Baal Shem Tov was known for his compassion and lovingkindness. One day one of his disciples approached him and dared to ask a question that had been troubling him. He dared to ask because it was a question that anyone other than the Baal Shem might have construed as sacrilegious. But the Baal Shem understood that the question arose as much from faith as from doubt.

"Forgive me, Rebbe," the disciple said, "but there is something that has been bothering me. I know we are taught that God is always near, closer to us than our own shadows. But I must confess to you that there are times when the Infinite One seems to be infinitely far. Can you help me with this?"

The Baal Shem thought for a moment and then replied, "Have you ever watched a father teach his child how to walk? For a while he will hold the toddler by the hand and walk at his side, guiding him and encouraging him every step of the way. But there comes a time when the father will let go, so that the little fellow may try to walk on his own toward him. It may be frightening at first, but soon they give each other a loving embrace, and then the father moves back again. Each time the child steps toward his father by himself he learns to walk a little better.

"Know, then, that God, who is the Father of all, teaches us to walk in the same manner. He moves away from us for a time, so that we may move toward Him. Moving toward Him, we learn to move toward life."

Love Him More

The teachings of the Hasidic masters can be summed up in two words: love more. But love is not a fuzzy feeling or one emotion among many. No, it is a living presence that rises up between people. Feelings dwell inside of us, Martin Buber once said, but we dwell in our love. Indeed, it is our love for one another that makes dwelling possible. Love, then, is a source of edification and an avenue of revelation. We cannot wait until we know what life is about before we love it, for it is only by loving life that we can ever hope to understand it.

This tale was included in the Siach Sarfei Kodesh *(Utterance of the* Holy Flame*), a collection published in Lodz in 1929.*

There was once a man whose adolescent son had fallen into sinful ways. The boy would stay out late at night, carouse with Gentiles, and chase after girls. He even spoke to his mother and father with disrespect. Finally, at a complete loss as to how he might lead his son back to the proper path, the father went to speak to the Baal Shem Tov.

"Rebbe," he said, "I am at my wits' end. My son has fallen into such evil that I fear for his soul. He has completely abandoned the teachings of our faith, and his behavior is disgraceful. I have threatened to beat him or to throw him out of the house, but nothing seems to work. How can I convince him to change his ways?"

"Love him more," the Baal Shem replied.

"But he deserves no love!" the father answered.

"That is all the more reason to increase your love for him," the Besht insisted. "Do you think God loves us because we deserve it? No. Love is the very essence of life. It is the light that illuminates the path to God. If you would have your son follow that path, then you must be such a light unto him. Love him more."

The Little Boy's Tune

This tale of the Baal Shem Tov is about prayer and about love. If love is the essential element in the relationship of one human being to another, it is because love is the essential component in the relationship between man and God. That makes love a fundamental feature of prayer, love for the One to whom our prayer is addressed and who, through our prayers, addresses us. If He addresses us through our prayers, He also addresses us through the many tales about prayer that have been passed down to us from our forbears—through tales like this one.

Rabbi Yisrael ben Eliezer, the Baal Shem Tov, once was about to enter a synagogue when he came to a sudden halt.

"It is impossible for me to go in there," he declared to the Hasidim who accompanied him.

"Why is that, Rabbi?" they asked.

"There is not enough room for me to squeeze in," he said.

"But there are only a few people here today," the Hasidim replied. "How could there be no room for you?"

"The building is crammed full of prayers," the master explained, "from floor to ceiling."

"Is that not as it should be?"

"Indeed not," the Baal Shem answered. "You see, these prayers are dead prayers. They possess neither the power nor the intensity to rise up to heaven. Instead, each new layer of prayer crushes the one beneath it."

The Baal Shem Tov returned home, greatly disturbed by the sight of the dead prayers that had filled the synagogue.

Not far from the Baal Shem's home in Medzibozh lived a simple shepherd. The shepherd had a twelve-year-old son David, who was rather slow-witted. In fact, after years of schooling, the child had not even learned the alphabet. Finally his father withdrew him from school and sent him out to the fields to attend to the flocks. At least there, he thought, the lad would be of some use.

One day, as he sat in the field looking after the sheep, David took a reed and made himself a flute. He played his flute for hours on end, and wherever he went he would take his flute with him.

When David turned thirteen his father decided that his son must be exposed to the Jewish ways. Thus, when Yom Kippur, the Day of Atonement, the holiest day of the Jewish year, arrived, David and his father set out for the synagogue in Medzibozh.

When they reached the synagogue, David sat down next to his father and kept very quiet throughout the morning service. When the men recited the musaf prayers—the additional service—raising their voices in song, David looked on in awe.

Overwhelmed by the passion of prayer, David tugged at his father's sleeve and said, "Father, I want to pray too!"

But his father scolded him, saying, "Do you want to anger Rabbi Yisrael? Be still!"

The boy struggled to sit quietly until the Minchah, afternoon, service. Once again David cried to his father, "Father, please let me pray too!"

"But you can't even read!" his father retorted. "Do you want to embarrass both of us? Just be quiet."

Once again, biting his tongue in shame, the boy sat in silence throughout the prayers that moved him so.

At last came the hour for Neilah, the concluding service of Yom Kippur. The worshipers trembled in the flickering candlelight. All through the house of prayer they could sense the Presence of the Holy One. Rabbi Yisrael stretched out his arms and recited the Eighteen Benedictions.

The vision of the Baal Shem lifting the prayers of the Jews to God was too much for the shepherd's son. He took his flute from his coat pocket and, aflame with the fervor of faith, began to play a tune.

The entire congregation fell silent, aghast at this effrontery that bordered on sacrilege. Staring at the impudent child, they looked as if they expected the walls of the synagogue to fall down upon them. Crushed with shame, David's father started to tear the flute from his son's mouth, when he noticed that the Baal Shem was transfixed by the music.

His face beaming with joy, Rabbi Yisrael rushed over to the child who was playing the flute and spread his palms over him in a gesture of benediction.

"Thanks to the passion of this little one," he cried, "the cloud of evil that has kept our prayers from Heaven has been penetrated! For the Evil One Himself could not prevail against such a prayer!"

The Scholar and the Laborer

This tale was related by one of the Baal Shem Tov's closest disciples, Rabbi Yaakov Yosef ha-Kohen Katz, in his work known as Toledot Yaakov Yosef (The Chronicles of Yaakov Yosef). *It teaches us that substance is more important than surface, devotion more crucial than gestures. For a Jew the decisive question is not only whether he studies Torah but*

whether he lives by it. That is why the Talmud tells us that one who has
only the Torah does not even have the Torah.

The Baal Shem Tov once told a story about two Jews and their families who shared a single house. One man was a scholar noted for his learning; the other was a poor and humble laborer. Each morning, like the pious men of old, the scholar would rise at dawn, go to the synagogue, and study a folio from the Talmud. At precisely the proper moment, he would turn his heart to heaven and begin the morning prayers. He recited his prayers slowly and carefully, concentrating on each word, so that it took him almost until midday to complete them. Having finished his study and prayers, the scholar would finally leave the synagogue, very pleased with himself for having been so observant in adhering to the will of God.

The poor laborer also rose at dawn. But instead of going to the synagogue, he set out for the backbreaking toil that filled his day. He had no opportunity to stop for morning prayers. It was only when he had a break at noon that he could at last hurry to the synagogue, where he would rush through his prayers, filled with guilt and pain for having been so late. Very often, as he was dashing to the house of prayer, he would pass his neighbor, who had already completed the morning service. Uttering a groan of regret, the laborer was invariably embarrassed that his neighbor had fulfilled the observance while he had not yet gotten around to it.

As for the scholar, each time he saw the laborer arriving so late for the morning prayers, he would declare to himself, "Master of the Universe, You see the difference between that impious man and myself. Each day I rise for Torah study and prayer, but just look at him! Already the hour for the morning prayers has passed, and he has not yet shown his face in Your house."

Thus the two of them passed their lives, one enjoying the luxury of Torah and prayer, the other forced into the toil of laboring for his bread. As it comes to all, death came at last to them both.

The scholar was summoned before the celestial tribunal to answer for his deeds.

"What have you done with the days of life that were allotted to you on earth?" a voice demanded of him.

His heart full of pride, the scholar declared, "I have devoted all of my days to the faithful study of God's Torah and to prayers of devotion."

At that, however, the heavenly accuser stepped forward and pointed out, "He may have said his prayers, but he mocked his neighbor, the poor laborer, for failing to say his."

The scales of justice were brought forward. On one side were placed all the Torah that the scholar had studied and all the prayers that he had said. On the other side was laid the trace of a smirk that had come over the scholar's face whenever he greeted his neighbor. The weight of that smirk tipped the scales to a verdict of "guilty."

Then the poor laborer was brought before the heavenly tribunal.

"What have you done with the days of life that were allotted to you on earth?" he was asked.

"I am afraid," he answered, "that I spent all my days laboring to provide food for my wife and children. I did not have time to pray with the congregation at the proper hour, nor did I have time to study very much of God's Torah."

At that the heavenly advocate spoke in his behalf, saying, "Every day, as he hurried to say his prayers, this man would utter a groan of regret for having failed to serve the Lord as he believed he should. It was a groan filled with longing for the Creator."

The scales of justice again were brought before the court, and the laborer's groan was placed on one side, with his tardiness to recite the prayers laid on the other. The weight of his groan was enough to tip the scales to a verdict of "innocent."

God Fulfills Our Needs

There is a great difference between what we desire and what we need. The point is made eloquently in this brief tale about one of the Baal Shem Tov's disciples, Rabbi Michal of Zlotchov. Hasidim say that it is better to want what you have than to have what you want. Along with their accent on joy, Hasidim place tremendous emphasis on gratitude—not just for what we have but for gratitude itself. As Rebbe Baruch of Medzibozh once cried out, "How could I live without gratitude?"

Of all the Hasidic masters, Rabbi Michal of Zlotchov was the most poverty-stricken. Yet he always considered himself rich in blessings.

One of the greatest Hasidic preachers, he was often heard to declare, "I have never felt any desire for anything that I did not have. If I do not have something, I do not need it. After all, God knows better than we do what our needs are."

Rabbi Michal insisted that his prayers always were answered. Indeed, it seemed that any time he prayed for heaven's intervention, it was granted. Never, however, did he seek anything for himself; he insisted that the wisdom of God's will was greater than his own. He continually praised God, saying, "Blessed art Thou, O Lord, King of the Universe, who has fulfilled my every want!"

One day a disciple heard the rabbi offer up this prayer of thanksgiving and could not help but ask the master, "Rabbi, how can you praise God for satisfying your every want? Just look at your dilapidated house, your ragged clothes, your empty pockets. You live in poverty!"

"What you say of me is true," the rabbi answered. "My pockets are empty. But know that if this is so, then what I want right now is my poverty, and the Holy One, blessed be He, has supplied me with just that."

The Prayer Itself Is Divine

Rabbi Pinchas Shapiro of Koretz was one of the Baal Shem Tov's closest disciples. This tale from his work Nofet Tsufim (Honey Flowing from the Honeycomb) conveys a lesson that is fundamental not only to Hasidism but to Judaism: it is God who draws us toward God. When we recite the Amidah prayer, the Shechinah enters into us and prays through us. That is why we begin the prayer by saying, "Oh, Lord, open my lips and I shall sing Your praise." It is God who moves our lips as we pray.

Rabbi Pinchas Shapiro, the Koretzer Rebbe, once sat and struggled with a passage from the prophet Isaiah: "It is written: 'Lift up thy voice as a shofar'" (Isaiah 58:1).

"What could it mean?" he wondered. "How can a voice become like a shofar?"

After pondering the verse further, Rabbi Pinchas suddenly realized that God was revealing to us something about the nature of prayer.

"The shofar remains silent," he said, "and cannot emit a sound unless the breath of a man passes through it. When we become like a shofar, the breath of the Holy One, the divine Shechinah, passes through us. That is how we pray: the breath of God's Indwelling Presence vibrates on our lips. We may think we pray to God, but that is not exactly so: the prayer itself is divine."

How to Serve God

This brief tale captures the substance of the Baal Shem's teaching on how we should serve God.

Rabbi Hersh, son of the Baal Shem Tov, was not the heir to his father's authority. After his father's death, in fact, little is known of Rabbi Hersh. It is said, however, that in his dreams Rabbi Hersh would visit his deceased father in order to speak to him and, above all, to learn from him.

Once, when the Besht came to Rabbi Hersh in a dream, his son asked the Master, "Tell me, Father, how shall I serve God?"

Saying nothing at first, the Baal Shem climbed up to the top of a high mountain that had emerged in the dream. Standing there, he cried to his son, "Like this!" and threw himself from the dizzying height into the yawning abyss.

Puzzled by this, Rabbi Hersh asked once again, "Father, tell me, please, how am I to serve God?"

This time the Baal Shem appeared to his son as a mountain of fire that rose up and exploded in a myriad of flaming fragments.

Whereupon the Baal Shem declared, "Like this!"

My Enemy Will Not Triumph

This story about Rabbi Shmelke of Nikolsburg, a disciple of the Maggid of Mezeritch, appeared in the Menorah ha-Tehorah (Lamp of Purity), *published in Prezemysl in 1911. It exemplifies the great love for one's fellow human being that characterizes the Hasidic movement. It is a love that enables the sacred to manifest itself where otherwise it would never appear; it is a love that transcends the confines of reason and nature: it is a love even for our enemies, who are also the children of God.*

There was once a man who despised Rabbi Shmelke of Nikolsburg and the Hasidic movement that he represented. Trying to devise a way to ruin the rabbi, the man came up with a plan that would plunge the rabbi into public disgrace. On the day before Yom Kippur, the Day of Atonement, the wicked man put his scheme into action and sent the rabbi a flask of very old, very strong wine.

"Shmelke will drink the wine prior to his fast," the scoundrel thought to himself, "and it will make him drunk. When he recites the prayers in the synagogue, everyone will hear his slurred speech and realize that he is intoxicated. The rabbi will be ruined."

When the wine was brought to Rabbi Shmelke, he took a small taste of it and realized what his enemy was up to.

That night the evil man went to the Yom Kippur service to see whether his wicked plan had worked. He waited throughout all the prayers, until, at the conclusion of the service, Rabbi Shmelke stood up and recited a verse from the forty-first Psalm over and over.

"By this I know," the Rabbi repeated, "that You delight in me, that my enemy does not triumph over me."

And each time that Rabbi Shmelke invoked the passage from the Psalm, he declared, "By this You teach me that those who wish to harm me shall suffer no harm because of me. Let this be my prayer to You!"

The man who had hoped to disgrace the rabbi was so moved by his prayer for his enemies that at last he rushed over to Rabbi Shmelke and cried, "Forgive me, please, I beg you!"

"There is nothing to forgive," Rabbi Shmelke calmed him. "Even if you had succeeded in your plan to have me fall into disgrace through public drunkenness, still you would have done me a great good. For such a disgrace would have helped me to pay for the many sins that I have committed. I only regret that my awe of the Holy One, blessed be He, sobered me."

Realizing the great holiness of the rabbi whom he had tried to disgrace, the man was completely transformed and became one of the rabbi's most faithful followers.

How He Ties His Shoes

One of the most basic principles of Hasidism is the idea that God abides in all things. Every act, no matter how small, can affirm our relation to God. That is what Rabbi Leib ben Sarah learned in Mezeritch, as told in this story from a collection titled Die Gemeinde der Chassidim (The Hasidic Community), *published in Vienna in 1920.*

"His sermons on the Torah must have been wonderful," a disciple once said to Rabbi Leib ben Sarah, commenting on his master's teacher, Rabbi Dov Ber of Mezeritch.

"Indeed they were," Rabbi Leib nodded. "But I did not undertake the long and hazardous journey to Mezeritch merely to hear the Maggid's sermons on the Torah."

"If not for his discourses on the Torah," his student asked, "then what?"

"I went to watch him tie his shoes," the rabbi replied.

"Tie his shoes?" the puzzled student repeated. "Rabbi, I do not understand."

"The wisdom of the Maggid," Rabbi Leib explained, "lay not only in his insights and interpretations of the Torah but in the many ways by which he expressed that understanding through every little thing he did. His every gesture, his every word, his very bearing articulated his love for God and man. And so it must be for us all. The Torah encompasses all. To the man of God, therefore, knowing how to tie your shoes is a great accomplishment."

Horror in the Night

The greatest Jewish stories ever told are forever contemporary. The times and places in which they take place are intricately and intimately tied to our own time and place. But some, like this tale of Rabbi Dov Ber's disciples, Rabbi Elimelech of Lizensk and his brother Rabbi Zusya of Onipol, are all too contemporary. This story links the two Hasidic masters to a time and a place that are terrible indeed.

Rabbi Elimelech and his brother Rabbi Zusya traveled throughout eastern Europe to bring Hasidic teachings to Jews near and far. One day as dusk was approaching and they began to fear that they might have to spend another night on the road, they came within sight of a small town. Quickening their steps, they reached the town and found their way to an inn.

Although they did not have enough money for a room, the innkeeper kindly allowed them to share a small space behind the stove. There they bedded down for the night and soon fell asleep.

But as the night wore on, the two of them suddenly awoke and stared at each other in inexplicable horror and panic. Overwhelmed by fear, neither of them said a word.

Unable to shake off their terror, they rose up in the dead of night, ran out of the inn, and fled from the village. Later they learned that the name of the place was Oushpitsin.

Their descendants would know the place as Oswiëcim.

Or: Auschwitz.

Protecting Others from Theft

This tale of Rabbi Zev Wolf of Zbarazh, from the nineteenth-century collection Miflaot ha-Tsadikim (Miracles of the Righteous), reminds us that if we can give others whatever they ask for, not only can no one ever steal from us, but we can actually reduce the level of sin in the world by protecting others from committing theft. We are not what we have—whatever we are lies in what we give.

Rabbi Zev Wolf of Zbarazh was famous for his generosity. Indeed, he belonged to the category of those whom the *Pirke Avot*, Ethics of the Fathers, describes as a "saintly person," one who by his actions declares, "What is mine is yours and what is yours is yours." Each night before retiring, he would go to his door and shout, "All that I have belongs to anyone who desires it."

One night Rabbi Wolf came home later than usual. When he arrived he found two men filling their bags with everything they could find—candlesticks, a menorah, anything in sight.

The rabbi did nothing to stop them but simply said, "In order that you might be spared from falling into the sin of thievery, please accept everything you take as my gift to you."

For a moment the two men looked at each other in surprise, then they continued about the business of filling their bags. Before long one of them happened upon a jar that contained a medicine that could be poisonous.

Noticing the man put the jar into his bag, Rabbi Wolf called out, "One moment! As I told you, all that you see I offer you as a gift. If you want the jar, then please take it—it is yours. But know that it contains a medicine that could be harmful to you if you should swallow too much. Be careful!"

So great was the rabbi's compassion that not only did he not want to see the two men found guilty of theft, but he wanted no harm of any kind to come to them.

It is not known whether the two men made off with the rabbi's possessions. Indeed, to Rabbi Wolf it did not matter.

The Sound of Babbling

One of the most famous disciples of the Maggid of Mezeritch, Rabbi Levi Yitzchak of Berdichev was known as a great defender of humanity. His teachings are included in the nineteenth-century work Kedushat Levi *(Sanctity of Levi). "When God gave the Torah," Rabbi Levi Yitzchak once said, "He gave not only the words but the silence between the words." Here we see the understanding that abides in the silence of the holy that surpasses words.*

One day during the morning prayer service Rabbi Levi Yitzchak of Berdichev overheard a young man mumbling the words of his prayers so that they were hardly intelligible. After the service was over, the rabbi sent for the young man on the pretext of wanting to ask him a question about the Torah. Of course, the man could not refuse such a request. However, when he came into the rabbi's study and greeted him, Levi Yitzchak responded by mumbling something.

"Forgive me, Rabbi," said the young man, "but I did not understand what you said."

Again the rabbi mumbled something or other. Again the man apologized, repeating that he could not understand what the rabbi was saying.

Then Rabbi Levi Yitzchak spoke very clearly and said, "Was that not just the manner in which you were speaking to God at this morning's prayer service?"

"Well, yes," the young man replied, "it's true. You see, I was in a hurry to get back home to my wife and children, who are not well today. I recited the prayers so quickly that it must have sounded like mumbling. But it was my hope that God would understand me all the same, just as a father can understand the mumbling of his children."

Hearing this explanation pleased the rabbi very much, and he quickly sent the young man home to his family. In his remarks to his followers on the following Sabbath the rabbi pointed out that love can take us to levels of understanding that exceed the most erudite scholarship.

"Have you ever noticed," he said to them, "how a babe who has not yet learned how to put words together will lie in his cradle babbling? 'Ma, ma, ma,' he says, 'wa, wa, wa.' If you were to gather around his cradle the most learned scholars and sages of the world, they would not understand anything that came out of that little one's mouth. And yet, when the infant's mother walks into the room, she understands immediately what that babbling means. Indeed, to her it is not babbling at all. It is the voice of an angel calling her to the most sacred of tasks. And in her mother's wisdom she knows just what to do."

Truth and Lie Reversed

In this tale about Rabbi Levi Yitzchak of Berdichev we have a riddle: when is lying preferable to telling the truth? The Berdichever Rebbe explains.

One Yom Kippur Rabbi Levi Yitzchak was reciting the confessional prayers with his congregation when a great sadness suddenly overcame him.

Seeing their rabbi stricken with such sorrow, the people in the congregation asked him, "Rabbi, what is the matter?"

Levi Yitzchak cried out, "The world has been turned on end, and I no longer understand anything! In days of old, when Jews walked the streets and through the marketplaces, they spoke the truth to one another. But when they gathered in the synagogue, they uttered lies. Now things have turned the other way around: in the streets and places of business they tell one lie after another, but when they enter the house of prayer, they pronounce the truth."

"But Rabbi," he was asked, "why should it sadden you that at least here in the synagogue we speak the truth?"

"I'll tell you why," said the rebbe. "In years past Jews were known for their honesty and integrity, and the light of truth illuminated their dealings with one another. Thus they adhered to what they were taught in the Torah, answering their neighbors and their customers with a righteous "Yes" and a truthful "No." Nevertheless, when they entered the synagogue for the confessional prayers, they would beat their breasts and cry out, 'We have lied, we have stolen!' In offering God this confession, indeed they were lying, for they had dealt fairly with their fellow human beings, in truth and good faith.

"But now it is the other way around. The ways in which they deal with one another are filled with falsehood and deception. And so, when they enter the house of prayer and proclaim, 'We have lied, we have stolen,' their words are all too true."

Hearing this explanation of the riddle, the rabbi's congregants understood very well why he was so sad. And in their hearts they determined that they would do everything in their power to relieve him of his sadness.

"She Says, But I Know"

A student once asked his rabbi how Maimonides could expect us to affirm that we believe with perfect faith when no one has perfect faith. The rabbi explained that it was not an assertion but a request that we bring to God: may I believe with perfect faith. This Hasidic tale, however, suggests that there may be some who indeed believe with perfect faith, who not only say God is at work in life but know it. If we can believe the tale, then among those who were possessed of such faith was Rabbi Levi Yitzchak of Berdichev.

When the time came for Rabbi Levi Yitzchak to enter into marriage, he made a match with the daughter of a very wealthy man who lived in the town of Lubertov. Noted for his vast knowledge of Talmud, Rabbi Levi Yitzchak brought his brilliance to this place, so that it soon became known as a center of Jewish learning.

Rabbi Levi Yitzchak was a great admirer of Rabbi Shmelke of Nikolsburg and always followed the advice that Rabbi Shmelke gave him. Therefore when Rabbi Shmelke suggested that he go to Mezeritch and meet with Rabbi Dov Ber, Rabbi Levi Yitzchak left his new wife for a time and set out immediately to visit with the great Maggid of Mezeritch.

Since he was newly wed, Rabbi Levi Yitzchak did not stay away from home for very long. When he returned from this first visit to the Maggid of Mezeritch, his father-in-law had him to dinner in order to ask him about his meeting with Dov Ber.

"So tell me," his father-in-law asked as they sat at the table, "did you learn anything special from the renowned rabbi?"

"Yes, I did," Levi Yitzchak replied. "He led me to realize that God is in the world."

"But that is common knowledge to even the simplest of Jews," his father-in-law commented. "Here, I'll show you." Turning to the maid who was serving them he said, "I have a question for you, my good woman. Is God in the world?"

"Why, of course He is, sir," the maid answered.

"There, you see," the father-in-law announced triumphantly to Levi Yitzchak. "What could be simpler?"

"She says," Levi Yitzchak shot back, filled with inspiration. "But I know."

The Timid Tailor

Ever since Abraham argued with God over the fate of Sodom and Gomorrah, it seems that part of Jews' living up to their side of the Covenant entails insisting that God live up to His side of it as well. The Talmud teaches us that God likes to be defeated by His children. And recall God's assertion at the end of the Book of Job that Job had spoken rightly. Why does He say this, just after having rebuked Job for his presumption? Because He likes the idea that Job was willing to speak up in the face of what he took to be an injustice in the world. In this tale Rabbi Levi Yitzchak would like to see a timid tailor speak up too.

Rabbi Levi Yitzchak of Berdichev stood before his congregation one Yom Kippur. Struggling in his heart to come up with a way to convey to his followers an important lesson, he turned to one of the congregants, a tailor by trade, and asked him to step before the assembly of the faithful. Heeding his rabbi's request, the tailor rose and went to stand next to Levi Yitzchak.

"I would like for you," the Rabbi asked, "to please offer your prayer of confession to the Holy One, blessed be He."

Without hesitation the tailor made his public confession: "I, Yankel, am a poor and simple tailor. I must say that this year there were times when I was not completely honest. Now and then I would keep remnants of cloth that were left over from my work. And more than once I have missed the Minchah prayer service. But is this worse than what You Yourself have done, O Lord? You have taken children from their mothers, wives from their husbands, and brothers from their sisters. What do you say we call it quits on this Day of Days, O Lord? If You can forgive me, then I shall find a way to forgive You."

Hearing this prayer, Rabbi Levi Yitzchak heaved a great sigh and said, "Yankel, O Yankel, why were you so timid? Why did you let God off so lightly?"

The King Who Loved Music

In this parable attributed to Rabbi Levi Yitzchak of Berdichev we learn that the devotion with which we try to serve God is more dear to Him than the skill that we bring to that service. No one is excluded from the opportunity to bring joy to the Holy One, blessed be He, for devotion requires not the erudite learning of the scholars but the burning passion of the believer.

A king took such great delight in music that he appointed the best musicians in his kingdom to play for him each morning. Those who arrived at the designated hour received a handsome reward, and those who came early were rewarded even more handsomely. The musicians, however, were so devoted to the king that they came not for the rewards he bestowed upon them but out of love for the monarch.

As the years went by, the musicians passed away one by one. Their sons tried to take their places in service to the king, but they did not have their fathers' skills, and their instruments were in very poor condition. Worse than their lack of skill and their ill-kept instruments was the fact that they did not have the same love for the king that had animated their fathers. They were interested only in the rewards that the king offered them for showing up at the designated hour. As one might expect, the sounds they made were so terrible that the king soon gave up listening to them.

Among the sons of the deceased musicians, however, were a few who were concerned not with rewards but with whether or not they were worthy of being the king's servants. Therefore they were determined to learn the art of their fathers and attend to the care of their instruments. Often they would rise in the morning to tune their instruments and practice their music, so that sometimes they would be late in arriving at the court. When they finally entered to the harsh sounds that were coming from the other musicians, they would go off into a corner and play as best they could. Long after the other musicians had departed they would continue to practice, so that they might better serve the king.

The king was well aware of these efforts—nothing escaped his attention—and he was very pleased by them. While they did not play with the same skill as their fathers, their devotion was just as great. And their music filled the king with joy.

More Important than Kol Nidre

Rabbi Moshe Leib of Sasov, one of the most noted disciples of Rabbi Shmelke of Nikolsburg, knew that the aim of all prayer, of all Torah study, is to bring us closer to our fellow human being. In drawing nigh unto another person, we draw nigh unto the Holy One, as this story retold from the Esser Tsachtsochot *(Ten Splendors; Piotrkov, 1910) teaches.*

The Jews of Sasov were gathered in the synagogue one Yom Kippur eve to hear Rabbi Moshe Leib chant the Kol Nidre, the most important prayer of the year. Then, as now, people who never regularly attended the synagogue at any other time were on hand for this prayer, and they eagerly awaited the appearance of their rabbi.

But, strange to say, as the moment for the recitation of the prayer approached, Rabbi Moshe Leib still had not shown up.

"Where could he be?" the congregants asked one another, growing more worried with each passing second. After all, Moshe Leib was known for being in the right place at the right time, for joining words with meaning at precisely the moment when words were called for. It was unthinkable that he should fail to be present for the Kol Nidre.

They began to fear that something terrible had happened to him. Indeed, some wondered whether they should go look for the rabbi, but no one was sure where to look. If he was not in the synagogue, with all the Jews of Sasov, where could he possibly be?

Among those who sat and waited for the rabbi was a young widow who lived near the synagogue. That evening she had left her infant son at home, sleeping in his cradle, just long enough to come and hear the chanting of Kol Nidre. Surely, she said to herself, it will not take too long for just this one prayer, the most important of all prayers. Five minutes went by and then ten, minutes that seemed like an eternity. Finally the young mother felt that she could wait no longer and hurried home to her little one.

When she walked into her house, whom should she behold but Rabbi Moshe Leib sitting in a rocking chair and singing a lullaby to the babe.

Somewhat apologetically, the rabbi looked up at the surprised woman and explained, "I was on my way to the synagogue for the Kol Nidre service. As I was passing by your house, I heard your child crying. What else could I do but come in and comfort the baby?"

What is even more important than praying Kol Nidre? Rabbi Moshe Leib knew: more important than the most important of prayers is the comfort given to a child in distress.

Beyond the Fiftieth Gate

This tale about Rabbi Baruch of Medzibozh (c. 1756–1810) contains a teaching concerning the dangers of proceeding too far too fast along the path of mysticism. According to Jewish tradition, the mystic passes through fifty gates in his endeavor to draw near God. Indeed, the fifty days between Passover and Shavuot, when we counter the omer in remembrance of those who went forth from Egypt and approached Mount Sinai, correspond to those fifty gates. Those who pass through the gates unprepared risk losing everything—even their faith. But, as we see in the words of Rabbi Baruch, the concern of one Jew for another may return one who is lost to the path of faith.

Among the disciples of Rabbi Baruch was a young man who ventured too soon into the realm of the esoteric, a realm that only the initiated may dare to breach. Like others who had entered into realms for which they were not yet chosen, he paid a very dear price for his impatient curiosity: the young man came to find himself teetering on the edge of apostasy.

When Rabbi Baruch found out about what the young man was involved in, he was greatly distressed. At first he told himself, "He will come to me in his anguish. I shall reprimand him for his actions and return him to God."

But, despite his anguish, the young man did not seek out the rabbi. Instead of struggling to return to God, he stopped praying, left off with his study of Torah, and broke off all his relations to the Hasidim.

Realizing that if he did not act quickly the youth would be lost forever, Rabbi Baruch took it upon himself to seek out the one who had turned away from God. When he arrived at the place where his former disciple now lived, he entered without waiting to be invited in, and he spoke without waiting to be asked why he had come.

"Do you think I do not know what you have been doing?" he asked the frightened and troubled student. "I know your innermost thoughts even before you think them. Already you have passed through all the gates but the fiftieth gate of knowledge and doubt.

"At each gate you posed a question and then went on to the next question, one after another, on and on. And now you stand before the fiftieth gate, terrified and seeking refuge from your terror in isolation. But isolation offers no refuge: it is a prison in which even now your soul languishes.

"I know why you are afraid, for I too have stood at the fiftieth gate. You are afraid because at the fiftieth gate you confront a question for which there is no human answer. And if you attempt to answer it, you are afraid that you will tumble into the abyss, where you will be lost forever."

Hearing these words, the young man cried out, "O Rabbi, you have seen into my trembling soul. But what am I supposed to do? Would you have me go back to the first gate?"

"No," replied the rabbi. "It is too late for that. What is done is done."

"Then what is to become of me?" the frightened man longed to know. "Where else can I turn?"

"You can turn to the gate that stands before you," the master answered. "Turn to the gate, cast your gaze beyond it, and move forward. One thing will keep you from tumbling into the void, and that is faith. Beyond the fiftieth gate yawns the abyss. But beyond that gate there is also faith. For faith and the abyss always lie next to one another."

At that the rabbi took the young man's hand and led him back to the community of the Hasidim—led him back to his own soul.

To Be at Home

Included in a work published in Warsaw in 1922 called the Sefer ha-Chasidut *(Book of Hasidism), this story relates an incident that transpired between Rabbi Baruch of Medzibozh and his brother Rabbi Ephraim of Sudlikov (1737–1800). It is about a problem fundamental to human life: the problem of presence. In order to live as a human being, we must be able to declare before our fellow human being, "Here I am." This presence before another, for the sake of another, opens up a path for God's presence to enter the world. And where God is present human beings have a home.*

During one of his journeys to raise money for the poor, Rabbi Baruch stopped in Sudlikov to spend the Sabbath at the home of his brother Rabbi Ephraim. When the time came for lighting the Sabbath candles, Rabbi Baruch noticed with dismay that his brother's candlesticks were made of clay and not of silver.

"Brother," he cried, "I had no idea you were so poor that you could not afford to buy silver candlesticks! Please, you must let me do something about this."

"It's a small matter," Rabbi Ephraim waved his hand. "What is important is not the shine of the candlesticks but the light that issues from the candles. Come, now, let us say the blessings on the bread and the wine."

Rabbi Baruch said nothing, but still he was troubled by his brother's candlesticks. As soon as the Sabbath was over, he went out and purchased a set of silver candlesticks.

"These are for you," he presented them to his brother Ephraim, "a small token of gratitude for your kind hospitality."

Rabbi Ephraim thanked his brother for the gift and spoke no more about it.

Some months later Rabbi Baruch happened once again to be passing through Sudlikov and once again decided to spend the Sabbath with his brother. When it came time to light the Sabbath candles, however, he noticed to his surprise that instead of the silver candlesticks he had given him, there stood the old candlesticks of clay.

"Where are your silver candlesticks?" Rabbi Baruch wanted to know.

"At the pawnbroker's," Rabbi Ephraim replied. "Money was needed, so I pawned them. I hope you'll forgive me."

"Of course," said Rabbi Baruch. "But doesn't it bother you that your beautiful silver candlesticks sit in the pawnbroker's shop, while you have to sit here at home with these sticks of clay?"

"Not really, my brother," Rabbi Ephraim smiled. "I would rather be here in my home and have my silver candlesticks elsewhere than the other way around. Come, now, let us say the blessings on the bread and the wine."

God Is Hiding

This Hasidic tale illustrates a classic Hasidic saying: God enters where He is allowed to enter. Indeed, in the Jewish tradition we find many examples of the idea that in order for God to make Himself known, human beings must initiate some kind of action. God lies in the seeking of God; He abides not just at the end of the road—He is the road itself.

One day Rebbe Baruch was busy studying Torah, when his little grandson Yechiel came running to him. The rabbi could see that the child was very upset and immediately asked him, "What is the matter, my young one?"

In tears, the little boy cried, "Grandfather, Grandfather, it isn't fair!"

"Tell your grandfather all about it," the rebbe replied. "What isn't fair?"

"I was playing hide-and-seek with my friend," Yechiel explained through his sobs. "He hid first, and I looked and looked for him until I found him. Then it was my turn. I hid in a good hiding place, Grandfather, and he started to look for me. But when he couldn't find me right away, he just gave up. He stopped looking for me and left me there all by myself! It just isn't fair!"

Rebbe Baruch gave his grandson a loving caress, and, with tears welling up in his own eyes, said, "There, now, Yechiel, I'll tell you a secret. You are not the only one who is sad because no one is looking for him. God is unhappy too, for the same reason that you are unhappy. You see, like you, He is in hiding, and no one is looking for Him. People look for and long for all sorts of things, for everything except God. Do you realize what that means, little one? Because we do not try to find Him, we ourselves are lost!"

The Mad Prince

This tale comes from the Hasidic master most famous for his tales: Rabbi Nachman of Bratslav (1772–1810). It teaches us that the way to convince another to speak our language is first to speak his language; the way to encourage another to see the world from our point of view is to look at the world from his point of view. This is what it means to work with another, and not against him.

A prince once took complete leave of his senses and imagined that he was a rooster. So convinced was he that he had become a rooster that he shed his clothes and crawled under a table, where he lived naked like a bird in his roost. Refusing to leave his new dwelling place, he insisted upon eating nothing but the grain set aside for the royal chickens.

After repeatedly pleading with the prince to come out from under the table and return to his life as a man, his father, the king, was at a loss as to how to restore his son's sanity. He sent for the best physicians and the most renowned experts in his kingdom, but none of them could help. Growing more desperate, he turned to the magicians known for their tricks and the monks famous for their miracles, but to no avail. The prince continued to squat under the table, crowing at the dawn and pecking at his grain.

One day, however, a sage unknown to anyone appeared in the king's court.

"I have received word of your dilemma," he told the king. "With your permission, I think I can cure the prince."

Willing to try anything, the king agreed. With his courtiers in tow, he led the sage to the table beneath which the prince lived as a rooster. The sage walked over to the prince, and, to the amazement of all, he removed his clothing, crawled under the table with the prince, and began to crow like a rooster. But the prince was not easily fooled.

"Who are you?" he demanded. "What do you think you're doing here?"

"I might ask you the same thing," the sage shot back. "Who are you and what are you doing here?"

"Why, I am a rooster," the prince answered. "Can't you see that?"

"Of course I can see that," the sage nodded. "But if you are a rooster, then surely you can see that I am a rooster too. I've come to keep you company in your roost."

"Splendid!" the prince shouted. Immediately the two men who acted like roosters became the closest of friends.

Before long, having won the prince's confidence, the sage said, "Excuse me for a moment, my friend." And at that he put on a shirt.

"What on earth are doing?" asked the prince. "Have you lost your mind? Surely you don't think you have turned into a man! Nothing could be more degrading to a rooster!"

"But don't you see?" the sage replied. "Dressing like a man does not make you a man. A rooster can wear a shirt and still be a rooster."

"That's true," the prince agreed, and the two of them put on the clothes of men.

The next day the sage sent for some delicacies from the palace kitchen. The dishes were laid under the table, and the sage began to eat.

"What is this?" the prince cried to his friend. "Don't tell you're going to eat as they do!"

"But a rooster can eat anything he wants and still be a rooster," the sage explained to him. "In fact, a rooster can sit at a table, walk among men, and remain a rooster nonetheless. Merely behaving like a man does not make you a man."

"Yes, I see!" the prince declared.

Having realized the truth of what the sage was saying, the prince crawled out from under the table and returned to his life as a prince.

The King's Daughter

Commenting on this tale that he adapted from an ancient folk tradition, Rabbi Nachman said, "Everyone who hears it has thoughts of repentance." This is a tale about the exile of the Shechinah, the Indwelling Presence of God, which can abide in the world only where people allow her to. The chamberlain's efforts to save the king's daughter are symbolic of the Jewish people's struggle to preserve the holy in the world of humanity. Since that struggle is an eternal one, its outcome remains to be decided.

There was once a king who had six sons and one daughter. Because she was his only daughter, she was especially dear to him. One day, however, he grew annoyed at her over some trifle, and before he could hold his tongue, he cried out in anger, "May the Evil One take you!"

The next morning, to the king's dismay and horror, his daughter was nowhere to be found. He had the palace searched from top to bottom, but in vain. Finally the king's chamberlain asked for permission to set out to look for her. After providing the chamberlain with a servant, a horse, and money, the king sent him on his way.

The faithful chamberlain searched everywhere, through forests, mountains, and deserts, but could not find the lost girl. He was all but ready to give up, when he decided to take one last road to a place beyond the realm, where he had never been. After traveling for some time, he came upon a beautiful castle with many soldiers standing guard around it. He went to the guards and explained his mission. They graciously allowed him not only to enter but to search the castle.

After looking in one room after another, the chamberlain came to a great hall, where he found a king surrounded by musicians, singers, soldiers, and servants. Neither the king nor anyone else asked him any questions, and when he saw a table laid with food, he went over to eat. Having eaten his fill, he lay down in a corner to see what would happen next.

Soon the king sent for his queen, and when she entered the hall everyone broke out in songs and shouts of joy. When she took her seat next to the king, the chamberlain suddenly recognized her: she was the daughter of his beloved king.

She, too, recognized the chamberlain. Very quietly she rose and went over to him. After exchanging greetings with her, the chamberlain asked, "How did you happen to come here?"

"It is because of the words that carelessly came from my father's lips," she explained. "He declared that the Evil One should take me, and this is the palace of the Evil One himself."

"How can I deliver you from this place?" the anxious chamberlain asked.

"There is only one way," she replied. "You must choose a place far from here and there spend a year of longing for my return. On the day that year is up, you must devote yourself to fasting and prayers and avoid all sleep."

The devoted chamberlain left the palace of the Evil One and did exactly as the king's daughter had said. When the year came to an end, he set out to release her from her prison. Along the way, however, he saw a tree full of delicious apples. Because his fasting had made him very hungry, he stopped to eat one of them. No sooner did he take a bite from it than he fell into a deep sleep.

When the chamberlain finally awoke—years later—he realized to his horror what had happened. Hoping against hope that it was not too late, he rushed to the palace of the Evil One, where he found his king's daughter in a state of great sorrow.

"You must spend another year of longing for me," she told him, "if I am to be delivered from this place. This time you may eat on the last day, but you must be sure to refrain from sleep. Remember: you must stay awake."

Once again the chamberlain did exactly as he was told. Once again, after his year of longing had passed, he set out to save the king's daughter. On his way to rescue her, however, he happened by a spring that looked like it was filled with fragrant wine. Unable to refuse the temptation, he went over to have a taste of it. No sooner did the wine cross his lips, than he fell into a sleep that lasted for seventy years.

As he slept, the king's daughter came by in a carriage surrounded by soldiers. Realizing what had happened, she was overcome with sorrow and began to weep. Then she took a kerchief from her head, wrote something on it with her tears, and laid it next to the slumbering chamberlain.

When the chamberlain awoke, once again in dismay, he found the kerchief and noticed that there was something written on it. He held it to the sun and read the message that the king's daughter had left him. In it she explained that she had been moved to a palace of pearls atop a golden mountain and that the chamberlain should seek her there.

Knowing that he would have to seek out some distant and enchanted land if he was to find a golden mountain, the chamberlain wandered the earth for many years. One day, as he was making his way across a desert, he met a giant.

"Who are you?" the giant asked.

"I am just a man," the chamberlain replied, "a man in search of a palace made of pearls on top of a golden mountain."

"There is no such thing," the giant scoffed.

"But there must be," the chamberlain insisted. "My king's daughter is held captive there, and I must free her."

"It is impossible," the giant declared. "And to prove it to you, I shall summon the winds that blow over the earth. They know every corner of every land and will tell you that the palace you seek does not exist."

The giant called forth the winds and asked them if they had ever heard of a castle like the one the chamberlain had described. Each in its turn said that it had never seen or heard of such a thing.

"There, you see," the giant declared triumphantly. "Someone has been telling you false tales about this castle of pearls."

Just at that moment one last wind arrived.

"Where have you been?" the giant demanded. "Why did you not come with the other winds?"

"I was delayed," the last of the winds explained, "for I had to carry a king's daughter to a castle of pearls high atop a mountain of gold."

"So there is such a place after all," the giant admitted. Then, turning to the chamberlain, he said, "I shall have this wind take you there, so that you may find the one you have been seeking."

The wind rose up, carrying the chamberlain over a great distance, until at last it brought him to rest at the gate of a city. The chamberlain entered the gate to discover a realm of unsurpassed beauty. Immediately he realized that, in order to obtain the knowledge necessary to rescue the king's daughter, he would have to reside in the city for a very long time. The chamberlain managed to find a man with whom he could board while he studied the ways of this wondrous place.

How he finally delivered the king's daughter from her captivity and found his way home, no one knows. All that is known is that in the end he succeeded.

Where Are You?

In this tale Rabbi Shneur Zalman of Lyady (1747–1813) explains the meaning of the first question that God put to the first man: Where are you? "Only as the You becomes present," philosopher Martin Buber once said, "does presence come into being." And the You becomes present only when we are able to declare, "Here I am, for you!"

Suspected of being a threat to the tsarist regime of Russia, Rabbi Shneur Zalman was once placed under arrest and taken to a prison in Saint Petersburg. There the chief investigator of the Tsar's police force visited him frequently and interrogated him on all sorts of matters. In the course of these interrogations the police investigator came to realize that the rabbi was not a dangerous criminal after all but was very likely a great sage. And so, as long as he had the rabbi in custody, the investigator decided to question him about various passages in the holy Scriptures.

"There is a verse in the Bible that has always puzzled me," he said to the rabbi one day. "We are told that 'the Lord God called unto Adam and said to him: "Where are you?"' Now why would a God who knows all things ask Adam where he was? Did not He who knows all know this?"

"The point of this passage is not that God does not know where Adam is," Rabbi Shneur Zalman explained, "but rather that Adam is the one who must declare where he is. It is he who must affirm his presence before God. Indeed, his name, Adam, means 'human being,' and a human being is a being who becomes present before the One in whose image he is created. Therefore this first question that God put to the first human being is the question that He puts to every human being. As He asked Adam, so He asks us all where we stand in relation to Him and to our fellow human beings. He asks us what we have done, how we have lived, and whether we have answered when we have been called."

The investigator was very pleased with this reply from the rabbi. He went on to discuss other issues pertaining to the Bible, until finally he was more convinced than ever that the rabbi was not only a wise man but also a saintly man. And so, thanks to the intervention of the investigator who had learned so much from the rabbi, Shneur Zalman was released from the Russian prison.

The Seer's Great Fall

This tale is shrouded in mystery. It is about Rabbi Yaakov Isaac, the Holy Seer of Lublin (d. 1815), and his efforts to summon his Hasidim to joy, so that he might battle a strange disaster that was to befall him. Holocaust survivor and author Elie Wiesel wonders whether the Holy Seer had not caught a glimpse of the horror that was to befall the Jews of Europe during the Holocaust, when Lublin became a center of destruction with the appearance of the death camp Majdanek on its outskirts. Others speculate that the Holy Seer came face to face with the Angel of Death and had a foretaste of the following Tishah b'Av, a day of mourning commemorating the destruction of the Temple, the day he would pass away. The tales of Rabbi Yaakov Yitzchak were collected in the nineteenth-century Niflaot ha-Chozeh (The Wonders of the Seer).

It was the eve of Simchat Torah, the holiday that marks the completion of the annual cycle of the reading of the Torah, and the Hasidim of Lublin had come to the house of study to dance and sing and rejoice. Gathered around their rebbe, Rabbi Yaakov Yitzchak, they were soon carried away in a fervor of ecstasy. But they also sensed that there was something different about this night, about this celebration, something unlike the celebration of any other Simchat Torah. On this occasion the rabbi seemed particularly insistent that they summon from their depths the deepest level of joy.

"Drink!" he cried to them. "Dance! Let your souls catch fire and ascend on high! If your joy is intense enough, if it rises high enough, humanity will suffer in anguish no more! Dance! Your salvation depends upon it!"

With these words he went into a dance of such fervor and frenzy that it seemed as though he might single-handedly bring redemption to all creation. Yes, this Simchat Torah was unlike any other. Something that had never happened would happen this Simchat Torah.

Obeying the master's command to take off in flights of unparalleled joy, the Hasidim danced in a state of such abandon that they did not notice the Rabbi slipping away to his private study. No one but his wife saw him enter the study, all alone, and no one, not even his wife, knew what he was doing there.

Suddenly she heard strange noises coming from the rabbi's study. The noises sounded rather like the weeping of a child, but she knew that there were no children in the room. Afraid that something might have happened to him, she rushed into his study and found—nothing. The room was empty. She let out a cry of terror.

"He's gone!" she shouted. "He's been taken away!"

Hearing her cry, the Hasidim were frozen with fear. Taken away? What could she mean? Where could the rabbi be? His wife had seen him enter, and she was careful to watch for him to come out. But he did not come out. Mysteriously, he had simply disappeared.

Fearful for their master, the Hasidim rushed into the streets to search for him. They searched for hours but could not find him anywhere. Having all but given up hope, they were on their way back to the house of study, when they heard a man moaning in pain. They raced to the poor fellow lying in the shadows of an alley only to discover that it was none other than Rabbi Yaakov Yitzchak.

"Rabbi, Rabbi," they cried, "are you all right? What happened to you?"

But instead of answering them, the Holy Seer repeated over and over, "The abyss. . . the abyss. . . it calls forth another abyss. . . the abyss. . . ."

What could he mean by those strange words? What had taken place in his study? Had he come face to face with the Evil One? Had he, like our father Abraham, had a vision more terrible than any other he had ever had?

When Two Are Gathered

One of the closest disciples of Rabbi Yaakov Yitzchak, the Seer of Lublin, was his namesake Rabbi Yaakov Yitzchak of Przysucha (1765–1813). Known as the Holy Jew, Rabbi Yaakov Yitzchak was noted for the emphasis he placed upon lovingkindness in human relationships. For it is there alone, between one human being and another, he maintained, that God shows Himself in the world. This tale is from a collection of stories about the Holy Jew known as the Niflaot ha-Yehudi *(Wonders of the Jew), published in Warsaw in 1908.*

The Holy Jew, Rabbi Yaakov Yitzchak of Przysucha, once recalled to his disciples how his father would study the prayer book with him.

"Not only did we examine the words," he said, "we pondered every letter of every word. One letter in particular caught my eye. It is hardly a letter at all, you see, little more than a dot. It is the letter *yud*. Unlike most of the other letters, two *yuds* were often written together, side by side. My father explained to me that two *yuds* formed a very special word: the holy name of God.

"But what if one *yud* is written above another? Does that spell the Holy Name?

"'No,' my father told me when I asked him, 'it does not. Written one above the other, two dots indicate an interruption, a break in the speech.'

"Suddenly I realized that through these letters that form His name God teaches us something very important, something that, indeed, the sages teach us in *Pirke Avot*, Ethics of the Fathers. When two Jews—two Yuden—are gathered together to study Torah, face to face and on the same level, the Shechinah, God's Indwelling

Presence, is there also. But whenever one places himself above the other, taking himself to be better than the other, God is absent. All that remains is a terrible emptiness.

"Therefore learn how to say 'you' to your fellow Jew. For in saying 'you' to our fellow Jew, we say 'You' to the Holy One Himself."

Those Who Defeated the Rebbe

Rabbi Naftali of Ropshitz (1759–1826) was famous not only for his intelligence but for his wisdom. With regard to his intelligence, it was known that no one could defeat him in a debate. But with regard to his wisdom, as this tale shows, he was wise enough to be defeated even by the most humble of the Hasidim. Various versions of this story can be found in works about the rabbi, such as Ohel Naftali *(Tent of Naftali; Warsaw, 1911) and* Shivchei Naftali *(In Praise of Naftali; Lublin, 1927).*

Everyone knew that it was impossible for even the most learned of rabbis to defeat Rabbi Naftali in an argument.

"Do not even try," people would advise one another. "His mind is too sharp and his wit too quick."

Indeed, Rabbi Naftali took a small measure of pride in his reputation and was always ready to prove himself in an argument with a learned scholar. There were, however, three occasions upon which the rabbi was defeated. And he was defeated by the most unexpected of opponents.

The first to defeat him was his little boy Eliezer.

One day the rabbi found his son idling away the hours doing nothing in particular. "Why do you sit around doing nothing?" he asked the child. "Do you not realize that the time God gives us is precious? You should be studying Torah or helping your mother."

"Yes, Father, I know," Eliezer answered him. "But the Evil Inclination is sometimes too hard for me to overcome. It's the Evil Spirit that has led me to be so lazy."

"Then you should follow the example of the Evil Spirit himself," his father replied. "After all, it is God's will that the Evil Inclination lead you astray. You too, then, should do God's will and study Torah or come to someone's aid."

"Yes, Father, you are right," said the little boy. "But for the Evil Spirit it is easy. You see, he has no Evil Inclination to tempt him into failing to do God's will!"

To that Rabbi Naftali had no answer.

The next person to defeat the learned rabbi was a little girl. He met her while traveling through a small village where very few Jews lived. It was so small, in fact, that only ten men were left in the village: just enough for a minyan, a prayer quorum. The village did, however, have a synagogue and a cemetery.

Tell me, child," the rabbi commented to the little girl, "isn't one of these, the synagogue or the cemetery, unnecessary? After all, if one of the ten in the minyan should pass away, you would have no need of the synagogue since there would not be enough men to hold a prayer service. If none of the men passes away, then why do you need the cemetery?"

"That's simple," the little one replied. "You may rest assured that the synagogue will always remain open. God dwells in His house, and He will see to it that His worshipers come to Him. As for the cemetery, it is there for strangers who pass through our village and die before they can leave. So you see, both are needed."

Pleased with the child's reply, the rabbi smiled and said nothing.

On a third occasion Rabbi Naftali met with defeat at the hands of a simple coachman. It happened on the eve of Simchat Torah, when the Hasidim celebrate the completion of the annual cycle of Torah readings. They were dancing in celebration of all the blessings that we receive from the holy Torah. When Rabbi Naftali joined in the festivities, he noticed among the Hasidim a coachman who was known to be so ignorant that some thought he was illiterate.

"What are you doing here?" the rabbi challenged him. "You never study Torah, and you break half of its commandments. What can this celebration held in the observance of the Torah possibly mean to you?"

"But Rebbe, the Sages teach us that the tablets of the Torah are like a bride and groom," the coachman surprised the rabbi with an allusion to the Midrash. "If my brother arranges a wedding, am I not allowed to participate in the celebration?"

"Indeed you are," the rabbi smiled, pleased at the man's insight. "Dance on! For you have defeated me!"

The Rebbe's Last Words

Rabbi Naftali of Ropshitz was known for his wit, but his end was not a happy one. Not all tales, not even all Hasidic tales, are happy ones. For the joy that permeates Hasidic tales is a serious matter. It is a joy that arises from a profound insight into what there is to be afraid of. Perhaps this can explain something about the terrible fear that overcame Rabbi Naftali during the last months of his life.

Strangely, suddenly, and without explanation, Rabbi Naftali of Ropshitz went into seclusion toward the end of his life. No longer did he counsel his followers. No longer did he entertain the Hasidim with his stories. No longer did he utter even a word.

Days went by only to turn into weeks. The weeks then stretched into months, and still the rabbi remained locked in his prison of silence. Every day his son Eliezer, later known as the Dzikover Rebbe, tried to speak to him, but to no avail. At first his father would answer him with the gestures of a mute. When Eliezer asked him, for example, whether there might be some mystical meaning to his silence, Naftali would shake his head "No." But as the silence dragged on, the rabbi left off even with this silent communication.

Finally the rabbi fell seriously ill and grew near to death. Realizing that his father's last day arrived, Eliezer went to him.

"I beg you, Father," he pleaded, "speak! Just a single word! Do not leave us with this unbearable silence!"

At first the aged rebbe persisted in his silence and said nothing. But his son continued to plead with him: "Father, I beg you, a word, just one word!"

Then, in a barely audible whisper, the rabbi declared, "I. . . I am afraid. Do you understand, Eliezer? Can you understand? I am afraid!"

And without any explanation of what had terrified him, Rabbi Naftali of Ropshitz breathed his last.

The Sign of Forgiveness

This tale about Rabbi Simcha Bunem of Przysucha (1765–1827) concerns both the need to seek forgiveness and the importance of knowing we are forgiven. The tradition teaches us that repentance is among the things that preceded the Creation, for repentance is a path to God that takes us beyond the confines of the world. The question for the believer, then, is: how do I know that my repentance has drawn me close enough to God to be forgiven? In this piece from Siach Sarfei Kodesh (Utterance of the Holy Flame) *Rabbi Bunem offers a reply.*

Rabbi Simcha Bunem of Przysucha was known for the love he offered not only to the righteous among his followers but also to the sinners. There was, however, one man among his congregants who seemed to be especially unrepentant. Since this greatly troubled Rabbi Bunem, he sought a way to turn the man back toward the path of holiness.

The sinner was noted to be an excellent chess player, and so Rabbi Bunem, who was himself a very good chess player, came up with a plan drawing on the man's devotion to chess in order that he might interest him in devoting himself to seeking forgiveness. Thus, setting his plan into motion, the rabbi invited the man to his home for a game of chess.

Their game was not long underway when the rabbi intentionally made a very foolish move. The man was about to take advantage of the move, when Rabbi Bunem stopped him and said, "Oh, I did not mean to move there. Would you please excuse my mistake?"

"No," the man replied. "A move is a move."

"But please," the rabbi persisted, "just this once."

"Oh, very well," the man reluctantly excused the move.

Before long the rabbi made another foolish move and once again asked to be forgiven for his error. Once again the man refused.

"Rabbi, please," he moaned. "I cannot allow you to take back every foolish mistake you happen to make!"

Then the rabbi stared hard at him and said, "You refuse to allow two little errors in a silly game, and yet you expect God to overlook your transgressions without taking so much as a single step toward repentance."

At these words the man was suddenly stricken by remorse and said, "Rabbi, you are right, of course. But if I should seek to repent, how can I know that I have been forgiven?"

"The sign that you have been forgiven," said the rabbi, "is that you sin no more."

Convinced more than ever of the truth and wisdom of Rabbi Bunem, the man became a true penitent and one of the rabbi's most devoted followers.

The Fabric of Self-Righteousness

The Baal Shem Tov said that one day soon there would be so many pious people that it would prevent the coming of the Messiah. Indeed, it was said that he had a kind word for everyone, high and low, except for those pious people who took themselves to be among the righteous. This brief tale about Rabbi Nachum of Stephanesht, son of the famous Rabbi Yisrael of Rizhin (1797–1850), represents the general Hasidic attitude toward a piety that is nothing but self-righteousness.

In his pursuit of righteousness, a disciple of Rabbi Nachum of Stephanesht once went to his teacher with a question.

"Can you tell me, Rabbi," he asked, "what piety is?"

"You raise a very good question," the rabbi replied. "I have thought long and hard about this matter, for you know that my father, Rabbi Yisrael of Rizhin, never spoke of it. I do not know what piety is, but I think I know what it can become. It seems to me that piety may be a kind of cloak with which the self-righteous conceal themselves. It is something pleasing to the eye that they parade before others and before themselves, never mindful of the eye of God that looks on and sees through every artifice. But the material of this cloak is made of arrogance, for only the arrogant would stoop to raising themselves above their fellow human beings. Its lining consists of grudges, for the self-righteous go through life feeling cheated by a world that has not given them their due. And it is sewn with the threads of bitterness and dejection, for piety of this sort always comes at the price of rejoicing in life."

"But how do we seek righteousness, as the Torah commands us to do?" the student pleaded.

"Seek righteousness," said the rabbi, "by seeking humility, gratitude, and joy. Seek righteousness by serving others. For true righteousness lies in the realization that our fellow human being opens up what is more than we are, what is better than we are. It lies not in hiding behind the cloak of piety but in moving into the openness of humility."

Opening the Door for God

Although this tale centers around a question asked by Rabbi Menachem Mendel of Kotzk (1787–1859), it is about Rabbi Moshe of Kobrin (1783–1858). Rabbi Moshe believed that God abides in all things and in every activity. Therefore Rabbi Moshe was intensely present in everything he did. Our every word and thought, our every gesture and deed, is an opportunity for worship and for the opening up of a portal through which God may show Himself in the world. In the words of the Kobriner Rebbe, "A Tsaddik is one in all of whose ways God is revealed, and a Hasid is one in all of whose works God is present." Rabbi Moshe's teachings can be found in a nineteenth-century text called Amorot Tehorot (Pure Words).

When Rabbi Moshe of Kobrin passed away there was a great deal of discussion about his message to the Hasidim and the things he emphasized in his teachings on how best to serve God and humanity. One of his contemporaries, the great Rabbi Menachem Mendel of Kotzk, had a close friend who had been among Rabbi Moshe's disciples.

When Rabbi Moshe passed away the Kotzker went to his friend and asked, "What was the most important thing to your teacher, Rabbi Moshe of blessed memory?"

"That's easy," his friend replied. "The thing most important to the Rebbe of Kobrin was whatever he happened to be doing at the moment. His every movement was a form of prayer. Therefore he was present, heart and soul, in his every action. I have never known anyone who was so fully present, before God and man alike, in everything he did."

Hearing these words, the Kotzker realized the truth of one of his own sayings: God enters where He is allowed to enter. And He can enter anywhere at any time. But it is our presence in our words and deeds that opens the door for Him.

The Treasure Beneath Our Feet

According to a Hasidic saying, in all the world there is but a single place where a great treasure is hidden. That place is the spot on which you stand. But sometimes, as this tale from the Kotzker Rebbe suggests, we must journey a great distance in order to behold the precious thing that is lying at our feet, sitting in our lap, or hugging us around the neck. How do we perceive the treasure hidden at the spot on which we stand, the treasure lying in our very homes? Through eyes filled with gratitude. This story is taken from the Kotzker Maasiot (Legends of the Kotzker), *a work published in Warsaw in 1924.*

There was once a Jew who lived in Cracow named Yitzchak, the son of Yekel. Yitzchak was a very simple man and a very poor man. At times he could be a very skeptical man. Therefore when he began having a certain dream night after night, he tried at first to dismiss it as nothing.

But as the dream persisted, he began to think, "Perhaps there is something to it. After all, the Talmud tells us that a dream unheeded is like a letter unopened."

In his dream he saw a certain bridge in the heart of the city of Prague. As the dream went on, he saw himself going down to a certain spot under the bridge, where he started to dig. After digging for a while, he suddenly unearthed a great treasure, so that in his dream he was no long poor Yitzchak the son of Yekel. He had become rich Yitzchak, the son of Yekel.

Since the dream would not leave him alone, Yitzchak decided one day that he would make the journey to Prague. Just in case the dream might be true, he packed a spade in his bag and set off. Since he was very poor, he had to set out on foot; whenever he could, he hitched a ride with a passing farmer.

When at last he came to the great city of Prague, Yitzchak went straight to the city's center, and, sure enough, he found the bridge that he had seen in his dream. Wasting no time, he went right to the spot beneath the bridge that he had dreamt of and started digging. Before he could find any treasure, however, he was discovered by a policeman. Recognizing him to be a foreigner and a Jew, the policeman became very suspicious of his actions, placed him under arrest, and took him to jail.

As soon as they arrived at the jail, the policeman sat him down and began to interrogate him, demanding, "What are you doing here?"

"Nothing, " the frightened Yitzchak replied. "I'm just a poor Jew passing through your city."

"Do you expect me to believe that?" the policemen barked at him. "People passing through don't go digging under bridges. Not only that, I know you foreign Jews. You're all alike: spies, every one of you. You might as well confess that you have come here to spy on us. You'll save me a lot of trouble and yourself a lot of pain."

"But I'm not a spy!" Yitzchak insisted.

"Then what are you doing here?" the policeman wanted to know. "And what were you doing under that bridge?"

Unable to come up with an excuse for himself, Yitzchak told the policeman the truth. He explained the details of his recurring dream about a treasure hidden under the bridge in Prague and how he had finally decided to come look for it.

The policeman found the story to be so fantastic that he believed the poor Jew and laughed, "That's just like you stupid Jews! You don't have an ounce of sense. Take me, for example. I have had a dream about a Jew in Cracow named Yitzchak, the son of Yekel. In my dream this Jew has a treasure buried under the stove in his house. But you don't see me running off to Cracow, now do you?

Besides, half the Jews in that city are named Yitzchak and the other half are named Yekel. I couldn't find such a house if I wanted to. So you see, I have the good sense to stay right where I am. You should do the same, you foolish Jew." And with that the policeman released him.

Grateful to God for having spared him any further misery, Yitzchak, the son of Yekel, hurried back to his home. There he went to his stove, looked underneath it, and—lo and behold—there was the treasure that the policemen had seen in his dream.

The Stork

In ancient times the Jews were perhaps the only people who included among their laws the commandment to treat the stranger, or the non-Jew, as well as they treated their own. In this Hasidic tale Rabbi Yitzchak Meir of Ger (1799–1866) explains, precisely in such terms, the difference between one who is righteous and one who is not. As the Hasidic masters have taught us, there are two ways to keep warm in a cold house: one is to wrap yourself in a coat; the other is to build a fire. Those who wrap themselves in a coat exclude others from their warmth. But one who builds a fire warms all who come near it.

Puzzled by a certain passage in the Talmud, a disciple of Rabbi Yitzchak Meir, the Gerer Rebbe, once came to his teacher with a question.

"Rabbi," said the disciple, "the sages tell us that in Hebrew the stork is called *chasidah*, which mean 'the pious one' or 'the loving one.' They go on to teach us that the stork is referred to by this name because it offers so much love to its mate and to its offspring. Indeed, it is said that the stork brings food to the nests of other storks as well. Now if this is so, why would the Torah declare the stork to be among the unclean birds?"

"You ask an excellent question," replied the rebbe. "Know that the Torah deems the stork to be unclean because it is kind only to its own and brings food only to the nests of other storks. While it offers its love to its own, the bird has no love for strangers. The Torah teaches us that those who are closest to God are the widow, the orphan, the poor, and the stranger. Why? Because these are the ones who have nowhere to turn. Therefore we must turn to them, lest God turn away from us. There is no human being, Gentile or Jew, who is not one of our own. We are all the children of Adam."

God Speaks in All Things

God never ceases from addressing us. If at times it seems that He has fallen silent, it is because we have ceased to hear, not because He has ceased to speak. God speaks in all things. This is the lesson that Rabbi Avraham Yaakov Friedman of Sadgora (1820–1883) offers to one of his disciples. Like many of us, the Rabbi's student looked around at some of the works of man and could not see or hear anything of value in them. But Rabbi Avraham Yaakov helped him to hear and helps us to hear as well.

"Know that God never leaves off speaking to us," Rabbi Avraham Yaakov Friedman of Sadgora would declare to his disciples. "Not only in the works of nature does He call out to us but also in the works of humanity. For those who are created in the image of their Creator participate in His creation. Which means: their works are part of His utterance."

There was a young man among the rabbi's disciples who had complete faith in the truth of his teacher's every word. No sooner would an utterance come from the rabbi's lips than the student would examine it, wrestle with it, and struggle to learn from it. But he had a great deal of trouble with this particular teaching, especially when he looked around and saw the work in which some people were engaged. So one day the young man gathered his courage and went to the rabbi to question him about this teaching.

"Rabbi," he said, "if you will forgive me, there is something I must ask you."

"Please ask," Avraham Yaakov replied, always glad to have a question from one of his students.

"You have told us that God addresses us in everything," he continued, "both in the wonders of nature and in the actions of man. But when I look around at the new inventions that have come into the world, I cannot see anything of value to be learned from them. The railroads that cut across the land foul the air with their smoke and their noise. The telephone removes us from the face of our neighbor. And the telegraph reduces words—the most holy of things—to mere dots and dashes. What can God possibly be teaching us through these things?"

The rabbi smiled patiently at the young man's concern and answered, "Oh, but the Holy One, blessed be He, is offering us His wisdom even through these new inventions. You may have noticed that people who tarry in idleness often miss their train. So you see, the railroad teaches us that a moment's hesitation will cause us to miss everything. As for the telephone, it enables us to speak with others over long distances. Therefore it reminds us that what is said here is heard there. And the telegraph? Here we have perhaps the most important lesson of all. The telegraph teaches us that every word is counted—and charged. Thus even in these new and strange inventions God is speaking to us."

And, hearing these words of his teacher, the young man could hear God's voice where he had thought there to be nothing.

Modern Tales

THE STORIES INCLUDED in this section come from storytellers who have lived in many different times and places. They wrote in a variety of languages, adopted a variety of world views, and grew up in a variety of cultures; indeed, some of them changed the cultures of their origin. And yet in each of these tales one can find the concern for human values and the value of the human being, for the relationship between God and humanity, that makes these tales distinctively Jewish. But what makes them distinctively modern?

The term *modern* in this sense refers to a time characterized by certain developments over the last three centuries. The modern age has seen, for example, the rise of secularism, nationalism, urbanization, technology, social and political revolutions, and other upheavals. For Jews the modern period has meant large-scale migrations; new opportunities in social, political, and cultural spheres; new forms of religious observance; and, at times, new forms of oppression. While the stories in this section are over fifty years old and have stood the test of time, they reflect the crises and conflicts of modern times.

For Jewish writers, the literary response to these crises and conflicts is characterized by confrontations between modern values and ancient traditions. Even when they challenge Jewish traditions, these authors generally maintain a connection with the truths and the teachings of tradition. Thus the Scriptures that contain the origins of all Jewish tales find echoes in these modern Jewish tales, as they have throughout the centuries of Jewish storytelling. These tales may help us, then, to endure the conflict between the meaningful and the meaningless, between the sacred and the profane, between light and darkness. Indeed, like all the greatest Jewish stories ever told, these storytellers and their stories help us to transform darkness into light—which is the reason for our existence.

The Prayers of Children

THE MAGGID OF DUBNO

Rabbi Yaakov ben Wolf Kranz (1741–1804), the storyteller known as the Maggid of Dubno, was born in Lithuania. Traveling throughout Poland and Germany, he carried his tales and sermons to Jews who lived far from his home. In this tale the Maggid offers us a teaching as old as the Talmud, namely that the world is sustained thanks to the breath of little children. From their lips, uncorrupted by the world, come the purest of prayers. It is our children, therefore, who take our prayers to the Holy One.

There once was a man who lived with his wife and a house full of children in a village carved out of a clearing in the forest. Each night, as his family prepared for sleep, the man would see to their security by barricading the door and sealing all the windows of the house.

"After all," this loving father would say to himself, "one never knows when danger might strike. A man cannot be too cautious where his family is concerned."

One night, however, the man and his wife were awakened by the fearsome smell of smoke: a fire had broken out in the house. Within minutes, it seemed, the smoke was everywhere. The parents frantically rushed to save their children. Once they had gathered the little ones together, they headed for the door. But, to their horror, it would not open. When the father tried the windows, they were locked from the outside and also could not be opened.

Suddenly the smallest of the children, a little boy of three, cried out, "Over here, Papa! This window is unlocked!" But, alas, the open window was too small for any of them to crawl through—except for the little toddler who discovered it.

Carefully lifting his youngest child up on his shoulders, the father helped the little fellow slip through the window. Immediately the boy ran to the villagers and brought help for his family. Soon the men of the village were there and, with the use of a battering ram, were able to break through the door to the house. Thus the man and his family were rescued from the blaze that surely would have killed them all, had it not been for the work of the child.

Just as that little boy was able to squeeze through the small opening in the house, so are little children able to offer up prayers to God that squeeze through the openings of heaven. Hearing the prayers that rise up from innocent lips, Gods comes to our aid and delivers us from evil.

The Seder

HEINRICH HEINE

The renowned German poet, Heinrich Heine (1797–1856), was a complicated and tragic figure. Barred from government service, his writings banned because he was a Jew, Heine had himself baptized in an effort to find a way into European society. He soon realized, however, that German antisemitism comprised more than a religious prejudice, and he came to regret having turned renegade. In this story taken from his novella Der Rabbi von Bacherach (The Rabbi of Bacherach) *it is evident that Heine was devoted to Judaism. He once said, "I never returned to Judaism, because I never left it." Perhaps just as Rabbi Abraham fends off the Angel of Death in this tale, so Heine averted the death that threatened his soul in his attempt to enter Christian European society.*

Gathered in his home with students, family, and other guests, Rabbi Abraham began the evening celebration of the Feast of Passover. Everything in the room shone more brightly than usual; a silk-embroidered cloth with fringes of gold hanging to the ground was spread over the table; engraved with images from the holy tales, the little plates with the symbolic foods and the tall goblets filled with wine had a warm glow about them; the men wore their black coats and hats; the women were in marvelously shimmering clothes made of fabric from Lombardy and wore pearls and gold jewelry on their heads and necks; and the silver Sabbath candelabra cast its festive light over the devoutly joyful faces of young and old alike. Leaning against a purple velvet cushion in his high-backed chair, Rabbi Abraham read and chanted the Haggadah, as the merry choir joined in or responded at the prescribed places. The rabbi too wore the black dress of the festival, his noble features looking milder than usual, his lips smiling through his beard as though they would relate many marvelous things, and his eyes awash with a mixture of sacred memories and anticipation. In the high-backed chair at his side sat the beautiful Sarah, who as hostess wore no jewelry, but only white linen, which enfolded her slender body and pious face. This face was movingly beautiful, just as the beauty of all Jewish women is of a strangely moving sort; the conscious-ness of the deep misery, of the bitter outrage and harsh conditions in which their friends and relatives live, spreads over their lovely faces a certain sad intensity and a watchful, loving anxiety that enchants the heart. So sat the beautiful Sarah today, as she gazed steadily into her husband's eyes; now and then she would also glance at the Haggadah that lay before her, a book bound in gold and velvet, an old heirloom with aged wine stains from the days of her grandfather; in it were the many bold and brightly painted pic-tures that she loved to look at on Passover eve ever since she was a little girl. They portrayed stories of the Bible, such as the one about Abraham when he took a hammer and smashed his father's idols of stone, about the angels who came to visit him, about Moses killing the Egyptian, about Pharaoh sitting pompously on his throne, about the frogs that would allow him no peace even at his table, about how he drowned, thank God, as the children of Israel crossed the Red Sea, about how they stood open-mouthed with their sheep and cattle and oxen at Mount Sinai, about the righteous King David playing his harp, and finally about Jerusalem with its towers and the pinnacles of the Temple illuminated by the sun.

The second cup had been filled, and the faces and the voices were growing more and more cheerful; taking hold of a piece of matzo, the Rabbi read the following words from the Haggadah: "Behold! This is the bread that our fathers ate in Egypt! Let all who are hungry come and eat, all who are sad come and join us in the joy of Passover! This year we celebrate the feast in this land but next year in the Land of Israel! This year we remain slaves, but next year we shall celebrate as the sons of freedom!"

With these words the door to the room opened, and two tall, pale men wrapped in broad black coats entered. One of them spoke: "Peace be with you. We are traveling believers and would like to celebrate the Passover feast with you." The rabbi quickly answered in his friendly manner: "With you be peace. Please, take a seat next to me." The two strangers seated themselves, and the rabbi continued with the reading. Sometimes, as the others responded after him, he would whisper words of affection to his wife, and, playing on the old adage that on this night the father of the house is a king, he said to her, "Rejoice, my queen!" But she answered with a melancholy smile, "Our prince is missing," by which she meant the son of the house who, according to the Haggadah, was supposed to ask the father about the meaning of the feast. The rabbi made no reply but pointed with his finger at one of the pictures on the open page of the Haggadah, which showed very nicely how the three angels came to Abraham to announce that a son would be born to him by his wife Sarah, as Sarah stood behind the door of the tent and, with the slyness of a woman, listened to the conversation. That hint brought a blush to the cheeks of his beautiful wife, who lowered her eyes and then looked joyfully at her husband as he went on to chant the wondrous tale. He sang of Rabbi Joshua, Rabbi Eliezer, Rabbi Azariah, Rabbi Akiva, and Rabbi Tarfon, who sat reclining in Bene Beraq and spoke all night about the deliverance of the children of Israel from Egypt, until their students came to inform them that it was daybreak and that the morning prayers were already being recited in the synagogue.

As the beautiful Sarah gazed upon her husband and listened reverently, she noticed that his face suddenly froze with horror: the blood disappeared from his cheeks and lips, and his eyes popped out like icicles. And yet, almost in the same instant, peace and cheer returned to his features, his lips and cheeks red once more, his eyes moving brightly about; indeed, his whole being seemed to be seized by a strange, mad mood. The beautiful Sarah was terrified as she had never in her life been terrified, and a cold dread rose up within her, less because of the signs of horror that for a moment had come over her husband's face than due to this merriment that was gradually turning into roaring exhilaration. The rabbi playfully shifted his kipah from ear to ear, stroked and curled his beard, and sang the text of the Haggadah as though it were a street song. As he counted off the ten plagues of Egypt, when one normally dips a finger into the wine glass and lets a drop of wine fall to the floor for each plague, the rabbi flicked the wine at the young girls; this was followed by grumbling over spoiled ruffles and a great deal of resounding laughter. Her husband's convulsive and effervescent merriment struck the beautiful Sarah as increasingly uncanny, and, seized by a nameless anxiety, she stared at the buzzing crowd of people who were rocking back and forth, nibbling at the matzo and gulping down wine, chatting with each other and loudly singing, and generally enjoying themselves.

When it came time for supper, everyone stood up to wash their hands; the beautiful Sarah brought in a large silver basin adorned with figures of gold and held it before each of the guests as they poured water over their hands. When she went to offer the rabbi this service, he gave her a meaningful look and slipped out the door. The beautiful Sarah followed him out; the rabbi took his wife by the hand, hurriedly dragging her through the streets of Bacherach, out the city's gate, and up to the country road that follows the Rhine to Bingen.

The rabbi moved his lips many times without uttering a sound, until at last he cried out, "Do you see the Angel of Death? He hovers down there over Bacherach. But we have escaped his sword. Praised be the Lord!" And in a voice that still shook with horror he explained how he was leaning back and joyfully chanting the Haggadah, when he happened to glance under the table, and there at his feet he caught sight of the bloody body of a child. "Then I noticed," he went on, "that our two guests who arrived late were not of the community of Israel but were from the assembly of the godless, who had plotted to secretly place that corpse in our house, so as to accuse us of child murder and incite the people to plunder and murder us. I could not let it be known that I had seen through this work of darkness; that would have hastened our destruction, and only by cunning were we both saved. Do not fear, my beautiful Sarah: our friends and relatives will also be spared. The evil ones thirsted only after my blood; since I have escaped from them, they will satisfy themselves with my silver and gold. Come with me, my beautiful Sarah, to another land, and let us leave this misfortune behind us. The God of our fathers will not forsake us."

If Not Higher

ISAAC LEIB PERETZ

Born in Poland during a time of cultural upheaval, Isaac Leib Peretz (1852–1915) explored the conflicts between the world of Hasidism and the secularism that was sweeping across Europe. He began work as an attorney but entered the literary scene when he published his first book at the age of twenty-seven. After moving to Warsaw, where he became a leader in the Jewish community, Peretz established himself as one of the most prominent figures in Yiddish literature. This story, like many of his stories, is taken from the Jewish folk tradition and reminds us that we draw nigh unto the Divine Being through the help we offer human beings.

Whenever it was time for the penitential prayers to be recited with the coming of the Days of Awe, the Rabbi of Nemirov would disappear. Nowhere to be found, he was not seen in the synagogue or in either of the houses of study or even in any of the minyanim of Nemirov. Absent from his home, he would leave his door open, so that anyone who wanted to could go in and out. But, of course, no one would ever think to steal anything from the rabbi.

Where could the rabbi have gone? Indeed, where should he have gone? Up to heaven, of course. After all, the rabbi has much to attend to as the Days of Awe draw nigh. Jews, may the Lord bless them, are in need of work, peace, health, and decent mates. They long to be good and devoted to God, but their sins are many. And the Accuser, with his thousand eyes, gazes upon the entire world, from end to end. He reports all he sees; he denounces and informs. Were it not for the rabbi, we would be lost!

So thought the people of Nemirov.

A Litvak, however, showed up one day and laughed at them.

You know how those Litvaks are. They are among the Mitnaggedim, those who are opposed to the Hasidim. Litvaks do not give a thought to the holy books, and yet they gorge themselves on Talmud and Halachah. So this Litvak throws in your face a passage from the gemara, where it says that even Moshe Rabbenu never ascended to heaven in all his life but rose up only to be left hanging two and a half handbreadths beneath the gates. And who can reason with a Litvak?

Well, then, where might the rabbi be?

"That's none of my concern," the Litvak shrugged. But all the while he is plotting to find out. You cannot put anything past a Litvak!

And so that very night, just after the Maariv prayers, the Litvak sneaks into the rabbi's room, crawls under the bed, and waits. There he'll wait all night if he has to, just to find out where the rabbi disappears to and what he does during the penitential prayers. Anyone else might have fallen asleep while waiting there through the night, but not a Litvak. He stays awake by reciting to himself an entire tractate from the Talmud.

As dawn breaks, he hears the call to prayer. The rabbi has long since been awake. This the Litvak knows, because he has heard him moaning for at least an hour. Anyone who has heard the moaning of the Rabbi of Nemirov realizes how deep is his sorrow and his suffering over Israel. The sound of it is enough to break a man's heart. But not the heart of a Litvak: his soul is made of iron. And so he listens and stays put beneath the bed where the rabbi, may he have long life, is lying.

Suddenly the Litvak hears the beds in the house creaking, as people rise, mumble a few words, pour water over their hands, and pass in and out of doorways. Finally everyone has gone. Once again it is dark and quiet, with a ray of moonlight shining through the shutters.

(The Litvak later confessed that when he was left alone with the rabbi, he was overcome with fear. His skin was covered with so many goose bumps that the roots of his peyot pricked him like needles. Being alone with the rabbi during the time for the penitential prayers is no small matter! But a Litvak is stubborn. And so he stayed where he was, trembling like a fish in water.)

The rabbi finally rises up from his bed. After doing what a Jew should do, he goes to his closet and takes out some clothing like the peasants wear: linen pants, boots, a coat, a large felt hat, and a wide leather belt with brass studs. The rabbi gets dressed. A heavy rope, the kind the peasants use, is dangling from his coat pocket. He leaves his room, with the Litvak close behind him. Stopping in the kitchen, the rabbi fetches an ax, slides it into his belt, and sets out on his way. The Litvak is frightened but nevertheless follows close behind.

The dark streets of Nemirov are shrouded in the hushed dread of the Days of Awe. Now and then a cry rises up from a sickbed or from one of the minyanim reciting the penitential prayers. The rabbi keeps to the sides of the streets and shadows of the buildings. He moves from house to house, and the Litvak is right behind him. He can hear the sound of his beating heart mingling with the sound of the rabbi's footsteps. But still he goes on, following the rabbi to the outskirts of town and into the woods.

The rabbi goes thirty or forty paces into the woods and stops at a small tree. The Litvak is amazed to see the rabbi take out the ax and chop down the tree. Then the rabbi cuts the tree into logs and the logs into sticks. Taking the heavy peasant's rope from his pocket, the rabbi ties the wood into a bundle and throws it over his back. After sliding the ax back into his belt, he heads back to town.

The rabbi walks until he comes to a side street, where he goes up so a small, broken-down shack and knocks on the window.

"Who is there?" a frightened voice asks. The Litvak can tell that it is the voice of a sick Jewish woman.

"It is I," the rabbi replies in a peasant accent.

"Who is 'I'?"

Pretending to be a Russian peasant, the rabbi says, "Vassily."

"Vassily? Who's that? What do you want?"

"I am selling wood, very cheap." And, without waiting for the woman to answer, the rabbi goes into the shack.

The Litvak sneaks in right behind him. In the gray morning light he sees a poverty-stricken room with pitiful, broken furniture. On the bed lies a sick woman wrapped in rags. She cries out bitterly, "How can I buy your wood? A poor widow like me has no money."

"You can take it as a loan," says the so-called Vassily. "It's only six kopeks."

"How am I supposed to pay you back?" the poor woman groans.

"Don't be so foolish," the rabbi reproaches her. "You are a poor, sick Jew, and I am ready to trust you for a bit of wood. I have no doubt that you will pay me back. But what about you? You have a great and almighty God, and you do not trust Him for six kopeks?"

"But who will light the fire for me?" the widow wants to know. "I am too weak to get up, and my son is at work."

"I'll light the fire," replies the rabbi.

At that the rabbi took the wood and arranged it in the widow's stove. As he did so, he recited the first part of the penitential prayers. Then he lit the fire in the stove, and as the wood began to burn, he recited the second portion of the penitential prayers, this time with added joy. And when the fire was burning strong and bright, the rabbi said the last portion of the penitential prayers.

The Litvak who witnessed the entire scene immediately became a disciple of the Rabbi of Nemirov. And ever since that time, whenever a fellow disciple comments on how the rabbi ascends to heaven during the penitential prayers, the Litvak laughs no more. Instead, he simply adds, very quietly, "If not higher."

The Golem

ISAAC LEIB PERETZ

This tale is one that I. L. Peretz adopted from the Jewish folk tradition surrounding the creation of an artificial human being, a golem. Those who are sufficiently righteous, it is said, and who know the secret incantation can bring a lump of clay to life. The golem thus created, however, remains mute, for only the Holy One can impart the power of speech. The story has its origins in the Kabbalah and has been retold in a variety of forms. Peretz's version is based on the most popular one, concerning the famous sixteenth-century rabbi Yehudah Loeb, the Maharal of Prague, who appears in the last of the Kabbalistic tales included in this volume. The tale is a commentary on the limitations of human powers and the dangers of growing too spiritually weak to summon divine intervention.

There was a time, a terrible time, when the ghetto of Prague was under assault. For the Jews had received word that their women were about to be raped, their children about to be burned alive, and their men about to be slaughtered. Just when the situation seemed beyond hope and the end imminent, the great Maharal of Prague, Rabbi Yehudah Loeb, set aside his studies of the gemara and went out into the street. He went up to a large pile of clay, took it into his hands, and fashioned the image of a man. The rabbi breathed into the nostrils of the golem, and the thing began to move. Then he whispered into its ear the name of the Holy One, and the golem rose up. The rabbi turned to go back into the house of prayer, and the golem turned to leave the ghetto. Once outside the ghetto, the golem fell upon our enemies and attacked them without mercy.

Soon Prague was littered with bodies. It is said that the golem's attack went on for days. When Friday came and the clock struck twelve, the golem was still hard at his bloody work.

The head of the ghetto went to the rabbi and cried, "Rabbi, the golem is slaughtering all the goyim of Prague! If this goes on, there will not be a single Gentile left to light our fires for the Sabbath or to remove the Sabbath lamps!"

Hearing this outcry, the Maharal left his studies once more. He approached the altar and there offered up the psalm called "The Song of the Sabbath."

As soon as the words of the psalm came from the rabbi's lips, the golem ceased its killing and returned to the ghetto. Once in the ghetto, it went to the house of prayer and walked up to the rabbi, where it stood motionless. The rabbi whispered into the golem's ear, and its eyes closed shut. Thus the soul that the rabbi had breathed into it fled, and the golem once again became a mere heap of clay.

Ever since that time, now covered with cobwebs, the golem has lain hidden in the attic of a synagogue in Prague. No living soul, especially pregnant women, may look upon it. Anyone who so much as touches the cobwebs dies. Now even the elders have forgotten all about the golem, all of them except the grandson of the great Rabbi Loeb, the wise man called Zvi. For he continues to ponder a question: is it permitted to count the golem in a minyan?

Therefore the golem has not been completely forgotten. It is still with us! But the divine name, the name by which the golem might be summoned to life in a time of danger, has vanished. The cobwebs continue to spread over the thing, and no one is allowed to touch them.

What, then, are we to do?

Hodel

SHALOM ALEICHEM

In his youth Shalom Aleichem (1859–1916), born Shlomo Rabinowitz, served as a rabbi in the Russian province of Poltava. One of the most prolific writers of Yiddish literature, he left Russia after the Kiev pogrom that took place in reaction to Jewish revolutionary activity in October 1905, when for three days rioters looted Jewish shops and homes while soldiers looked on. From Kiev Shalom Aleichem went to Switzerland; from there he went to Denmark, and in 1914 he settled in the United States.

Most famous for his tales about Tevye the milkman, which formed the basis for Fiddler on the Roof, *Shalom Aleichem was noted for his endearing portraits of Jewish life in Eastern Europe. Many of his stories convey the ways in which modern life begins to overwhelm the more traditional customs and beliefs of the shtetl. Here, for example, the young Jewish man named Feferl has chosen to align himself with the revolutionary movement that was on the rise in Russia; for those activities, which come into conflict both with the Russian government and Jewish tradition, he is sent to prison. Translated from a 1940 Yiddish edition, this Tevye tale reveals the pain that can enter into a parent's heart when his love for a child and devotion to his tradition come into conflict.*

Are you surprised to see me, Mr. Shalom Aleichem, after such a long time? You're perhaps thinking that Tevye's hair has turned gray overnight? Oh, oh, oh! If only you knew what heartaches, what troubles, Tevye has had to bear lately! As it is written in our Scriptures: Man is made from dust, and to dust he shall return. A man is weaker than a fly and stronger than iron. Indeed, that is a description of me! Whatever the blow, whatever the trouble, whatever the nuisance, for me there is no way out. Why is it like that? Is it because Tevye is such a fool that he believes everything everyone tells him? Tevye forgets what our wise men have told us a thousand times: *Kavdihu vechashdihu.* In the Ashkenazic language that means: "Beware of dogs." But what am I supposed to do, if that's how I am, if, after all, that's Tevye? As you know, I am a person of great faith, and, as the Eternal One lives, I never doubt Him. After all, whatever He ordains, He ordains for the good. Besides, what good does it do to complain? What is a man, and where lies his dignity? Like I am constantly saying to my wife, "Golda, I tell you, you are sinning. You know, we have a midrash. . ."

"What do I care about a midrash?" she says. "We have a daughter to marry off. And after that daughter we have two more daughters to go. And after them three more, may the Evil Eye bring them no harm!" "So what, Golda?" I say to her. "That's nothing. Our sages have also spoken about that. There is a midrash on that too. . ." But she doesn't let me speak. "Daughters," she says, "who are all grown up are themselves a good midrash." Just try to explain something to an old woman!

So here we are with a house full of young ladies to choose from, the Lord be blessed, each one more beautiful than the other. It may not be proper for me to praise my own children, but I am only repeating what all the world says: "What beauties!" Especially Hodel, the one who comes next after Tseitl, who, you recall, fell in love with the tailor. But what can I say of my Hodel? She is like the one described in the Holy Megillah: Beautiful of form and fair to gaze upon. And, as if that were not trouble enough, she has a head on her too. She reads and writes, both Yiddish and Russian, and devours books like they were holishkes. I know what you must be thinking: what is a daughter of Tevye doing with books, when her father is nothing but a peddler of cheese and butter? I'd like to know the answer to that question myself. But just look at youngsters these days. They can't afford a pair of trousers, and yet they want only to study, as it is said in the Haggadah: And you shall learn, and you shall study. Ask them, "What are you studying? Why are you studying?" They can't say. It's their nature, that's all, just as it is a goat's nature to jump into a garden. And who are they? The children of laborers, tailors, and cobblers, so help me God, every one of them! They go off to Yehupets or Odessa, sleep in attics, eat a little here, have a bite there, go for months on end without so much as seeing a piece of meat. They can make a feast out of a single loaf of bread and a piece of herring.

The short of it is, one of that "chevurah" wound up in our corner of the world, a real shlimazl of no account. I used to know his father, a cigarette maker, without a kopek to his name. But that's nothing against the lad. If it wasn't beneath the tanna Rabbi Yochanan to repair shoes, then there can be no harm in having a father who makes cigarettes. The only thing that bothers me is: why should a pauper be so eager to learn and study? True, the boy has a good head on his shoulders, a really good head. His name is Pertshik, the shlimazl, but we called him Feferl, "Peppercorn," and he looked like a peppercorn: small, dark, and dried up, but with a quick, sharp tongue.

One day I was on my way home from Boiberik, where I had unloaded my milk and butter and cheese. As usual, I was daydreaming about all sorts of things, about the rich people of Yehupets, who get everything they want, while the shlimazl Tevye and his horse work like slaves and go hungry all their life. It was summer, the sun was burning down, the flies were biting, and the world stretched out all around me. I felt like spreading my arms and flying off!

I glanced up and saw a young fellow trudging along with a package under his arm, huffing and puffing. "Rise up, Reb Yokel ben Flekel!" I said to him. "Climb into the wagon, and I'll give you a ride. There's plenty of room. For it is written: If you see the ass of your enemy lying under its burden, you shall not pass it by. If that's how it is for an ass, how much more so for a man?" He laughs, the shlimazl, and climbs into the wagon. "Where," I ask, "might the young fellow come from?" "From Yehupets." "And what," I ask, "is there for a young fellow like you in Yehupets?" "A young fellow like me is preparing for his examinations." "And what," I ask, "might a young fellow like you be studying?" "A young fellow like me," he says, "has no idea what he is studying." "Then why," I ask, "does a young fellow like you trouble his head?" "Don't worry, Reb Tevye," he says, "a young fellow like me knows what he must do." "So tell me," I say, "since you know who I am, who are you?" "Who am I?" he says. "I am a man." "I can see you're not a horse," I say. "I mean whose are you?" "Whose should I be?" he says. "I am a child of God." "I know," I say, "that you're a child of God. It is written: All creatures and all living things are His. What I mean is, who are you descended from? Are you from around here. Are you a Lithuanian?" "I am descended," he says, "from Adam, the first man. And I come from right here. You know me." "Well, tell me," I say, "who is your father?" "My father," he says, "was called Pertshik." "Why, then," I say, "did you make me suffer like this? So you're the son of Pertshik the Cigarette Maker?" "That's right," he says, "the son of Pertshik the Cigarette Maker." "And you are taking classes?" I ask. "And I am taking classes," he says. "Well," I say, "men and birds are all trying to improve themselves. But tell me, lad, what do you live on?" "I live on what I eat," he says. "Oh," I say. "Very good. And what do you eat?" "Whatever people give me," he says. "I understand," I say. "You eat whatever there is to eat. And if you have nothing to eat, you bite your lip and go to bed hungry. But it's worth it, as long as you can go on studying in your classes. You're like those rich people in Yehupets." And I quoted him a Bible verse and a midrash as only Tevye can. "Don't ever compare me to them!" he cries out. "You seem to have something against them," I say. "What did they do, steal your father's inheritance?" "Let me tell you something," he says. "It may well be that you and I and all of us will have a share in their inheritance." "You should let your enemies talk like that," I say. "But I can see one thing: you're not shy, and you have a sharp tongue. If you have the time, you can come by my house tonight and we can chat a little more. You'll have supper with us."

The lad accepted the invitation immediately and showed up right on time, just as the borsht was laid on the table and the knishes were in the oven. "Right on time!" I say. "You can wash your hands, or you can eat without washing your hands. Your punishment in the next world is your own, not mine." As we chat, I take a liking to the young fellow for some reason. Maybe it's because I like a man I can have a word with, as you know, one who can follow a Bible verse or a midrash, who can follow an argument about one thing and another. That's the kind of man Tevye is. From that moment on the young fellow came to our house almost every day. After tutoring a few students, he would come to our house to visit for a bit. He couldn't have been paid much for his lessons. Those who were rich used to pay their tutors three rubles a month and expect them to read telegrams, write out addresses, and run errands for them. And why not? Like the verse says: If you want to eat, you must earn your bread. It was a good thing for him that he ate with us most of the time, and in exchange for this he would give our daughters lessons too. Like it says: One good turn deserves another. And so he soon became part of our household. My girls would bring him a glass of milk, and my wife saw to it that his shirts were cleaned and his socks mended. That was when we changed his name to Feferl, giving him a Yiddish name instead of Pertshik. It could truly be said that we came to love him like one of our own. He was likable, simple, honest, and generous. Whatever was ours was his, and whatever was his was ours.

The only thing that troubled me about him was the way he would up and vanish without warning. We would look up and suddenly, no Feferl! "Where were you, my friend?" I would ask, and he would keep as silent as a fish. I don't know about you, but I don't care for a person who has secrets. I like someone who can tell you where he's been and what he's done. But I'll say this for him: he could speak beautifully, and, come fire or water, when he started, you couldn't stop him! He spoke against the Lord and His anointed and had the wildest notions. Everything was turned upside down. For example, according to his crazy ideas, a poor man is better than a rich man, and if he happens to be a worker to boot, he is the shiniest jewel in the crown! The most valuable ones of all, he says, are those who labor with their hands. "That's all very well," I say, "but will it bring you any money?" Then he gets angry and tries to tell me that money is a curse on the world. All the lies in the world, he says, come from money, nothing good can come of it, and as long as money matters, there will be no justice. "Is there no justice" I ask, "in the fact that my cow gives milk and my horse pulls a load?" I didn't let him get away with anything and followed him word for word, step by step, as only Tevye can! But my Feferl can argue too. Can he ever! If he has something in his heart, he says so. One evening we were sitting on the porch discussing various things, philosophy they call it. Suddenly he said, "Do you know something, Reb Tevye? You have very lovely daughters." "Oh, really?" I say. "Thank you for letting me know that. They have someone lovely to take after." "The oldest one is especially bright," he says. "She's a complete human being." "I know what you mean," I say. "The apple doesn't fall far from the tree." My heart swelled with pride, and why not? What father isn't pleased to hear his children praised? How was I to know that from such an innocent remark a passionate love would arise?

Well, as I was going through Boiberik with my wares one evening, from one house to the next, as I do day and night, someone stopped me. I looked up and saw Ephraim the Matchmaker. As you know, Ephraim the Matchmaker, like all matchmakers, thinks about nothing but making matches. So when he sees me there in Boiberik, he stops me and says, "Pardon me, Reb Tevye, but I have something I must tell you." "Go ahead, if it's something good," I say, as I stop my horse. "Reb Tevye," he says, "you have a daughter, a daughter!" "I have seven," I say, "as it should be." "I know," he says, "I have seven, too." "Then between us," I say, "we have fourteen." "Yes, well, this is what I have to tell you," he says. "As you know, I am a Jew and a matchmaker, and I have a young man for you, a real prince. There is no one like him anywhere." "That's nice," I say, "but what do you mean by a real prince? If he's a tailor or a shoemaker or a teacher, he can stay put. I'll have one who is like me, or no one at all, from a farmer's stock, as the midrash says." "Ah, Reb Tevye," he says, "you're starting with your midrashim already. A man has to be learned to talk with you! You spread your midrashim all over the world. You would do better to listen to Ephraim to see what sort of match he can offer. Just listen and be quiet." And he reads off all his client's good points from a slip of paper. And he sounds very good. First of all, he comes from a good family, which is very important to me. After all, I'm not a nobody myself. In my family there are people of all sorts, both workers and landowners. Secondly, he is an educated man, who can read large print and small and who knows all the commentaries. To me that is no small thing, as I cannot stand an ignoramus! To me an illiterate man is a thousand times worse than a criminal. You can walk around with your head bare, you can even walk on your head, with your feet in the air, but if you know what is written in Rashi, then you are a man after my own heart. That's the kind of Jew Tevye is. And on top of everything else, says Ephraim, the fellow is rich, loaded with money. He goes around in a carriage drawn by two horses so spirited that steam rises up from them. And that's not such a terrible thing. Better rich than poor. God Himself must have no use for a poor man. Otherwise, why would He have made him poor? "Well," I ask, "what else do you have to say?" "What else is there to say?" he asks. "The man wants me to arrange a match with you. He can't wait to make a match. Not with you, of course, but with one of your daughters. He wants a pretty one." "Is that so?" I say. "And who is this great find of yours? A bachelor? A widower? A divorced man? A smuggler?" "He's a bachelor," he says, "no longer young, but a bachelor." "And what is his holy name?" I ask. But he wouldn't tell me. "Bring her to Boiberik," he says, "and then I'll tell you." "What do you mean 'bring her'?" I say. "You bring a horse or a cow to sell, not a girl."

Well, you know how these matchmakers are: they can talk a wall into moving. We agreed that early the following week I would bring her to Boiberik. And all sorts of wonderful thoughts ran through my mind as I was driving home, about how my Hodel would ride about in a fine carriage drawn by spirited horses. The whole world would envy me, not just for the carriage and the horses but for the good deeds I could bring about through my wealthy daughter. I would help the poor, this one with twenty-five rubles, that one with fifty. How does the saying go? "They have a soul too." That's what I was thinking as I rode home that evening, whipping my horse and speaking to him in his language. "Hurry up, my little horse," I say. "The faster you go, the sooner you'll have your oats. As it is written, those who don't work don't eat."

And as I'm talking to my horse, I see two people, a man and a woman, coming out of the woods. Their heads are together, and they are whispering something to each other. Who could they be? Looking through the bright rays of the setting sun, I swear the man is Feferl. But who could he be walking with, that shlimazl, so late? I place my hand on my forehead and look more closely. Who is that young lady? Oy! Could it be Hodel? Yes, as I am a Jew, it's Hodel! So? Is that the way they've been studying their grammar and their books?! Oy, Tevye, what a fool you are! I stop the horse and call out to them. "Good evening," I say. "What are you two doing out so late? What are you looking for, the day before yesterday?" The two of them stop, at a loss for what to do or say, their eyes looking down, their faces blushing. They look at me, I look at them, they look at each other.

"Well?" I say. "You look at me as though you haven't seen me in ages. I'm the same Tevye as always. Not a hair on my head has changed." I speak to them half in anger and half joking. Then my daughter Hodel, blushing more than ever, speaks up and says, "Father, you can wish us a mazel tov." "What mazel tov?" I say. "What happened, did you discover treasure in the woods? Or were you just saved from some great danger?" "Wish us a mazel tov," says Feferl. "We're engaged." "What do you mean 'engaged'?" I say. "Engaged," he says. "Don't you know what that means? It means she is to be my bride." Feferl looks me in the eye, and I look him in the eye, and I say to him: "When was the contract signed? And why haven't I been invited to the wedding? Didn't you suppose that I might have a little interest in the matter?" I make jokes, but my heart is breaking. Tevye is no weakling. Tevye wants to hear it out to the end. I cry out to them: "How can you get married without a matchmaker, without an engagement feast?" "What do we need matchmakers for?" says Feferl. "We arranged the engagement ourselves." "Oh?" I say. "A miracle of God! Why were you so quiet about it?" "Why should we shout it out?" he says. "We wouldn't have said anything now, but we must part soon, and we've decided to get married first."

That really weighed down on me, as it is said: water pressed in on my soul. It was bad enough that they should get engaged without my knowledge, but I could bear it. After all, he loves her, and she loves him. But standing as a bride under the chupah? That was a bit too much for me. "When are you leaving?" I ask. "Soon." "Where are you going?" "I can't tell you," he says. "It's a secret." You hear? A secret! This young Feferl—small, dark, and homely—presents himself as a bridegroom, wants to stand with my daughter under the chupah and then leave, and he won't even say where he's going! Wouldn't that drive you out of your mind? "Okay," I say to him, "a secret is a secret. With you there are nothing but secrets. But let me understand one thing, young man: you are a man of integrity, devoted to humanity. How does it happen, then, that you want to take Tevye's daughter in marriage and then leave her? Is that what your integrity is about? Your humanity? I'm lucky you didn't decide to rob me or burn my house down!" "Father!" says Hodel. "You don't know how happy we are, now that we've told you our secret. It's like a stone lifted from our hearts. Come, give me a kiss." And they both take hold of me, she on one side and he on the other, and start hugging and kissing me. I kiss them back, and, in their excitement, they kiss each other. I felt like I was at the theater! "All right," I say, "maybe you've done enough kissing already? It's time to discuss more practical matters." "Like what?" they ask. "Like the dowry, clothes, wedding arrangements, and such," I say. "We don't need any of those things," they say. "Well, then," I say, "what do you need?" "Just a chupah," they say. What do you think of that?

The short of it is that nothing I said made a difference. They had their wedding, if you can call it that. Of course, it wasn't the sort of wedding that would suit Tevye, a quiet affair, and that was all there was to it. On top of that I had a wife who was hounding me to know why they were in such a rush. Go try to explain that to a woman! So I made up a story about a rich aunt in Yehupets, an inheritance, and such nonsense. A couple of hours after this beautiful wedding the three of us—I, she, and he, my son-in-law—got into my horse-drawn wagon and set out for the station in Boiberik. As I'm sitting in the wagon with the young couple, I steal a glance at them and think: what a good and powerful Lord we have, and how cleverly He rules His world! What odd and wondrous creatures He has made! Here are a couple of newlyweds, and he is going off to God knows where, leaving her all alone, and you don't see either of them so much as shedding a tear! But never mind. Tevye is not some curious old woman. He can wait and see. . . . When we get to the station, I see a couple of young fellows in ragged clothes and worn-out shoes there to see the bridegroom off. One of them is dressed like a goy, with his shirt hanging over his pants, and the two of them are whispering mysteriously to each other. "Watch out, Tevye," I say to myself. "You may have fallen in with a bunch of horse thieves, pickpockets, home wreckers, or counterfeiters!"

On the way home from Boiberik with my Hodel I can't hold it

in any longer, and I tell her plainly what I think. She bursts out laughing and assures me that they are upstanding people, honest men, whose entire lives are spent living for the sake of humanity and whose own welfare means nothing to them. "The one with his shirt hanging over his pants," she says, "is the son of a rich man. He renounced his father's riches and left his parents in Yehupets. He won't take a cent from them." "Oh?" I say. "One of God's wonders! What a fine young man! With his shirt hanging over his pants and his long hair, all he needs now is a harmonica or a dog to follow him around, and then he'll be a wonderful sight!" I thought I was getting even with her for the suffering that she and her new husband had caused to my bitter heart. But did she care? Not a bit! I would say to her, "Feferl." And she would answer me, "The cause of humanity," or "The workers," and such. "What good is this cause of humanity," I say, "if it's all done in secret? There's a saying: 'Where there are secrets, there are scoundrels.' Tell me, then, where has Feferl gone and what is he up to?" "Anything but that," she says. "It's better not to ask about it. Believe me, in time you'll know everything. You'll hear the news, perhaps very soon, and it will be good news!" "Amen, halvay," I say, "from your mouth to God's ears. But our enemies understand as little of it as I do." "That's the whole problem," she says, "you don't understand anything." "Is it so complicated?" I say. "With God's help, I think I can understand even more difficult things." "You can't understand these things," she says, "with your intellect alone. You have to feel them, feel them in your heart." And when Hodel said that to me, her face was aflame and her eyes burned. These daughters of mine! With them, nothing is halfway. Everything is done body and soul, with all their hearts and minds!

In short, a week went by, then two, then five, six, and seven, and not a word. No letter, no news. "Feferl is gone for good!" I said and glanced over at my Hodel. There wasn't a hint of color in her face. She was trying to forget her troubles and didn't need such a reminder. She tried to act as though there were no Feferl anywhere in the world! One day, when I came home from work, I saw that my Hodel had been crying. I asked around and found out that a young man with long hair had come and spoken to her for some time. "Aha!" I said to myself. "That must be the fellow who renounced his riches and pulled his shirt over his pants." And with-out waiting a minute longer, I called Hodel from her room and took her outside. "Tell me, daughter, have you received word from him?" "Yes." "Where is he, your intended one?" "He is far away," she says. "What is he doing?" "He's in prison." "He's in prison?" "He's in prison." "Why is he in prison? For what?" She is silent. She looks at me straight in the eyes and remains silent. "Just tell me, my daugh-ter," I say. "As I understand it, he's not in prison for stealing. I real-ize that he's not a swindler. If he's neither a thief nor a swindler, then why is he in prison? For his good deeds?" She remains silent. "Okay," I say to myself, "don't say anything. He's your shlimazl, not mine." But my heart aches for her. I'm still her father, no matter what anyone says. A father is still a father.

To make it short, it was the evening of Hoshanah Rabah. It's my custom to rest on a holiday, and my horse rests too, as it is written in the Torah: Thou shalt rest from thy labor, thy wife and thine ass. . . and your horse. Besides, there was not much to do in Boiberik at that time. As soon as the shofar sounds, all the houses close up and Boiberik is like a desert. At that time of year I like to stay at home and sit on my stoop. For me it's the best time of year. Each day is like a gift. The sun no longer beats down on you, the woods are still green, and the pines smell nice. In the yard stands the sukkah I've built for the holidays, and the forest around me looks like a sukkah made for God Himself. This is where God observes Sukkot, I think to myself, here, and not in town, where people bustle about in the noise, and all you hear is money, money, money! As I said, it is the evening of Hoshanah Rabah. The sky is dark blue, the stars are twinkling, shimmering, blinking like a man does with his eyes. Now and then a star falls from the heavens, leaving behind it a long green trail: that means someone's luck has fallen, some Jew's luck. "I hope it isn't mine," I murmur to myself, and for some reason I think of Hodel. She has changed in the last few days; life has returned to her face once more. It seems that some-one has brought her a letter from him, from her shlimazl. I wish I knew what he wrote to her, but I won't ask. If she remains silent, so will I. Tevye is not an old woman. Tevye has time.

And, as I sit and think about Hodel, she comes out of the house, sits down next to me on the stoop, looks around, and whispers,

"Father, I have something to tell you: I must say goodbye to you . . . for good."

She spoke so softly I could hardly hear her, and she gave me a look such a look that I shall never forget it. She gives me a hug and asks if I would like something to drink. What do I need with something to drink? Not far from us, in the village, a peasant was cooking something. . . you know what it was. I once heard about a young maiden who had fallen ill and died, and her father was utterly broken. His daughter had passed away, and someone brought him water to drink.

"What do you mean you have to say goodbye for good?" I say and look away from her, so that she wouldn't see me die. "I mean," she says, "I'm going away tomorrow morning, and we may never see each other again. Never. . ."

My soul grew sick at these words, even though it is written: This too is for the good. "Where are you going," I ask, "if I may have the right to know?" "I'm going to him," she says. "To him?" I say. "Where is he?" "He's still in prison," she says. "But soon he'll be sent away." "So you're going to say goodbye to him?" I say to her, pretending not to understand. "No," she says, "I'm going to follow him." "Follow him where?" I ask. "What is the place called?" "We don't know the name of the place yet," she says. "We only know that it is far, far away."

It seems to me that she is speaking with great joy and pride, as though he had done something for which he deserves a medal! What can I say to her? A father scolds a child for such talk, punishes her, maybe even beats her. But anger gets you nowhere. "I realize, my daughter," I say, "that in the Torah it is written: Thus shalt thou leave thy father and mother. So for a Feferl you are ready to abandon your father and mother and go off to who knows where, to some wilderness, to some frozen wasteland, where Alexander of Macedon, as I read somewhere, once found himself among a bunch of wild men."

I speak to her half in anger and half in jest, my heart weeping all the while. But Tevye is no weakling, Tevye keeps a hold on himself. Hodel doesn't lose control either. She answers me word for word, calmly and thoughtfully. And Tevye's daughters know how to talk.

My head is bowed and my eyes are closed, but somehow I can

see Hodel. Her face is as pale and flat as the moon, and her voice is trembling. Should I throw myself around her neck and beg her not to go? I know it would do no good. When my daughters fall in love, it's with their whole being, body and soul, heart and mind!

The short of it is, we sat on the stoop for a long time, maybe all night. We were silent more than we spoke, and when we did speak, it was only a word here and there. She would say something, and I would say something. I asked her only one thing: who ever heard of a girl taking a husband just so she could go off and follow him to some remote end of the earth? She answered me: "With him I would go to the ends of the earth." I tried to make her understand how foolish that was. She tried to make me understand that I would never understand. So I told her a fable about a hen who hatched some ducklings only to have them take to the water and swim away from her, leaving her sadly clucking on the shore. "What do you say to that, my dearest daughter?" I ask. "What am I supposed to say to that?" she asks. "I feel sorry for the hen, but should the ducklings stop swimming just because she is clucking?" Do you hear those words? Tevye's daughter doesn't talk nonsense.

Meanwhile, time never stands still. The day was breaking, and my old woman could be heard mumbling in the house. She had already called out several times that it was time to go to bed. Realizing that it did no good, she stuck her head out the window and, with her usual blessing, shouted, "Tevye! What's keeping you?" "Be still, Golda," I say. "As it says in the Psalms: Why are the people in an uproar? Have you forgotten that today is Hoshanah Rabah? Hoshanah Rabah is the Day of Judgment. On Hoshanah Rabah a man should be up. Listen, Golda, you light the fire under the samovar and make some tea, and I'll go get the horse and wagon ready. I'm taking Hodel to the station." Once again I make up some story about Hodel going to Yehupets because of the inheritance. I tell her that Hodel may have to stay there the whole winter, and maybe the summer and another winter, so we need to give her some clothes, a couples of pillows, and such to take along with her.

As I'm giving her these orders, I tell her not to cry, as it's Hoshanah Rabah. "One shouldn't cry on Hoshanah Rabah," I say. "It's a law!" But, of course, no one pays any attention to me, and when the time comes to say goodbye, they're all crying—the mother, the children, even Hodel herself. And when she said goodbye to her older sister, Tseitl (Tseitl and her husband were spending the holidays with us), the two sisters threw themselves around each other's necks, and you could hardly tear them apart.

I was the only one who controlled himself, as firm as iron and steel—on the outside, that is: inside I was boiling like a samovar. But Tevye is no weakling. We rode all the way to Boiberik in silence. When we were not far from the station, I asked her one last time to tell me what Feferl had done. "He must have done something," I said. She got angry and swore that he was innocent. "He is a man," she said, "who has no concern for himself. Everything he does is for the good of all humanity, especially for the workers who labor with their hands." It made no sense to me. "So he worries about the whole world?" I ask. "Why doesn't he worry about his own world? Anyway, give him my regards, that Alexander of Macedon of yours, and tell him I rely on his integrity—he is a man of integrity, right?—to be good to my daughter. And write to your old father once in a while."

As soon as I finish talking, she falls on my neck and starts to cry. "Goodbye, Father," she says. "Be well. God knows when we shall see each other again!" Well, at that I could no longer control myself. You see, I was thinking of when my Hodel was just a little baby and of how I carried her in my arms. . . . I carried her in my arms . . . Oh, if you only knew what a daughter my Hodel is! You should see the letters she writes! She is a Hodel from God! For me she is a kind of . . . of . . . I can't explain it to you . . . .

You know what, Mr. Shalom Aleichem? It would be better to talk about something more cheerful. Have you heard any news about the cholera in Odessa?

Hopes and Dreams

ISRAEL ZANGWILL

Perhaps the most internationally famous Jewish author of the nineteenth century, the British-born Israel Zangwill (1864–1926) combined great wit with a great love for the Jewish people—indeed, for all people. He was both an ardent Zionist and a social activist, and he never failed to speak out on behalf of oppressed peoples, even when it was unpopular to do so. This story is taken from his collection Children of the Ghetto, *in which there is a mixture of ancient and modern names, ancient and modern rituals, ancient and modern passions. In this tale Zangwill captures a late nineteenth-century Jewish world in a state of transition, torn between nostalgia for the past and longing for a future filled with new possibility, which is the stuff of hopes and dreams. The setting is London, where the community of both Ashkenazic and Sephardic Jews had undergone major changes. In the 1840s the Reform movement had established itself in this city, which by the 1860s had become the center of Jewish emancipation in England. The 1880s brought a huge influx of Russian Jews—like the character Strelitski in this story—which resulted in an increase in the Jewish population from 47,000 to over 150,000. Many of those who immigrated to London had their eyes turned toward America.*

The morning of t he Great White Fast broke bleak and gray. Esther, alone in the house save for the servant, wandered from room to room in dull misery. The day before had been almost a feast-day in the Ghetto—everybody providing for the morrow. Esther had scarcely eaten anything. Nevertheless she was fasting, and would fast for over twenty-four hours, till the night fell. She knew not why. Her record was unbroken, and instinct resented a breach now. She had always fasted—even the Henry Goldsmiths fasted, and greater than the Henry Goldsmiths! Q. C.'s fasted, and peers, and prize-fighters and actors. And yet Esther, like many far more pious persons, did not think of her sins for a moment. She though of everything but them—of the bereaved family in that strange provincial town; of her own family in that strange distant land. Well, she would soon be with them now. Her passage was booked—a steerage passage it was, not because she could not afford cabin fare, but from her morbid impulse to identify herself with poverty. The same impulse led her to choose a vessel in which a party of Jewish pauper immigrants was being shipped farther West. She thought also of Dutch Debby, with whom she had spent the previous evening; and of Raphael Leon, who had sent her, via the publishers, a letter which she could not trust herself to answer cruelly, and which she deemed it most prudent to leave unanswered. Uncertain of her powers of resistance, she scarcely ventured outside the house for fear of his stumbling across her. Happily, every day diminished the chance of her whereabouts leaking out through some unsuspected channel.

About noon, her restlessness carried her into the streets. There was a festal solemnity about the air. Women and children, not at synagogue, showed themselves at the doors, pranked in their best. Indifferently pious young men sought relief from the ennui of the day-long service in lounging about for a breath of fresh air; some even strolled towards the Strand, and turned into the National Gallery, satisfied to reappear for the twilight service. On all sides came the fervent roar of prayer which indicated a synagogue or a *Chevrah*, the number of places of worship having been indefinitely increased to accommodate those who made their appearance for this occasion only.

Everywhere friends and neighbors were asking one another how they were bearing the fast, exhibiting their white tongues and generally comparing symptoms, the physical aspects of the Day of Atonement more or less completely diverting attention from the spiritual. Smelling-salts passed from hand to hand, and men explained to one another that, but for the deprivation of their cigars, they could endure Yom Kippur with complacency.

Esther passed the Ghetto school, within which free services were going on even in the playground, poor Russians and Poles, fanatically observant, forgathering with lax fishmongers and welshers and without which hulking young men hovered uneasily, feeling too out of tune with religion to go in, too conscious of the terrors of the day to stay entirely away. From the interior came from sunrise to nightfall a throbbing thunder of supplication, now pealing in passionate outcry, now subsiding to a low rumble. The sounds of prayer that pervaded the Ghetto, and burst upon her at every turn, wrought upon Esther strangely; all her soul went out in sympathy with these yearning outbursts; she stopped every now and then to listen, as in those far-off days when the Sons of the Covenant drew her with their melancholy cadences.

At last, moved by an irresistible instinct, she crossed the threshold of a large Chevrah she had known in her girlhood, mounted the stairs and entered the female compartment without hostile challenge. The reek of many breaths and candles nearly drove her back, but she pressed forwards towards a remembered window, through a crowd of be-wigged women, shaking their bodies fervently to and fro.

This room had no connection with the men's; it was simply the room above part of theirs, and the declamations of the unseen cantor came but faintly through the flooring, though the clamor of the general masculine chorus kept the pious au courant with their husbands. When weather or the whims of the more important ladies permitted, the window at the end was opened; it gave upon a little balcony, below which the men's chamber projected considerably, having been built out into the back yard. When this window was opened simultaneously with the skylight in the men's synagogue, the fervid roulades of the cantor were as audible to the women as to their masters.

Esther had always affected the balcony; there the air was comparatively fresh, and on fine days there was a glimpse of blue sky, and a perspective of sunny red tiles, where brown birds fluttered and cats lounged and little episodes arose to temper the tedium of endless invocation; and farther off there was a back view of a nunnery, with visions of placid black-hooded faces at windows; and from the distance came a pleasant drone of monosyllabic spelling from fresh young voices, to relieve the ear from the monotony of long stretches of meaningless mumbling.

Here, lost in a sweet melancholy, Esther dreamed away the long gray day, only vaguely conscious of the stages of the service— morning dovetailing into afternoon service, and afternoon into evening; of the heavy-jowled woman behind her reciting a jargon-version of the Atonement liturgy to a devout coterie; of the prostrations full-length on the floor, and the series of impassioned sermons; of the interminably rhyming poems, and the acrostics

with their recurring burdens shouted in devotional frenzy, voice
rising above voice as in emulation, with special staccato phrases
flung heavenwards; of the wailing confessions of communal sin,
with their accompaniment of sobs and tears and howls and gri-
maces and clenchings of palms and beatings of the breast. She was
lapped in a great ocean of sound that broke upon her conscious-
ness like the waves upon a beach, now with a cooing murmur, now
with a majestic crash, followed by a long receding moan. She lost
herself in the roar, in its barren sensuousness, while the leaden sky
grew duskier and the twilight crept on, and the awful hour drew
nigh when God would seal what He had written, and the annual
scrolls of destiny would be closed, immutable. She saw them loom-
ing mystically through the skylight, the swaying forms below, in
their white grave-clothes, oscillating weirdly backwards and forwards, bowed as by a mighty wind.

Suddenly there fell a vast silence; even from without no sound
came to break the awful stillness. It was as if all creation paused to
hear a pregnant word.

"Hear, O Israel, the Lord our God, the Lord is One!" sang the
cantor frenziedly.

And all the ghostly congregation answered with a great cry,
closing their eyes and rocking frantically to and fro:

"Hear, O Israel, the Lord our God, the Lord is One!"

They seemed like a great army of the sheeted dead risen to testify to the Unity. The magnetic tremor that ran through the synagogue thrilled the lonely girl to the core; once again her dead self
woke, her dead ancestors that would not be shaken off lived and
moved in her. She was sucked up into the great wave of passionate
faith, and from her lips came, in rapturous surrender to an over-
mastering impulse, the half-hysterical protestation:

"Hear, O Israel, the Lord our God, the Lord is One!"

And then in the brief instant while the congregation, with ever-
ascending rhapsody, blessed God till the climax came with the
sevenfold declaration, "the Lord, He is God," the whole history of
her strange, unhappy race flashed through her mind in a whirl of
restless emotion. She was overwhelmed by the thought of its sons
in every corner of the earth proclaiming to the sombre twilight
sky the belief for which its generations had lived and died—the

Jews of Russia sobbing it forth in their pale of enclosure, the Jews of Morocco in their mellah, and of South Africa in their tents by the diamond mines; the Jews of the New World in great free cities, in Canadian backwoods, in South American savannahs; the Australian Jews on the sheep-farms and the gold-fields and in the mushroom cities; the Jews of Asia in their reeking quarters begirt by barbarian populations. The shadow of a large mysterious destiny seemed to hang over these poor superstitious zealots, whose lives she knew so well in all their everyday prose, and to invest the unconscious shuffling sons of the Ghetto with something of tragic grandeur. The gray dusk palpitated with floating shapes of prophets and martyrs, scholars and sages and poets, full of a yearning love and pity, lifting hands of benediction. By what great highroads and queer by-ways of history had they travelled hither, these wandering Jews, "sated with contempt," these shrewd eager fanatics, these sensual ascetics, these human paradoxes, adaptive to every environment, energizing in every field of activity, omnipresent like some great natural force, indestructible and almost inconvertible, surviving—with the incurable optimism that overlay all their poetic sadness—Babylon and Carthage, Greece and Rome; involuntarily financing the Crusades, outliving the Inquisition, illusive of all baits, unshaken by all persecutions—at once the greatest and meanest of races? Had the Jew come so far only to break down at last, sinking in morasses of modern doubt, and irresistibly dragging down with him the Christian and the Moslem; or was he yet fated to outlast them both, in continuous testimony to a hand moulding incomprehensibly the life of humanity? Would Israel develop into the sacred phalanx, the nobler brotherhood that Raphael Leon had dreamed of, or would the race that had first proclaimed— through Moses for the ancient world, through Spinoza for the modern—"One God, one Law, one Element," become, in the larger, wilder dream of the Russian idealist, the main factor in "One far-off divine event To which the whole Creation moves"?

The roar dwindled to a solemn silence, as though in answer to her questionings. Then the ram's horn shrilled—a stern long-drawn-out note, that rose at last into a mighty peal of sacred jubilation. The Atonement was complete.

The crowd bore Esther downstairs and into the blank indifferent street. But the long exhausting fast, the fetid atmosphere, the strain upon her emotions, had overtaxed her beyond endurance. Up to now the frenzy of the service had sustained her, but as she stepped across the threshold on to the pavement she staggered and fell. One of the men pouring out from the lower synagogue caught her in his arms. It was Strelitski.

A group of three stood on the saloon deck of an outward-bound steamer. Raphael Leon was bidding farewell to the man he reverenced without discipleship, and the woman he loved without blindness.

"Look!" he said, pointing compassionately to the wretched throng of Jewish emigrants huddling on the lower deck and scattered about the gangway amid jostling sailors and stevedores and bales and coils of rope; the men in peaked fur caps, the lacklustre eyes, the majority brooding, despondent, apathetic. "How could either of you have borne the sights and smells of the steerage? You are a pair of visionaries. You could not have breathed a day in that society. Look!"

Strelitski looked at Esther instead; perhaps he was thinking he could have breathed anywhere in her society—nay, breathed even more freely in the steerage than in the cabin if he had sailed away without telling Raphael that he had found her.

"You forget a common impulse took us into such society on the Day of Atonement," he answered after a moment. "You forget we are both Children of the Ghetto."

"I can never forget that," said Raphael fervently, "else Esther would at this moment be lost amid the human flotsam and jetsam below, sailing away without you to protect her, without me to look forward to her return, without Addie's bouquet to assure her of a sister's love."

He took Esther's little hand once more. It lingered confidently in his own. There was no ring of betrothal upon it, nor would be, till Rachel Ansell in America, and Addie Leon in England, should have passed under the wedding canopy, and Raphael, whose breast pocket was bulging with a new meerschaum too sacred to smoke, should startle the West End with his eccentric choice, and confirm its impression of his insanity. The trio had said and resaid all they had to tell one another, all the reminders and the recommendations. They stood without speaking now, wrapped in that loving silence which is sweeter than speech.

The sun, which had been shining intermittently, flooded the serried shipping with a burst of golden light, that coaxed the turbid waves to brightness, and cheered the wan emigrants, and made little children leap joyously in their mothers' arms. The knell of parting sounded insistent.

"Your allegory seems turning in your favor, Raphael," said Esther, with a sudden memory.

The pensive smile that made her face beautiful lit up the dark eyes.

"What allegory is that of Raphael's?" said Strelitski, reflecting her smile on his graver visage. "The long one in his prize poem?"

"No," said Raphael, catching the contagious smile. "It is our little secret."

Strelitski turned suddenly to look at the emigrants. The smile faded from his quivering mouth.

The last moment had come. Raphael stooped down towards the gentle softly-flushed face, which was raised unhesitatingly to meet his, and their lips met in a first kiss, diviner than it is given most mortals to know—a kiss, sad and sweet, troth and parting in one: Ave et vale—"hail and farewell."

"Goodbye, Strelitski," said Raphael huskily. "Success to your dreams."

The idealist turned round with a start. His face was bright and resolute; the black curl streamed buoyantly on the breeze.

"Goodbye," he responded, with a giant's grip of the hand. "Success to your hopes."

Raphael darted away with his long stride. The sun was still bright, but for a moment everything seemed chill and dim to Esther Ansell's vision. With a sudden fit of nervous foreboding she stretched out her arms towards the vanishing figure of her lover. But she saw him once again in the tender, waving his handkerchief towards the throbbing vessel that glided with its freight of hopes and dreams across the great waters towards the New World.

The Rebbe and His Wife

LAMED SHAPIRO

*Noted for his excellent literary craftsmanship, Lamed Shapiro (1878–
1948) is one of the first of the truly modern Yiddish writers. What distinguishes him as a modern author are his themes of conflict between a higher
truth and a human void and his situating himself within the contexts of
European literature, and not just Jewish literature. He was born in the
Ukraine, where the harrowing experiences of his childhood and youth are
reflected in his early tales of the pogroms. His later writings demonstrate
the influence of Anton Chekhov and Gustave Flaubert, from whom he learned
the principles of narrative organization and an economic care for the words
he used. While many of his tales deal with life in the past, they are written
in a clearly modern style; while they are often about life in the shtetl, they
are removed from the folkloric style of early Yiddish literature. This story
is a good example of how Shapiro was able to capture an entire way of life,
a life steeped in faith, using just a few words.*

There was once a rebbe who lived alone with his wife.

Whenever the rebbe was engaged in the study of Torah, his
wife would claim that she could hear the angels singing on high.
And whenever his wife was cooking fish for the Sabbath meal, the
rebbe would insist that he could smell the aroma of Paradise. Thus
each of them, the rebbe and his wife, was just as good, just as
righteous, just as wise as the other. If one might say that there was
one difference between the two of them, it would be that the rebbe's
wife could all but pronounce rabbinical judgments, while the rebbe
himself made no claims in the matter of preparing fish.

It happened, however, that God had closed the womb of the
rebbe's wife. The rebbe would sit in one corner, while she sat in
another, and the two of them would offer up to God their silent
pleas.

Creator of the Universe, lend an ear to Your servant's prayer
and bless me with a son, so that I may teach him Your Torah and
the way of good deeds. . . .

Creator of the Universe, Lord of the World, hear the prayer of
Your servant and gladden my heart with a child, so that I may

instill in him the ways of what is good and teach him to live by Your will . . . .

The rebbe would take a seat next to his wife and say, "As soon as our son learns to speak, I shall teach him how to read and what every word means."

And his wife would add, "When our sacred little one wakes up each day, I shall recite the morning prayers with him, and just before he goes to bed each night, the two of us will say the evening prayers together."

But the years went by, and the people of the village began to whisper among themselves, saying, "A husband should not go on living under the same roof with a woman who bears no children after ten years of marriage."

When word of this grumbling reached the rebbe's ear, he declared, "I shall never put my wife away. For God will yet grant me a son."

The people of the village complained and at first wondered if they should not get rid of the rebbe. Later, however, they decided that if his wife's barrenness did not bother him, it certainly should not bother them. And so the years continued to pass.

Sitting across from one another, the rebbe and his wife would talk.

"When our little boy grows tall, I shall teach him the gemara and all the commentaries."

"When our son returns from the mikvah on Fridays, I will serve him fresh fish. And when he comes home from the synagogue for the Sabbath, I will greet him with the sacramental wine."

After a time the people of the village once again reflected on the rebbe and his wife. They decided to give them some advice: "You should adopt a child and raise him as your own. And a hundred years from now he will be there to say Kaddish for you."

But the rebbe and his wife both refused such an idea. Said the rebbe, "How am I supposed to teach a strange child Torah and good deeds, if I am not accountable for his transgressions?" And his wife added, "How am I to go and offer a strange child all my love and devotion, if I have not borne him into the world through my blood?"

And together they declared to all, "We have no doubt that God will bless us with our own child!"

The people of the village complained that the rebbe and his wife were stubborn and would not listen to reason. But after some time had passed, they forgot all about it once again.

Meanwhile the elderly couple affirmed, "Our precious treasure will grow up to pronounce judgments on rabbinical matters. He will author many holy books. And in the year when he turns eighteen, we shall have the joy of leading him to the wedding canopy."

Year after year went by, as they do with the never-ending passage of time. One morning it was discovered that the rebbe and his wife had died. Found sitting on their beds, they were facing one another with their hands clasped around their knees, like little children. On their faces was the hint of a smile, and in the air the words seemed to vibrate still:

When our son has grown up . . .
When our Kaddish comes of age . . .

The Rabbi's Son

ISAAC BABEL

Isaac Babel (1894–1941) was born in Odessa, but when he was three years old his family moved to Nikolayev, a place from which they fled back to Odessa during the pogroms of 1905. Babel served in the cavalry during the Russian Revolution and, encouraged by Maksim Gorky, wrote many tales about his experiences during that time. In the late 1930s Babel fell prey to the Stalinist purges and perished in a Soviet camp under circumstances unknown. While he played an active role in the revolution, tales like this one show his sensitivity toward the plight of the Jews, whose traditions collided with the changing times, both in tsarist Russia and in Soviet Russia. Set in the time of the Russian Revolution, the story combines two short pieces translated from Babel's collection of tales Konarmiya *(Red Cavalry).*

"All is mortal. Only the mother is destined to immortality. And when the mother is no longer among the living, she leaves a memory which no one has yet dared to violate. The memory of the mother instills a compassion in us that is like the ocean—and the limitless ocean feeds the rivers that cut through the universe—"

Such were Gedali's words, spoken with great solemnity, as the fading evening shrouded him in the rosy haze of its sadness.

The aged Gedali said, "The passion-filled house of the Hasidim has had its doors and widows broken down, but it is as immortal as the soul of the mother. Ever increasing its orbit, Hasidism still stands at the crossroads of the stormy winds of history."

Thus spoke Gedali. And, having finished his prayers in the synagogue, he took me to Rabbi Motaly, the last rabbi of the Chernobyl dynasty.

We went up to the main street, Gedali and I. White churches gleamed in the distance like fields of buckwheat. The wheel of a gun carriage creaked past a corner. A couple of pregnant Ukrainian women emerged from a doorway, their coin necklaces jingling as they took a seat on a street bench. From the orange colors of the sunset a timid star emerged, and peace, the peace of the Sabbath, settled on the rooftops of Zhitomir.

"This is the place," Gedali whispered, as he pointed toward a tall building with a broken facade.

We entered a room that was stony and empty, like a morgue. Rabbi Motaly was sitting at a table surround by liars and souls possessed. He wore a white robe tied around the middle with a cord and a sable hat. The rabbi sat with his eyes closed, running his thin fingers through his yellow beard.

"Where are you from, Jew?" he asked me, raising his eyelids.

"From Odessa," I replied.

"A God-fearing city," said the rabbi with unexpected anger, "the star of our exile and, against its will, the source of our distress. What is your occupation, Jew?"

"I am setting the adventures of Hersh of Ostropol to verse."

"A formidable task," the rabbi commented and then closed his eyes. "The jackal whines when it is hungry. Every fool has enough folly for despair, and only the wise man can penetrate the veil of being with his laughter. What are you studying, Jew?"

"The Bible."

"What are you seeking, Jew?"

"Amusement."

"Reb Mordecai," said the tsaddik, shaking his beard, "let the young man have a seat at the table, let him eat with the other Jews this Sabbath eve, let him rejoice in being alive and not dead, let him clap his hands as his neighbors dance, let him have some wine, if you will."

And up jumped Mordecai, a jester of old, hunchbacked, with eyes turned up, no taller than a boy of ten.

"Oh, my dear and very young man," said the ragged Mordecai, as he winked at me. "Oh, how many rich fools I once knew in Odessa! And how many penniless wise men I once knew in Odessa! Do sit down, young man, and drink the wine you won't be given!"

And so we all sat down, side by side: the liars, the possessed, and the idlers. In the corner there were some very stout Jews who looked like fishermen moaning over their prayer books. Dressed in his green coat, Gedali was dozing next to the wall. Suddenly I caught sight of a youth behind him, a lad with the face of Spinoza, with Spinoza's strong forehead, and the face of a nun. He was smoking and looked like a prisoner returned to his cell after a long chase. The ragged Reb Mordecai crept over to him, snatched the cigarette from his mouth, and came back over to me.

"That's Ilya, the rabbi's son," he declared in his hoarse voice. "He's the cursed son, the last son, the unruly son."

At that Mordecai shook his fist at the young man and spat in his face.

"Blessed be the Lord!" rang out the voice of Rabbi Motaly Bratzlavsky, as he broke the bread with his monkish fingers. "Blessed be the Lord, God of Israel, who has chosen us from among all the nations of the earth!"

The rabbi blessed the food, and we all sat down at the table. Outside the windows horses were neighing and Cossacks were shouting. There the wilderness of war yawned. As for the rabbi's son, he went on smoking one cigarette after another in the midst of the silence and the prayers. When the meal came to an end, I was the first to rise.

"My dear and very young man," Mordecai pulled me by the belt, "if there were no one in the world except the evil rich and the poor vagabonds, how would the saints live?"

I gave the old man some money and went out into the street.

After saying goodbye to Gedali, I headed for the station. Waiting for me in the train of the First Cavalry was the flare of many lights, the magical brilliance of the wireless station, the endless drone of the printing machines, and my unfinished article for the *Red Trooper*.

Do you remember that night, Vassily? Outside the window horses were neighing and Cossacks were shouting. The wilderness of the war yawned on the other side of the windows, as Rabbi Motaly Bratzlavsky prayed at the eastern wall, his fingers wrapped in his tallis. Then the curtain of the ark was drawn to one side, and in the funereal candlelight we beheld the Torah scrolls covered in purple velvet and blue silk. And bent over the Torah scrolls was the beautiful face of Ilya, the Rabbi's son, the last heir to the dynasty.

Well, Vassily, just the day before yesterday the regiments of the Twelfth Army advanced the front lines as far as Kovel. The conquerors bombarded the town mercilessly. The train crawled over the bodies that littered the fields. And monstrous, unimaginable Russians tramped along either side of the train cars in bast shoes, like a swarm of bugs. Typhus-ridden peasants jumped on the steps of the cars only to be knocked down by our rifle butts.

When I had no more potatoes to offer them, I tossed Trotsky's leaflets at them. But only one man among them held out a lean and dirty hand to take those leaflets. It was Ilya, the son of the rabbi of Zhitomir. I recognized him immediately, Vassily. It was so heartrending to see the prince with his trousers sagging, bent double under his soldier's pack, that we defied our orders and took him onto the train with us.

His bare knees, as frail as an old woman's, banged against the rusty iron steps. We took the shamed body of this dying man and laid it in a corner in the editor's office; Cossacks dressed in red, loose trousers straightened the clothes that were falling off of him. Two full-bosomed typists rested their legs—the legs of dull-witted females—on the floor and stared at him. And I began placing the shattered belongings of the Red Army soldier Bratzlavsky in a box.

His things were strewn about: mandates from the propagandist and books of Jewish poetry. Portraits of Lenin and Maimonides lay side by side, the knotted iron of Lenin's skull next to the dim silken image of Maimonides. There was a lock of a woman's hair in a book and the Resolutions of the Party's Sixth Congress. In the margins of Communist leaflets were scrawled lines of Hebrew verse. And all about were pages from the Song of Songs scattered among revolver cartridges.

As the dreary rain of evening washed the dust from my hair, I said to the boy who was dying on a wretched mattress in a corner, "One Friday evening four months ago the aged Gedali took me to your father, Rabbi Motaly, but you were not a member of the Party at that time, Bratzlavsky."

"I was," the boy insisted, scratching his chest and tossing with fever, "but I couldn't leave my mother."

"And now, Ilya?"

"When there's a revolution going on, a mother is just a passing episode," he whispered, less and less audibly. "My letter came up, the letter B, and I was sent to the front."

"And did you reach Kovel, Ilya?"

"I reached Kovel!" he cried in despair. "The profiteers let the enemy through the front. I took over the command of a small regiment, but it was too late. I didn't have enough artillery."

He died before we arrived at Rovno. He, the last of the princes of Zhitomir, died amidst his poetry, phylacteries, and coarse linen leggings. We buried him at some forgotten station or other. And I, who can scarcely contain the storms of my imagination within this primeval body of mine, was at my brother's side when he breathed his last.

The Messiah at the Gates of Rome

DER NISTER

Der Nister (1884–1950), a Yiddish pen name meaning "the Hidden One," was born Pinchas Kahanovich in the famous Hasidic town of Berdichev, and his writings reflect the influence of his Hasidic surroundings. Containing all the elements of allegory, this story demonstrates his skill at weaving mystical, messianic tales. It is based on a tradition, according to which the Messiah sits at the gates of Rome where, disguised as a leprous beggar, he wraps, unwraps, and wraps again the sores that cover his body. Here Der Nister casts the Messiah in the role of one who is rather like himself, in the role of a singer. The genius of this author lies in his ability to take us through his singer's eyes into a place where none of us can go: into the soul of the suffering Messiah.

The dawn breaks, and the singer's eyes stare into the fog. As it lifts, a city unfolds before him: houses and walls, each one higher than the next, one rising above the other. He sees entire quarters of the city, some stretching across the hillsides, others lying in the valleys.

It is early. The city sleeps. But there is a tremendous uneasiness in its sleep. For soon the city will awaken after a night of sin, its eyes open wide to yet another day and another night of debauchery.

As the morning light grows brighter, the people of the city appear on the streets. And into the city, traveling roads from near and far, on foot and wagon-drawn, the peasants from the surrounding villages come laden with their foodstuffs. Merchants, peddlers, soldiers, cripples, tax collectors, magicians, beggars, and whores arrive from every corner of the land to make ready for another night of pleasure in the city. All who leave and all who enter pass through the city's gates and for some reason feel compelled to spit on the sores of the one who is sitting there. Some spit on his head, while others spit in his face. Still others spit on his clothes and his rags. Now and then he wipes the spittle from his sores, but most of the time he sits motionless and mute, as though they were not spitting at him at all.

Suddenly the singer cries out, his limbs trembling all over. He gazes into that shining face covered with the spittle of the crude and coarse soldiers, merchants, peddlers, cripples, and whores. Bits and pieces of lines borrowed from the liturgies, from sad and ancient songs, pass through his mind. He moves to their rhythm, and, like one who is wounded, he sings:

My wounds have not grown soft
And my bruises are terrible indeed
And my eyes have grown dim
From seeking my redeemer.

The one sitting at the city gates longs to be comforted, but in vain. And so he is left to imagine himself in the place of another, and if it were the other who was covered with sores and spat upon, as if it were he who would then take upon himself the other's shame, the other's silence, and the other's knowledge that his destiny was decided by a will from on high, that it is a destiny most blessed, bestowed by the grace of loving hands.

The Tale of Rabbi Gadiel the Infant

S. Y. AGNON

In 1966 Polish-born Shmuel Yosef Agnon (1888–1970) was awarded the Nobel Prize for Literature. By that time he had long been regarded as one of the most prominent twentieth-century Hebrew authors. His tales contain a wealth of wisdom and insight into Jewish traditions as those traditions have unfolded in every realm of Jewish life. While the life of the Jews of Poland prior to the Enlightenment is one of his favorite topics, he does not confine himself to that period. Indeed, part of Agnon's genius lies in his ability to weave together timeless traditions and timely topics. In this tale from his collection Sipurim *(Stories), for example, Agnon works out new variations on a figure from Jewish lore, Gadiel the Infant, to create a mystical vision of judgment and redemption.*

Rabbi Gadiel the Infant was born by virtue of the Torah that his father taught to the infants of Israel. When he entered the world, he was so small that one could hardly tell whether he was a son of man. Once Rabbi Gadiel reached the age of instruction, his father began to teach him the commandments. He made him a *tallit katan* with woolen fringes and on Lag b'Omer shaved the hair off his head at the grave of Rabbi Shimon bar Yochai, leaving him with side curls. His father carried him in the pocket of his clothing to the morning and evening services at the Great Synagogue to say, "Blessed is He and blessed be His Name," and to respond, "Amen, Blessed be His great Name." And when the cantor pronounced the blessing, Rabbi Gadiel would respond, "Blessed is He and blessed be His Name," and then with all his might would answer, "Amen." His voice would rise up until the threshold would shake, and no one knew where the voice came from, since Rabbi Gadiel was hidden inside his father's pocket.

When he reached the age of Torah study, his father set him on a tobacco box and opened up before him the five books of the Torah. His father interpreted for him the words of the living God, until he had studied the entire Torah and was reading the Targum and had mastered the commentaries. He learned Mikra, Mishnah, Halachah, and Aggadot, the Babylonian Talmud and the Jerusalem Talmud, Sifra and Sifre, Tosefta and Mechilta, the Sefer Yetzirah, the letters of Rabbi Akiva, and the Sefer Hatmunah. And if his father should doze off while they were studying, Rabbi Gadiel would rise up from the tobacco box and sit beside the pages of the book to examine the crowns and the curves of the letters, large and small. When his father woke up and did not see him, he thought the infant was sitting in his mother's lap. Not realizing that the infant was standing between the pages of the book, he would close the book and attend to his business, so that Rabbi Gadiel was left in the midst of the letters, repeating all he had learned. Thus he was diligent in his study and very successful in acquiring Torah and its wisdom. In order that these matters may not appear to be exaggerated, God forbid, let us relate how small Rabbi Gadiel really was. It happened once that a jar of olive oil was set down for the Chanukah candles, and Rabbi Gadiel fell into it and sat there until his father came to light them. Only when he poured the oil into the menorah was Rabbi Gadiel able to jump out, his face shining and scented with the aroma of good oil. Because Rabbi Gadiel was so small, his father was afraid to set him down in public, lest he be trampled by the passersby. Whenever he went to the market to trade with the Gentiles, he would carry Rabbi Gadiel in the folds of his clothing; lying in a corner of his father's tallis, Rabbi Gadiel would listen to his father's conversations and to the conversations of the people, to what he said to them and what they said to him. Thus he learned the languages of Greece and Edom and Ishmael, as well as the languages of all the other peoples of the world, and could speak them all fluently.

One day some of the most wicked men from among the Gen-

tiles, men who were envious of Rabbi Gadiel's father, gathered together and said, "How long will this Jew keep us under his heel and
get in the way of our livelihood? The time has long since come to
remove him from the world." Said one to the other, "Were it not
for fear of our rulers, we would eat him alive."

Another stood and said, "Passover is coming for these Jews. Let
us take a corpse, slip it into this Jew's house, and say, 'He has killed
one of us to bake his matzo in our blood! He has killed one of us!'
Then we will go to the city's judges and the elders of the community; they will arrest him, put him in iron chains, and take him out
to be executed, and then we shall have our revenge. After that, we
can divide his wealth and his property among us." But they did not
know how to go about it. So one of them who was very determined advised the others, "It is their custom to drink four cups of
wine on their Passover eve, with one large cup left on the table,
the cup of Elijah the Prophet they call it. Let us take a skin and fill
it with blood and create a disturbance in their house on the eve of
Passover, and while he and his family are in a state of confusion,
we will pour out the wine from Elijah's cup and fill it with blood.
Then we will summon the king's police and the elders of the community, and they will arrest him, shackle him, put him in jail, pronounce judgment on him, and kill him. Thus we shall have our
revenge." Having heard this, they all said, "Yes, let us do it." They
spread a rumor that a boy had been lost and stirred people up over
the imaginary loss, until they had incited the evil men from among
the Gentiles to take revenge on Israel.

When the eve of Passover came all the evil and wicked men
from among the Gentiles gathered with hatchets and axes to kill,
destroy, and wipe out all the seed of Israel. And since Rabbi Gadiel's
father was the head of the community that year, they went to him
first, in keeping with the adage "start at the top." That evening
Rabbi Gadiel's father and all his family were reclining and telling
the story of the liberation from Egypt, when the door opened with
an evil crash, and a group of soldiers broke in and threw the house
into a state of confusion. The family looked on fear, and they were
overwhelmed with a terror of the Gentiles. As one wailed and another wept, the little Rabbi Gadiel jumped into Elijah's cup. No
one knew that he was there, and there he stayed, until their priest

came and drank down the wine, so that the cup could be filled with blood.

Rabbi Gadiel remained inside the bowels of the wicked man without his knowing it. His intestines had grown coarse from eating a thousand pigs and drinking a thousand bottles of wine, so that the evil priest could not feel him. Rabbi Gadiel remained inside the bowels of the wicked man, but did not wait to become one with the evil one's body and die; instead, he concentrated on the seven forms of wisdom and the seventy languages of the world, so as not to dwell on words of Torah in such a place.

After the Gentiles had filled the cup with blood, they placed guards all around it and ran off to fetch the elders of the community and the city's judges and show them the blood. They said, "Look at how the Jews take our lives and suck our blood to drink it on their holy days!" Immediately the elders of the community grew very angry, and they seized Rabbi Gadiel's father and mother and his brothers and sisters; they put them in iron chains, lowered them into a pit, and tortured them in various ways while they waited for the king to order their execution.

The matter was brought before the king and his ministers, as Rabbi Gadiel lay inside the body of the evil one and concentrated on words of wisdom, rhetoric, the proverbs of the nations, and such things. But at that time the kingdom was a just one, and crimes were not judged without investigation and examination. They investigated and examined everything very carefully, summoning all who were there to stand and bear witness, and chief among the witnesses was the priest. The priest took the traditional oath, and they told him, "Open your mouth and offer your testimony." The priest swore that all the words he was about to speak were true and just and stood to give his testimony. And what did Rabbi Gadiel do? He rose up to the evil one's throat and began to poke around the wicked man's gullet with his finger. The evil one felt the poking in his throat and could not utter a single word. And so the wicked man could not testify, and he was disgraced. The king shouted at him in a loud voice, saying, "Open your mouth!" And what did Rabbi Gadiel do? He began to speak from inside the throat of the evil one, and in the wicked man's language related everything that had happened. The evil men all lowered their faces in shame, and the king and his ministers were greatly alarmed that they had nearly spilled innocent blood and, God forbid, had almost destroyed the great community of Israel when they had committed no crime. Immediately they set free those who were in chains and punished the evils ones, hanging the priest from a tree. Thus God paid him in full for what he had intended to do to the Jews.

The priest hung there the whole day, until the prophet Elijah, of blessed memory, came and kicked him, took Rabbi Gadiel from his belly, and wrapped him in a corner of his cloak. He took him to the hot springs of Tiberias and there washed him, anointed him in pure olive oil, and dipped him in the flowing waters of the river. Then he dressed him in a shirt made of light and took him to one of the caves of the righteous, where they discussed the prosecution of the wicked who oppress the children of the Holy One, blessed be He.

Rabbi Gadiel still sits in the Yeshivah of the Righteous and faithfully records all the ways in which the nations of the world slander the children of the Holy One, blessed be He. And when the great and awesome Day of the Lord comes, Rabbi Gadiel will come forth from his place clad in garments of revenge and cloaked in zeal, to speak to the Gentiles and cry out against the nations, saying, "Thus have you done, and thus have you slandered!" And the ministers of the nations will have no way out and will be unable to deny it. And they will be led to caves of rock and holes in the dust, as it is written: "Flee to the rocks and hide in the dust from the terror of the Lord before the brilliance of His glory as He rises up to shake the earth!" (Isaiah 2:10).

So ends the tale of Rabbi Gadiel the Infant, and yet all his tales are unfinished.

The Tale of a Nanny Goat

S. Y. AGNON

This brief selection, also from S. Y. Agnon's collection Sipurim, *contains a wealth of teachings on the importance of communicating, of paying heed to the people and the world around us. It teaches us something about the wonder and the holiness of the Land of Israel, a land that might be a heaven on earth, if only we knew how to dwell in its midst. And it teaches us something about the things most precious that are always so near and yet so far.*

This is the story of an old man who groaned from the depths of his heart. Doctors were sent for and consulted. They told him that he should drink the milk of a nanny goat. And so he went out and bought a nanny goat and brought her to his shed. Not many days went by before the goat disappeared. They went out to look for her but could not find her, neither in the yard nor in the garden, neither on the roof of the synagogue nor by the spring, neither in the hills nor in the fields. She was gone for several days and then returned on her own, her udder full of milk that had the taste of the garden of Eden. Not just once but many times did she disappear from the house. They would go looking for her, but in vain, until at last she would return on her own, her udder full of milk sweeter than honey and teeming with the taste of the garden of Eden.

On one occasion the old man said to his son, "My son, I want to know where she goes to get this milk that is sweet to my palate and to all my bones." His son said to him, "Father, I have a plan." "What is it?" His son stood up and fetched a piece of cord and tied it to the goat's tail. His father said to him, "What are you doing, my son?" He told him, " I am tying a cord to the goat's tail, so that when I feel her pull on it, I will know that she is leaving. Then I can take hold of the end of the cord and follow her." The old man nodded his head and cried out to him, "My son, if your heart is wise, then my heart will be glad." The lad tied the cord to the goat's tail and watched it very carefully. When the goat stood up to go, he took the cord in his hand and did not let go of it, until the goat finally led him all the way to a cave.

The goat went into the cave, and, holding on to the cord, the youngster went into the cave after her. Thus they walked for an hour or two, or perhaps it was for a day or two. The goat wagged her tail and bleated, until the cave came to an end.

When they emerged from the cave, the youth caught sight of lofty mountains and hills covered with delicious fruit, with a fountain of living waters flowing down from their sides, and the wind was full of all sorts of fragrances. The goat climbed up to where the branches were full of carob fruits dripping with honey; she ate the fruits and then drank from the garden's fountain. The boy saw some passersby along the road and called out to them, "Can you please tell me, good people, where I am and what the name of this place is?" They said, "You are in the Land of Israel, near Safed." The youth raised his eyes upward and declared, "Blessed be the Omnipresent, that He has brought me to the Land of Israel!" He kissed the dust and sat down under the tree. He said to himself, "Until the day comes to an end and the shadows fade away, I shall sit on this hill under this tree. Then I shall go home and bring my father and mother into the Land of Israel." As he was sitting and savoring the holiness of the land, he heard someone cry out, "Come, let us greet the Sabbath Queen!" And he saw men who looked like angels wrapped in shawls of white with myrtle branches in their hands, and all the houses were aglow with candlelight. He realized that the Sabbath eve was coming with the darkening of the day and that he would be unable to go back. He uprooted a reed and dipped it in gallnuts, from which the ink for writing Torah scrolls is made; then he took a piece of paper and wrote a letter to his father: "From this corner of the earth I sing a song of joy to tell you that I have come in peace to the Land of Israel. I am sitting here near Safed, that holy city, and I am awash in its holiness. Do not ask how I got here, but take hold of the cord tied to the goat's tail and follow on the heels of the goat. Then you will travel the road in safety and come to the Land of Israel." The lad rolled up the note and placed it in the goat's ear. He said to himself, "When she reaches my father, he will stroke her head. She will flick her ears, and the note will fall out. Father will pick up the note and read what is written in it. Then he will take hold of the cord and follow the goat to the Land of Israel."

The goat returned to the old man, but he did not stroke her head, and she did not flick her ears. And so the note did not fall out. Since the old man saw the goat come back without his son, he clasped his hands to his head and began to weep and wail, "My son, my son, where are you? Would that I had died in your place, my son, my son!" And so he went on, weeping and mourning over his son. He said, "An evil beast has devoured him and has torn my son to pieces!" And he refused all comfort, saying, "I shall mourn my son, who has passed away, even as I go down to the grave!" And every time he looked at the goat he said, "Woe to the father who has exiled his son, and woe to her who drove him from the world!" And the old man could find no comfort, until he sent for the butcher to slaughter the goat. The butcher came and slaughtered the goat. As they were removing her hide, the note fell from her ear. The old man picked up the note and said, "It is my son's handwriting!" And when he read all that his son had written to him, he clasped his hands to his head and wept, "Woe is me! Woe to the man who steals away his good fortune with his own hands, and woe to the man who returns evil for good!" For many days he mourned over the goat and refused all comfort, saying, "Woe is me, for I could have gone up to the Land of Israel in a single leap, but now I must spend my days in the torment of this exile!"

Since that time the entrance to the cave has been hidden from sight, and there is no more shortcut. And, if he has not died, the lad will bear fruit in his old age, in the peace and calm of the Land of Life.

Soap and Water

ANZIA YEZIERSKA

Anzia Yezierska (1885–1970) was sixteen when she and her parents immigrated to New York from Russia. Her life is representative of the lives of many Jewish children who came to the United States with their parents at the turn of the century. Her mother and father were very traditional, while young Anzia rebelled against her parents' orthodoxy and pursued the secular lifestyle of her new land. Soon after her arrival in New York, she found work in a tailor's sweatshop and lived in poverty until her first collection of stories, Hungry Hearts, *came out in 1920. Taken from that volume, this tale of the immigrant's experience tells us what she seeks when she seeks to come to America.*

What I had so greatly feared, happened! Miss Whiteside, the dean of our college, withheld my diploma. When I came to her office, and asked her why she did not pass me, she said that she could not recommend me as a teacher because of my personal appearance.

She told me that my skin looked oily, my hair unkempt, and my finger-nails sadly neglected. She told me that I was utterly unmindful of the little niceties of the well-groomed lady. She pointed out that my collar did not set evenly, my belt was awry, and there was a lack of freshness in my dress. And she ended with: "Soap and water are cheap. Any one can be clean."

In those four years while I was under her supervision, I was always timid and difficult. I shrank and trembled when I had to come near her, I mumbled and stuttered, and grew red and white in the face with fear.

Every time I had to come to the dean's office for a private conference, I prepared for the ordeal of her cold scrutiny, as a patient prepares for a surgical operation. I watched her gimlet eyes searching for a stray pin, for a spot on my dress, for my unpolished shoes, for my uncared-for finger-nails, as one strapped on the operating table watches the surgeon approaching with his tray of sterilized knives.

She never looked into my eyes. She never perceived that I had a soul. She did not see how I longed for beauty and cleanliness.

How I strained and struggled to lift myself from the dead toil and exhaustion that weighed me down. She could see nothing in people like me, except the dirt and the stains on the outside.

But this last time when she threatened to withhold my diploma, because of my appearance, this last time when she reminded me that "Soap and water are cheap. Any one can be clean," this last time, something burst within me.

I felt the suppressed wrath of all the unwashed of the earth break loose within me. My eyes blazed fire. I didn't care for myself, nor the dean, nor the whole laundered world. I had suffered the cruelty of their cleanliness and the tyranny of their culture to the breaking point. I was too frenzied to know what I said or did. But I saw clean, immaculate, spotless Miss Whiteside shrivel and tremble and cower before me, as I had shriveled and trembled and cowered before her for so many years.

Why did she give me my diploma? Was it pity? Or can it be that in my outburst of fury, at the climax of indignities that I had suffered, the barriers broke, and she saw into the world below from where I came?

Miss Whiteside had no particular reason for hounding and persecuting me. Personally, she didn't give a hang if I was clean or dirty. She was merely one of the agents of clean society, delegated to judge who is fit and who is unfit to teach.

While they condemned me as unfit to be a teacher, because of my appearance, I was slaving to keep them clean. I was slaving in a laundry from five to eight in the morning, before going to college, and from six to eleven at night, after coming from college. Eight hours of work a day, outside my studies. Where was the time and the strength for the "little niceties of the well-groomed lady"?

At the time when they rose and took their morning bath, and put on their fresh-laundered linen that somebody had made ready for them, when they were being served with their breakfast, I had already toiled for three hours in a laundry.

When college hours were over, they went for a walk in the fresh air. They had time to rest, and bathe again, and put on fresh clothes for dinner. But I, after college hours, had only time to bolt a soggy meal, and rush back to the grind of the laundry till eleven at night.

At the hour when they came from the theater or musicale, I

came from the laundry. But I was so bathed in the sweat of exhaustion that I could not think of a bath of soap and water. I had only strength to drag myself home, and fall down on the bed and sleep. Even if I had had the desire and the energy to take a bath, there was no such things as bathtubs in the house where I lived.

Often as I stood at my board at the laundry, I thought of Miss Whiteside, and her clean world, clothed in the snowy shirt-waists I had ironed. I was thinking—I, soaking in the foul vapors of the steaming laundry, I, with my dirty, tired hands, I am ironing the clean, immaculate shirt-waists of clean, immaculate society. I, the unclean one, am actually fashioning the pedestal of their cleanliness, from which they reach down, hoping to lift me to the height that I have created for them.

I look back at my sweatshop childhood. One day, when I was about sixteen, someone gave me Rosenfeld's poem, "The Machine," to read. Like a spark thrown among oily rags, it set my whole being aflame with longing for self-expression. But I was dumb. I had nothing but blind, aching feeling. For days I went about with agonies of feeling, yet utterly at sea how to fathom and voice those feelings—birth-throes of infinite worlds, and yet dumb.

Suddenly, there came upon me this inspiration. I can go to college! There I shall learn to express myself, to voice my thoughts. But I was not prepared to go to college. The girl in the cigar factory, in the next block, had gone first to a preparatory school. Why shouldn't I find a way too?

Going to college seemed as impossible for me, at that time, as for an ignorant Russian shop-girl to attempt to write poetry in English. But I was sixteen then, and the impossible was a magnet to draw the dreams that had no outlet. Besides, the actual was so barren, so narrow, so strangling, that the dream of the unattainable was the only air in which the soul could survive.

The ideal of going to college was like the birth of a new religion in my soul. It put new fire in my eyes, and new strength in my tired arms and fingers.

For six years I worked daytimes and went at night to a preparatory school. For six years I went about nursing the illusion that college was a place where I should find self-expression, and vague, pent-up feelings could live as thoughts and grow as ideas.

At last I came to college. I rushed for it with the outstretched arms of youth's aching hunger to give and take of life's deepest and highest, and I came against the solid wall of the well-fed, well-dressed world—the frigid whitewashed wall of cleanliness.

Until I came to college I had been unconscious of my clothes. Suddenly I felt people looking at me at arm's length, as if I were crooked or crippled, as if I had come to a place where I didn't belong, and would never be taken in.

How I pinched, and scraped, and starved myself, to save enough to come to college! Every cent of the tuition fee I paid was drops of sweat and blood from underpaid laundry work. And what did I get for it? A crushed spirit, a broken heart, a stinging sense of poverty that I never felt before.

The courses of study I had to swallow to get my diploma were utterly barren of interest to me. I didn't come to college to get dull learning from dead books. I didn't come for that dry, inanimate stuff that can be hammered out in lectures. I came because I longed for the larger life, for the stimulus of intellectual associations. I came because my whole being clamored for more vision, more light. But everywhere I went I saw big fences put up against me, with the brutal signs: "No trespassing. Get off the grass."

I experienced at college the same feeling of years ago when I came to this country, when after months of shut-in-ness, in dark tenements and stifling sweatshops, I had come to Central Park for the first time. Like a bird just out from a cage, I stretched out my arms, and then flung myself in ecstatic abandon on the grass. Just as I began to breathe in the fresh-smelling earth, and lift up my eyes to the sky, a big, fat policeman with a club in his hand, seized me, with: "Can't you read the sign? Get off the grass!" Miss Whiteside, the dean of the college, the representative of the dean, the educated world, for all her external refinement, was to me like that big, brutal policeman, with the club in his hand, that drove me off the grass.

The death-blows to all aspiration began when I graduated from college and tried to get a start at the work for which I had struggled so hard to fit myself. I soon found other agents of clean society, who had the power of giving or withholding the positions I sought, judging me as Miss Whiteside judged me. One glance at my shabby clothes, the desperate anguish that glazed and dulled my eyes and I felt myself condemned by them before I opened my lips to speak.

Starvation forced me to accept the lowest-paid substitute position. And because my wages were so low and so unsteady, I could never get the money for the clothes to make an appearance to secure a position with better pay. I was tricked and foiled. I was considered unfit to get decent pay for my work because of my appearance, and it was to the advantage of those who used me that my appearance should damn me, so as to get me to work for the low wages I was forced to accept. It seemed to me the whole vicious circle of society's injustices was thrust like a noose around my neck to strangle me.

The insults and injuries I had suffered at college had so eaten into my flesh that I could not bear to get near it. I shuddered with horror whenever I had to pass the place blocks away. The hate which I felt for Miss Whiteside spread like poison inside my soul, into hate for all clean society. The whole clean world was massed against me. Whenever I met a well-dressed person, I felt the secret stab of a hidden enemy.

I was so obsessed and consumed with my grievances that I could not get away from myself and think things out in the light. I was in the grip of that blinding, destructive, terrible thing—righteous indignation. I could not rest. I wanted the whole world to know that the college was against democracy in education, that clothes form the basis of class distinctions, that after graduation the opportunities for the best positions are passed out to those who are best-dressed, and the students too poor to put up a front are pigeon-holed and marked unfit and abandoned to the mercy of the wind.

A wild desire raged in the corner of my brain. I knew that the dean gave dinners to the faculty at regular intervals. I longed to burst in at one of those feasts, in the midst of their grand speech-making, and tear down the fine clothes from these well-groomed ladies and gentlemen, and trample them under my feet, and scream like a lunatic: "Soap and water are cheap! Soap and water are cheap! Look at me! See how cheap it is!"

There seemed but three avenues of escape to the torments of my wasted life, madness, suicide, or a heart-to-heart confession to some one who understood. I had not energy enough for suicide.

Besides, in my darkest moments of despair, hope clamored loudest. Oh, I longed so to live, to dream my way up on the heights, above the unreal realities that ground me and dragged me down to earth.

Inside the ruin of my thwarted life, the unlived visionary immigrant hungered and thirsted for America. I had come a refugee from the Russian pogroms, aflame with dreams of America. I did not find America in the sweat-shops, much less in the schools and colleges. But for hundreds of years the persecuted races all over the world were nurtured on hopes of America. When a little baby in my mother's arms, before I was old enough to speak, I saw all around me weary faces light up with thrilling tales of the far-off "golden country." And so, though my faith in this so-called America was shattered, yet underneath, in the sap and roots of my soul, burned the deathless faith that America is, must be, somehow, somewhere. In the midst of my bitterest hates and rebellions, visions of America rose over me, like songs of freedom of an oppressed people.

My body was worn to the bone from overwork, my footsteps dragged with exhaustion, but my eyes still sought the sky, praying, ceaselessly praying, the dumb, inarticulate prayer of the lost immigrant: "America! Ach, America! Where is America?"

It seemed to me if I could only find some human beings to whom I could unburden my heart, I would have new strength to begin again my insatiable search for America.

But to whom could I speak? The people in the laundry? They never understood me. They had a grudge against me because I left them when I tried to work myself up. Could I speak to the college people? What did these icebergs of convention know about the vital things of the heart?

And yet, I remembered, in the freshman year, in one of the courses in chemistry, there was an instructor, a woman, who drew me strangely. I felt she was the only real teacher among all the teachers and professors I met. I didn't care for the chemistry, but I liked to look at her. She gave me life, air, the unconscious emanation of her beautiful spirit. I had not spoken a word to her, outside the experiments in chemistry, but I knew her more than the people around her who were of her own class. I felt in the throb of her voice, in the subtle shading around the corner of her eyes, the color and texture of her dreams.

Often in the midst of our work in chemistry I felt like crying out to her: "Oh, please be my friend. I'm so lonely." But something choked me. I couldn't speak. The very intensity of my longing for her friendship made me run away from her in confusion the minute she approached me. I was so conscious of my shabbiness that I was afraid maybe she was only trying to be kind. I couldn't bear kindness. I wanted from her love, understanding, or nothing.

About ten years after I left college, as I walked the streets bowed and beaten with the shame of having to go around begging for work, I met Miss Van Ness. She not only recognized me, but stopped to ask how I was, and what I was doing.

I had begun to think that my only comrades in this world were the homeless and abandoned cats and dogs of the street, whom everybody gives another kick, as they slam the door on them. And here was one from the clean world human enough to be friendly. Here was one of the well-dressed, with a look in her eyes and a sound in her voice that was like healing oil over the bruises of my soul. The mere touch of that woman's hand in mine so overwhelmed me, that I burst out crying in the street.

The next morning I came to Miss Van Ness at her office. In those ten years she had risen to professorship. But I was not in the least intimidated by her high office. I felt as natural in her presence as if she were my own sister. I heard myself telling her the whole story of my life, but I felt that even if I had not said a word she would have understood all I had to say as if I had spoken. It was all so unutterable, to find one from the other side of the world who was so simply and naturally that miraculous thing—a friend. Just as contact with Miss Whiteside had tied and bound all my thinking processes, so Miss Van Ness unbound and freed me and suffused me with light.

I felt the joy of one breathing on the mountain-tops for the first time. I looked down at the world below. I was changed and the world was changed. My past was the forgotten night. Sunrise was all around me.

I went from Miss Van Ness's office, singing a song of new life: "America! I found America."